T4-AFY-306

"I Will Give Them One More Shot"

Endowed by

TOM WATSON BROWN

and

THE WATSON-BROWN FOUNDATION, INC.

"I WILL GIVE THEM ONE MORE SHOT"

RAMSEY'S 1ST REGIMENT GEORGIA VOLUNTEERS

George Winston Martin

Mercer University Press
Macon, Georgia

MUP/H818

1400 Coleman Avenue
Macon, Georgia 31207

First Edition.

Books published by Mercer University Press are printed on acid free paper that meets the requirements of American National Standard for Information Sciences—Permanence of Paper for Printed Library Materials.

Mercer University Press is a member of Green Press initiative (greenpressinitiative.org), a nonprofit organization working to help publishers and printers increase their use of recycled paper and decrease their use of fiber derived from endangered forests. This book is printed on recycled paper.

ISBN 978-0-88146-219-7

Cataloging-in-Publication Data is available from the Library of Congress
Martin, George Winston, 1954-
"I will give them one more shot" : Ramsey's 1st Regiment Georgia Volunteers / George Winston Martin. -- 1st ed.
p. cm.
Includes bibliographical references and index.
ISBN 978-0-88146-219-7 (hardback : alk. paper)
1. Confederate States of America. Army. Georgia Infantry Regiment, 1st (1861-1862) 2. Georgia--History--Civil War, 1861-1865--Regimental histories. 3. United States—History—Civil War, 1861-1865—Regimental histories. 4. West Virginia—History—Civil War, 1861-1865—Campaigns. 5. United States—History—Civil War, 1861-1865—Campaigns. 6. Ramsey, James N. (James Newton), 1821-1870. I. Title. II. Title: Ramsey's 1st Regiment Georgia Volunteers.
E559.51st .M37 2010
973.7'13--dc22

201003363

CONTENTS

To Cecile,

who opened the door,

and Jean,

who encouraged me to go through.

When in the circle of lov'd friends once more
Soldiers were wont to fight their battles o'er,
And tell of marches fraught with hardship-sore.
Those Georgians who, cut off from ev'ry friend,
'Mid perils that appeared to have no end,
Resolving not to yield, took their rough way
Over the rugged mountains night and day,
Ne'er tired of telling how a path they made
Through the dense laurels, dark with gloomy shade,
Nor how, when famine stared them in the face,
A friendly mountaineer their path did trace,
Supplied their needs and led them a safe way
To join their comrades, camped at Monterey:
And, wheresoe'er they gave this tale to fame.
With gratitude they mentioned Parson's name.

—Joseph Tyrone Derry, 1904[1]

---

[1] Joseph Tyrone Derry, *The Strife of Brothers, a Poem* (Atlanta GA: The Franklin Printing and Publishing Company, 1904) 16.

Preface

My journey of discovery concerning the 1st Georgia Infantry began with a letter. With an abiding passion for all things "Civil War" since childhood, I was curious whether any of my ancestors had served. In response to a query, my Aunt Cecile Costine (the family historian) wrote back, providing information that launched my quest for the story of two distant cousins from north Georgia.

Their father, Abel Cummings Marshall, the brother of my great-great grandfather, had traveled from the forests of northern New England to Dahlonega in the early 1800s, lured by the gleam of gold discovered in the north Georgia mountains. There, he met and wed Lucinda Hawkins of South Carolina, raising a family of two sons and two daughters. The younger son, Cummings, went north to New Hampshire in the 1850s. Abel disappeared from records during that time—whether he died or simply went away is unknown. In any event, when the war began, the eldest son, William Henry, enlisted in the Dahlonega Volunteers, which became Company H of Ramsey's 1st Georgia. Cummings enlisted in the 1st New Hampshire Heavy Artillery in 1864, serving at Battery Reno outside of Washington. After the war, both brothers, as well as their mother and one sister, made their way to New Hampshire. They rest side by side in a cemetery in the little village of Colebrook, near the Canadian border.

The power of this story brought home the concept of the "Brothers' War" in an immensely personal way. I set out to discover as much as possible about the brothers and their units. Digging for material, I discovered a book-length history of the 1st Georgia was not to be found. Therefore, as a way to honor my ancestor who served in that unit, and at the urging of several friends, I decided to try my hand at a regimental history.

My intention was to create neither a coldly analytical military history nor a definitive genealogical composition. Rather, this is the story of the *men* of the 1st Georgia, related in large part through their own words. I wish to give their history a human face—to not lose the soldiers themselves in a sea of statistical analysis. As I spent hours in libraries and archives, digging through stacks of books, manuscripts, and microfilm, I realized the best way to tell the story of these soldiers was to let them speak for themselves. In using the men's own words to describe the events surrounding them, I hope to allow them to live once again, if only in the pages of this work.

Material about the 1st Georgia was found scattered in books, diaries, letters, and newspapers, as well as in university and archival repositories. Compounding the difficulties of the search was the fact that there were several "1st Georgias." *The Organizational Summary of Military Organizations from Georgia in the Confederate States of America*, compiled from extensive research of the holdings of the Georgia Department of Archives and History, lists no fewer than ten "1st Georgia Infantry" units. There were also three "1st Georgia Battalions," a "1st Regiment Georgia Army," the "1st Regiment Georgia Light Duty Men," and the "1st Regiment Georgia Troops and Defenses." There was even a *Union* 1st Georgia Regiment! Confusion arose over unit designations arose as early as 1861, as noted in the 16 August edition of the *Rome Weekly Courier*: "The Georgia Regiments.—There seems to be no little confusion in the numbers by which the Georgia regiments are designated. An irregularity that may lead to important, if unjust, mistakes in history."

By far, the most daunting task was attempting to unravel the confusion surrounding the change of officers that took place in early December 1861. Much conflicting information exists regarding when Colonel James N. Ramsey and Lieutenant Colonel James O. Clarke left the regiment. Some records show Ramsey resigning, elevating Clarke to the colonelcy; others state quite the reverse. My own opinion of the events swung back and forth as each new piece of information surfaced. (See Appendix D for a more detailed explanation.)

Translating the words from old letters (either the originals or copies) proved very much a challenge. As Bell I. Wiley observed in his landmark study *The Life of Johnny Reb*, "The handwriting of most letters was bad, but the spelling was worse. When these deficiencies are combined with haphazard punctuation, promiscuous capitalization, inferior paper and pale ink, the deciphering becomes indeed a task."[2] Every effort has been made to be true to the original content of the correspondence, especially in the spelling used by the participants. I have avoided the use of the [*sic*] notation; I have always found it a distraction while reading quotations. All correspondence is reproduced as from the originals. Any errors that have been made are entirely my own.

On a shelf above my desk stands a miniature version of the Washington Rifles flag, along with a photographic copy of Colonel Ramsey's portrait.

---

[2] Bell Irvin Wiley, *The Life of Johnny Reb: The Common Soldier of the Confederacy* (Baton Rouge: Louisiana State University Press, 1943) 203.

As the colonel stared down at me with his steely gaze, I found myself promising I would do my utmost to be true to him and his comrades-in-arms. I earnestly hope that I have succeeded.

Acknowledgments

A work such as this would be impossible to complete without the help of numerous individuals. I am exceedingly grateful to director Marc Jolley, editor Kevin Manus-Pennings, and the rest of the staff of Mercer University Press for their belief in me and for the opportunity to tell this fascinating story.

I received enthusiastic assistance at every step of my research. I am especially indebted to W. Hunter Lesser, author of *Rebels at the Gate: Lee and McClellan on the Front Line of a Nation Divided.* Hunter took time from a busy Fourth of July weekend to have lunch with me and my family, then escorted us on a private tour of the route followed by General Robert S. Garnett's retreating army from Laurel Hill toward Corricks Ford. As we stood at the site along the Shavers Fork River where Garnett was killed, we could feel the "ghosts" of the past swirl around us. A year later, Hunter and I spent a rainy September day tramping through the brush along the banks of Shavers Fork, working out positions held by the Georgians during Colonel Ramsey's rearguard action. I am grateful for his patience during the numerous times I pestered him with questions.

Dr. David Wiggins, author of *Remembering Georgia's Confederates* and *Georgia's Confederate Sons*, helped me connect with others who held pieces of this story and supplied much appreciated encouragement. His unflagging efforts tracking down images have greatly enhanced the work.

Loretta Andrews was a most gracious contributor. Ms. Andrews, a descendent of Colonel James N. Ramsey, allowed me into her home twice to photograph an imposing portrait of the colonel. She related that the original painting was of Ramsey as a civilian, and at some later occasion his Confederate colonel's uniform was painted over his civilian clothes. (The pigment used was not as good as the original, for the image of his civilian clothes has bled through over time.)

Henry Persons, Jr., of Maryland provided a marvelous bibliography of material he has collected on the 1st, which was of immense help in locating important information. O. Lee Sturkey of South Carolina donated his extensive research on burial sites of 1st Georgia soldiers. Dr. Keith Bohannon of Western Georgia University compiled another excellent bibliography for me.

Dr. Steven Enggerrand and the staff of the Georgia Department of Archives and History in Morrow, Georgia, were most courteous, pointing me toward several works and collections that I might have missed otherwise. Research assistants Chris Kersten, Tony Cable, and the other employees at the Henderson County (NC) library reference desk aided greatly by acquiring materials. Chris was an absolute wizard, coming up with obscure books and rare microfilm through interlibrary loan.

Others who provided direction and valuable assistance include Bruce Allardice, author of *Confederate Colonels: A Biographical Register*; research assistants Nathanial King and Matthew Turi, Wilson Library at the University of North Carolina at Chapel Hill; Kathy Shoemaker, Research Services associate archivist, Manuscript, Archives, and Rare Book Library (MARBL), Emory University; Mary Linnemann, Hargrett Rare Book and Manuscript Library, University of Georgia; John McClure and Lee Shepard, Virginia Historical Society; Timothy Frilingos, curator of exhibits, Georgia Capitol Museum; Amy Schindler of the College of William and Mary; Tom Redwine, senior administrator, Male Academy Museum, Newnan, Georgia; Nancy Dupree, Alabama Department of Archives and History; Guy Robbins, curator, Augusta Museum of History; Gordon Jones, senior military historian, Atlanta History Center; Robert Ambrose, vice president, Bath-Romney Campaign Historical and Preservation Association; Robert Faye, Lumpkin County (GA) Historical Association; Wynella Martin and Ernest Morgan, Monroe County (GA) Historical Society; Debra Capponi and Kyler McCoy, information specialists, Chestatee Regional Library System; Becky Sims, park ranger, Gulf Islands National Seashore, Fort Barrancas Unit, Warrington, Florida; Dr. Terry F. Hambrecht, senior technical advisor, National Museum of Civil War Medicine, Frederick, Maryland; Greg Biggs; William Smedlund; Francie Ramsey Thornton; Morgan Merrill; Cynthia Coan; William Fleming; Richard Wilson; Professor John E. Woods; Lt. John Powell; Al Medcalf; Barry Colbaugh; Jeff Youngblood; David W. Vaughan; D. Mark Baxter; William Bragg; the Evans Family; David Lewis; Susan Patton Hamersky; Kerry Elliot; Gerald D. Hodge; Cheryl Brundell; Harold Fox; Joe White; and Shanna English. I would also like to extend my thanks to a very understanding and accommodating manager, Susan Ledford.

Most of all, I would like to thank the love of my life, my wife, Cathy. She and our daughters, Amanda and Alicia, patiently tolerated my research trips and my long sessions of writing behind the closed door of my den. Reading through reams of pages thrust into her hands, Cathy provided much-appreciated suggestions to improve the manuscript. More than that, she always encouraged me to keep going.

Above: **Colonel James Newton Ramsey**, commander of the 1st Georgia Regiment. Formerly 1st Lieutenant of the Columbus Southern Guards, Ramsey was elected Colonel on April 3, 1861. (Image courtesy of Loretta Andrews)

Left: **Private Isaac Hermann**, Washington Rifles. Hermann came to Georgia from France in 1859. When he enlisted in Confederate service, he exclaimed "I want to fight like an American!" (Memoirs of a Confederate Veteran 1861–1865).

Governor Joseph E. Brown of Georgia. "May the God of Battles go with you," Brown told the soldiers of the 1st Georgia. (*The History of the State of Georgia, From 1850 to 1881*)

James W. Anderson. 1st Lieutenant of the Newnan Guards, Anderson was appointed Regimental Adjutant on April 3, 1861, and promoted Major on December 11. (Courtesy of Kerry Elliot)

Unidentified soldier of the Oglethorpe Infantry, in fatigue dress.
(Photo courtesy David Lewis)

The Oglethorpe Infantry of Augusta. This image was probably taken the day of their departure for Macon. The officer in front is most likely Captain James O. Clarke, who would become Lt. Col. of the 1st Georgia. (Courtesy of the Augusta History Museum)

Private Benjamin Campbell of the Dahlonega Volunteers.
(Image courtesy of Cynthia Coan)

Private Benjamin McCowen of the Quitman Guards. (Photo courtesy of D. Mark Baxter)

Above: **Lieutenant Andrew P. Brown** of the Newnan Guards, shown in his later artillery uniform. The Guards became part of the 12th Battalion Light Artillery after mustering out of the 1st Georgia. Brown was killed at Fort Sumter, South Carolina, on October 28, 1863. (Image courtesy Coweta County Historical Society)

Left: **Private Lavender R. Ray**, Newnan Guards, in his dress uniform. (*Letters and Diary of Lieut. Lavender R. Ray 1861-1865*)

Above: **Private William McDaniel Felder** of the Southern Rights Guard. (Photo courtesy of David W. Vaughan)

Left: **Private William S. Askew**, wearing the fatigue uniform of the Newnan Guards. Askew joined the 1st Georgia on May 7, 1861. He was discharged on August 21 at Monterey Virginia. (Library of Congress)

Left: **Lieutenant William O. Fleming**, Bainbridge Independents. Fleming would later become Lieutenant Colonel of the Fiftieth Georgia Infantry. In his letters home, Fleming constantly entreated his wife to write. (Image courtesy of William L. Fleming)

Below: **The King brothers** of Houston County; (seated) Francis Marion and Alfred A.; (standing) John Hamblin, Sylvester Capers. John served in Company G of the 8th Georgia. His brothers were members of the Southern Rights Guard, later the Southern Rights Battery. (Photo courtesy of Susan Patton Hamersky)

Above: **First Lieutenant Beverly D. Evans** of the Washington Rifles. After his service with the 1st, Evans was elected Captain of Company H, 2nd Regiment State Troops, then later Lieutenant Colonel. (Image courtesy of the Evans Family and William Bragg)

Left: **Sergeant John Thomas Youngblood**, Washington Rifles. Youngblood was both color bearer and commissary sergeant for the company. (Image courtesy of Jeff Youngblood)

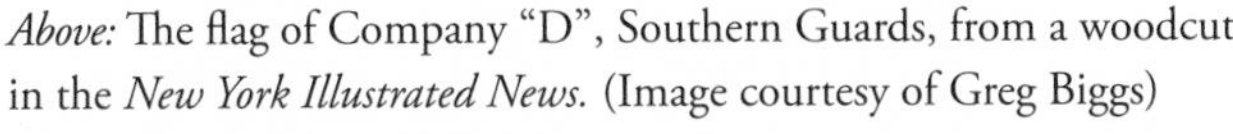

Above: The flag of Company "D", Southern Guards, from a woodcut in the *New York Illustrated News.* (Image courtesy of Greg Biggs)

Right: Model 1816/1822 Springfield musket .69 caliber smoothbore, altered from flintlock to percussion. The 1st Georgia was issued weapons like these at Macon. (Photo courtesy of Collectors Firearms, Houston, Texas.)

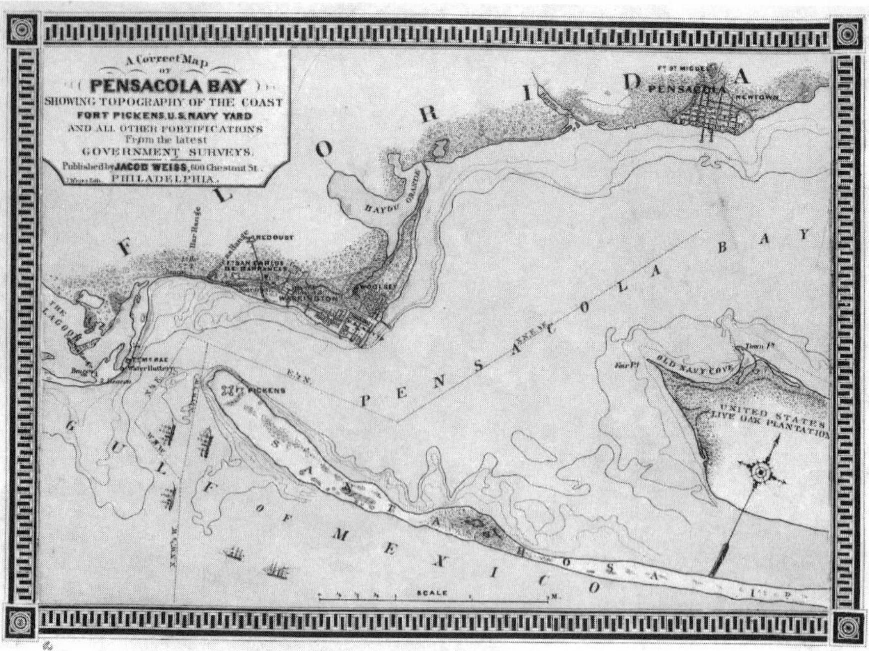

Pensacola Bay in 1861. (Jacob Weiss, Philadelphia, circa 1861)

View from Fort Barrancas across Pensacola Bay toward Fort Pickens. The Georgians wondered when they would cross over to attack the Federal fort. (Photo by the author)

Entrance to Fort Barrancas. The camp of the 1st Georgia was nearby.
(Photo by the author)

Bayside face of Fort Barrancas. The white structure is an earlier Spanish battery.
(Photo by the author)

Brigadier General Braxton Bragg, commander of the Confederate forces at Pensacola. When Colonel Ramsey complained about the division of his regiment, Bragg threatened to send him to Virginia. (Library of Congress)

Brigadier General Robert Seldon Garnett. Upon his assignment to Western Virginia, he feared he was being sent to his death. (Library of Congress)

Columbiads at entrance to Pensacola Bay, February 1861.
Several companies of the 1st Georgia were set to work drilling on guns such as these, much to the displeasure of Colonel Ramsey. (National Archives)

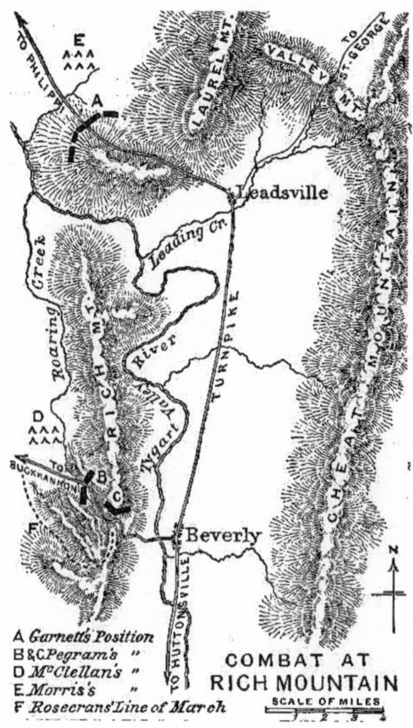

Confederate and Federal positions at Laurel Hill and Rich Mountain.
(*Battles and Leaders of the Civil War*)

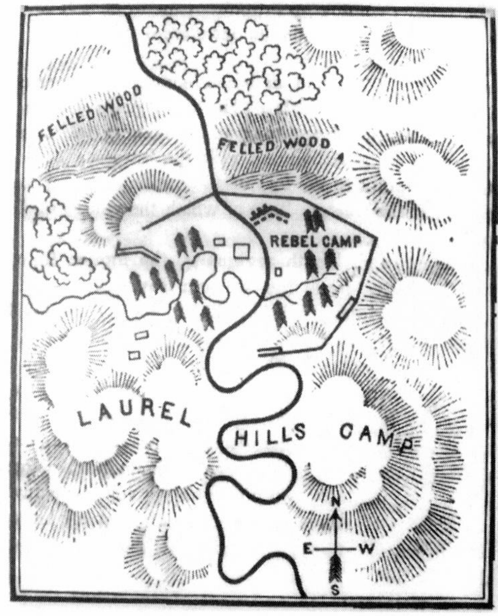

Confederate camp at Laurel Hill, drawn by William Fletcher of the Union Army.
(*The Soldier of Indiana in the War for the Union, Volume I, page 43*)

Major General George B. McClellan. His victories in Western Virginia helped propel him to command of the Union armies. (National Archives)

Engagement between Federal troops and the 1st Georgia Regiment at Laurel Hill. (*Frank Leslie's Illustrated Newspaper*)

Site of Camp Laurel Hill, looking toward the scene of the engagement between the 1st Georgia and the Federal army. Lt. Col. Clarke led his detachment up the hill to the right, yelling "Remember you are Georgians!" (Photo by the author)

Captain Henry W. Benham (shown in his later rank of Brigadier General). With 1800 Ohio and Indiana soldiers, Benham pursued Garnett's retreating army with dogged determination. (Library of Congress)

Brigadier General Thomas Morris. His instructions were to "amuse" the Confederates at Laurel Hill while General Rosecrans attacked Rich Mountain. (Library of Congress)

Battle flag of the Washington Rifles, Company E. Captured by the 9th Indiana, it was returned to the State of Georgia by the United States Government in 1905. (Courtesy Georgia Capitol Museum, Office of Secretary of State)

While Garnett's wagons retreated across this ford at the lower end of the Shavers Fork valley, Colonel Ramsey fought his delaying action. It was here, after the four remaining companies of the 1st Georgia had retreated, that the Washington Rifles' flag was discovered in an abandoned wagon. (Photo by the author)

General Robert E. Lee on Traveler. His legacy from the Western Virginia campaign was the nickname "Granny", a beard, and a legendary mount. (Library of Congress)

Brigadier General Henry Rootes Jackson of Georgia.
(*The History of the State of Georgia, From 1850 to 1881*)

Brigadier General William W. Loring. Angered at finding most of the 1st Georgia absent on furlough, Loring had Colonel Ramsey arrested. (Photo courtesy of W. Hunter Lesser)

Kalers Ford. Garnett's retreating army first crossed Shavers Fork of the Cheat River here, passing from right to left. (Photo by the author.)

View northward down the Shavers Fork valley. To the left in the trees is the remains of the road followed by the retreating Confederates. To the right is the "mountain spur", edged by trees, where six companies of the 1st Georgia waited to ambush the advancing Union column. (Photo by the author)

View down the Greenbrier Valley. To the left was posted Colonel Albert Rust's Arkansas Regiment. The tree to the right is on the edge of the site of Yaeger's tavern. Colonel Ramsey's pickets were about a mile to the north. (Photo by the author)

Valley of the Greenbrier River. The Twelfth Georgia was posted along the ridge to the left of the white barn, with the 1st Georgia behind it in support. (Photo by the author)

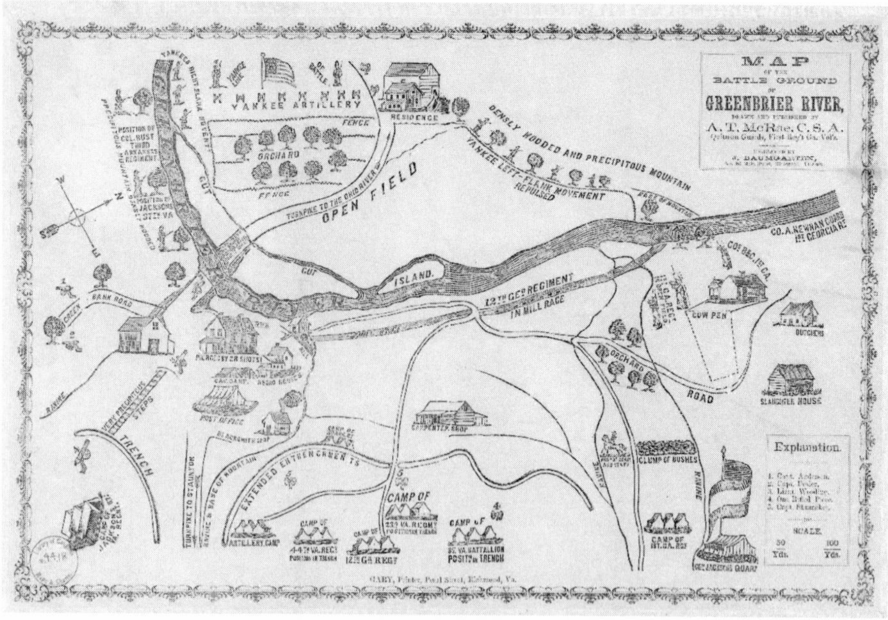

Battle of Greenbrier River, drawn by A. T. McRae of the Quitman Guards. (Library of Congress)

Camp Bartow – Confederate entrenchments behind Traveler's Repose. Rolling down the slopes while asleep was a constant worry of the troops. (Photo by the author)

General Thomas J. "Stonewall" Jackson. Jackson drove the soldiers of the Army of the Northwest (including the 1st Georgia) almost to mutiny. (National Archives)

Colonel William Booth Taliaferro. Bad relations between this rigid disciplinarian and the 1st may have led to the colonel being assaulted by a Georgia soldier. (*The Photographic History of the Civil War, Volume Ten*, page 105)

Romney, Western (now West) Virginia, as sketched by artist Alfred Waud.
(Library of Congress)

Monument to the Bainbridge Independents, Bainbridge, Georgia. The plaque reads: "The Bainbridge Volunteers, later the Bainbridge Independents, organized 1859 by Captain Charles G. Campbell, assembled here in March 1861 and entered service under the command of Captain John W. Evans as Company G, 1st Georgia Regiment."
(Photo by the author)

Monument in Forsyth, Georgia, commemorating companies raised in Monroe County, including the Quitman Guards. (Photo by the author)

The Peace Monument to the Gate City Guard in Atlanta, dedicated October 10, 1911, symbolized reconciliation between North and South. (Photo by the author)

Georgia Counties

which provided companies for the

First Georgia Volunteer Infantry (Ramsey's)

(County borders as of 1861)

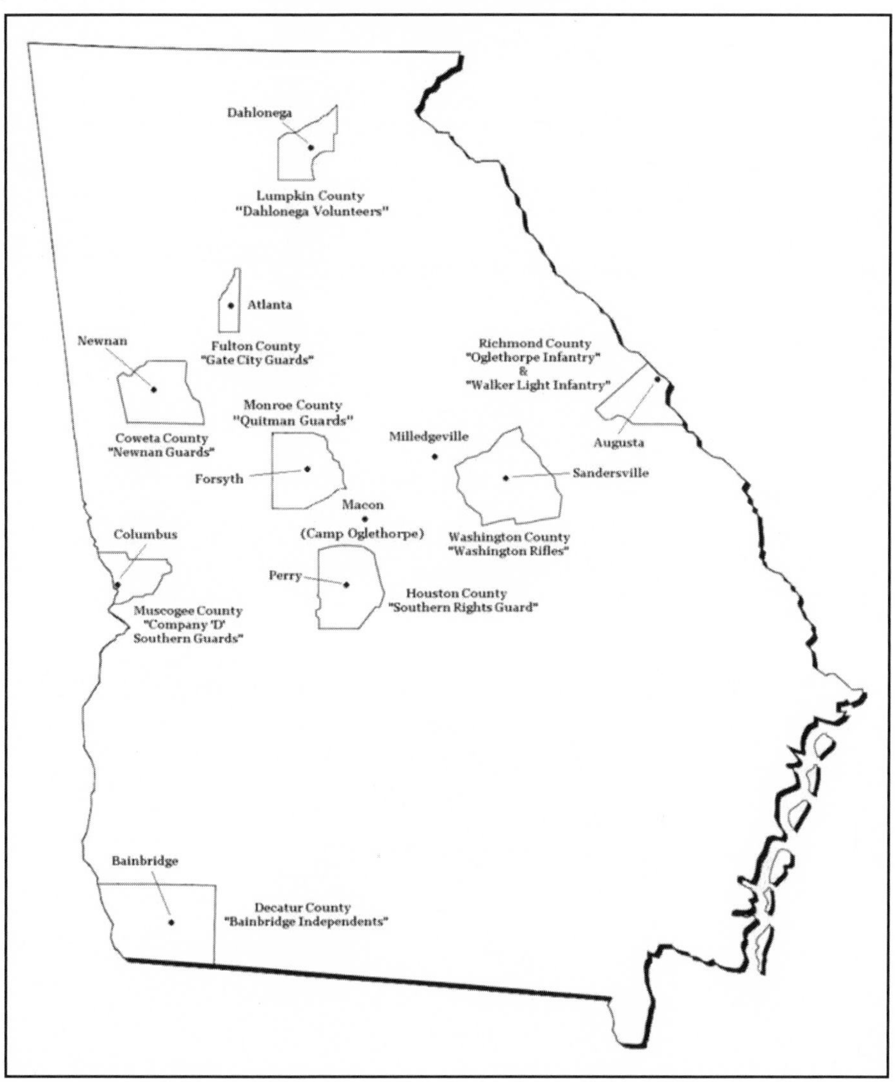

On to Pensacola

April, 1861

Virginia Theater of Operations of First Georgia Regiment

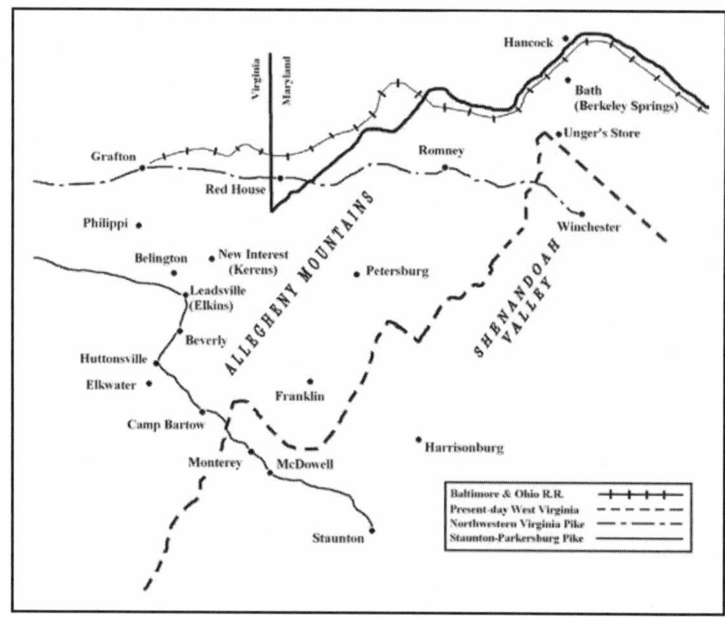

West to the Alleghenies

June, 1861

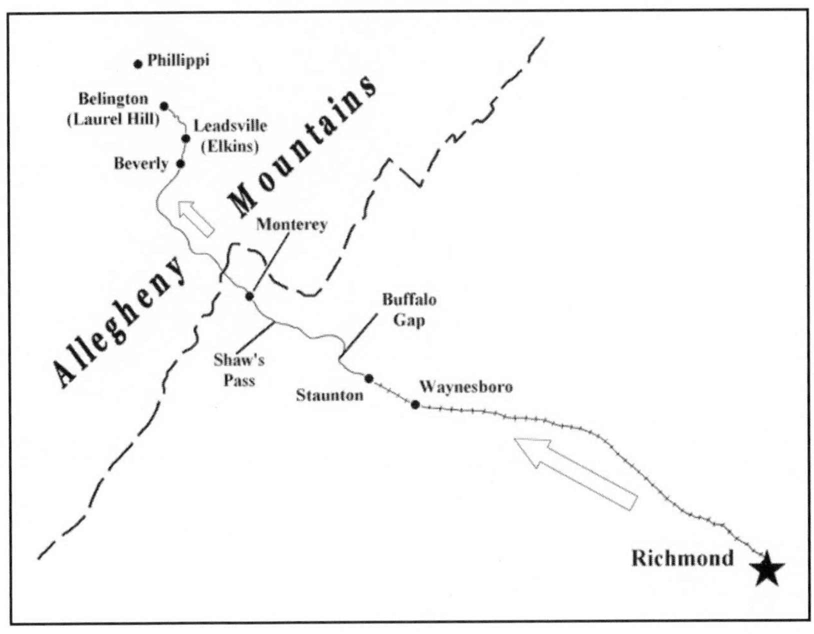

First Skirmish

The First Georgia at Laurel Hill

July 7, 1861

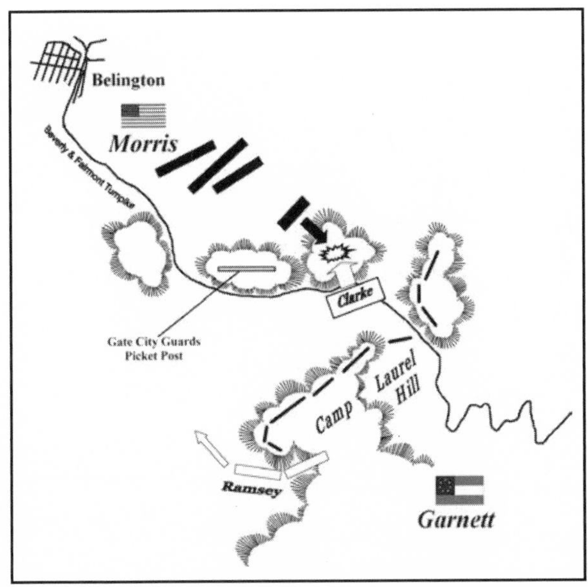

Garnett's Retreat

July 12-13, 1861

= Engagement

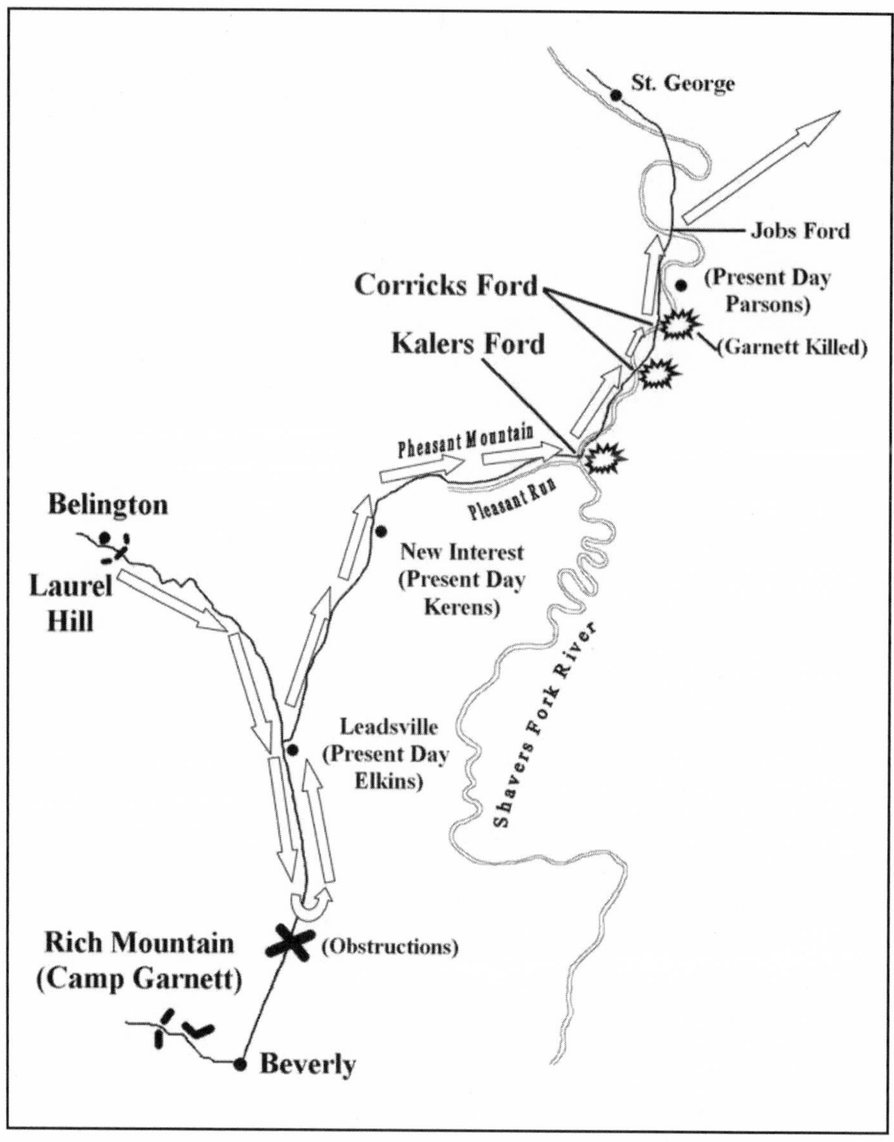

Action at Kalers Ford

Approximately 10:30 a.m.

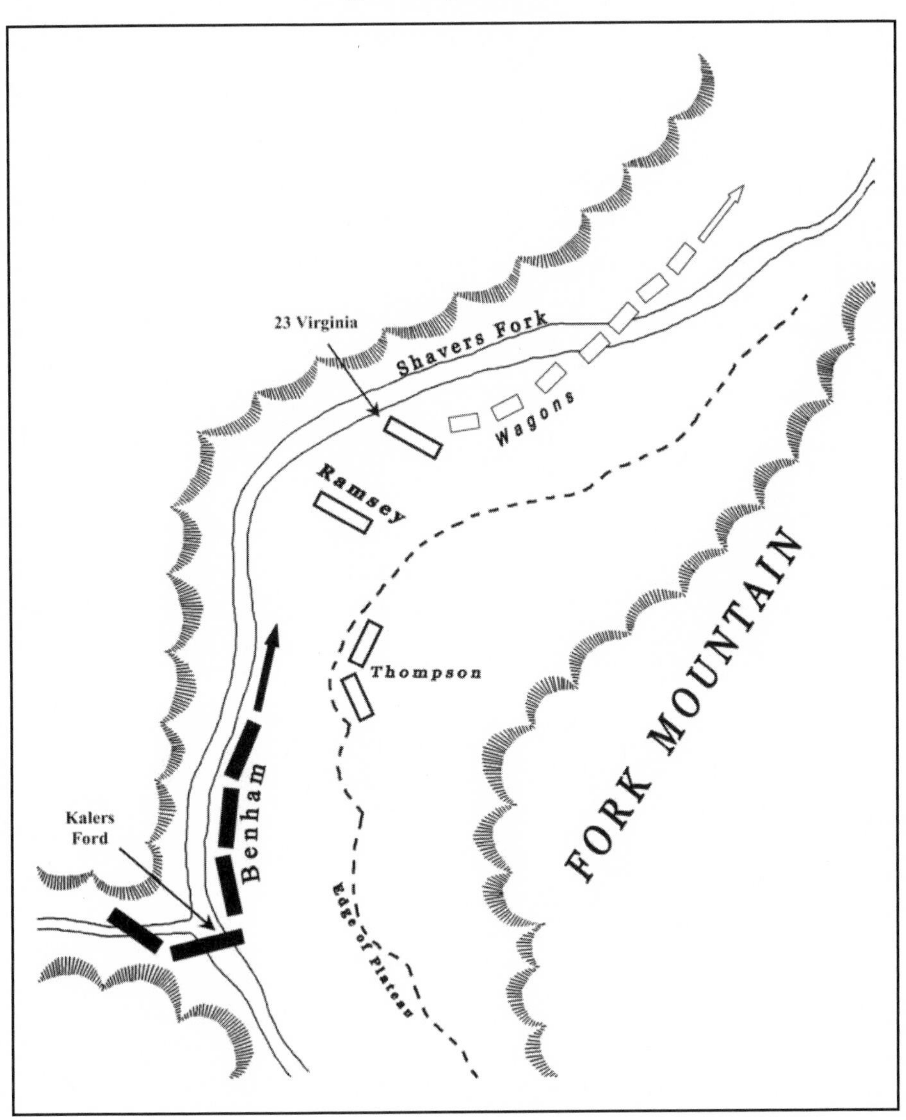

Action at Kalers Ford

Approximately 11:30 a.m.

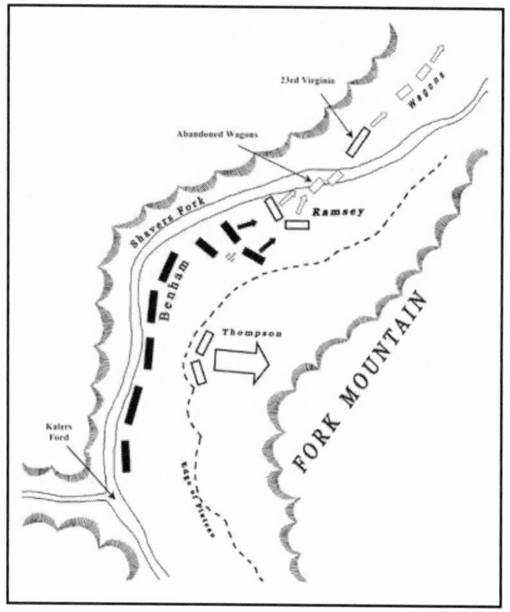

Ramsey's Retreat

and the Ordeal in the Wilderness

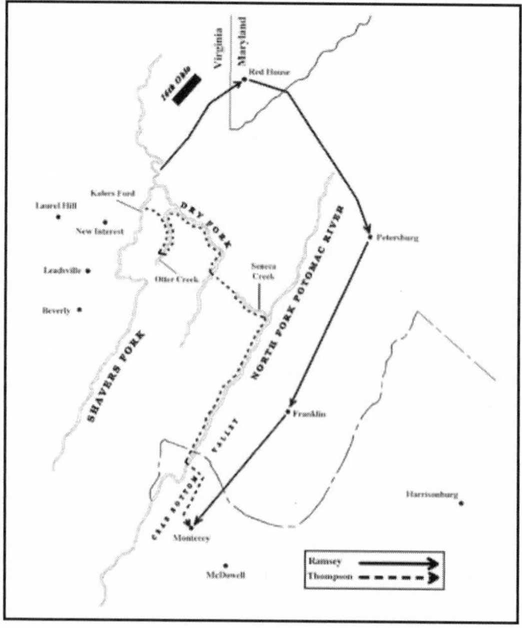

Assault on Cheat Mountain

September 9-16, 1861

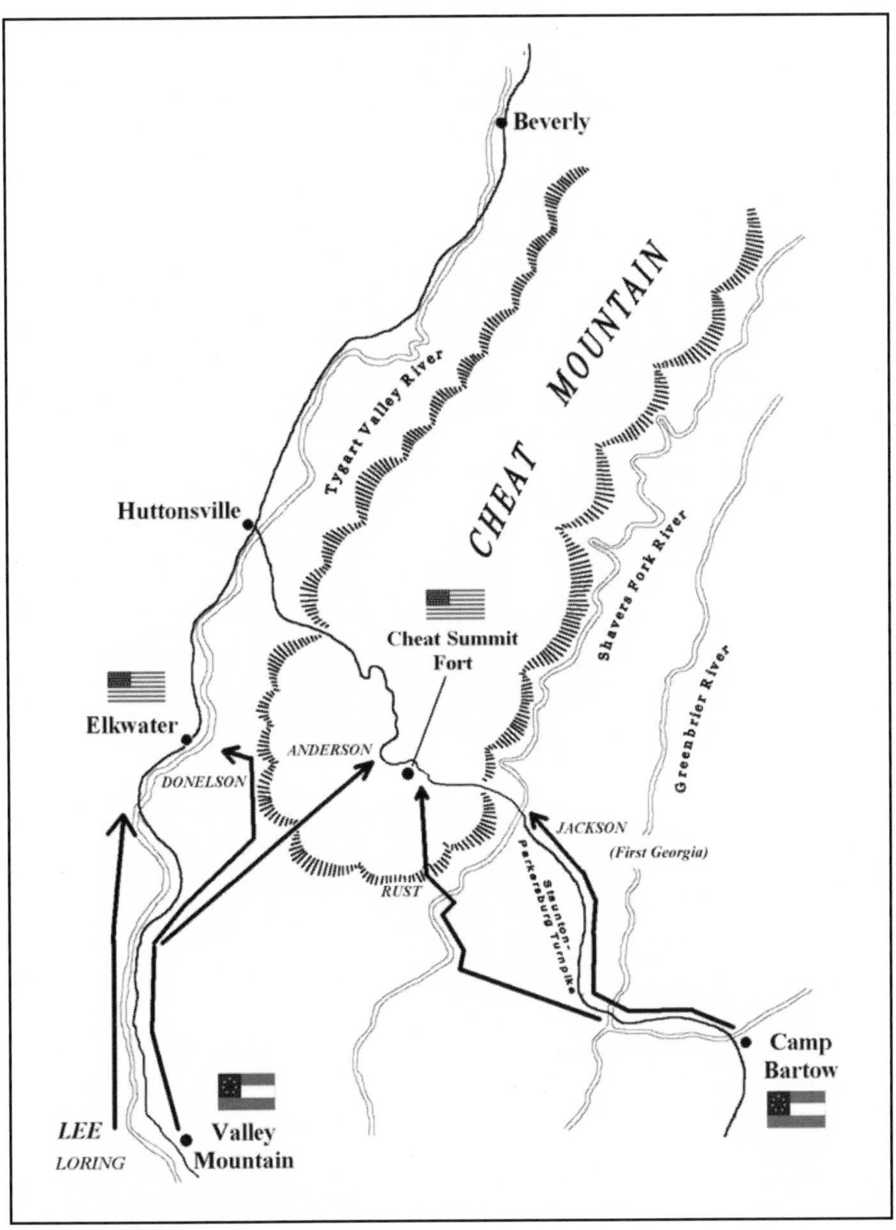

Georgians vs. Georgians

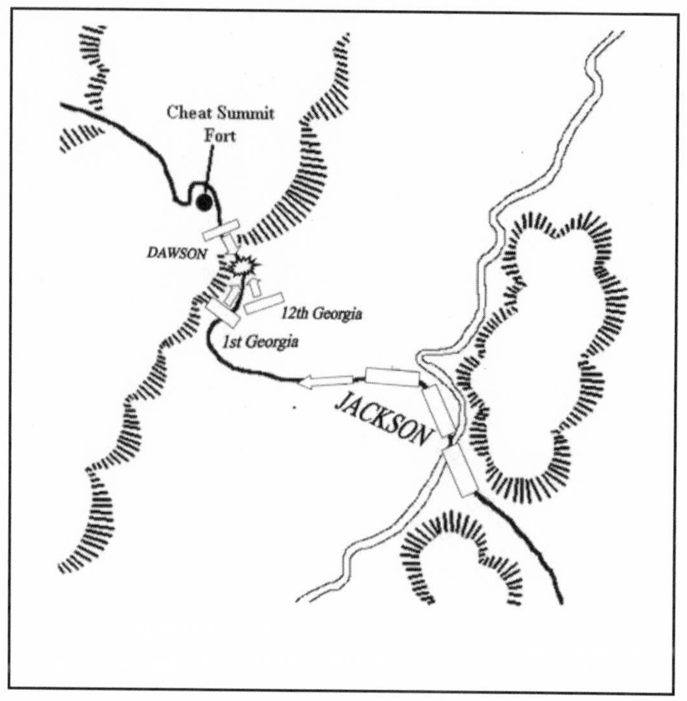

Battle of Greenbrier River

Confederate Positions Prior to Federal Attack

October 3, 1861

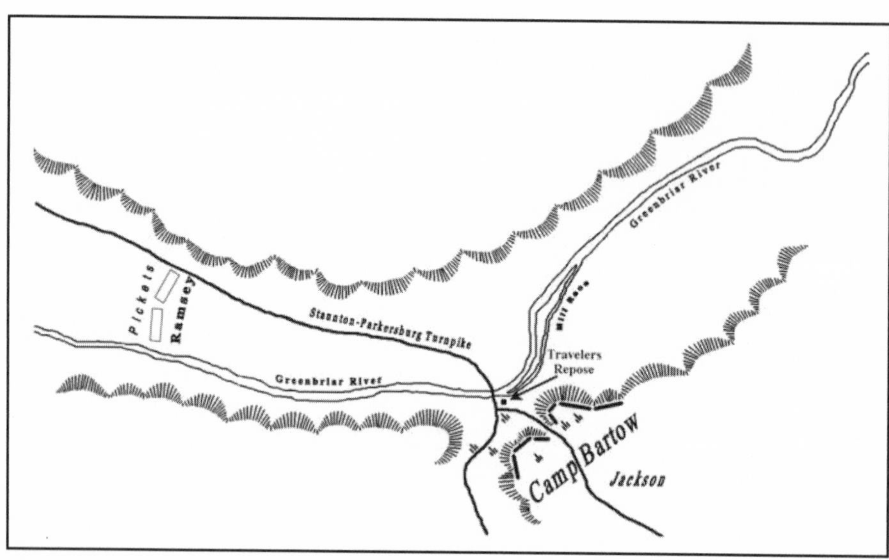

Battle of Greenbrier River

Approximately 7:00 a.m.

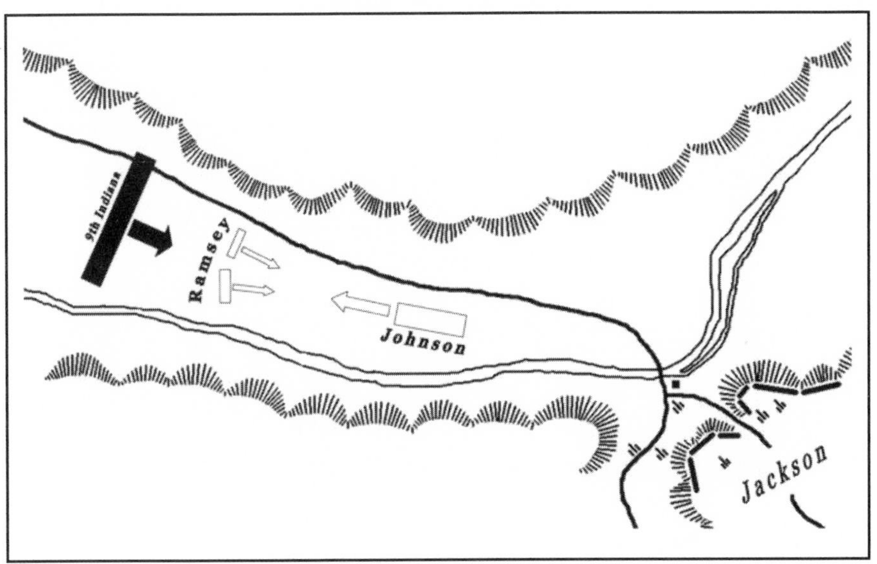

Battle of Greenbrier River

About 8:00 a.m.

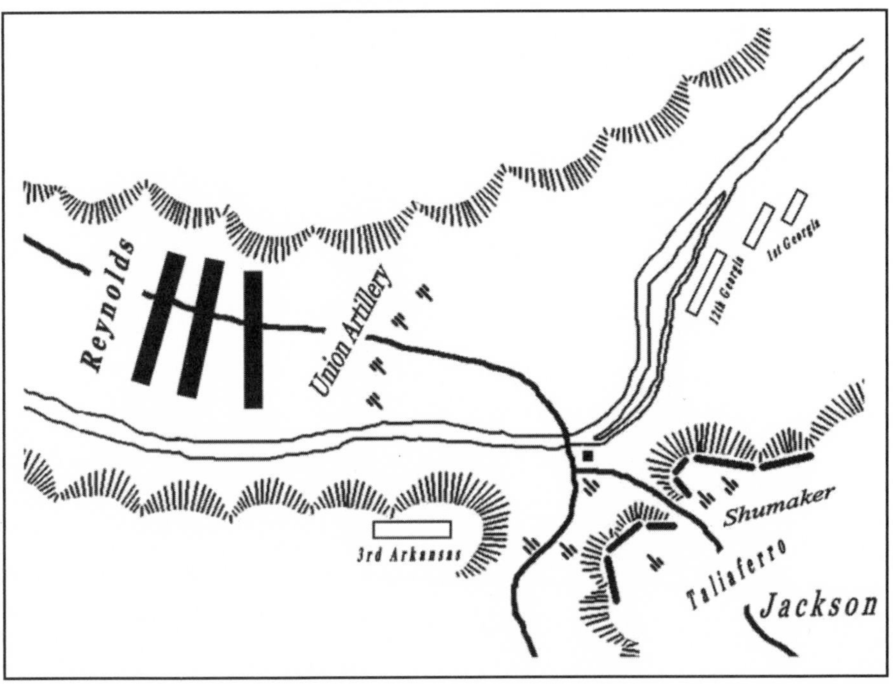

Battle of Greenbrier River

About 1:00 p.m.

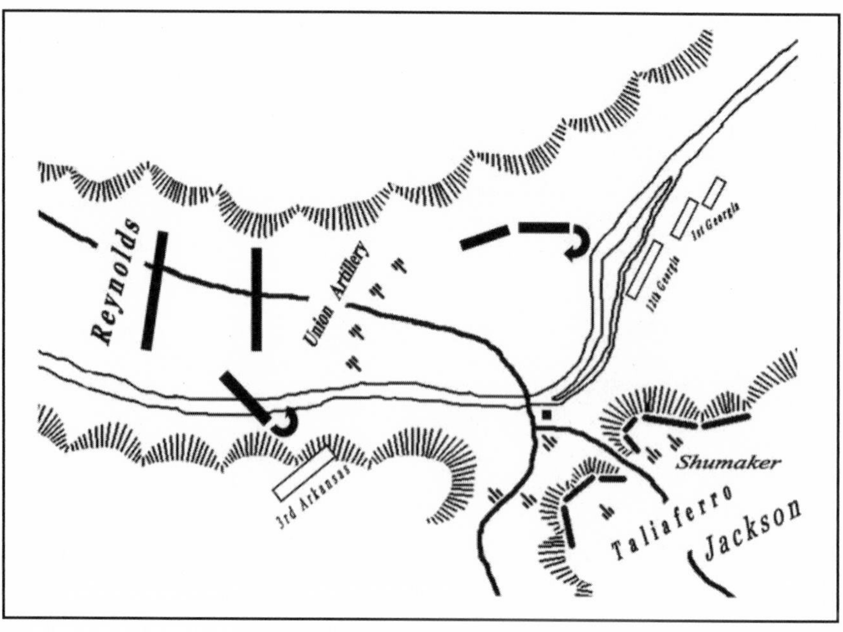

Advance on Bath

January 1-4, 1862

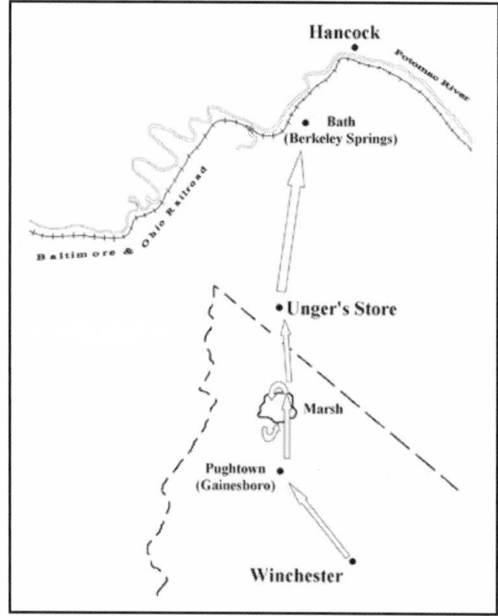

Jackson's Attack on Bath
January 4, 1862

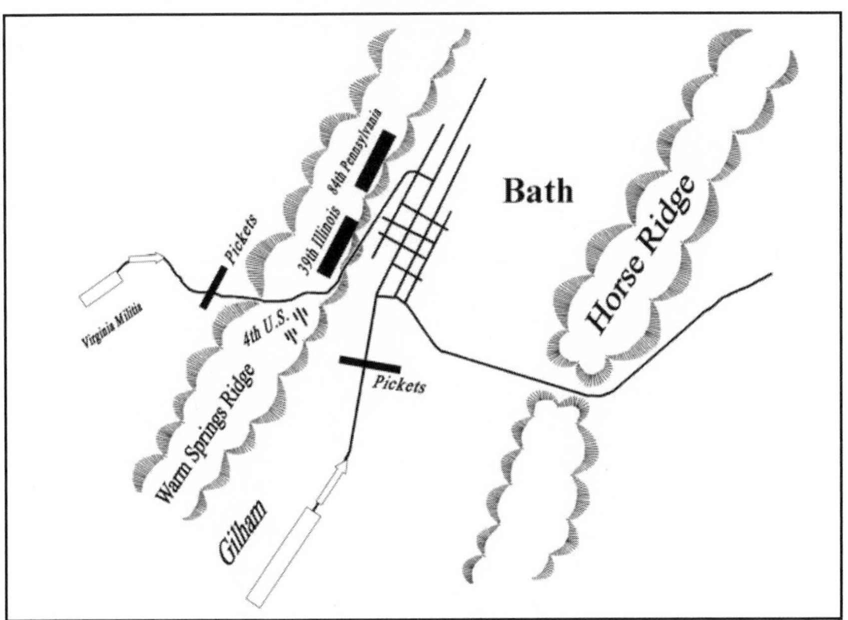

Jackson's Attack on Bath
January 4, 1862

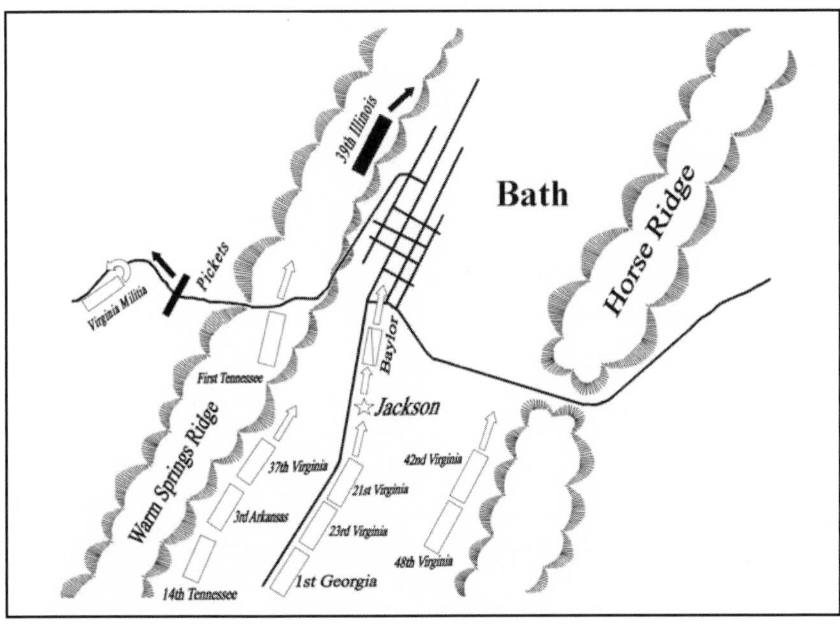

Jackson's Advance on Hancock

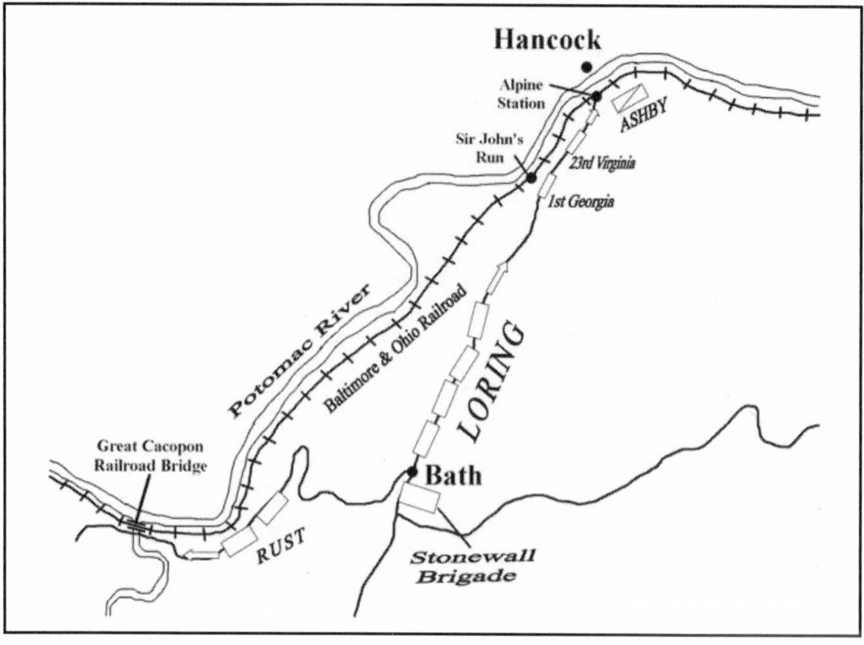

Withdrawal from Hancock and Occupation of Romney

January 7-17, 1862

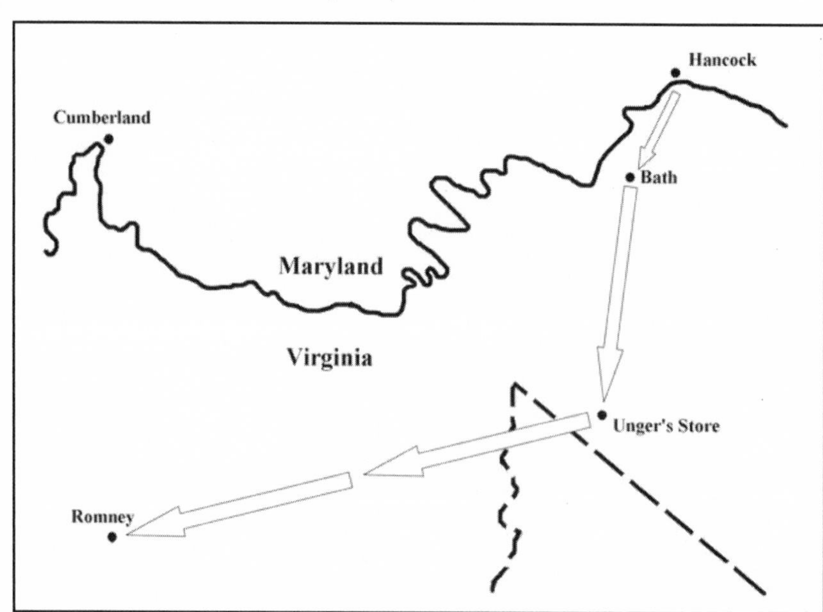

INTRODUCTION

> "My apology for asking space in your valuable columns...," the letter began. Appearing in the 20 June 1883 issue of the *Atlanta Constitution* was an appeal for survivors of the 1st Georgia Volunteer Infantry to attend a veteran's reunion, to be held 3 July near Gainesville. Penned by Confederate veteran William H. Norwood, formerly of the Southern Rights Guard, the missive implored his old comrades in arms not to pass up this chance to gather one more time. "Many a poor fellow of our regiment has no doubt missed all and either from chagrin or the hope of more pleasant and fruitful fields wandered away beyond the knowledge of his old comrades, and perchance his eye may catch this with an invitation to return again, if only to say howdy and goodbye, is the object I have in view."
>
> "The history of the first Georgia regiment," Norwood declared, "if correctly written, would show a compound of freaks, fights and flights peculiar only to itself, or more properly expressed, an enigma unsolvable by even its own members. While peculiar circumstance prevented hard fought battles, yet those same peculiar circumstances caused it to cover in one year about ten thousand miles of territory and to suffer trials and privations almost beyond the endurance of the hardiest of soldiers."[1]

Near the end of March 1861, several companies of Georgia militia journeyed to Macon, called out by Governor Joseph E. Brown in response to a summons by the Confederate States War Department. These young citizen-soldiers came from every walk of life; they were students, lawyers, newspapermen, miners, shopkeepers, and farmers. Coming from nine counties scattered through the state, they marched forth enthusiastically, many motivated by an overwhelming sense of duty and patriotism. They were eager to defend their state against a new foe—their former countrymen, the people of the northern states of the United States of

---

[1] William H. Norwood, "The First Georgia Volunteers," *Atlanta (GA) Constitution*, 20 June 1883.

America. Many looked forward to a great adventure. Few had any real sense of what trials awaited them.

Some of these men had seen service with the militia for a number of years. The Oglethorpe Infantry of Augusta, for example, was chartered in 1850. An even older organization was the Monroe County Musketeers. This company was originally authorized by the Georgia General Assembly in 1826 and saw service in Florida against the Seminole tribes. The Musketeers were reorganized as the Quitman Guards on 16 January 1859, in honor of Governor John A. Quitman of Mississippi.[2]

In Fulton County, the Gate City Guard was constituted in early January 1855. The title came from Atlanta's nickname, the "Gate City," bestowed in recognition of its importance as a point of access beween the eastern seaboard communities and territories to the west. The company's officers received their commissions from the governor on 28 March 1859. The Guards were called out in July of that year to provide security for the execution of John Cobb, Jr., who was convicted of robbery and murder. Rumors persisted that friends of the condemned man would try to foil the hanging.[3]

As the country drifted toward division, the enrollment of new militia units accelerated. The year 1858 saw the establishment of the Bainbridge Fusiliers (later renamed the Bainbridge Volunteers) in Decatur County, as well as Washington County's namesake Rifles. The following year several new companies were formed, among them Houston (pronounced HOW-ston) County's Southern Rights Guard.[4]

Upon Abraham Lincoln's election to the presidency on 6 November 1860, Georgia responded with a rush to arms. Additional companies, such as the Muscogee County Southern Guards, Coweta County's Newnan Guard, the Dahlonega Volunteers of Lumpkin County, and the newly created

---

[2] Gordon Burns Smith, *Counties and Commanders, Part 2*, vol. 3 of *History of the Georgia Militia, 1783–1861*, 4 vols. (Milledgeville GA: Boyd Publishing, 2000–2001) 158; Monroe County Historical Society, "History of Quitman Guards and Monroe Musketeers," http://www.thegagenweb.com/mchs/military-history.htm. Twice governor of Mississippi, major general during the Mexican War and US congressman, Quitman was involved in the planning of a filibustering expedition to Cuba that never came to fruition.

[3] Henry Clay Fairman, *Chronicles of the Old Guard of the Gate City Guard, Atlanta, Georgia, 1858–1915* (Atlanta GA: Byrd Printing Company, 1915) 7–8.

[4] William Warren Rogers, *A Scalawag in Georgia, Richard Whitely and the Politics of Reconstruction* (Champaign: University of Illinois Press, 2007) 15.

Walker Light Infantry of Augusta, stood ready to answer their state's call for troops. When Governor Brown issued his summons, they set out for Macon. From there, these eager volunteers marched into the pages of history. Unfortunately, those pages are often read only in footnotes.

The campaigns in which the 1st Georgia served are little remembered or celebrated today. With so much attention on the siege of Fort Sumter in Charleston Harbor, few realize that the Civil War almost began at Fort Pickens, near Pensacola, Florida; indeed, shots were fired at citizen militia attempting to take nearby Fort Barrancas on 8 January 1861. The stories of the first land battles of the war, which took place in what is now West Virginia, are eclipsed by the Battle of First Manassas (or "Bull Run"), which occurred within days of fights at Laurel Hill and Corricks Ford. Robert E. Lee is deservedly eulogized as one of the greatest generals of all time, but in September 1861 he was taunted as "Granny Lee," having failed to coordinate feuding generals and retake northwestern Virginia. Much is written about "Stonewall" Jackson's Shenandoah Valley Campaign, where the general's lighting thrusts toward McDowell, Front Royal, and Winchester gave rise to the legend of Jackson's "Foot Cavalry." In his preoccupation to capture Bath and Romney during the initial stage of that movement, Jackson was vilified as being insane, and the soldiers of the Army of the Northwest (including the 1st Georgia) came close to mutiny.

While their movements were not among the "grand" battles of the war, the soldiers of the 1st fulfilled their commitment with a high sense of duty and patriotism, as well as a resolve to see it through. Many perished of sickness and battle wounds; several bore scars and disabilities for the rest of their lives. There were a few rogues and thieves, and even a murderer. But for the most part, these soldiers served their regiment honorably. After the regiment was mustered out, nearly all the veterans of the 1st reenlisted in other commands, fighting on for their state and country until the Confederacy was overwhelmed in 1865.

The saga of the 1st Georgia Infantry is unique within the annals of the American Civil War. It was the first regiment formed by the state of Georgia for service in the Confederate army. It was the first Georgia regiment to see actual combat. And it was the only Georgia regiment to be mustered out after the end of its term of service, disbanding just one month before the First Confederate Conscription Act was enacted. (This legislation, passed on 16 April 1862, required all Confederate military units existing as of that date to remain in service for three years or for the duration of the war.)

Before their single year term of service was complete, Colonel James N. Ramsey's 1st Georgia Volunteer Infantry would experience boredom and hard labor along the coasts of Florida; arduous marches in rain, snow, and ice in the Allegheny Mountains and Shenandoah Valley; and the terror and confusion of battles along the Shavers Fork and Greenbrier Rivers. They would suffer through anguish and disappointment from retreat, and they would enjoy the sweet taste of victory at least once. Through it all, though, these citizen-soldiers displayed unquestionable courage. This is their story.

1

To the Edge of a Chasm

"The triumph of the Northern section of the Union over the Southern section, upon a platform of avowed hostility to our rights, does, in my opinion, afford ample cause to justify the South in withdrawing from a confederacy where her equality, her honor, and the rights of her people, can no longer be protected."—Georgia governor Joseph E. Brown, speaking shortly after the election of Abraham Lincoln[1]

Sunday evening, 14 July 1861. Along a windswept ridgetop high in the Allegheny Mountains of western Virginia, ragged and exhausted soldiers lay in wet grass and on flat boulders as they struggled to catch a few hours of fitful slumber. Many huddled under scraggly laurel and spruce trees as a frigid rain poured, spattering already drenched uniforms. The kindling of fires to soothe tired muscles was impossible; dry wood for fuel was nonexistent.

Seated amidst the miserable, disheartened men was Corporal Nathan Pugh, a member of the Walker Light Infantry, late of Augusta, Georgia. Pugh sat hunched over his diary, hands shaking from the cold and wet as he reviewed his entry from earlier in the day:

> This morning at day light we started on our march through the hills, weak from hunger, and somewhat discouraged with the gloomy prospect of finding food to-day. It is thought by those of our company having maps in their possession that we are within twelve miles of the turn pike, and that we will reach it this evening. Marching through a laurel range of mountains, almost impassable, nearly all day, we halted in the afternoon, and ate freely of birch bark, and a kind of grass or weed called "sheep-sorrel." It will be remembered that a large number of our company have had nothing

---

[1] "Letter from Gov. Brown," *Macon (GA) Weekly Telegraph*, 13 December 1860.

> to eat since Thursday morning, and have been on a tedious and tiresome march since that time.

Pugh probably took a few moments to massage his shivering fingers while mentally sorting through the rest of the day's events. "After a brief rest," he wrote, "we renew our gloomy march, eating bark and grass as we journey." He continued,

> Night finds us in a rough, rocky ravine near one of the many small, swift mountain streams that course their way through the laurel forests of this cold, dismal, and uninhabited portion of the mountains of northern Virginia. It is raining. Who can imagine our condition? our feelings? We are only kept from suffering severely from the cold, during the day by the most active exercise; and now night is upon us, and such a night! Nothing heard except the falling of the rain drops, the running of the aforesaid brook, and the croaking of a raven in some hollow tree farther up the mountains. Here we must rest for the night. We cannot move, or we might pitch from the top of a precipice into eternity. How shall we sleep? We have no blankets! We have divested ourselves of everything except what we wear, and many have had their clothes nearly torn from them by the brush in passing through the laurel thicket.

Despair welled up as Pugh continued to scribble.

> What would our mothers and sisters think, and say, if they knew our condition? I have just heard a member of the Walker Light Infantry say that he would not have his wife know of his present sufferings for a million of dollars; another said he would not have his mother made acquainted with his present situation for twice that amount. I feel around in the dark for a place to sleep. I prop myself against a tree to prevent my rolling down the mountain, and soon I am asleep. I dream—but *not* of HOME. Here I shiver with cold, half sleep, and half awake, until morning.[2]

By the time Corporal Pugh scrawled these anguished words, the American Civil War had passed into its fourth month. Less than a year

---

[2] Nathan S. Pugh, "A Letter from Western Virginia," *Augusta (GA) Daily Constitutionalist*, 9 August 1861.

before, Pugh and his comrades were civilians, living normal lives, safe and secure in such diverse Georgia communities as Atlanta, Columbus, Forsyth, Perry, Newnan, Sandersville, and Augusta. From Dahlonega, in the northeast Georgia mountains, to Bainbridge, close to where the Florida and Alabama lines form the southwest corner of the state, merchants, farmers, and other ordinary citizens enjoyed a modest and happy existence. Few realized how close they were to the edge of a yawning chasm, one which would split the country, produce cataclysmic destruction, and cause the deaths of thousands of Georgia's youth.

We Have Just Cause for War

As the 1850s drew to a close, sectional differences between North and South over issues such as tariffs, trade, control of Congress, and slavery were threatening to tear the United States apart. By 1859, the southern tier of states was becoming increasingly estranged from its northern counterpart. Across the South, citizens viewed the presidential election of 1860 as a litmus test; the result would determine whether they would continue to be associated with a government perceived by many as destroying their rights and their way of life.

Joseph Emerson Brown, beginning his second term as governor of Georgia in November 1859, gave voice to the raw emotions of the period in his inaugural address: "Our fathers consented to enter the confederacy of these states only upon terms of perfect equality; and we, as their sons, would be unworthy of our sires if we consented to remain in the confederacy a day longer than this principle of equality is recognized. But should this organization be broken down, and Georgia's constitutional rights be denied, and her equality in the Union destroyed, I would then advise her citizens to strike for independence out of the Union."[3]

In the nine counties which would send their sons to join the 1st Georgia, citizens watched the rending of the national fabric. Like the nation, Georgia was herself split on the question of secession. Most citizens viewed the likelihood of separation from the United States with exultation. Fire-eaters such as Senator Robert Toombs were adamant in their belief that the state's destiny would be better served apart from the Union. Toombs condemned the principles of the Republicans, railing against the party in an

[3] Newnan-Coweta Historical Society, *History of Coweta County, Georgia* (Roswell GA: Wolfe Associates, 1988) 13.

address before the United States Senate in which he said, "I denounce the Republican party as enemies of the Constitution and enemies of my country, and I shall treat them as such. I submit it to the judgment of the Senate, the country and the civilized world, if according to the public law of all civilized nations, we have not just cause of war against our confederates."[4]

There were many, however, who watched events unfold with great trepidation. Statesmen such as former congressman Alexander Stephens and former governor Herschel V. Johnson counseled against secession, urging Georgia and the other Southern states to compromise with the North. Labeled "cooperationists," Stephens and his associates agreed the South was in danger of losing its influence in Washington. They felt strongly, however, the national government should be given the chance to address the South's concerns, with secession employed only as a last resort. Differences of opinion divided this group as well. Though most agreed retaliation in the form of secession must remain an option, some felt secession should occur only when and if compromise with the North proved futile. Others were convinced disunion should come about only after an overt act of federal belligerence.

Governor Brown, convinced the North could not do without the agricultural production of the South, did not expect that secession would lead to war. "If the fifteen Southern States of the Union should meet in Convention," he wrote on 7 November 1860, "and determine to secede from it, there would be no war, no bloodshed. So many of the Northern people are dependent upon our Cotton, and our Trade, for employment; and for the necessaries, as well as the luxuries of life, that they could neither afford to fight us, nor to stand by and see others do it."[5]

While the central and southern parts of the state tended to align with the secessionists, Lumpkin and other mountain communities leaned more toward the Union. Trade between this region and states to the north had been expanding over the previous decades, helped by the construction of rail lines into the mountains. The federal mint, which opened in Dahlonega in 1838, stamped gold coins that fueled commerce across the United States. Unionist and cooperationist sentiment had a strong foothold in the northern

---

[4] Walter G. Cooper, *Official History of Fulton County* (Atlanta GA: W. W. Brown, 1934) 103. "Fire-eaters" referred to radical pro-seccessionist and pro-slavery politicians.

[5] Allen D. Candler, *The Confederate Records of the State of Georgia*, 6 vols. (Atlanta GA: Charles P. Byrd, State Printer, 1909–1911) 1:51.

section of the state. This was of special concern to Governor Brown, for he had been raised in the region.

There was also great difference between the counties in regards to slavery. While black servitude was common in all areas of the state, the numbers of African Americans varied widely. In the 1860 census, slaves accounted for barely 9.3 percent of the population of Lumpkin, with only 432 blacks recorded. By contrast, Muscogee County tallied 6,164 slaves out of a total population of 17,039. The city of Augusta, the largest manufacturing center in Georgia and one of only ten cities in the South with a population of more than 10,000, counted 3,663 slaves and 386 free blacks.[6]

Discord was found even within the various state militia units. Members of Atlanta's Gate City Guards quarreled about the flying of the United States flag over their armory. After one angry exchange, there was agreement to raise the state flag. Discontent simmered, though. While voting whether to offer their services to the governor, the issue rose once again. Nearly half the company threatened to resign if a United States banner did not replace the Georgia flag. The resignations were accepted, and only forty-six members remained.[7]

Regardless of the turmoil enveloping the country, life moved on. Georgians of all stripes tried to maintain a semblance of normalcy in the face of the brewing storm. In Columbus, attorney James N. Ramsey and his partner, Albert R. Lamar, practiced law in their office located above the Columbus Bank. On the opposite side of the state, Augustans proudly watched as a fire bell weighing more than four tons was installed at the top of a five-story iron tower. A lookout would be positioned in the tower—if he spotted a fire, he would ring the bell, affectionately dubbed "Big Steve."[8]

---

[6] John H. Martin, *Columbus, Geo., From Its Selection as a "Trading Town" in 1827, to Its Partial Destruction by Wilson's Raid, in 1865* (Columbus GA: Thomas Gilbert, Book Printer and Binder, 1874) 119; Florence Fleming Corley, *Confederate City: Augusta, Georgia, 1860–1865* (Columbia: University of South Carolina Press, 1960) 14–15; Jonathan Dean Sarris, *A Separate Civil War: Communities in Conflict in the Mountain South* (Charlottesville: University of Virginia Press, 2006) 42.

[7] Henry Clay Fairman, *Chronicles of the Old Guard of the Gate City Guard, Atlanta, Georgia, 1858–1915* (Atlanta GA: Byrd Printing Company, 1915) 17.

[8] Advertisements, *Columbus (GA) Daily Times*, 5 March 1861; Corley, *Confederate City: Augusta, Georgia*, 20.

Attorney William O. Fleming, recently arrived in Decatur County after marrying Georgia Williams of Bainbridge, was trying his hand at being a planter, practicing law while at the same time worrying about his peach trees and beet crop.[9]

Newcomers to the state also worked to make a living. Recent Jewish immigrant Isaac Hermann, along with his brother Abram, was trying to make a go of a shop in the small crossroads known as Fenn's Bridge, northeast of Sandersville. Traveling from the French province of Alsace, Isaac and Abram had made their way to Washington County after arriving in New York City in 1859.[10]

Displaced Georgians also kept close track of the goings on in their state. Lavender R. Ray, son of a distinguished Newnan judge and a student at the University of North Carolina at Chapel Hill, burned with impatience as he observed the events taking place in his native Coweta County.

We Are Ready to March

Apprehension gripped Georgia as election day arrived 6 November. The candidates for president on the ballot included former vice president John C. Breckenridge of Kentucky, congressman John Bell from Tennessee, and Illinois senator Stephen Douglas. The three represented a split in the Democratic Party; Douglas had been nominated by the national party, but other groups had splintered off. Breckenridge was supported by the Southern Democrats, while Bell was running under the banner of the Constitutional Union Democrats. The Republican candidate, Abraham Lincoln, was noticeably absent from the Georgia ballot.

As the voting progressed, Augustans were aroused with anger and excitement by a rumor of shots being fired in Charleston, South Carolina. Those still friendly to the Union found themselves increasingly in danger. A

---

[9] "Inventory of the William Oliver Fleming Papers, 1860–1930," Manuscripts Department, Wilson Library, University of North Carolina at Chapel Hill, http://www.lib.unc.edu/mss/inv/f/Fleming,William_Oliver.html; William O. Fleming to his wife, 8 May 1861, in the William Oliver Fleming Papers, #2292-z, Southern Historical Collection, the Wilson Library, University of North Carolina at Chapel Hill (hereafter cited as Fleming Papers). Quoted with permission of William Fleming, descendent.

[10] Anny Bloch, "Mercy on Rude Streams: Jewish Emigrants from Alsace-Lorraine to the Lower Mississippi Region and the Concept of Fidelity," *Southern Jewish History Journal* 2 (1999): 98; Ella Mitchell, *History of Washington County* (Atlanta GA: Byrd Press, 1924) 135.

town meeting in City Hall to discuss the ramifications of disunion was disrupted as secessionists threatened violence against cooperationists. William Henry Talbot Walker, a veteran of the Mexican War and a supporter of separation, stood to address the throng. Speaking passionately about disunion, he convinced the secessionists to follow him out to the front steps to conduct their own meeting. "I was against fanaticism and not against Georgia," he said later.[11] Inside the hall, the remaining moderates passed resolutions in favor of cooperation. A letter to the pro-Union *Chronicle and Sentinel* pleaded for reason and for respect for the United States flag: "It still waves with its stars and stripes, and might long continue to wave as our own if we would manfully hold on to it and not retreat from it and the Union it represents and weakly and despairingly abandon it to traitors who threaten to desecrate it."[12]

With the Democratic vote divided, the Republicans gained a majority of electoral votes, and thus the presidency. In the days and nights immediately following Lincoln's election, secession meetings were held in Augusta, Perry, Bainbridge, and other cities. Speaker after speaker joined the call for a convention to consider separation from the United States and to implement plans for the security of Georgia. There was great fear of what a Republican administration might do once it took office. Howell Cobb of Athens, who would resign as President James Buchanan's secretary of the treasury on 8 December spoke to these anxieties: "Equality and safety in the Union are at an end.... The Union formed by our fathers was one of equality, justice and fraternity. On the 4th of March it will be supplanted by a union of sectionalism and hatred."[13]

Most in Georgia's military establishment were eager to offer their services in defense of the South. Captain George M. Hanvey of Coweta County wrote to outgoing South Carolina governor William H. Gist on 8 November: "I am instructed as The Commanding officer of The 'Newnan Guards' to tender to your Excellency Their Services in The event our State

---

[11] Corley, *Confederate City: Augusta, Georgia*, 31–32.

[12] Edward J. Cashin, *The Story of Augusta* (Augusta GA: Richmond County Board of Education, 1980) 115.

[13] "Letter of Secretary Cobb to the People of Georgia," *Macon (GA) Weekly Telegraph*, 20 December 1860. President Lincoln was inaugurated on 4 March 1861.

withdraws from the Federal Government and an attempt on the part of the Same to coerce South Carolina back into the union."[14]

Officers in a few companies were uneasy with the impetuous rush to separation. During a caucus of militia officers held soon after Lincoln's election, a canvas was taken regarding establishing an armory, doing away with the Georgia military system as it stood, and seceding from the United States immediately. While voting in favor of the first two items, the officers of Augusta's Oglethorpe Infantry opposed the motion for secession.[15]

Other units campaigned for new recruits to fill their ranks. In an open letter to the community posted in the *Sandersville Central Georgian*, a committee from the Washington Rifles scolded county residents. The 1860 census of Washington County listed 1,460 white citizens within the military ages of fifteen to fifty, out of a total of 6,143. Why was the county not supporting their militia more fully? "In view of the unsettled condition of our country," wrote the members, "and of the gathering storm, which may burst in rain upon our heads, does not the voice of patriotism call upon all to prepare for the conflict—and shall Georgia call and Washington not answer? or shall our rights demand our service in the field, and we be unprepared for the conflict? Patriotism and honor alike forbid."

"In behalf of our corps," the letter continued, "we invoke the aid of our young countrymen—we invite you to join our ranks to aid us by your co-operation—to you your country looks for protection, to the youthful, the gallant, the brave! Will you be laggard? Will you shrink from the conflict? Will you prefer inglorious ease? Shall your country call in vain? Sons of Revolutionary sires, shall your country's call be unheeded?"[16]

The Georgia legislature voted 16 November to fund the state's military preparations. The next day that body unanimously approved a proposition calling for a special convention to address whether the state should remain within the Union. Next a bill was passed that decreed elections for assembly

---

[14] Capt. George Hanvey to South Carolina governor William H. Gist, 8 November 1860, in the George M. Hanvey papers, Ms 494, Hargrett Rare Book and Manuscript Library, University of Georgia Libraries, Athens GA (hereafter cited as Hanvey Papers).

[15] Corley, *Confederate City: Augusta, Georgia*, 30.

[16] Mitchell, *History of Washington County*, 69; J. R. Smith and B. D. Evans, "To the People of Washington County," *Sandersville (GA) Sandersville Central Georgian*, 20 November 1860.

delegates would be held 2 January 1861. Milledgeville, the state capital, was to be the conference site. Governor Brown quickly signed the edict.[17]

Throughout the state, rallies were held to agitate for separation from the union. In Atlanta, a large secession meeting was called for the evening of 10 December. Gathering in front of Dr. Joseph Thompson's hotel, the torch-bearing group cheered fiery speeches given by several citizens, including one of the hotel owner's sons, Captain George Harvey Thompson of the Gate City Guard.[18]

Placards appeared calling on patriotic citizens to elect delegates to the secession convention. One such advertisement in Houston County reads:

ATTENTION
RESISTENCE MEN
ALL THE CITIZENS OF HOUSTON COUNTY
WHO WHEN DEMANDS SHALL BE MADE OF THE NORTHERN STATES FOR THE REPEAL OF ALL THE PERSONAL LIBERTY BILLS, FOR CONSTITUTIONAL GUARANTIES FOR THE SECURITY OF OUR SLAVES, AND FOR THE LOSS OF THE SAME, BY THOSE STATES INTO WHICH THEY HAVE ESCAPED—FOR THE EQUAL RIGHTS OF THE SOUTH IN THE TERRITORIES OF THE UNION, AND SUCH DEMANDS SHALL NOT BE COMPLIED WITH, ALL IN FAVOR OF SUCESSION, ARE REQUESTED TO MEET AT THE COURT HOUSE IN PERRY ON SATURDAY THE EIGHTH OF DECEMBER TO SELECT CANDIDATES TO REPRESENT THIS COUNTY IN THE STATE CONVENTION, TO ASSEMBLE ON THE 16TH OF JANUARY NEXT.
DECEMBER 3, 1860.
MANY CITIZENS[19]

The crisis between North and South came to a head on 20 December 1860, when South Carolina passed an Ordinance of Secession, formally withdrawing from the United States and declaring itself a sovereign entity. Other states of the Deep South followed in rapid succession: Mississippi, 9 January 1861; Florida, 10 January; and Alabama on 11 January. Pressure was building for Georgia to join her neighbors.

---

[17] Thomas Conn Bryan, *Confederate Georgia* (Athens GA: University of Georgia Press, 1953) 3–4.

[18] Cooper, *Official History of Fulton County*, 99.

[19] Warren Grice, ed. *A History of Houston County, Georgia* (Perry GA: n.p., 1934) 143–44.

Many did not want to wait for Georgia's secession to go to war. In Perry, the members of the Southern Rights Guard passed a series of resolves:

> 1st: That we, the Southern Rights Guard, be placed on a war footing;
>
> 2nd, That we inform Gov. Brown that we are ready for service and that if our State does not require our service we are ready to march to South Carolina or any other Southern State that may be attacked or threatened by Federal forces;
>
> 3rd, That a copy of these resolutions be forwarded immediately to Gov. Pickens of South Carolina and Gov. Brown of Ga.

In Columbus, "President" F. W. Dillard of the Southern Guard likewise offered his company's assistance to Pickens.[20]

The impending likelihood of armed conflict spurred enlistment. "The 8th of January was celebrated by the Washington Rifles with full ranks, Captain Jones commanding," exclaimed the *Central Georgian* with pride. "The question was submitted to the company, as to who was ready to march for the defense of Georgia when her Governor should call for volunteers? All who would go were request to march five paces to the front. At the command, march! every soldier stepped boldly forward with a determination which manifested that they were in earnest. And when Georgia does call, we predict that the Rifles will not be the last to rally to her defense."[21]

Brown continued to prepare the state for defense. The governor received warning from Senator Toombs of President Buchanan's plan to garrison Fort Pulaski, near Savannah. Reacting quickly, on 2 January the governor directed Colonel Alexander Lawton, commanding a militia force styled the 1st Volunteer Regiment of Georgia, to take possession of the lightly guarded installation.[22]

---

[20] Ibid., 156; Gordon Burns Smith, *Counties and Commanders, Part 2*, vol. 3 of *History of the Georgia Militia, 1783–1861*, 4 vols. (Milledgeville GA: Boyd Publishing, 2000–2001) 311. Francis W. Pickens was elected governor by the South Carolina General Assembly on 16 December 1860 and inaugurated the next day.

[21] Untitled article, *Sandersville Central Georgian*, 16 January 1861.

[22] Ulrich Bonnell Phillips, *The Life of Robert Toombs* (New York: The MacMillan Company, 1913) 215–16.

The Union Is Hereby Dissolved

On 16 January, the secession convention assembled in Milledgeville. Day after day speakers addressed the delegates on the pros and cons of leaving the Union. If separation from the United State were to be ratified, warned Alexander Stephens, dire consequences would ensue:

> This step [of secession] once taken, can never be recalled; and all the baleful and withering consequences that must follow will rest on the convention for all coming time. When we and our posterity shall see our lovely South desolated by the demon of war, which this act of yours will inevitably invite and call forth; when our green fields of waving harvest shall be trodden down by the murderous soldiery and fiery car of war sweeping over our land; our temples of justice laid in ashes; all the horrors and desolations of war upon us; who but this convention will be held responsible for it? and who but him who shall give his vote for this unwise and ill-timed measure, as I honestly think and believe, shall be held to strict account for this suicidal act by the present generation, and probably cursed and execrated by posterity for all coming time, for the wide and desolating ruin that will inevitably follow this act you now propose to perpetrate?[23]

Among those attending the convention was William O. Fleming, who fretted about the sick wife and child he had left back in Bainbridge. On 18 January he penned an anxious letter: "I am afraid you have a good reason for not writing me (viz) the sickness of yourself and or dear little Lila. Perhaps I am too easily frightened but such are my surmising."

Almost as an afterthought, Fleming described the momentous events taking place. He wrote, "A secession resolution passed the convention today by a majority of thirty five. Tomorrow it is thought the ordinance of secession will be signed almost unanimously. I do sincerely hope so. There are a great many here from all parts of Georgia & in fact from other states there is a large representation."

Fleming ended his letter with a tease to his young wife: "Plenty of pretty girls here but I have not even spoken to one."[24]

---

[23] Alexander H. Stephens, *The Reviewers Reviewed: A Supplement to the "War Between the States," etc., With an Appendix in Review of "Reconstruction," So Called* (New York: D. Appleton and Company, 1872) 182.

[24] William O. Fleming to his wife, 18 January 1861, Fleming Papers.

Cooperationists made one last attempt to forestall separation, proposing a convention of the slave states of the Deep South to address the injustices of the federal government, and to propose several amendments to the Constitution that would deal with their grievances. Time would be allowed for the United States Congress to respond. These resolutions were voted down, albeit by a slim margin.[25]

A "test vote" indicated a majority of the delegates would vote in favor of disunion. The next day, 19 January, a roll call of the delegates was taken—208 voted for secession, and 89 were against the measure.[26]

Quickly, a document was readied for presentation to the citizens of Georgia:

> AN ORDINANCE. To dissolve the Union between the State of Georgia and the other States united with her under a compact of Government entitled "The Constitution of the United States of America."
>
> We, the people of the State of Georgia, in Convention assembled, do declare and ordain, and it is hereby declared and ordained, That the ordinance adopted by the people of the State of Georgia in Convention, on the second day of January, in the year of our Lord seventeen hundred and eighty-eight, whereby the Constitution of the United States of America was assented to, ratified and adopted; and also all Acts and parts of Acts of the General Assembly of this State ratifying and adopting amendments of the said Constitution, are hereby repealed, rescinded and abrogated.
>
> We do further declare and ordain, That the Union now subsisting between the State of Georgia and other States under the name of the "United States of America," is hereby dissolved, and that the State of Georgia is in full possession and exercise of all those rights of sovereignty which belong and appertain to a free and independent State.
>
> GEORGE W. CRAWFORD, President.[27]

---

[25] Allan Nevins, *Prologue to Civil War 1859–1861*, vol. 2 of *The Emergence of Lincoln* (New York: Charles Scribners Sons, 1947–1950) 415–16.

[26] Ibid., 416.

[27] Candler, *Confederate Records of the State of Georgia*, 1:706–707.

Realizing they would be unable to sway the convention to their side, most cooperationists accepted the inevitable and joined the secessionists. The two delegates from Lumpkin County, who had come with strong cooperationist views, had voted against seceding. But when it came time to sign the ordinance, they both affixed their signatures.[28]

The news flashed across the state. Fireworks and cannon fire lit the night sky. The Georgia states' rights flag, a red star on a white field, was raised. "Big Steve," the huge fire bell in Augusta, began to toll in celebration. In Newnan, the Guards pranced about in their dress uniforms, firing their muskets heavenwards for hours. Even in Dahlonega, where secession had been opposed, the music of hammers ringing on anvils filled the air.[29]

Newspapers blared their support for the new nation. "THE SOVEREIGNITY OF THE STATES" blazed out from the masthead of the *Columbus Daily Times*. "The die is cast," reported the *Central Georgian*; "the deed is accomplished, and the great State of Georgia is no longer a member of the 'United States of America.'"[30]

Go We Must

The takeover of federal facilities escalated, but Union sentiment in the northern counties threatened to start a civil conflict within the state. In Dahlonega, local rabble-rouser Harrison W. Riley declared his intention of occupying the United States Mint to defend it for the federal government. Pro-Southern men took up positions guarding the mint, warning that anyone who attempted to occupy the buildings would be shot. Governor Brown was urged to send troops. Knowing Riley was more bluster than violence, Brown took a more tactful approach, appealing to Riley's sense of honor. Riley backed down, and the governor advised the officers of the mint he was taking control in the name of the state. The takeover netted $50,000 in gold.[31]

---

[28] Sarris, *A Separate Civil War*, 49–51.

[29] Corley, *Confederate City: Augusta, Georgia*, 32; Bryan, *Confederate Georgia*, 10; Sarris, *A Separate Civil War*, 44.

[30] "Georgia Adrift," *Sandersville Central Georgian*, 16 January 1861.

[31] Joseph H. Parks, *Joseph E. Brown of Georgia* (Baton Rouge: Louisiana State University Press, 1977) 135; Sarris, *A Separate Civil War*, 52, 59; Anonymous, "Important from Georgia," *New York Times*, 29 January 1861.

Three days after the Secession Ordinance was signed, Brown turned his attention to an even greater prize: the federal arsenal in Augusta, with its immense supply of arms and munitions.

Arriving in the city on Tuesday, 22 January, Brown reviewed the Augusta Battalion, commanded by Lieutenant Colonel Alfred Cumming. The governor then sent a message to the arsenal's commandant, Captain Arnold Elzey, demanding the surrender of the facility. Elzey refused. On Wednesday, Brown advised Cumming to have his troops prepared for action the next morning against the Federals. By 8:00 A.M. on 24 January, more than eight hundred soldiers were formed, eagerly awaiting their chance for glory. Their disappointment was great when they were dismissed an hour later, having learned the governor and his aide Henry Rootes Jackson, along with state militia brigadier generals Robert Harris and Charles H. Williams, had negotiated with Captain Elzey for the post's surrender. At 3:00 P.M., General Harris marched contingents of the Oglethorpe Infantry and Washington Artillery to the arsenal to take possession. There was little, if any, animosity between the two sides; in fact, Captain Elzey provided refreshments for Brown, his aides, and officers upon completion of the surrender proceedings. That evening, the Oglethorpes stacked their muskets, sharing a meal with the federal soldiers they were supposedly guarding.[32]

Men and boys from all corners of the state rushed to arms. Schools and colleges emptied as students deserted their classrooms to join regiments. Montpelier Springs, a school for boys in Monroe County, lost its entire student body. Though written in late April, an Emory University student's letter aptly described the enthusiasm engulfing most college campuses following secession: "There is a great deal of excitement prevailing here. We are expecting the college to close in a few days. President Thomas says if the excitement continues, he will be compelled to disband. One of the Professors is Captain of a Company, and is looking for orders every day to leave for Pensacola or Fort Pulaski...and about 20 leave tonight for Pensacola. A great many of the students are going home. I think by Friday, the college will be broken up entirely; what boys are not going to the wars, are going home."[33]

---

[32] Corley, *Confederate City: Augusta, Georgia*, 36–37.

[33] Monroe County Historical Society, *Monroe County, Georgia: A History* (Forsyth GA: n.p., 1979) 151, 195; Bryan, *Confederate Georgia*, 218.

Lavender Ray watched from afar as his state left the Union. Though North Carolina was resisting secession for the moment, expectations ran high among the youth in the state's colleges that the Old North State would soon join the Confederacy. "There is great excitement here," Ray would report soon after; "Everybody talks, thinks and dreams of war.... The students petitioned the Trustees at Raleigh for a suspension of regular duties, as it is almost impossible for us to study during the excitement."[34]

The ranks of military organizations swelled as eager new recruits signed up. Units materialized almost overnight. In Richmond County, two companies of "minutemen" were combined to create the Walker Light Infantry, named for the W.H.T. Walker who led the secessionists out of Augusta's City Hall. The entire male population of some families enlisted—in Perry, the Southern Rights Guards included four Felder brothers, along with a fifth soldier bearing the same surname (possibly a cousin). The Gate City Guards had little trouble obtaining new members to replace those who had resigned; within a few days, the company's strength was back to near eighty, and by late March, when Governor Brown would issue a call for troops, the Guard would assemble with 104 men.[35]

So many men were determined to join the ranks it was impossible to arm them all, so many were turned away. Company commanders frantically requested weapons from the state. In a letter to Adjutant General Henry C. Wayne regarding the condition of his company's equipment, Lieutenant Joseph Palmer of the Southern Rights Guard advised he had only forty-seven Harpers Ferry pattern rifles. Informing Wayne of his intention to distribute these weapons to selected soldiers, Palmer begged for more guns. "If you will send us more rifles," he wrote, "we will get more men. We already have more men than we have arms & several applications for admission with our company."[36]

Eager for action, Captain Jonathon Evans of the Bainbridge Independents (recently having changed its name once again, from the Bainbridge Volunteers) wrote Wayne on 24 March of his company's want of arms:

---

[34] Lavender Ray to his sister, 28 April 1861, in Mills Lane, ed., *"Dear Mother: Don't grieve about me. If I get killed, I'll only be dead.," Letters from Georgia Soldiers in the Civil War* (Savannah GA: The Beehive Press, 1977) 6–7.

[35] Fairman, *Chronicles of the Old Guard of the Gate City Guard*, 17–18.

[36] Corley, *Confederate City: Augusta, Georgia*, 35; Grice, *A History of Houston County, Georgia*, 158.

> I desire to report that our citizens have made up for us eighty temporary fatigue suits; & that no excuse from the President will ever ever satisfy us, if we do not put to work immediately. Do not let the report which I have made of the condition of our arms occasion any delay or uncertainty in our departure. Go we must. We will be content with the things we now have in the shape of arms, & be considered as supplants even for them if a change is to retard us, they have good bayonets on them. We also have some forty old musketoons with the sabre bayonet. We even will go if you allow us pikes.[37]

Throughout Georgia, militiamen stepped up preparations as they waited for the call from Milledgeville. The Gate City Guard of Atlanta shined and oiled their specially ordered Springfield rifled muskets. Drills and parades were scheduled with increasing frequency. "APPEAR at your Armory," read a notice in the *Atlanta Gate City Guardian*, exhorting the guards to assemble "on Friday next, 22d February, at 10 o'clock, A.M., in full uniform, for Parade." Other units were "respectfully invited to unite with the Guards in celebrating the Day."[38]

Impatient to try out new tents, the Washington Rifles laid out a campsite next to the Sandersville Methodist Church on 8 March. There they spent the night under strict military rules, with guards posted around the camp. Rising early the next morning, the company formed ranks to salute the new Confederacy, firing a volley for each of the seceded states. A "dismal groan" rose for Tennessee, North Carolina, and Virginia, in rebuke for those states' apparent hesitation to secede and join the new Southern nation.[39]

Companies ramped up their recruiting efforts. "VOLUNTEERS WANTED IMMEDIATELY," declared an advertisement in the *Columbus Daily Times*. "TWENTY FIVE OR THIRTY able bodied young men wanted to fill up the ranks of Company D, Southern Guard, for immediate service in the field. All those who are desirous to enter the service of their

---

[37] Frank S. Jones, *History of Decatur County Georgia* (Spartanburg SC: The Reprint Company, Publishers, 1980) 366, William Warren Rogers, *A Scalawag in Georgia, Richard Whitely and the Politics of Reconstruction* (Champaign: University of Illinois Press, 2007) 15.

[38] Advertisement, *Atlanta (GA) Gate City Guardian*, 19 February 1861.

[39] Anonymous, "The Encampment," *Sandersville Central Georgian*, 13 March 1861.

country can now have an opportunity of doing so, by calling up on the officers and enrolling their names."[40]

The drills attracted much attention from the populace and enticed many to enlist. The evolutions of the newly formed Walker Light Infantry so entranced Henry Hill of Augusta, a seventeen-year-old free black man, he implored its officers to allow him to join. Convincing them with his sincerity and fervor, as well as his musical skill, Hill was appointed company drummer.[41]

The company from Augusta was not the only one to include a black musician. The Gate City Guards employed a slave by the name of Glasgow as a fifer. Sam Fisher, who had accompanied Hamblin R. Felder as a cook, was appointed company drummer for the Southern Rights Guard.[42]

Expectation of a short, single-battle conflict led to company rosters swelling with enlistees, anxious for their chance to confront the now hated Yankee before their chance for glory slipped away. Captain A. C. Rogers from Upson County offered ten men from his company to the Gate City Guard. More men attempted to join than some companies could absorb, resulting in many being turned away. "Five patriotic citizens of Griffin also attached themselves to the Guards this morning," reported the *Atlanta Southern Confederacy.*"Verily, the spirit which actuated the Sires of '76 is again rife in the land. As the Guards cannot enlist a greater number than eighty, rank and file, we fear some of the young men most anxious to 'smell gunpowder,' will have to wait until a further call for volunteers shall be made."[43]

Look Out for the Bombshells

Not everyone was eager to send their sons to war. Captain Hanvey of the Newnan Guards received a letter from one friend which began with patriotic flourishes: "In case of an attempt on the part of the late United

---

[40] Advertisement, *Columbus (GA) Daily Times*, 21 March 1861.

[41] Corley, *Confederate City: Augusta, Georgia*, 108.

[42] "B.," "A Southern Rights Negro from Atlanta, Goes to Fight the Abolitionist," *Macon (GA) Daily Telegraph*, 9 April 1861; Bobbe Hickson Nelson, *A Land So Dedicated: The History of Houston County, Georgia* (Perry GA: Southern Trellis, 1998) 172.

[43] Anonymous, "Gate City Guards," *Atlanta (GA) Southern Confederacy*, 29 March 1861.

States to coerce the Confederate States it had been my wish that Abner should do his part in the defence of the section where providence had cast his lot. In the event of a war breaking out it has been my ardent desire that he should perform his part in defence of his own section. I know this to have been his wish. It has ever been mine since the commencement of our difficulties with the Gov. of the United States."

The writer's true intent soon became apparent, however. "It is my earnest desire," he explained,

> to give him a thorough Collegiate education—he is now about Sixteen years of age if he should volunteer for the purpose merely of guarding some fort, which would be the only duty he would be called on to perform unless we should be engaged in actual war, & should he continue in that kind of service for one two or three years, I should loose all hope, from the damaged condition of his mind before returning home, of ever having him well educated. I have not the time to write you fully at present & give you in detail all the reasons which would influence me in objecting to his being mustered in service now. You have the main reasons & as a parent yourself will know how to appreciate them. If a war breaks out it will be all up in a very few days—in that case so far from wishing him excused, if he even hesitates to go I would disown him forever son as he is. I have written him today & have informed him that I have written to you. Be good enough to have him excused exempt for active service.

The letter was signed, "Truly Your Friend, A. B. Cabiness."[44]

Using the various military units as a nucleus, the governor began to build a state defense force. Brown selected officers from the militia to serve in the "State Army of Georgia." Among these was George Harvey Thompson of the Gate City Guards, who received a commission as captain in the state army. Applauding Thompson's selection, as well as other Atlanta officers, the *Gate City Guardian* crowed, "These are admirable appointments, and shows that His Excellency has a keen appreciation of true merit."[45]

By March 1861, with hostilities imminent between North and South, the newly established Confederate government in Montgomery, Alabama,

---

[44] A. B. Cabiness to Capt. G. M. Hanvey, 15 March 1861, Hanvey Papers.

[45] Anonymous, "Appointments," *Atlanta Gate City Guardian*, 14 February 1861.

was scrambling to organize, equip, and train regiments for its fledgling army. Secretary of war Leroy P. Walker sent urgent appeals to the governors of the seceded states, asking for troops. Walker wrote to Governor Brown on 9 March requesting 1,000 soldiers for Fort Pulaski and another 1,000 for Pensacola "to be sent forward to those points with as little delay as possible." Brown replied on 12 March, "I will furnish you two regiments of 1,000 each as soon as they can possibly be organized."[46]

Rumors of the impending troop buildup quickly reached local editors, who wasted little time proclaiming the news in enormous headlines. "GEORGIA VOLUNTEERS GET READY," cried the *Columbus Times*. "We learn from a gentleman direct from Montgomery," the article continued, "that President Davis will issue an order for five thousand Volunteers for Pensacola. Of this number Georgia will furnish, perhaps, two thousand. We consider the information reliable, and believe that the order will be issued to the Governors of the Confederate States immediately. President Davis does not regard the withdrawal of the troops from Fort Sumter, (as it is a case of life and death with the Government troops) as any indication of peace."[47]

"Put on your knapsacks, boys, and look out for the bombshells and cannon balls at Pickens," warned the *Times*. The advice was fitting. Georgia's sons were about to be summoned to war.[48]

---

[46] Candler, *Confederate Records of the State of Georgia*, 3:20–22.

[47] Anonymous, "Georgia Volunteers Get Ready," *Columbus (GA) Times*, 14 March 1861, as reported in the *Sandersville Central Georgian*, 20 March 1861.

[48] Ibid.

2

The Regiment Forms

"Nothing could induce me to leave the quiet & enjoyment of my own domestic hearth for this life of turmoil & confusion save the call of my country for the services of her sons. I am now enlisted in that service & will never no never desert my post, but this does not prevent my heart yearning for the dear ones at home as God grant that we may soon meet again."— Lieutenant William Oliver Fleming, Bainbridge Independents[1]

We Have Given Up a Brother

Governor Brown would not suffer for lack of troops while trying to fill Secretary Walker's request, for some 250 companies had offered their services to the state. It was decided the units selected for this first Confederate regiment would be accepted in the order their tender was received by the government—with one exception. Brown wanted a North Georgia company in the regiment, feeling that having a mountain unit would increase sentiment in Lumpkin and the surrounding mountain counties in support of secession. Thus, orders were sent for the Dahlonega Volunteers to report to Macon.[2]

When Brown's call for troops arrived, militiamen closed up shops; took leave of sweethearts, wives, and families; and rushed to join their companies. In Coweta County, 2nd Lieutenant Thomas Swint of the Newnan Guards placed an advertisement in the local newspaper: "I have closed out my entire stock of groceries, and leave this day for the service of

---

[1] William O. Fleming to his wife, 1 April 1861, in the William Oliver Fleming Papers, #2292-z, Southern Historical Collection, the Wilson Library, University of North Carolina at Chapel Hill (hereafter cited as Fleming Papers). Quoted with permission of William Fleming, descendent.

[2] Joseph H. Parks, *Joseph E. Brown of Georgia* (Baton Rouge: Louisiana State University Press, 1977) 137; Jonathan Dean Sarris, *A Separate Civil War: Communities in Conflict in the Mountain South* (Charlottesville: University of Virginia Press, 2006) 47.

the Confederate States. My books and notes will be found in the office of J. E. Dent. Those who have no money can call and give notes."[3]

For some, the sacrifice of leaving their families was agonizing. Private Vincent Ogletree of the Southern Guards bade farewell to his wife and three children with a heavy heart, for he was leaving them with no income save his army pay and with no one to watch over them. Some two weeks after his departure, the family's plight was discovered and publicized in the *Columbus Daily Times*:

> While we cannot appreciate the patriotism that would make so great a sacrifice as this yet the fact exists and we would be pleased to see the Citizens give some relief to the family. The lady's name is Mrs. Ogletree and she has three children to support. She is unable to provide for her family and it would be an act of charity and true benevolence for our citizens to step forth and see that she does not suffer. A soldiers wife, (and we learn she has been a good one,) with three small children appeal to the sympathy of a patriotic people. Will it be heeded?[4]

Joseph M. G. Medlock, editor of the *Sandersville Central Georgian*, left his newspaper to join the Washington Rifles. His final editorial was a poignant goodbye to his subscribers:

> FAREWELL! Ere this reaches our readers we shall be far on our way toward the field of battle. In time of peace we united with some of our fellow citizens of this county in forming a volunteer company. Our country now calls for our services on the tented field. We heed that call, and the pen must now be exchanged for the sword. We go, trusting, we hope, in Divine Providence for the result. Behind us, we leave those who are dearer to us than life. In the hands of Providence and our fellow country men we leave them, believing that should we fall in defence of our country, they will be taken care of.[5]

Atlanta's City Hall served as worship center on Sunday, 31 March, with the Reverend Dr. J. S. Wilson offering prayers for the protection of the

---

[3] Newnan-Coweta Historical Society, *History of Coweta County, Georgia* (Roswell GA: Wolfe Associates, 1988) 13.

[4] Anonymous, "Relief to the Poor," *Columbus (GA) Daily Times*, 11 April 1861.

[5] J. M. G. Medlock, "Farewell!" *Sandersville Central Georgian*, 3 April 1861.

Gate City Guard. The next morning, despite dark clouds and showers, a large crowd gathered on the platform of the Macon and Western Railroad Depot, as well as in and around the nearby Franklin Printing House. There to celebrate the departure of the Guards, they were also eager to witness a ceremony bestowing a new flag to the company. Marching in through mud-lined streets, the Guards were escorted to the depot by four other companies. After listening to a speech brimming with vitriol against the United States government and northern abolitionists, the Guard was presented with its new standard. In turn, a representative from the company presented a gold watch to the young lady who oversaw the women's group which had lovingly sewn the banner. The timepiece was inscribed "Gate-City Guards, to Miss J. E. Hanleiter, April 1, 1861."[6]

As the Guardsmen waited to board their train, another young lady, Miss Sallie Avery, spoke to the crowd: "Soldiers, your country has called for your services, and with a promptness never excelled by Greek nor Roman you grasped your swords, buckled on your armor, and now wait but the neighing of the iron horse to bear you on with thunder tread to the scene of action, and it may be to the field of bloody glory. In you we present to the sacred cause of patriotism the jewels of Georgia." After several more speeches, 223 girls from the Atlanta Female Institute distributed small flags to each of the soldiers.[7]

While the departure of the Guards saddened many, in at least one household it signaled a much deeper strain on family ties. Chester A. Stone had come to Atlanta from Vermont around 1856, joining his brother and sister-in-law, Amherst and Cyrena. Eager to join Atlanta's social circle, Chester joined the Gate City Guard. When several Guardsmen resigned over flying the United States flag, Chester chose to remain in the unit. Though they were likely part of the crowd seeing the Guards off, Amherst and Cyrena were deeply dismayed at Chester's decision to throw his lot in with the Confederacy. Both strong Unionists, the couple could not understand why Chester would choose to fight against his native region and state.[8]

---

[6] Anonymous, "A Sermon Before the 'Gate-City Guards,'" *Atlanta Southern Confederacy*, 1 April 1861; Anonymous, "Flag Presentation to the Gate-City Guards," *Atlanta Southern Confederacy*, 1 April 1861.

[7] Henry Clay Fairman, *Chronicles of the Old Guard of the Gate City Guard, Atlanta, Georgia, 1858–1915* (Atlanta GA: Byrd Printing Company, 1915) 26.

[8] Thomas G. Dyer, *Secret Yankees: The Union Circle in Confederate Atlanta* (Baltimore: The Johns Hopkins University Press, 1999) 64–65.

Young Sarah Rice watched with admiration as the Southern Rights Guard departed Houston County. Afterwards, she wistfully recorded the event in her diary: "Never while memory holds her place will we forget the 1st day of April 1861—it has taken from Perry many of her most prominent men to go off in defense of southern rights. We have given up a brother brave and true. He was our principal support and protector but we could not say nay, when his country called and his patriotism bade him go."[9]

The Dahlonega Volunteers received their orders Saturday, 30 March. The next evening, each member of the company was presented with a Bible by the local Methodist church. Before dawn on 1 April, they huddled inside the old brick courthouse, unable to load their wagons because of a cold rain. While waiting for the drizzle to slacken, the soldiers were regaled with speeches by prominent citizens. Shortly before noon the company finished packing their equipment, then formed ranks. Once again, the ringing of hammers on anvils filled the air as the Volunteers marched away.[10]

Although their columns had decried secession, the editors of the *Augusta Chronicle and Sentinel* revealed their high regard for the troops as they bade farewell to the Oglethorpe and Walker Light Infantries: "While we shall part with our military friends with much regret—a regret that is natural, inasmuch as we shall miss many familiar faces and daily friendly recognitions upon the street, in the circles of business, and the social circle—we feel a glow of pride at these representatives of our Volunteer Soldiery. We are not ashamed to "pit" them against similar organizations in the whole Confederacy. They are brave, well disciplined and effective men, and will command the respect and admiration of their fellow-soldiers wherever they may be called."[11]

Likewise, the *Atlanta Daily Intelligencer* lauded its local company: "The Gate City Guards, has always been one of the crack companies of Atlanta, and should they be called into actual service, to make a reputation at the cannon's mouth, we have strong faith that they will acquit themselves

[9] Bobbe Hickson Nelson, *A Land So Dedicated: The History of Houston County, Georgia* (Perry GA: Southern Trellis, 1998) 112.

[10] Anonymous, "Military Surprise," *Atlanta Southern Confederacy*, 4 April 1861; Andrew W. Cain, *History of Lumpkin County, 1832–1932* (Atlanta GA: Stein Printing Company, 1932) 143.

[11] Anonymous, "Under Marching Orders," *Augusta (GA) Chronicle and Sentinel*, 29 March 1861.

with honor to Atlanta, the State of Georgia, and the Government of the Confederate States."[12]

"The Newnan Guards have orders to march immediately and rendezvous at Macon," reported the *Newnan Banner*. "Destination Fort Pickens. They will leave here on Monday next. The Guards will muster between sixty or seventy brave men, well officered, and all prepared to take a hand in the work of ridding Southern soil and forts of the presence of the old Federal Troops of Lincoln. If a fight is necessary and nothing else will satisfy the Black Republicans, we guarantee a good account from the Guards when the ball opens."[13]

Similar scenes were enacted as other companies bid adieu to their communities. Escorted to the train by other city militia, Company D of the Southern Guards departed Columbus to the sound of musket volleys and the boom of a small cannon dubbed the "Baby Waker." In Sandersville, the ladies of the town treated the Washington Rifles to a "sumptuous dinner" at the courthouse, after which the leftovers were packaged for the soldiers' journey. Following the meal, the company was presented with a "handsome flag of the Confederate States." The evening concluded with a round of speeches, which exhorted the soldiers "never to permit the flag confided to their keeping by the angel band of [w]omen to be tarnished by one unpatriotic act, or soiled by the hand of a foe."[14]

As the whistles of engines faded in the distance and the footsteps of marching soldiers could no longer be heard, a profound sense of emptiness gripped the soldiers' hometowns. The silence in the streets of Sandersville was overwhelming. The day after the Rifles left, a columnist wrote,

> When we see so many of our friends and acquaintances,young, old and middle-aged, leaving us on such a mission—their wives and children, parents, brothers and sisters remaining behind and praying for their success and safe return—may we not be pardoned for the involuntary exhibition of this little infirmity. In truth, we are almost idealess this week; are troubled and confused, and until the farewells of those friends and patriot soldiers from whom we parted

---

[12] Anonymous, "Gate City Guards," *Atlanta (GA) Daily Intelligencer*, 26 March 1861.

[13] Anonymous, "Orders to March," *Newnan (GA) Banner*, 29 March 1861.

[14] Anonymous, "The Military Leaving," *Columbus Daily Times*, 2 April 1861.

yesterday—some of them probably for the last time—cease to resound in our ears, the effort at resurrection will be fruitless.

"Our town wears an appearance of gloom," observed another journalist, "The 'soul-stirring drum and ear-piercing fife' are no longer heard in our streets."[15]

God Bless the Ladies of Macon

The troops' path to Macon was lined with adoring throngs. An enthusiastic crowd greeted the Gate City Guards, Newnan Guards, Ringgold, and Etowah Infantry when their train pulled into the depot in Griffin. The Griffin Light Guard paraded in full dress to honor the troops. Determined not to miss this auspicious occasion, the Spalding Greys formed in civilian clothes, not yet having received their uniforms.[16]

Stopping for the night near Fort Valley, the Southern Rights Guard was met by two local companies who escorted the troops from the depot into town. After an impassioned address by Professor Thomas Russell, one of the village's leading citizens, the townspeople gave the Guard three cheers. Once camp was set up, the company was invited to a levee being held in its honor. "The evening was pleasantly spent," it was reported, "and until the 'clock told the hour for retiring,' the moments sped as a marriage bell; and as we saw the firm shake of the hand, and the hearty 'good-bye—God bless you,' we did feel, and do felt that God will bless this noble band of patriot soldiers, the Southern Rights Guard, of Houston."[17]

From the four points of the compass, the citizen-soldiers converged on Macon. First to turn up were the Quitman Guards—so early, in fact, they were parading through Macon before the citizens became aware of their arrival. The Guard's early appearance ensured them a choice spot of ground at Camp Oglethorpe. Later in the morning, a crowd of townspeople waited impatiently at the depot for the train carrying the Atlanta and Newnan companies. As the Newnan Guards stepped down from the cars, their sheer size amazed the citizens—at least thirty members of the company were more than six feet tall.[18]

---

[15] Anonymous, "Departed," *Columbus (GA) Daily Enquirer*, 2 April 1861; Anonymous, "Gone to the Wars," *Sandersville Central Georgian*, 3 April 1861.

[16] Anonymous, "The Departure," *Sandersville Central Georgian*, 3 April 1861.

[17] Anonymous, "Military," *Griffin (GA) Middle Georgian*, 2 April 1861, 3 April 1861.

[18] "W. J. S.," "Southern Rights Guard," *Macon Daily Telegraph*, 4 April 1861.

Constructed in 1843 on the southwest side of Macon, Camp Oglethorpe occupied twelve acres near the Macon and Western Railroad. Bounded by city streets on three sides and a swampy area on the fourth, the camp boasted a wide, level parade ground, storage buildings , and enough water to provide for up to one hundred companies of soldiers. "The location is a beautiful one, situated some mile or more from the business part of the city," reported a correspondent from the *Augusta Chronicle and Sentinel*, writing under the pseudonym "Lennox."[19] Already encamped were Macon's own Floyd Rifles, Brown Infantry, and Independent Volunteers.[20]

Most of the troops came in by train, though some arrived footsore. Tramping almost non-stop from Decatur County, the Bainbridge Independents covered the distance in less than two days. Shortly after reaching the camp, Lieutenant William O. Fleming wrote to his wife: "We arrived in this place about two hours ago. I never was so hungry in my life as I have been today. Only a half meal at breakfast & not another mouthful until ten oclock tonight. I have just finished my supper & feel decidedly better tho' very sleepy."[21]

The facilities at Camp Oglethorpe failed to impress many soldiers. "I did not sleep a wink the 1st night I was here," complained William J. Miller of the Oglethorpe Infantry; "We could not get our tents and were put in an old shanty with one or two more companys....We have crackers or sea biscuits which are so hard that I can not brake some of them with my hands. We have to boil them before we can eat them. I am content with what I can get or at least have to be so."[22] Sergeant Medlock, a former editor, also found time to complain about the food: "Our fare is none of the best. We are furnished with side bacon of the fattest kind, pilot or light bread, (according to choice), sugar and coffee."[23]

---

[19] "Lennox," "Correspondence of the *Chronicle and Sentinel*," *Augusta Chronicle and Sentinel*, 7 April 1861.

[20] Anonymous, "Military," *Macon Daily Telegraph*, 2 April 1861; Anonymous, "More Troops Gone Forward," *Macon Daily Telegraph*, 8 April 1861.

[21] William O. Fleming to his wife, 1 April 1861, Fleming Papers.

[22] William J. Miller to his mother, 6 April 1861, in the A. J. Miller Papers, #510-z, Southern Historical Collection, The Wilson Library, University of North Carolina at Chapel Hill (hereafter cited as Miller Papers).

[23] J. M. G. Medlock, letter to the editor, *Sandersville Central Georgian*, 10 April 1861. Pilot bread was a hard cracker, also known as hard tack.

For the most part, Macon welcomed the volunteers. Committees were formed to minister to the troops' needs. "The ladies of Macon, God bless them," wrote one Augusta soldier, "have showered down attentions upon us, and baskets upon baskets of the 'substantial' of this life in the way of eatables are continually being sent in, with the compliments of some fair donor accompanying them."[24] One civic group provided hams and beef tongues each day for lunch.[25]

A few of Macon's businessmen took advantage of the influx to boost sales, leading to complaints of shady practices. One soldier wrote, "One would think that, under the circumstances, the merchants of Macon would sell us such things as we need very cheap. But, on the contrary, some of them are disposed to put the tariff on us."[26] A correspondent for the *Sandersville Central Georgian* noted "that they had to pay exorbitant prices for a good many things which they had to pay, a fact which we scarcely could believe of the Macon storekeepers."[27]

Camp Oglethorpe buzzed with activity as the companies settled in. "Macon is all astir," wrote Lieutenant Fleming;"martial music is heard in every direction."[28] The goings-on attracted a legion of curious spectators. "Camp Oglethorpe is visited every afternoon by large numbers of ladies and gentlemen," reported Lennox, "boys and girls, from Macon and the adjoining country, all of who take an active interest in the drills and manoeuvres of the Companies." The reporter was amused by the dizzying array of uniforms worn by the volunteers: "[T]o a stranger or spectator just now presents an interesting scene, with the red shirts, blue shirts, gray shirts, and shirts without order and indescribable to an unpractised eye in such descriptions."[29]

---

[24] "Letters by the Volunteers," *Augusta Chronicle and Sentinel*, 7 April 1861.

[25] Richard W. Iobst, *Civil War Macon: The History of a Confederate City* (Macon GA: Mercer University Press, 1999) 26.

[26] J. M. G. Medlock, letter to the editor, *Sandersville Central Georgian*, 10 April 1861.

[27] Ibid.; "N.," "A Day in Camp," *Sandersville Central Georgian*, 10 April 1861.

[28] William O. Fleming to his wife, 1 April 1861, Fleming Papers.

[29] "Lennox," letter to the editor, *Augusta Chronicle and Sentinel*, 7 April 1861.

Not for Ourselves Alone

Visitors to the encampment beheld a confusing hodgepodge of dress and fatigue uniforms. The Quitman Guards of Monroe County wore a short gray jacket with three rows of buttons, with red epaulettes adorning their shoulders. Their headgear was trimmed in red with the letters "Q G," and the Georgia coat of arms fastened on front, and adorned with a yellow plume. Their accoutrement hung from white cross-belts.[30]

Atlanta's Gate City Guardsmen were clothed in "dark blue Prince Albert coats, red breast, with three rows of brass buttons and cross bars of gold lace; light blue pants with red stripes, and dark beavers with nodding plumes of red and white." The Guards' fatigue uniforms were of gray material. The Bainbridge Independents came "uniformed in coarse flannel shirts, and pantaloons of the coarsest negro cloth," while the Washington Rifles arrived garbed in green service jackets.[31]

The uniform of the Oglethorpe Infantry was federal blue; dark for their single-breasted frock coats and light for their trousers. Silver epaulettes festooned their shoulders. Dressed in a gray coatee adorned with three rows of buttons and black piping on their collars and sleeves, the Newnan Guards

---

[30] Gordon Burns Smith, *Counties and Commanders, Part 1*, vol. 2 of *History of the Georgia Militia, 1783–1861*, 4 vols. (Milledgeville GA: Boyd Publishing, 2000–2001) 242. Smith describes the coat as blue with gold epaulettes. His description comes from a black and white photo of Benjamin McCowen of the Quitman Guards. McCowen's picture has evidently been reproduced several times, causing the image to be somewhat distorted. A much clearer image of another Guardsman taken about the same time, uncovered by Dr. David N. Wiggins and Dr. Keith Bohannon, displays the Guards' uniform more distinctly. This photograph has most of its original hand tint, showing the correct colors. The soldier, Stephen W. Nolen, was not with the Quitman Guards when they traveled to Macon. Nolen enlisted in the 6th Georgia Infantry. For a color reproduction of Nolen in his uniform, see David N. Wiggins, *Georgia's Confederate Sons, Volume 1* (Carrollton GA: University of West Georgia Press, 2007) 46, 94.

[31] Anonymous, "A Great Company—A Running Sketch of the Gate City Guard," *Atlanta Constitution*, 18 January 1889; Philip Katcher, *American Civil War Armies (5): Volunteer Militia* (Oxford: Osprey Publishing, 1989) 7; Gordon Burns Smith, *The Companies*, vol. 4 of *History of the Georgia Militia, 1783–1861*, 4 vols. (Milledgeville GA: Boyd Publishing, 2000–2001) 298; Isaac W. Avery, *The History of the State of Georgia from 1850 to 1881* (New York: Brown & Derby, 1881) 195; J. M. G. Medlock, letter to the editor, *Sandersville Central Georgian*, 10 April 1861.

wore gray shakos topped by a red and white pompon, with the letters "NG" surrounded by a wreath, and like color trousers highlighted with black stripes. Blue frock coats were worn by the Newnan officers, with the pompon fastened to a blue cap. Soldiers of the Southern Rights Guard sported drooping yellow plumes on their felt hats and wore dress blue frock coats trimmed with silk lace. A white stripe ran down the sides of their blue pants. The Guards' fatigue uniform was a gray single-breasted frock coat with black trim.[32]

While their outfits were not altogether "uniform," the flags borne by several companies followed the pattern of the new national banner, the "Stars and Bars"; consisting of an upper and lower red stripe with a central white stripe; the canton blue with a pattern of stars. The standard Miss Hanleiter presented to the Gate City Guards was of fine silk surrounded by a silk fringe, and was modified from a United States flag the company had received the previous April. The canton featured a circle of gold stars on each side surrounding an inscription. Printed on one side was the phrase "Gate City Guards, from the Ladies of Atlanta, 1861." On the reverse was written "In Hoc Signo Vinces" (By This Sign You Shall Conquer).[33]

The Quitman Guards carried a standard with gold stars, fringed with white silk.[34] The Volunteers coming from Lumpkin County (who were still enroute) bore a silk "Confederate Flag" presented "in behalf of the young ladies of Dahlonega."[35] The banner of the Washington Rifles differed in that, instead of stars, the right side canton contained the three-columned Georgia state coat of arms. A red scroll above the arms proclaimed "Washington Rifles"; a lower scroll read, "Organized May 17 1858." The

---

[32] Florence Fleming Corley, *Confederate City: Augusta, Georgia, 1860–1865* (Columbia: University of South Carolina Press, 1960) 33; Thomas G. Rodgers and Richard M. Harrison, *Never Give Up This Field, Georgia Troops in the Civil War* (Norcross GA: Wordsworth Group, 1989) 8; Ron Field, *The Confederate Army 1861–1865 (2), Florida, Alabama and Georgia* (Oxford: Osprey Publishing, 2005) 22; Nelson, *A Land So Dedicated*, 112; Warren Grice, ed. *A History of Houston County, Georgia* (Perry GA: n.p., 1934) 154. A shako is a tall, cylindrical military hat.

[33] Anonymous, "That Flag," *Atlanta Southern Confederacy*, 1 April 1861; Fairman, *Chronicles of the Old Guard of the Gate City Guard*, 15.

[34] Anonymous, "Reunion Echoes," *Atlanta Constitution*, 6 July 1883.

[35] Cain, *History of Lumpkin County*, 143.

canton's reverse side displayed a circle of stars with red scrolls top and bottom proclaiming "We Yield Not To Our Countrys Foes."[36]

Not every banner followed the pattern of the national flag. An exception was the flag borne by Company D of the Southern Guards. Constructed of white silk, the face side displayed the state coat of arms centered, with the addition of a slave sitting on a bale of cotton. Above the state emblem was emblazoned *"Non suibus solum sed patriae et amicis."* The translation, "Not for ourselves alone but for country and friends," was printed along the bottom. The other side of the banner bore a wreath of acorns and cotton bolls surrounding the words "Southern Guard" above a large letter "D." The flag was bordered with a three-inch wide fringe.[37]

The flag of the Walker Light Infantry was described as "...a beautiful banner, the work of fair hands... the flag is of white ground, having the coat of arms of Georgia on one side, with the motto, 'Dear our country: our liberty dearer.' On the other side is an uplifted arm grasping a sword. The flag is trimmed with a neat fringe."[38]

Drills and military discipline began to mold the disparate companies into a cohesive organization, though duty was surprisingly light. Drums rolled reveille at sunrise, and "our soldiers [hurried] from their tents, some without hats, others without shoes, and still others without—well, as a truthful chronicler we must tell it—without their unmentionables, but all wide awake, answering to their names as they were called from the roll by the Orderly Sergeant." With roll call completed, breakfast was cooked, followed by an hour of leisure during which the soldiers smoked their pipes and "segars," visited friends or penned letters to loved ones. Sergeants put new recruits to work learning "evolutions," or the proper way to march in ranks.[39]

Preparations for dinner (as the noon meal was called) began about 11:00 A.M. Companies divided up into groups, or "messes," of seven to ten

---

[36] Keith Bohannon et al., *Hallowed Banners, Historic Flags in the Georgia Capitol Collection* (Atlanta GA: Georgia Capitol Museum, Office of Secretary of State, 2005) 16–17, 94; Philip Katcher, *Flags of the American Civil War (1), Confederate* (Oxford: Osprey Publishing, 1992) 8.

[37] Anonymous, "Banner Presentation," *Columbus (GA) Weekly Times*, 11 February 1861.

[38] Anonymous, "Flag Presentation," *Augusta (GA) Daily Constitutionalist*, 21 March 1861.

[39] "N.," "A Day in Camp," *Sandersville Central Georgian*, 10 April 1861.

men who shared tents and cooking duties. The government warehouses issued bacon, pilot bread, sugar and coffee. Other food items purchased in Macon supplemented the men's bill of fare. Meals varied widely between each mess, depending on the culinary ability of the volunteers and the degree of ingenuity and financial wherewithal. A visitor to the camp of the Washington Rifles gave the following menu for one mess: "Fried bacon, boiled eggs, fried potatoes, corn bread, cabbage, turnips, light bread and butter, pickles, onions, cheese, and for desert sponge cake and water in place of wine."[40] Another group dined on "fried bacon, boiled peas, boiled eggs, light-bread, pilot bread and coffee."[41] The officer's mess, consisting of Captain S. A. H. Jones, three lieutenants, an ensign, and the company color bearer, was, as might be expected, provided with a much more bountiful choice: "Fried bacon, from the Government storehouse; cold ham, turnips, fresh lobsters, pickled lobsters, duck eggs boiled, cornbread, lightbread, pilot bread, cheese and coffee."[42]

The afternoon was filled with company and regimental drill, as the green soldiers learned to maneuver together in large formations. Visitors sometimes found themselves in danger of being run over as the troops struggled to learn wheels and countermarches. After a few hours of such exercises the men were dismissed to their camps for supper. The drums again beat out at 9:00 P.M., this time calling the soldiers for final roll call. Guards were posted, and the rest of the troops crawled into their tents for the night.[43]

Between the drills, various activities kept the soldiers from succumbing to boredom. "Many amusements are resorted to by the men in camp," wrote Lennox,

> to while "dull care away," among which may be mentioned foot races, leap-frog, and town-ball. Here are some asleep—here some writing—some reading—some trying their new guns—and some as I now write, are washing the frying-pans, while others are preparing eatables for the many amusing themselves. The men "fall in" with much eagerness at meals, and "Bridges" and "Schneider" may look to

[40] Ibid.

[41] Ibid.

[42] Ibid.

[43] Ibid.; Anonymous, "Camp Oglethorpe," *Atlanta Daily Intelligencer*, 6 April 1861.

> their laurels, for the members of the Oglethorpe and Walker Light Infantry are becoming efficient cooks. The work they have to do, namely—eat, sleep, loll, laugh, rise early, and have one or two short drills during the day, is certainly stimulus enough to make any one hungry for the next meal.[44]

Boyish pranks abounded. Whitson Johnson of the Oglethorpe Infantry found himself flat on the ground as the carpet seat of his campstool ripped. Johnson's tent-mate William Miller fastened the pieces back together, scheming to swap the stool to some other unsuspecting soldier, "so as to give some one a fall."[45]

The Honor, Glory and Fame of Georgia

On Wednesday, 3 April, ten of the companies were selected to form the 1st Regiment of Georgia Volunteers. Their enlistment was recorded as from 18 March, the date which most of the companies offered their services to the governor. Each company was assigned a letter designation:

"A"Newnan Guards, Captain George M. Hanvey
"B"Southern Guards, Captain Francis G. Wilkins
"C"Southern Rights Guards, Captain John Andrew Houser
"D"Oglethorpe Infantry, Captain James O. Clarke
"E"Washington Rifles, Captain Seaborn A. H. Jones
"F"Gate City Guards, Captain William L. Ezzard
"G"Bainbridge Independents, Captain Jonathon W. Evans
"H"Dahlonega Volunteers, Captain Alfred Harris
"I"Walker Light Infantry, Captain Samuel H. Crump
"K"Quitman Guards, Captain James S. Pinckard.[46]

Of the remaining companies, four (Macon Independent Volunteers, Ringgold Volunteers, Brown Infantry, and Etowah Infantry) were combined

---

[44] "Lennox," "Camp Oglethorpe," *Augusta Chronicle and Sentinel*, 6 April 1861.

[45] William J. Miller to his mother, 6 April 1861, Miller Papers.

[46] "Organization of 1st Regiment Georgia," n.d., in the George M. Hanvey papers, Ms 494, Hargrett Rare Book and Manuscript Library, University of Georgia Libraries, Athens GA (hereafter cited as Hanvey Papers). As the letter "J" sounds too much like a "G" when spoken and looks too much like an "I" when written, it was not used in regimental company designations.

to form the 1st Battalion Georgia Volunteer Infantry. The Floyd Rifles would remain in Macon, much to their chagrin.[47]

One company was noticeably absent, for the Dahlonega Volunteers had yet to arrive in Macon. Marching all the way from Lumpkin County, Captain Alfred Harris and his men appeared in Atlanta at 2:30 P.M. on 4 April, much to the surprise of the city leaders. The company was directed to the recruiting rooms of the Georgia State Army, where they rested for several hours. Roused late that night, they marched to the depot to catch a midnight train to Macon. To Atlantans, these mountain men appeared ready for a brawl. "The members of this Company are a hardy looking set of men, and they would no doubt prove ugly customers in a fight," reported a local newspaper. The Volunteers would not reach Camp Oglethorpe until the 5th.[48]

Following the tradition of mid-nineteenth-century militia, campaigning began in earnest for the election of the regimental officers. Adjutant General Wayne issued instructions for the election, specifying the order in which each company would vote. "The voting will be conducted by Companies, and under the immediate direction of the Captain of each Company, who will, after depositing his own vote, call the roll of his Company, officers, non-commissioned officers, musicians and privates, until all shall have voted, or been called to vote, when depositing his roll with the Superintendents, he will march his Company to draw arms and equipage."[49]

Standing for colonel were Captain James S. Pinckard of the Quitman Guards, Southern Guards First Lieutenant James N. Ramsey, and Captain S. A. H. Jones from the Washington Rifles. Captain James O. Clarke, Oglethorpe Infantry, was encouraged to vie for the position, but he declined, wanting to stay with his company. Pressed by several to run, he finally agreed to try for second in command, "because the Oglethorpes being on the

---

[47] The Floyd Rifles would not have to wait long for their opportunity. Later that month they would join the 2nd Battalion Georgia Volunteer Infantry in Norfolk VA.

[48] Anonymous, "Military Surprise," *Atlanta Southern Confederacy*, 4 April 1861; Anonymous, "Dahlonega Volunteers," *Atlanta Daily Intelligencer*, 5 April 1861.

[49] Henry C. Wayne, "General Orders No. 2," *Macon Daily Telegraph*, 3 April 1861.

right of the regiment, and the Lieutenant Colonel occupying generally a position on that wing, he will be near his company."[50]

Voting began at 8:00 on the morning of 3 April. After a spirited campaign, Lieutenant Ramsey was chosen to be colonel, receiving 320 votes to Jones's 270 and Pinckard's 84. Captain Clarke was unopposed, becoming lieutenant colonel by default. The major's commission went to Georgia State Army captain George H. Thompson, who beat Captain Frances H. Wilkins of the Southern Guards, Private Charles J. Munnerlyn of the Bainbridge Independents, and Captain C. G. Campbell.[51]

Ramsey may have had an inside track for the colonelcy. Howell Cobb, former secretary of the treasury under Buchanan, now president of the Confederate Provisional Congress and eager for a line command himself, had written to his wife on 28 March: "I would give freely five hundred dollars to beat Jim Ramsey for Col."[52]

Born 21 June 1821 in Newton County, Georgia, James Newton Ramsey attended Randolph-Macon College in Virginia, taking up the practice of law in Harris County, Georgia, in 1841. In 1842, he was elected as the Harris County representative to the Georgia State Senate. He wed Mary Elizabeth Pollard in 1844, and the couple had two sons, William Pollard and Lucius Curran. With a piercing, steely gaze, Ramsey radiated fierce determination.

Along with Henry Benning and M. J. Crawford, Ramsey was selected to represent Georgia at the 1850 Convention of the Southern States in Nashville, an early attempt to sound out the slave-holding states on the subject of possible secession. Moving his family to Columbus in Muscogee County in 1857, he resumed his law practice and continued to be outspoken on the matter of states rights. He and Mary celebrated the birth of a daughter, Ada, on 25 November 1859.[53]

As did many leading citizens, Ramsey joined the local militia, being appointed 2nd Lieutenant in the Southern Guards, Company D. Nominated as a delegate to the Milledgeville convention, he was elected as one of three from Muscogee County. There, he was appointed to the "Committee on the

---

[50] Anonymous, "The Troops in Macon," *Augusta Daily Constitutionalist*, 5 April 1861.

[51] Anonymous, "Military," *Macon Daily Telegraph*, 4 April 1861.

[52] Iobst, *Civil War Macon*, 60.

[53] Nancy Telfair, *A History of Columbus, Georgia, 1828–1928* (Columbus GA: Historical Publishing Company, 1929) 121; Loretta Andrews, *Timeline of James Newton Ramsey*, private collection of Loretta Andrews, Asheville NC.

Constitution of the State, and Constitution and Laws of the United States." One delegate dubbed Ramsey "the Patrick Henry of the South" for his rhetoric in favor of disunion.[54]

The other elected senior officers were more seasoned in military matters. An influential and popular citizen of Augusta, James O. Clarke was a veteran of the Mexican War, having served in General Zachary Taylor's army as sergeant major of the US 13th Infantry.[55]

George Harvey Thompson was the son of prominent Atlanta citizen Dr. Joseph Thompson, who had opened and still operated the Atlanta Hotel. Harvey, as he was frequently called, had been instrumental in the creation of the Gate City Guard, being elected its first captain. Thompson received his soldier's education at the Georgia Military Institute in Marietta, though his ratings were less than stellar. In 1853, his sophomore year, Thompson ranked 23rd out of 31 cadets in academics (though he scored eighth in French, he posted a mediocre grade in English, and was near the bottom of his class in math and drawing), and as 78th out of 114 cadets in conduct, receiving 74 demerits.[56]

First Lieutenant James W. Anderson of the Newnan Guards was selected to be company adjutant. To replace Clarke, the members of the Oglethorpe Infantry chose Horton B. Adams. In addition to the officers for the 1st Regiment, Captain Peter H. Larey of the Etowah Infantry was elected major of the 1st Battalion.

Once the results were known, the troops were eager to hear from their new commander. Colonel-elect Ramsey rose to give "one of those short, eloquent, stirring speeches, which won for him at once the love of his men."[57] Newspapers immediately began to shower the new commander with accolades. "He enters upon the duties of his office under a full knowledge of the responsibility of his position," read an article in the *Columbus Daily*

---

[54] Allen D. Candler, *The Confederate Records of the State of Georgia*, 6 vols. (Atlanta GA: Charles P. Byrd, State Printer, 1909–1911) 1:274.

[55] "Mexican Veterans," *Augusta Chronicle and Sentinel*, 1 September 1874; "Col. Jas. O. Clarke Dead," *Augusta Chronicle and Sentinel*, 7 December 1889; James O. Clarke service record, roll 143, Compiled Service Records of Confederate Soldiers Who Served in Organizations from the State of Georgia, National Archives Microfilm Publication M266, Georgia Department of Archives and History, Morrow GA.

[56] Gary Livingston, *Cradled in Glory: Georgia Military Institute, 1851–1865* (Cooperstown NY: Caisson Press, 1997) 175, 189, 196–97.

[57] "Macon Correspondence," *Columbus Daily Times*, 6 April 1861.

Times, "and with the heroic determination that the honor, glory and fame of Georgia will not suffer in his hands." "He is a gallant fellow," reported the *Macon Citizen*, "bold, unpetuous, and chivalrous. He is also eloquent of speech, and if a little talk is necessary to arouse the patriotic spirit of his command on the eve of battle, he is 'the right man in the right place.'"[58]

As each company finished voting, its captain marched the men to another part of the camp to receive weapons, as directed in Adjutant General Wayne's order. The troops were issued old caliber .69 smoothbore muskets from the cache seized at the Augusta arsenal. These model 1816/22 muskets had been converted from flintlock to percussion and were equipped with lethal-looking socket style bayonets. Guns brought from some companies' home counties were appropriated and replaced with the Augusta weapons, ostensibly in the interest of standardizing the regiment's arms. The troops of the Walker Light Infantry were required to give up their .54 caliber Mississippi rifles, received only a few weeks before.[59]

One company bridled at the idea of re-arming with such ancient and cumbersome weapons. Ordered to turn in their Springfield rifles, the members of the Gate City Guard seethed with resentment. The Guard had no intention of relinquishing their prized rifles. A scheme was hastily devised; the new weapons were crated and shipped off to Atlanta to be hidden. The Guardsmen planned to recover their cherished Springfields whenever they might return to their home city.[60]

May the God of Battles Go with You

Governor Brown arrived in Macon on Wednesday, 3 April, intending to review the regiment that afternoon, but the officers' election took more time than expected. Rescheduling for the next morning, Brown settled into the Lanier House Hotel, appearing later on the front porch to enjoy a serenade provided by a military band.[61]

On Thursday, despite occasional rain, the new regiment paraded for Governor Brown, Adjutant General Wayne, and their aides. Once the review was finished, Brown boarded his barouche drawn by two white horses. As

---

[58] "The Georgia Regiment at Camp Oglethorpe," *Macon (GA) Citizen*, as reported in the *Augusta (GA) Daily Constitutionalist*, 7 April 1861.

[59] Anonymous, "The Mississippi Rifles," *Augusta Daily Constitutionalist*, 17 March 1861.

[60] Fairman, *Chronicles of the Old Guard of the Gate City Guard*, 27.

[61] Iobst, *Civil War Macon*, 65.

he rode out onto the parade ground, the 1st formed a three-sided square around the coach. Spectators crowded the open side of the square, straining to hear the governor speak. Tree limbs groaned under the weight of dozens of young boys attempting to get a better view of the proceedings.[62]

Standing in the carriage, Brown glanced solemnly over the assembly. "Officers and Soldiers," he began,

> the circumstances which have called for this rendezvous are of a peculiar character. Our fathers bequeathed to us the wisest and best Government on the face of the earth. The foundations upon which that Government was based, were the equality of the states, and the equal protection of the rights of the citizens of every section of the Union. Equality of sovereignty, equality of rights, and equality of protection, are all the South ever demanded. She has borne much, endured long, but her stern decree has at last gone forth, that with less than these she never will be content. In the hope of a returning sense of justice on the part of the people of the Northern States, and for the sake of the Union, the South has long submitted to unjust Congressional legislation, which has plundered her of millions of dollars annually, to build up and enrich her Northern Confederates.

Brown expounded about how the Northern states had benefited from Southern bounty, while denying the South its rightful rewards. "We demanded an equal participation in the common property. They refused to allow it. We then offered to divide it by a line giving them much the larger portion. They spurned the offer and by superior numbers in Congress attempted to drive us from every inch of it."

His passion rising with every word, the governor discoursed about the new nation just born and of his pride in the officials selected to lead it. Turning his attention directly to the regiment, he spoke to their cause and mission by asking a question:

> But why are you *here* soldiers? Is it for the purpose of invading the territory of the United States, or plundering their people? No. We are not the aggressors. We rally only in defence of Southern homes, Southern firesides, and Southern altars, which are threatened with invasion and destruction. We deprecate war. But if war is forced upon

---

[62] See, e.g., ibid.; "Oglethorpe," "Letters from the Volunteers," *Augusta Chronicle and Sentinel*, 7 April 1861.

> us, we are prepared for it, and when once commenced, we swear by our altars, it shall never terminate till those who provoked it shall have been the greatest sufferers by it.

Declaring his desire to march to war with them, Brown concluded with a rousing sendoff to the troops, which was met by thunderous applause: "Go then, and may the God of battles go with you, and lead, protect and defend you, till the last foot-print of the invader shall be obliterated from the soil of our common country."[63]

Eager to reap a few more sales from the troops before their departure for Florida, storeowners enthusiastically promoted their wares towards the regiment. "Attention 1st Regiment," exclaimed one advertisement, "the officers and members First Regiment Georgia Volunteers, now encamped in Macon, and all others enlisting in the Army, who desire fine likenesses to leave with their friends, can obtain them at Pugh & Brother's celebrated Gallery, Triangular Block, at *one half their usual price,* making only 50 cents for Ambrotypes in neat cases, (a dollar being usual price.)." Zeilin & Hunt's Drug Store promoted sure cures for any malady the troops might encounter: "BEFORE taking up the line of March, each man should supply himself with a bottle of *HENRY'S EXTRACT OF GINGER*, to prevent bad effects of change of Climate, Water and Diet, a sure preventative of Dysentery Cholera, &c. We will sell it twenty per cent less than the usual price to any of the Regiment."[64]

Friday morning, 5 April, the Oglethorpes escorted the Walker Light Infantry and Brown Infantry to the Macon Depot for their departure to Pensacola. The Dahlonega Volunteers, who finally reached Camp Oglethorpe that morning, discovered they had arrived just in time to find everyone else preparing to leave. The Newnan Guards and the Gate City Guards boarded their train at 11:00 A.M. Saturday. Over the next few days, the remaining companies bid farewell to Macon. The Washington Rifles and the Oglethorpes marched to the depot on Tuesday the 9th. The final two

[63] "Gov. Brown's Address to the Departing Volunteers," *Atlanta Southern Confederacy*, 9 April 1861.

[64] Advertisements, *Macon Daily Telegraph*, 4 and 6 April 1861.

companies to leave Camp Oglethorpe, they would have the honor of escorting Colonel Ramsey and his staff on their way to Pensacola.[65]

Those soldiers who had to wait for departure could hardly contain their impatience. One member of the Southern Guard was overheard telling a friend in another company "not to take Fort Pickens before he got there, for says Company D., the Columbus boys are bound to have a hand in 'them Pickens.'"[66]

Several companies expressed their thanks to the citizens of Macon by posting notices in the local newspapers. "Such manifestations of regard and attention are highly appreciated," wrote Captain Pinckard of the Quitman Guards, "and for them we will cherish a grateful remembrance amid the privations and dangers we may be call upon to endure."[67] The Washington Rifles adopted a series of resolves, including "our thanks to the ladies and gentlemen of Macon, for their polite attentions and disinterested kindness to the members of this corps. Such kindness, attention and liberal hospitality as we have received, deserves, and will ever receive our gratitude."[68] The Southern Rights Guard directed its attention to the women of the town and their donations of food: "*Resolved*, That though the rich viands with which the ladies furnished us were enjoyed with a zest such as none but a hungry soldier knows, yet the *motives* which prompted their generous conduct was more appreciated by us. The citizens of Macon—particularly the ladies—will never be forgotten by the Southern Rights Guard."[69]

---

[65] Anonymous, "More Troops Left," *Macon Daily Telegraph*, 6 April 1861; Anonymous, "Letters from the Volunteers, *Augusta Chronicle and Sentinel*, 23 April 1861.

[66] Anonymous, "Flag Presentation," *Macon Daily Telegraph*, 6 April 1861.

[67] T. M. Killin, "To The Citizens of Macon," *Macon Daily Telegraph*, 8 April 1861.

[68] Anonymous, "Camp Oglethorpe," *Macon Daily Telegraph*, 9 April 1861.

[69] J. S. Pinckard, "A Card," *Macon Daily Telegraph*, 9 April 1861.

3

Pensacola

"General Bragg has at his command seven or eight thousand men, not only ready, but anxious and impatient for the conflict that will sweep from our soil her unnatural invaders and wipe out their degrading foot-prints from our sister State."—Correspondent "Ensign" to the Sandersville Central Georgian, *18 April 1861*[1]

We Spent a Disagreeable Night

Pressed by Jefferson Davis and Secretary Walker, Brigadier General Braxton Bragg had been pondering ways to capture Fort Pickens. Prior to the bombardment of Charleston's Fort Sumter, an uneasy truce had prevailed between the federal stronghold on Santa Rosa Island and the Confederate forces surrounding it. Since early January, there had been an agreement between both sides to avoid hostile action, with the Confederate government pledging the fort would not be attacked so long as it was not reinforced. President James Buchanan had directed no troops be landed from a squadron of ships holding position outside of Pensacola Bay.[2]

With the inauguration of Abraham Lincoln on 4 March 1861, the likelihood of a showdown between the Confederacy and the United States grew dramatically. Lincoln's pledge "to hold, occupy and possess these, and all other property and places belonging to the government" was directed squarely toward both Forts Pickens and Sumter. In Montgomery, discussions intensified between Davis and his cabinet over whether, and when, to use force to gain possession of the forts. Bragg was directed to come up with plans for taking Pickens. The general advised Montgomery he had three options: direct attack, a flank attack by landing troops on the opposite end of Santa Rosa Island, or siege. Worried his forces were still

---

[1] "Ensign," "For the Sandersville Central Georgian," *Sandersville Central Georgian*, 1 May 1861.

[2] Grady McWhiney, *Braxton Bragg and Confederate Defeat, Volume I* (Tuscaloosa: University of Alabama Press, 1969) 159.

unprepared to commence such operations, Bragg worked to strengthen his fortifications along the bay front while he waited for orders.[3]

Down the rails rumbled trains carrying the 1st Georgia Regiment on its way to Florida. Anxious for their chance to thrash the Yankees in open battle, the soldiers could hardly wait to reach Pensacola. For many, this would be their first journey outside the state. Excited throngs lined the tracks to cheer the troops. "The ride from Macon to Montgomery was exceedingly pleasant," wrote correspondent Lennox, "interrupted on the route, as it was, by many agreeable and encouraging welcomes and shouts of greeting along the road. At every stoppage there were gathered crowds of true Southerners to bid us go onward; all were enthusiastic—men, women, children, white and black."[4]

The new Confederate capital at Montgomery, Alabama, was to be the first major junction for the troops, though necessary stops to take on wood and water for the engines provided some with a final chance to see their friends and family. During a brief halt in Fort Valley, relatives and acquaintances came out to meet the Southern Rights Guards. "It was quite an affecting scene, especially with the young married couples, as every one brought some thing to their friends," wrote Private Edwin Collier, who was disappointed to find no one he knew in attendance.[5] A basket filled with treats was passed around to those soldiers without someone to meet them. Captain John A. Houser began to speak to the crowd, but his words were drowned out by the locomotive's whistle, blowing to announce its imminent departure.[6]

While stopped in Butler, Georgia, Captain S. A. H. Jones of the Washington Rifles received a bouquet of flowers from the wife of a local physician. "Wait not for the slow process of preventing the reinforcement of Fort Pickens," urged an attached note, "but, with true Southern chivalry, wrest it immediately from tyrants."[7]

Any problems cropping up during the journey were instantly attributed to Northern sympathizers. Private Collier and several other Guardsmen had

---

[3] Ibid., 165.

[4] "Lennox," letter to the editor, *Augusta Chronicle and Sentinel*, 23 April 1861.

[5] Edwin S. Collier, letter to the editor, *Macon Daily Telegraph*, 13 April 1861.

[6] Ibid.

[7] J. M. G. Medlock, letter to the editor, *Sandersville Central Georgian*, 17 April 1861.

just settled down for the night, "when we were awakened by an awful noise which proceeded from the door of the car. Upon examination, it was found to have been locked by an infernal Yankee conductor named McDonald. This conductor treated us badly, for he did not give us any water nor time to get any."[8] Arriving in Montgomery just before midnight, the Guards had a long march along muddy streets to the depot of the Alabama and Florida Railroad. Grumbling arose over lack of preparations to house and feed the soldiers. "Found no water but of the very worst description," wrote Collier. "No one to show us any—asked one young man to show us some, but he said that he was not in the habit of visiting filthy soldiers. We took seats in rough box cars exposed to the night air which tells pretty severely on some of the boys for they are coughing considerably."[9]

"At Montgomery no arrangements had been made for our accommodations," complained Joseph Medlock to his newspaper, "and we all slept as best we could in the open air, not being able to get our tents erected until next morning. However, no one took cold from this unusual exposure. I must say that our men fared worse in Montgomery than any point we have yet stopped. No arrangements whatever had been made to transport our baggage, or for our comfort. As a matter of course, all of us were glad to get away from that place."[10]

"We spent a very disagreeable night," wrote Medlock, "not being able to procure our baggage and consequently to pitch our tents. We lit our camp fires and lay upon the soft side of some plank—as some of our men expressed themselves—save a few who threw themselves upon the sand. The universal covering of all was the broad canopy of heaven. There were no sentinels posted save the thousand beautiful and bright stars that keep eternal vigilance over the sleeping patriot soldier."[11]

The Washington Rifles were scheduled to leave Montgomery at 6:00 A.M. on 10 April, but their departure was delayed for twenty-four hours, giving the troops an opportunity to explore the city. Soldiers swarmed through the streets, visiting the bars, billiard halls, and the State House. "It is not so large and roomy as our capitol," wrote Medlock, "but is of much neater finish and displaying more taste in its architecture and consequently

---

[8] Edwin S. Collier, letter to the editor, *Macon Daily Telegraph*, 13 April 1861.

[9] Ibid.

[10] J. M. G. Medlock, "Editorial Correspondence," *Sandersville Central Georgian*, 17 April 1861.

[11] "Ensign," letter to the editor, *Sandersville Central Georgian*, 1 May 1861.

more attractive to the visitor." Barbershops filled with men eager for a professional shave and cleansing. Several soldiers attended an evening performance by celebrated actress Maggie Mitchell. The troops returned to their camp refreshed and happy, though Sergeant Medlock reported that "most of them were upon the verge of bankruptcy."[12]

The Walk Was Considerably Fatiguing

Boarding cars of the Alabama and Florida Railroad, the troops continued until they reached the small hamlet of Garland. From there to Evergreen, Alabama, a distance of about fifteen miles, the tracks were still under construction. Detraining, the men bivouacked. "Garland is a newly settled place," wrote a member of the Gate City Guards, "containing four stores, two boarding houses, a depot, and a few dwellings. I understand from an inhabitant that the place is quite healthy. The water is bad—being rotten limestone." Rain was falling when the Southern Guard arrived, forcing the troops to make camp over sodden, marshy ground.[13]

With the food put up by the ladies of Macon being rapidly depleted, the soldiers began to "forage" for rations. While out in the woods, one of the Gate City Guards, nicknamed "Mr. McAfee," shot a pig and carried it back to camp. When questioned about where he acquired the pork, "he replied that it attempted to *bite* him, and he could not do otherwise than shoot it—*that he allowed no man's pig to bite at him.*" Shortly afterwards the owner appeared, demanding payment for his appropriated livestock. McAfee was ordered to reimburse the farmer.[14]

After a night of rest, the companies formed up for the march to Evergreen. Some of the soldiers had never before walked so far in one stretch. "It was their first march," recalled Private Joseph T. Derry of the Oglethorpe Infantry. He continued, "Their feet grew sore and their untried muscles wearied by the unaccustomed strain upon them."[15] A Gate City

[12] See, e.g., ibid.

[13] "F.," letter to the editor, *Atlanta Southern Confederacy*, 11 April 1861; Anonymous, "From Company D," *Columbus (GA) Daily Sun*, 11 April 1861. Letters from the soldiers varied the distance marched from six to twenty miles.

[14] "Our Special Warrington Correspondence," *Atlanta Southern Confederacy*, 19 April 1861.

[15] Walter A. Clark, *Under the Stars and Bars: Or Memories of Four Years Service with the Oglethorpes, of Augusta, Georgia* (Augusta GA: The Chronicle Printer, 1900) 11.

Guardsman wrote: "We left Garland at 3 o'clock on the evening of the 9th, and reached Evergreen about 8 o'clock, P.M. Most of the company were not enured to such exercise as walking such a distance with a heavy gun and fixtures, and to such the walk was considerably fatiguing."[16]

Dust rose, coating the uniforms of the weary soldiers as they trudged down the road. The men queried locals they encountered as to how much farther it was to Evergreen. One civilian told an Oglethorpe: "After you pass the next hill and reach the rise of another it will be five miles." Reaching the second hill, the soldier asked another individual the distance. "Six miles," was the answer. Plodding along, they came upon another person. "How far to—." Private Tom Eve interrupted the soldier before he could finish the question. "For the Lord's sake," exclaimed Eve in frustration, "don't inquire again. The road gets longer every time you ask."[17]

Finally arriving at Evergreen, the regiment was once again able to ride the cars on the final leg of their journey. Over the course of several days the companies of the 1st Georgia arrived in Pensacola. "Pensacola is a dingy looking old Spanish town," wrote one soldier, "the people present the appearance of Spanish and French extraction." The Georgian added, "They are kind and hospitable to strangers."[18]

Boarding steamers, the soldiers traveled down the bay, passing perilously close to the guns of Fort Pickens. The Union garrison made no attempt to stop them, and they reached Fort Barrancas without incident.

Homefolks waited anxiously to hear their men had reached Pensacola safely. In Columbus, family and friends of Captain Francis Wilkins fearfully watched the mails for word from the officer and the Southern Guard. A horrid rumor floated around the town that Wilkins had been shot by a soldier from his own company. Relief was profound when the report was found to be untrue.[19]

Waiting in Pensacola was the regiment's new spiritual adviser. Methodist pastor James McDonald Campbell had been ministering in Warrington and offered his services to the Confederacy. "The soldiers need the Gospel," Campbell wrote his mother in Alabama, "and I can preach to

---

[16] "F.," "Our Special Warrington Correspondence," *Atlanta Southern Confederacy*, 19 April 1861.

[17] Clark, *Under the Stars and Bars*, 11.

[18] "Florida," letter to the editor, *Augusta Daily Constitutionalist*, 19 April 1861.

[19] Anonymous, "Arrival of Company D," *Columbus Daily Sun*, 15 April 1861.

them, do good and fight for my country." Campbell was assigned as chaplain for the 1st Georgia.[20]

On 12 April Bragg's acting adjutant general, Colonel John H. Forney, ordered the three companies that had arrived up to then (Walker Light Infantry, Gate City Guards, and Southern Guards) to ready themselves for action. The Georgians leapt to arms, certain they were being called on to attack Fort Pickens. "Every man was immediately call up," wrote Private Thomas Larns of the Walker Light Infantry, "donned his uniform, belt, cartridge box, &c. The Augusta and Georgia boys were prompt in responding, and were ready and in time in five minutes after the order was communicated. Not a man was missing."[21]

Around 8:00 P.M., several artillery pieces were fired from Pickens, and Congreve rockets launched from the fort lit up the sky. Reports of Union troops being landed on Santa Rosa Island soon reached Bragg. The Georgians were dismissed back to their camps, where speculation abounded as to what had happened. Many soldiers were certain they were to scale the walls of Fort Pickens, and were disappointed their chance had passed. Private Harry Krous of the Gate City Guard wrote that the Federals had planned an attack on the Warrington Navy Yard, but Lieutenant Chester A. Stone of the same company reported the guns were a distress signal from one of the Union warships having run up on a sand bar. Perhaps Bragg had intended to assault the fort, but the coincidental landing of federal reinforcements dissuaded him from carrying out his attack.[22]

That same day, the Confederate batteries ringing Charleston Harbor opened on Fort Sumter. For thirty-six hours, shot and shell rained down on the federal defenders. The troops in Pensacola and those still enroute from Macon cheered as they received the news of Sumter's surrender on the 13th.

---

[20] John Wesley Brinsfield, William C. Davis, Benedict Maryniak, and James I. Robertson, Jr., *Faith in the Fight: Civil War Chaplains* (Mechanicsburg PA: Stackpole Books, 2003) 68.

[21] "T. P. L.," "Letter from Pensacola," *Augusta Daily Constitutionalist*, 19 April 1861.

[22] Harry Krous, "Letter from Harry Krous, of the G. C. G.," *Atlanta Southern Confederacy*, 17 April 1861; Anonymous, "Pensacola News," *Columbus Daily Times*, 17 April 1861; C. A. Stone, "Letter from Lieut. Stone, of the G. C. G.," *Atlanta Southern Confederacy*, 18 April 1861; "F.," letter to the editor, *Atlanta Southern Confederacy*, 19 April 1861.

The Georgians were convinced Fort Pickens would soon be in Southern hands as well.

Over the next few days, the rest of the regiment reached Pensacola. Unloading at a wharf in front of Fort Barrancas, the company quartermasters set about to find transportation for their equipment. Washington Rifles quartermaster John Thomas Youngblood (also the color bearer) had a particularly difficult time finding wagons. The soldier finally encountered a freight company owner who had wagons but no drivers. An expert driver himself, Youngblood soon had a team of mules hitched, then drove the wagon down to the wharf.[23]

Other companies were not so fortunate. "The first day we arrived we had to shove our baggage up hill," wrote Ellis H. Hull of the Oglethorpe Infantry, "on a railroad, about one mile and a quarter; then we had to put up our tents, and clear off the undergrowth; and finally went to bed at 10 o'clock P.M."[24]

Dubbing their encampment "Camp Georgia," the soldiers set to work raising their tents among the sand dunes behind Fort Barrancas. Construction on the stronghold had begun in 1839 on the site of earlier Spanish and British fortifications and was completed in 1844. The fort was built in a roughly triangular shape, the long side facing the bay. The rampart and exteriors were constructed of brick. Entrance to the fort was across a drawbridge over a dry moat on the northeast side. The parade ground was filled with earth, topped with a parapet along the walls, on which the fort's artillery was emplaced. Numerous vaulted casemates (gun rooms) were positioned under the fill along the outside walls to allow musket and rifle fire in all directions. Between the bayside wall and the beach was located a semicircular "water battery," constructed in the 1700s by the Spanish, and connected to the primary fortification by a tunnel.[25]

---

[23] J. M. G. Medlock, letter to the editor, *Sandersville Central Georgian*, 24 April 1861.

[24] "E. H. H.," "Letter from Pensacola," *Augusta Daily Constitutionalist*, 24 April 1861.

[25] James C. Coleman and Irene S. Coleman, *Guardians on the Gulf: Pensacola Fortifications, 1698–1980* (Pensacola FL: Pensacola Historical Society, 1982) 61–62; US Government, National Park Service, "Gulf Islands National Seashore," Fort Barrancas, http://www.nps.gov/guis/planyourvisit/fort-barrancas.htm.

The Georgians quickly settled into camp life. One soldier, his tongue firmly planted in cheek, wrote to the *Augusta Chronicle and Sentinel* on 18 April to give a recitation of the regiment's activities:

> At last we are here—settled on "this camp ground"—and what do you suppose the Georgia volunteers are doing? They are no longer the idlers at Camp Oglethorpe, near Macon—but something more romantic—none of your material practicalism—but the fascinating employment of wood-cutters, brush-burners, entertaining brass buttoned officers with filling empty sand bags to catch Lieut. Adam Slemmer's cannon balls. Nor is this all; your Augusta volunteers are up to their elbows in soap suds over military "duds;" and when the game of rubbing, washing, sunning and ironing a tea-cup flat-iron, or such other utensil as may be most convenient, the butt of your gun for instance—is played out. Some of your fashionable laundresses will certainly be found behind the age of least a quarter of a century. All are at work, you may rest assured, and are working with a vim.[26]

We Have to Storm the Fort

Relations with the inhabitants of Escambia County were not always cordial. "I never saw a community so generally *hated* as are the people of this place by the volunteers encamped hereabouts," observed Private George Cooper of the Southern Guard. "The Louisiana boys swear that when the fight with Pickens opens they intend to have a settlement with those on main land. I assured them that if matters continued as they were, I had no doubt but the Georgia boys would lend a willing hand."[27]

---

[26] "Lennox," letter to the editor, *Augusta Chronicle and Sentinel*, 23 April 1861. 1st Lt. Adam Slemmer was second in command of the Federal troops at Pensacola. His situation was much like that of Maj. Robert Anderson at Charleston. In the absence of his commanding officer, Capt. John H. Winder (who would later become a Confederate general and be placed in charge of the South's prison camps), Slemmer decided his positions at Fort Barrancas and the Warrington Navy Yard were untenable, so on 9 and 10 January he relocated his small force to Fort Pickens on Santa Rosa Island. (Mark M. Boatner, *The Civil War Dictionary* [New York: David McKay Company, Inc., 1959] 641; Coleman and Coleman, *Guardians on the Gulf*, 40.)

[27] George Cooper, "Pensacola Correspondence of the Sun," *Columbus Daily Sun*, 21 May 1861.

If he detested the male population of Pensacola, Cooper had a much different opinion of the women: "For three months the ladies of this place have met daily and worked for the soldiers. They will do anything a soldier wants—make uniforms, cap covers, shirts, drawers, mend clothing, and they have in the past few days fitted up some old houses very comfortably as a hospital, where they invite any soldier that may be in need of kind attention to come. They have a corps of nurses, who give all attention to their patients. There appears to be nothing in their power but they will do to add to the comfort and well being of the soldier."[28]

On 16 April, Colonel Forney issued General Order #19, formally mustering the regiment into Confederate service. The 1st was attached to Colonel Henry D. Clayton's 2nd Brigade, which included Clayton's own 1st Alabama Infantry along with the 2nd Alabama Battalion. A few days later, the Dahlonega Volunteers found themselves in need of a new captain. Deemed too old for service at age sixty, Captain Alfred Harris had resigned on 22 April. Thomas B. Cabiness, a private in the Quitman Guards, was selected to replace Harris.[29]

Nearing the end of his studies in North Carolina, Lavender Ray wrote home, his letter crackling with annoyance at what he perceived as the university's plodding. "The Senior speaking commenced today and will continue until Friday," he wrote on 29 April. "As the Faculty would not agree to omit it and permit the Seniors to return home and join the army, they are determined to hasten through and return home."

Ray's yearning to come home and enlist heightened when he heard of his brother's enlistment. "I received John's letter this eve announcing his

---

[28] See, e.g., ibid.

[29] Officers of the 1st Georgia Regiment to Gov. Joseph E. Brown, 21 January 1862, typewritten transcript, personal papers of Barry Colbaugh, Lula GA; Frank Moore, ed., *The Rebellion Record: A Diary of American Events, With Documents, Narratives, Illustrative Incidents, Poetry, Etc.* (New York: G. P. Putnam, 1861) 188; Lillian Henderson, ed., *Roster of the Confederate Soldiers of Georgia, 1861–1865*, 6 vols. (Hapeville GA: Longing & Porter, Inc., 1959–1964) 1:224, 232, 240, 252, 265, 289, 296, 297. There is some ambiguity in these records as to the actual date the regiment was accepted into the Confederate Army. The entries in Henderson's *Roster* for several companies state that Forney swore them in on 10 June near Richmond. This is unlikely, as by then Forney was colonel of the 10th Alabama Infantry, having been commissioned 4 June 1861. (Boatner, *The Civil War Dictionary*, 288; Stewart Sifakis, *Who Was Who in the Civil War* [New York: Facts On File, 1988] 223–24.)

intention of going to Pensacola. I heartyly wish that I could accompany him."[30]

John D. Ray joined the Newnan Guards on 7 May, arriving in Pensacola shortly afterward. Along with his new comrades-in-arms, Ray gazed across the bay at the high, brooding brick walls of Pickens, wondering when they might be called on to attack the fort. The prospect filled many with foreboding. John dashed off a letter to Lavender, his pen dipped in dread, "Cap Hanvey says if half of us return he will be satisfide for myself I am afread that I neve will see you again—but I am redy to die know if God calls me—I am going to sell my life as dear as posible. We have to storm the fort and it is doutful wheather we ever return any of us at all."[31]

Others were confident of ultimate victory. "This will say to you that I am well," wrote Quitman Guards Corporal John L. Tyus, "& have stood the duty of a Soldier in camp exceedingly well, as good as any one of our Company, though the Labors & duties connected with the preparation & fortification of this point for the battle has been arduous. But I can now say that we are fully prepared for the fight & I for one say let it come & the Sea will be made to heave its wild billows & the walls of Fort Pickens will sink under the heavy fire of our guns from Batteries & forts."[32]

"Tell me when the conflicting forces will meet & I will tell you within a few days the date of a victory for the confederate forces," trumpeted Lieutenant Fleming.[33] "After the fight opens here my judgement is that the confederate flag will be waving over Pickens or where *Pickens was* in about five days." During a review of the Georgia regiment, General Bragg spoke

---

[30] Lavender Ray to his sister, 28 April 1861, in Mills Lane, ed., *"Dear Mother: Don't grieve about me. If I get killed, I'll only be dead.," Letters from Georgia Soldiers in the Civil War* (Savannah GA: The Beehive Press, 1977) 7.

[31] John D. Ray to Lavender Ray, 14 May 1861, in the Lavender Ray Papers, 1791–1954, Accession 1949 0012M, Georgia Department of Archives and History, Morrow GA.

[32] John L. Tyus to his brother, 24 May 1861, private collection of Lt. John Powell, USN.

[33] William O. Fleming to his wife, 10 May 1861, in the William Oliver Fleming Papers, #2292-z, Southern Historical Collection, the Wilson Library, University of North Carolina at Chapel Hill (hereafter cited as Fleming Papers). Quoted with permission of William Fleming, descendent

to Captain Adams of the Oglethorpe Infantry, saying he "would have use for them before long." Adams replied emphatically, "We *are* ready."[34]

Bainbridge Independents 2nd Lieutenant Len Griffin, unimpressed with Bragg's preparations, lambasted the general in a letter to his father. Griffin wrote,

> On our arrival we found things in a bad condition. You know that the impression was that fort Pickens could not be reinforced but it was a false impression that went abroad. I made use of this observation as soon as I arrived at this point and views the premises—that Gen. Bragg was an ass and every day I heard this same thing repeated by older men. He has lain idle here in command of 5000 men and allowed the Yankees to go on and fortafie their position every day and get reinforcement and he has done nothing to prevent them. Instead of throwing over a force to occupy the Island of Santa roza opposite our camp and the navy yard, he has allowed our enemy to take that position and fortafie the land and from the point they can distroy the navy yard and contents worth forty millions of dollars.... Before you see this, the fight will commense—that you may rely upon. Many of our brave men will be made to bite the dust, but the fort will be taken, but when taken it will be worthless to us for after fighting us as long as they can and after they see they must be whipped, they will blow up the fort and retreat on their vessels and leave.[35]

Raucous celebrations erupted when news reached Pensacola of Virginia joining the Confederacy. "The cannons are roaring and the whole army are in a state of the wildness enthusiasm," wrote Private Archibald Sneed to his wife. "We have just heard of the secession of Virginia. The fight in Baltimore between the 7th Regiment of New York and the Baltimoreans and the capture of the Star of the West. And we are firing a salute for the same.

---

[34] "Edward," "Letter from a Private 'O. I.,'" *Augusta Daily Constitutionalist*, 27 April 1861.

[35] Len M. Griffin to his father, 3 April 1861, in the Len Mitchell Griffin papers, box 3, accession 3339–17, Civil War unit files, Georgia Department of Archives and History, Morrow GA. Griffin's company was still in Macon on 3 April, so he most likely wrote this letter on 13 April.

When the first gun was fired from Barrancas (opposite Fort Pickens) in a few minute the walls of Fort Pickens was covered with Federal troops."[36]

Constant alarms kept the green soldiers on edge. Nervous sentinels discharged their muskets at shadows. "The other night we were ordered out," reported Private William Peay, "and heard a great deal of musketry. We were ordered to load, fix bayonets, and march. We thought we were off for Pickens, to take it by storm, but when I saw the Colonel smoking a cigar I knew there was nothing unusual." The musket fire turned out to be a volley fired by another regiment, in celebration of Virginia's secession.[37]

A few days later, more volleys fired by nearby Mississippi troops brought the regiment out once more, ready to repel the supposed attackers. Editor Medlock reported to his newspaper "Col. Ramsey was promptly at his post; the call to arms was to be heard from every quarter; men hurrying hither and thither; commands issuing; big guns and rammers jingling; and in almost as short a space of time as it takes me to write it, the Georgia Regiment, with Col. Ramsey at its head, was ready to march." Once it was determined there was no assault, the troops were dismissed, disappointed at seeing no fighting, but ready to spring to action again at any time. "The men were rejoiced to think that the battle was to be fought so soon—if fight we must," concluded Medlock.[38]

I Can Not Believe You Have Not Written

Florida's unfamiliar climate and sandy landscape were the source of many laments in letters home. Fleming wrote to his wife, "Georgia, this is the most dusty place you ever saw. It is impossible to keep clean more than two or three hours at a time & then you must by at the greatest trouble to do so.... Last night was the most unpleasant night that any of us have had since we left home. We had what is called a land breeze & the mosquitoes oh! Thought they would eat me up."[39]

---

[36] Archibald Sneed to his wife, 20 April 1861, private collection of Cheryl Brundle, Macon GA. The actual regiment involved in the Baltimore riot was the 6th Massachusetts.

[37] W. E. Peay, "Letter from Private Peay," *Augusta Daily Constitutionalist*, 26 April 1861.

[38] J. M. G. Medlock, letter to the editor, *Sandersville Central Georgian*, 24 April 1861.

[39] William O. Fleming to his wife, 10 May 1861, Fleming Papers.

The relentless, intense sun prompted William Miller of the Oglethorpes to write: "I would like to have a pr of connade pants and a pr of Green Goggle like Bro Franks if you can get any in town. I want them to protect my eyes from the glare of the sun and the dust."[40]

Soldiers of all ages have grumbled about heavy labor, and the Georgians continued the tradition. After removing eight small cannon from Fort Barrancas, they worked to mount larger eight-, ten-, and eleven-inch columbiads. They also toiled constructing several of Bragg's gun emplacements. Private Miller griped about the drudgery in his letters:

> Our Regiment is kept working hard all the time. We have to do guard duty, Picket guard, work on the Sand Batteries, pull powder over the Rail Road (such as one as it is, the sand in some cases being a foot above the iron on the track) guard the Redoubt, where they keep the powder, and do mule duty and any thing they the young...head officers of the Regiment say do, In addition we have to drill at 8 o'clock and at 3 1/2 o'clock, and have a dress parade at 6 o'clock every day. I don't mind the fighting part of the Regiment business but I hate the menial work.[41]

"Soldiering is a hard life," complained a Gate City Guardsman. "Hard work—fat bacon and hard crackers. My hands are blistered badly. No time to fish yet. Plenty of oysters at forty cents a hundred. Martial law was declared here to-day, and everybody notified to take up arms immediately or leave. *Nothing to drink here at all.*"[42]

Restricted access to alcohol was particularly detestable to the Georgians. Private Elias Hull of the Oglethorpes wrote to a friend in the Clinch Rifles that "Gen. Bragg has destroyed all the liquor within five miles of this place, consequently there are about eight hundred involuntary members of the Temperance Society."[43]

---

[40] William J. Miller to his Mother, 10 May 1861, in the A. J. Miller Papers, #510-z, Southern Historical Collection, The Wilson Library, University of North Carolina at Chapel Hill (hereafter cited as Miller Papers).

[41] See, e.g., ibid.; handwritten note in Joseph T. Collier Papers, Civil War Miscellany, Personal Papers, drawer 283, reel 21, Georgia Department of Archives and History, Morrow GA.

[42] Anonymous, "Life at Pensacola," *Atlanta Southern Confederacy*, 23 April 1861.

[43] "E. H. H.," "Letter from Pensacola," *Augusta Daily Constitutionalist*, 24 April 1861.

Military rations were another source of gripes. Sergeant Joe Thompson, Jr., brother of Major George H. Thompson, described the rough fare for the editor of the *Atlanta Southern Confederacy*: "We lived awfully hard for the first week—nothing to eat but hard sea biscuits in a bucket of water at night and let them soak until morning. By this means we were enabled to get our teeth through them."[44]

Many soldiers supplemented their provisions with locally caught or purchased seafood. "Oysters sell at fifteen cents per dozen. They are the largest I ever saw. You can get anything in Pensacola for fifty cents. I can go to the sea beach and catch as many crabs as I want with a stick, but I don't like to handle the varmints. I can buy those large red fish, about as large as a four year old boy, for seventy-five cents. They make splendid chowder."[45]

With sparse rainfall and relentless sun, finding safe sources of drinking water was a constant concern. "We have very poor water here," wrote Sergeant Thompson, "and when we go after it, we have to wait sometimes till some fellow gets through washing his dirty clothes in the spring."[46]

Several companies sank wells to find water, but digging in the sandy soil was dangerous in itself, as Lieutenant Fleming explained:

> The company next to us came very near losing a man this evening. They were digging a well on their grounds. They had got about ten feet deep & were fixing a barrel at the bottom when it caved in completely covering up one man. He was standing erect, which was all that saved his life as it enabled those standing near by to get to his head.... When I saw him first his nose & forehead were all that could be seen. He could have been covered up again if some of the officers hadn't taken command & put out guards to keep the crowd off.[47]

It took almost two hours to extricate the man from the sand.

Letters from friends or loved ones were a delight to the men, many of whom had never been so far from home before. Soldiers who lacked

---

[44] Joe Thompson, Jr., letter to the editor, *Atlanta Southern Confederacy*, 27 April 1861.

[45] W. E. Peay, "Letter from Private Peay," *Augusta Daily Constitutionalist*, 26 April 1861.

[46] "Our Correspondents from Warrington," *Atlanta Southern Confederacy*, 27 April 1861.

[47] William O. Fleming to his wife, 6 May 1861, Fleming Papers.

sweethearts at home were envious of those receiving packages from wives and families. "There is one thing certain," lamented H. M. Wylie of the Gate City Guard, "if I get home from this trip, I never will leave on another till I get me a wife! Then I will be all right. It makes me feel badly to see these married men around me, getting all kinds of nice things from home. True, they are all kind, and divide with us, to the very last bit they have; but I would feel better if I knew I ever would have an opportunity to return the compliment."[48]

The absence of word from home for long periods left many bitter. Lieutenant Fleming remonstrated continually about what he perceived as his wife's lack of correspondence:

> My dear wife I can not believe you have not written me, without there being some cause for your not doing so beyond your control. I attribute my not hearing from you to some defect in the mail. Though it is strange that every one else that I know have heard from home. Not a married man in our company but has recd a letter or letters from his wife. It is generally known that I have not & I am sympathized with by all the married men—particularly those in tent with me. You certainly have written before this time—if not & it has been in your power to do so before I say candidly I do not beg you to do so now. Excuse this expression, Georgia, for my mortification in not receiving a line from you has compelled me to it.[49]

Southern Guard Private George Cooper bemoaned the lack of packages from Columbus in a letter to the *Daily Sun*:

> The boys are rather hurt at being slighted by folks. Every company in the regiment get *good* things sent them from home, but Company D never does. We are ashamed to tell where we hail from, as those we left behind appear to care nothing for us, only for the display of departure. We may have the *heart* of Columbus *when there*, but they do not allow it to follow us far.—This citizens of the different places from whence the various companies come (except Columbus) are

---

[48] H. M. Wylie, letter to the editor, *Atlanta Southern Confederacy*, 27 April 1861.

[49] William O. Fleming to his wife, 26 April 1861, Fleming Papers.

constantly sending some box *or* package to *their* company, but Company D has never had a chance to thank *home* for any favors.[50]

In addition to the artillery emplacements bearing down on Fort Pickens, General Bragg also sought ways to keep federal warships from entering the harbor. Four barges were sunk in the channel between Fort Barrancas and Pickens on the night of 4 May. Rockets launched from the Union post lit the sky over the Confederates as they worked, but no shots were fired.[51]

The next day, a boat bearing a flag of truce set out from the navy yard for Santa Rosa Island. The vessel was watched intently by the Confederate troops as it returned about forty-five minutes afterward. Later in the day several federal officers delivered a letter to General Bragg. After the Union officers left the dock to return to Pickens, Colonel Ramsey was instructed by headquarters to immediately advise as to the shape of his troops' weapons. Lieutenant Fleming reported "Col Ramsey stated to the regiment this evening that every man must have his gun ready & canteen full of water as the attack was expected at any moment." No attack materialized, however, and the regiment stood down once again.[52]

The barges were only partially successful inhibiting transit of the Northern ships, so Bragg turned to another resource. The pride of the pre-war navy yard was an enormous wooden dry dock, "a tremendous floating mass of timbers and irons and cost the old Government over a million of dollars." The barge's purpose was to repair naval vessels, but General Bragg decided to include it as part of his defenses. He ordered two hundred men from the 1st Georgia to report to the navy yard at 7:00 A.M. on 12 May. Once assembled, the Georgians set to work packing the structure with rocks, bricks, pieces of iron, and other heavy scrap. Bragg intended to sink the dry dock in the channel as a further barrier to the federal men-of-war.[53]

Late in the evening of 22 May, the Confederates began towing the dry dock into Pensacola Bay. As federal sentries sounded an alarm, Union artillerymen sprang to their guns. Reports had reached the Pickens garrison that the Rebels might be using the barge as a floating battery, or possibly a

---

[50] George Cooper, "Pensacola Correspondence of the Sun," *Columbus Daily Sun*, 21 May 1861.

[51] "F. R. P.," "Pensacola Correspondence," *Columbus Weekly Times*, 20 May 1861.

[52] William O. Fleming to his wife, 6 May 1861, Fleming Papers.

[53] "Pensacola Correspondence," *Columbus Weekly Times*, 20 May 1861

transport to ferry assault troops to Santa Rosa Island. Before the vessel moved very far, though, it grounded fast on a shoal. Unable to free the massive craft, the Confederates abandoned the effort.[54]

The Officers Came Very near Mutiny

Shortly before the Georgians began filling the dry dock, four companies received orders transferring them to the Warrington Navy Yard. Those who went were quite pleased with their new surroundings. "It is one of the most beautiful spots in the world," wrote Fleming. "The Navy yard is a perfect fairy land."[55]

The Georgians were placed under the command of Lieutenant Colonel John B. Villepigue, and began training on the siege cannon bearing on Fort Pickens. "We are to be drilled six hours at least in Artillery at some of the sand batteries," wrote a member of the Southern Guards, "and would be held in reserve to be sent to different points as occasion might require, and to cover the advance or retreat of the storming party, so it seems we will not be expected to scale the walls of Fort Pickens."[56] Working with the heavy guns was exciting to many of the soldiers. Captain Hanvey of the Newnan Guards went so far as to ask General Bragg to transfer his company permanently to the artillery.[57]

William Miller wrote of the redeployment: "We have only half of our Regiment in the camp now. Through the interposition of the higher

---

[54] George F. Pearce, *Pensacola During the Civil War: A Thorn in the Side of the Confederacy* (Gainesville FL: University Press of Florida, 2000) 82–83. Pearce states that another possibility for Bragg's ordering the movement of the dry dock might have been to protect it from bombardment, but this is doubtful, given that other sources report it was filled with debris and rubble in order to sink it in the channel. See John L. Tyus to his brother, 24 May 1861, in the personal collection of Lt. John Powell, USN; "Pensacola Correspondence," *Columbus Weekly Times*, 20 May 1861; Boatner, *The Civil War Dictionary*, 641. The dry dock was destroyed by Union forces on 2 September. See Boatner, *The Civil War Dictionary*, 641.

[55] William O. Fleming to his wife, 10 May 1861, Fleming Papers.

[56] "F. R. P.," "Pensacola Correspondence," *Columbus Weekly Times*, 20 May 1861.

[57] John H. Woods, ed., "Soldier and Prisoner, Two Confederate Memoirs by Robert H. Little," unpublished typescript, (University of Chicago, 2000) 17; "Pensacola Correspondence," *Columbus Weekly Times*, 20 May 1861; Captain G. M. Hanvey to General Braxton Bragg, 14 May 1861, in the George M. Hanvey papers, Ms 494, Hargrett Rare Book and Manuscript Library, University of Georgia Libraries, Athens GA (hereafter cited as Hanvey Papers).

authorities 1/2 of it has been ordered to the Navy Yard. Col. Ramsey is very mad about it."[58]

Ramsey was indeed livid at having his regiment split. His complaint was not well received by General Bragg, however. When the colonel protested about the deployment to the navy yard, Bragg informed Ramsey "if he was not satisfied to work under him he would send him to Virginia." "To Virginia it is," Ramsey retorted.[59]

Regardless of how irritated Bragg might have been, he acceded to Ramsey's demand to have the 1st reunited. Now it was the soldiers who were angry, furious at having to move from the comfortable barracks back to their tents. Wrote Lieutenant Fleming, "Our Col kicked up a fuss about his regiment being divided and General Bragg issued his order for us to return. You never saw such mad officers & men in your life. The officers came very near mutiny and passing condemnatory resolutions of the conduct of our Col."[60]

When the Newnan Guards received instructions to return to Camp Georgia, a disappointed Captain Hanvey wrote to Ramsey, requesting his company be allowed to remain at the navy yard: "So far as my command is concerned officers and men were pleased at the change at first, And now sincerely regret the order sending us back to Camp Georgia. We desire you to detach us to any point at which our services may be deemed most effective even though we be thusly entirely separated from the Regmt."[61]

The dull routine of camp and garrison life fed boredom and anger. Fights broke out among the troops. On 19 May alone, three soldiers were arrested for brawling. In another instance, a member of the Newnan Guards received two stab wounds, from which he was not expected to recover. "It is a bad turn to be using our weapons on our own brother soldiers," lamented Lieutenant Fleming.[62]

To prevent such occurrences, military order was rigidly enforced. "For sleeping on post," wrote Lieutenant Griffin, "a chain and ball to one leg or 80 days imprisonment is considered a lite punishment and in less than 5 days some of the men will be shot for sleping on post which is just

[58] William J. Miller to his mother, 14 May 1861, Miller Papers.

[59] Woods, "Soldier and Prisoner," 17–18.

[60] William O. Fleming to his wife, 19 May 1861, Fleming Papers.

[61] Capt. G. M. Hanvey to Col. James N. Ramsey, 14 May 1861, Hanvey Papers.

[62] William O. Fleming to his wife, 1 May 1861, Fleming Papers.

according to rules of war." An example was made of one soldier who slipped out of camp to visit his wife, who was staying in Warrington. Arrested for being absent without leave, the private was sentenced to march in place in front of his captain's tent for half an hour. Lieutenant Fleming, even though he was officer of the guard, regretted the need for such severe discipline, writing, "I tell you Georgia a private in this army is not a bit better than a negro—this is true of a volunteer—in the regular service a private is not half as good. They can do nothing without permission & the smallest of offences will subject them to a heavy penalty."[63]

Illness struck hard at men not used to living outside. Diarrhea, dysentery, and other diseases ran unbridled through the camp. "A great many in our company are sick," wrote Fleming. "There has been a few deaths in the regiment—none as yet in our company. Some are very sick now. There is a great deal of the sickness owing, I think, to the sudden changes in the weather. Last night it was very warm—tonight fire would be comfortable.... A great many of our men have the mumps."[64] Private Jason T. Smith of the Southern Guard died on 16 May, and William Swift of the Southern Rights Guard succumbed on the 29th.[65]

Disease left its mark in the officer corps as well—and not always in camp. Near the end of May, Colonel Ramsey received agonizing news—his daughter Ada had died on the 20th. Granted leave, Ramsey rushed back to Columbus to comfort his wife and attend his daughter's funeral.[66]

President Jefferson Davis arrived at Bragg's headquarters on the evening of 14 May, accompanied by his wife, Varina, and Senator James Chestnut, Jr., of South Carolina. Davis spent the next day inspecting the Confederate forts and batteries. After conferring privately with General Bragg, Davis and his entourage left on the 15th. It was rumored the

---

[63] Len M. Griffin to his father, 3 April 1861, in the Len Mitchell Griffin papers, box 3, accession 3339–17, Civil War unit files, Georgia Department of Archives and History, Morrow GA; William O. Fleming to his wife, 19 May 1861, Fleming Papers.

[64] William O. Fleming to his wife, 21 May 1861, Fleming Papers.

[65] Henderson, *Roster of the Confederate Soldiers of Georgia*, 1:231, 240.

[66] Brent H. Holcomb, ed., *Marriage and Death Notices from the "Southern Christian Advocate,"* 2 vols. (Greenville SC: Southern Historical Press, 1979–1980) 2:17.

government was no longer pushing for an attack on Fort Pickens, for other arenas were taking precedence.[67]

During this period, the Confederate government relocated from Montgomery to Richmond, Virginia. To counter the massive federal buildup across the Potomac in Washington, regiments poured into the new capital from throughout the South. On the 17th, Secretary Walker wrote to Bragg, asking if it would be possible to send some of his troops to Virginia. "For offensive operations I require all I have," Bragg replied, "For mere defense I can send three regiments—one from Alabama and two from Georgia." After more correspondence from Jefferson Davis, Bragg wrote on 28 May: "I can spare twenty-five hundred men for Virginia and can start them immediately, well armed."[68]

Not everyone was pleased to see the 1st leave. Colonel Clayton dictated an affectionate farewell message to Ramsey, the words couched in formal military prose. "COLONEL—The Colonel commanding this Brigade, directs me to express to you his feelings of profound regret at being called on, so soon, to sever the connection with you and your excellent Regiment. During the whole time your Regiment has been under his command not a single unpleasant incident has transpired, with any member of the same, to mar, so far as he is concerned, the pleasant intercourse between him and you and your command."[69]

Colonel Ramsey replied with equal formality. "SIR:—In response to your complimentary communication, accompanying General Orders No. 48, from Headquarters, I am gratified to assure you of a sincere reciprocity on the part of my command and myself. A bright period in the dark trials of a soldier's life is ever a source of pleasant reflection. Such a one it has been our good fortune to pass under your command. If it be our lot to meet the enemies of our common country, we will endeavor to prove ourselves worthy of your esteem."[70]

---

[67] Pearce, *Pensacola During the Civil War*, 80.

[68] US War Department, comp., *The War of the Rebellion: A Compilation of the Official Records of the Union and Confederate Armies*, 128 vols. (Washington DC: Government Printing Office, 1880–1901) (hereafter cited as *OR*) ser. 1, vol. 1, pt. 1, p. 468.

[69] "Correspondence between Colonels Clayton and Ramsey," *Columbus Daily Sun*, 3 June 1861.

[70] Ibid.

4

West to the Alleghenies

"Col. Ramsay addressed the regiment in a few remarks, the last of which were worthy of Patrick Henry. He said that the invader now pollutes the soil of the Old Dominion by his presence, and that the regiment was here to wash out his foot-prints in his heart's blood. He then concluded by pointing his sun-burnt hand to the north-west and saying, "There is the road that leads to the enemy—to-morrow we march."'—Correspondent of the Savannah Republican, *writing from Richmond on 18 June 1861*[1]

The Boys Look as if They Had Seen Some Service

Drums rolled early on the morning of 30 May. Grabbing their weapons, troops at Fort Barrancas and the navy yard rushed from their tents, certain the long foreseen attack on Fort Pickens was about to take place. As the 1st Georgia waited nervously in the predawn darkness, officers appeared bearing new orders—the men were to break camp and make ready to leave Florida. Their destination: the new Confederate capital at Richmond. Cheers rose from the ranks as the soldiers realized they would be traveling to the very seat of war. Surely they would be part of the one big battle that would decide the conflict. Within an hour, the Georgians had struck their tents.[2]

Set to depart along with the Georgians were the 5th Alabama and Lieutenant Colonel G. A. Gaston Coppen's regiment of New Orleans Zouaves. The Georgians regarded the Louisianans as "a desperate and hardy

---

1 Anonymous, "Virginia Correspondence," *Savannah (GA) Republican*, 13 June 1861.

2 Anonymous, "Departure of the Troops," *Pensacola (FL) Tribune*, 30 May 1861, as reported in the *Columbus Daily Sun*, 3 June 1861; James McDonald Campbell to his mother, in Edmond Lee Rice, ed. "Compiled Civil War Letters of James McDonald Campbell of the 47th Alabama Infantry Regiment with a Brief Sketch of His Life," facsimile copy of unpublished typescript, 197-, p. 35, Alabama Department of Archives and History, Montgomery AL.

set of men, whose trade is war, and war only. Somebody will get hurt, if care is not exercised, when they meet the enemy."[3]

Loading their tents and other camp gear back onto boats, the regiment sailed up Pensacola Bay. Arriving at the depot, the troops boarded rail cars, retracing their route to Montgomery. Happily, the gap in the railroad between Evergreen and Garland had been completed. Each day more companies climbed aboard trains bound for Montgomery, packing the cars so tightly space inside was at a premium. As the Quitman Guards traveled northward, several soldiers climbed onto the roof. Private Mark Brantley lost his hold and tumbled under the train. He was killed instantly.[4]

That same day, several companies of the 1st already encamped outside Montgomery were ordered into ranks and rushed into the city. A drunken riot was in progress. Soldiers from Coppen's Zouave regiment were breaking into stores and private homes in search of liquor. The city officials, unable to stop the destruction, desperately called on the officers of the 1st Georgia for help.

After leaving Pensacola, the train bearing the Zouaves made a breakfast stop at Garland. While the officers ate inside the station, the Louisiana soldiers uncoupled their special car from the rear of the train. The officers rushed from their meal, but were unable to catch up as the rowdy troops forced the engineer to steam away up the tracks. Once the gaily-dressed soldiers reached Montgomery, they roamed the streets in search of spirits. The 1st Georgia took position with loaded muskets and fixed bayonets, then commenced driving the Louisianans back. A murderous confrontation was averted at the last moment when the Zouaves' officers arrived. Swinging their pistols like clubs, they charged into the midst of the rowdies, "crackling French oaths rolling over their tongues with a snapping intonation, and their pistols whirling right and left like slung-shot, and dropping a mutineer at every blow."[5]

---

[3] Anonymous, "Departure of the Troops," *Pensacola Tribune*, 30 May 1861, as reported in the *Columbus Daily Sun*, 3 June 1861; Anonymous, "A Military Ovation," *Augusta Chronicle and Sentinel*, 4 June 1861.

[4] Anonymous, "Georgia Volunteer Accidentally Killed," *Augusta Chronicle and Sentinel*, 4 June 1861.

[5] T. C. DeLeon, *Four Years in Rebel Capitals* (Mobile AL: The Gossip Printing Company, 1890) 73; Terry L. Jones, *Lee's Tigers: The Louisiana Infantry in the Army of Northern Virginia* (Baton Rouge: Louisiana State University Press, 1987) 14–15.

Service on the Gulf Coast had wrought many changes in the troops' appearance. "They are bronzed and hardy," reported one newspaper of the Gate City Guards, "and are the very picture of perfect health and manhood. Their camp-life and labors have certainly been conducive to their physical development."[6] The skin of some soldiers had darkened so much, that while in Montgomery, one Guardsman was passed off as a slave, even being offered for sale. When an offer was made, the soldiers had a difficult time explaining the joke.[7]

Continuing on to Augusta, the regiment was welcomed by excited crowds, especially for the hometown companies. The *Chronicle and Sentinel* reported, "The Augusta boys had such an enthusiastic reception given them on their arrival, as one seldom sees. Thousands of people had gathered at the Georgia Depot to greet them, and as the huge train came on, the most joyous shouts, mingled with the salvos of artillery rent the air."[8]

Family and friends of the Oglethorpe and Walker Light soldiers were startled by the changes in their men. "The boys look as if they had seen some service," exclaimed the *Sentinel*, "being much bronzed by exposure, and their hands hardened by severe manual labor. The work has been hard, but they say they like it, and express the highest gratification with their experience, thus far, of a soldier's life."[9]

Several of the companies returned to their hometowns, greeted by adoring crowds. Atlanta citizens turned out to welcome the Gate City Guards. "Such a throng as was at the car shed has not been there in many days. The wives, mothers, sisters and sweethearts of the Guards were there—and they make a large crowd. It was more than a heart of adamant could endure to look on the scene and remain unmoved."[10] Dr. Joseph Thompson, father of Major George H. Thompson, invited the company to the Atlanta Hotel for breakfast. Before leaving for Richmond, the

[6] Anonymous, "Arrival of the Gate-City Guards," *Atlanta Southern Confederacy*, 2 June 1861.

[7] Anonymous, "A Great Company—A Running Sketch of the Gate City Guard," *Atlanta Constitution*, 18 January 1889.

[8] Anonymous, "A Military Ovation," *Augusta Chronicle and Sentinel*, 4 June 1861.

[9] Ibid.

[10] Anonymous, "Arrival of the Gate-City Guards," *Atlanta Southern Confederacy*, 2 June 1861.

Guardsmen retrieved their treasured Springfield rifled muskets from concealment.[11]

The Washington Rifles arrived in Sandersville on Monday, 3 June, to spend two days before continuing on to Virginia. "The members of the Rifles were in fine health," the *Central Georgian* informed its readers, "and much increased in flesh, but sunburnt and tough." The visit was all too brief. "The Rifles left on the one o'clock train yesterday for Virginia," reported the *Georgian* sadly, "and were accompanied to the depot by an immense crowd. Farewells were exchanged, they sprang upon the train, and soon the gallant corps was on its way to battle against our country's invaders, determined to meet victory or death. They have gone from among us, many hundred miles, to fight for our cause; let us not forget them nor their kindred who are left behind. May the God of battles be their God."[12]

On 6 June, as the Oglethorpe Infantry prepared to leave Augusta, the soldiers assembled at City Hall for a special ceremony. Prior to leaving for Macon, they had ordered a fine sword for then Captain James O. Clarke. The saber was not completed before the company's departure from Augusta, so it was kept in storage until the Oglethorpes returned. The weapon was a beautiful piece:

> The handle is formed in the shape of a lion's head, while the hilt is ornamented with the coat of arms of Georgia. The dress scabbard is of silver with gilt bands—the engraving being on the bands, the first representing "Excelsior" onward and upward—the rise and progress of this gallant company. The second representing "Liberty"—the object for which freemen are ever ready and willing to fight, and in whose cause this sword is to be drawn and used; third, justice at the "shoe" or point of the scabbard, significant of the fact that justice is to

---

[11] The Guardsmen came to regret retrieving their weapons: "Probably, if we had been more experienced soldiers…we would not have been so anxious to take the long-range rifles when the rest of the regiment had short-range guns, for when there was any skirmishing or sharp-shooting to be done, the Gate City Guard rifles were ordered to do it, as they were more on an equality with the Federals, who were well armed." See Henry Clay Fairman, *Chronicles of the Old Guard of the Gate City Guard, Atlanta, Georgia, 1858–1915* (Atlanta GA: Byrd Printing Company, 1915) 28.

[12] "The Washington Rifles at Home," *Sandersville Central Georgian*, 5 June 1861.

> be demanded and obtained at the point of the sword.... The service scabbard is bronzed, with silver bands.[13]

Lieutenant J. V. H. Allen presented the sword to Clarke, who was overcome with emotion as he offered his thanks to the Oglethorpes: "Pleased and surprised at this unexpected mark of approval and affection on the part of those whom I have had the honor to command, I am only prepared to say that such a gift from such a company, makes our heart swell with the emotions of gratitude, and in the hour of battle, the recollection of the source whence it came will give me inspiration, like the smiles of beauty, which drives the hero into the hottest of the fight! I take it, and swear it shall never be dishonored."[14]

Traveling a circuitous route by way of Wilmington and Goldsboro, North Carolina, the companies arrived in Richmond, coming in over a period from 6 to 10 June. The regiment set up camp at Howard's Grove, "about a mile from the center of the city in a beautiful pine grove," joining other Georgia regiments.[15] Oscar Cantrell, newly arrived recruit for the Newnan Guards, described the encampment as being on "a beautifully elevated plane."[16]

Soldiers took advantage of every chance to tour Richmond. Chaplain James Campbell marveled at the city's burgeoning war industry. Visiting a weapons factory, he "saw in one building about one hundred and fifty girls and women making cartrige and caps for guns. In another room men making boxes for said cartriges. Pass into another room machinery is boaring out ten inch columbiads, next room molding some other rooms making gun carriages and everything else that we want."[17]

---

[13] Anonymous, "A Handsome Gift," *Augusta Daily Constitutionalist*, 6 June 1861. A sword carved on the top of Clarke's burial monument in Magnolia Cemetery in Augusta GA matches this description very closely.

[14] Ibid.

[15] Anonymous, "By Telegraph," *Augusta Chronicle and Sentinel*, 7 June 1861; Anonymous, "Oglethorpe Infantry," *Augusta Daily Constitutionalist*, 8 June 1861; William S. Smedlund, *Camp Fires of Georgia's Troops, 1861–1865* (Marietta GA: Kennesaw Mountain Press, 1994) 158.

[16] Oscar A. Cantrell, *Sketches of the First Regiment Georgia Vols.: Together with the History of the 56th Regiment Georgia Vols., to January 1, 1864* (Atlanta GA: Intelligencer Steam Power Presses, 1864) 5.

[17] James McDonald Campbell to Bro Joe, 6 June 1861, in Rice, "Compiled Civil War Letters of James McDonald Campbell," 36.

President Jefferson Davis and Virginia governor John Letcher visited the Georgians' encampment on 14 June. Following a review of the troops, the president gave a short speech of "a few soul-stirring words, in the course of which he paid them, and the gallant State from whence they came, a high compliment."[18] Colonel Ramsey called for his men to raise three cheers, "which were given by the regiment with a heartiness that almost made the ground tremble beneath their our feet. Though not the usual way of manifesting respect in military circles, still, it seemed to gratify the President, who gracefully bowed his acknowledgements."[19] Governor Letcher ("a round-headed, fussy-looking sort of a personage," recalled one correspondent) also spoke briefly to the regiment.[20]

Virginia Is a Beautiful Country

Travelers heading from Richmond towards the northwestern part of Virginia cross the Blue Ridge Mountains into the Shenandoah Valley, also known as the "Valley of Virginia." West of Staunton rise the majestic Allegheny Mountains, a series of long, high ridges arranged roughly southwest to northeast. Rivers such as the Cheat, Tygart, and Greenbrier flow northerly between the mountains to their confluences with the Potomac River, in some areas winding like serpents along flood-plain valleys. Dense stands of laurel, spruce, and fir cover the steep slopes of the mountains. During the summer and fall months, the weather often changes dramatically, from hot and dry to cloudbursts lasting for days or even weeks. Though unusual, snow can make its appearance on the higher peaks as early as August.

In the mid-nineteenth century, three important roads cut across the area from east to west: the James River and Kanawha Turnpike in the south, the Staunton-Parkersburg Turnpike in the center, and the Northwestern Turnpike. An even more crucial transportation link, the Baltimore and Ohio Railroad, followed the Potomac River along the Maryland border. These avenues were of vital interest to Richmond, for they were not only essential

---

[18] Anonymous, "Special Army Correspondence," *Atlanta Southern Confederacy*, 15 June 1861

[19] Ibid.

[20] Anonymous, "Virginia Correspondence," *Savannah Republican*, 13 June 1861.

for transporting supplies, but could also be used as a path of invasion by Union forces.[21]

This section, known at the time as the Trans-Allegheny region, or simply "Western Virginia," held radically different views from the eastern reaches of the state. Populated by independent mountain folk, who politically and economically had more in common with neighboring states Ohio and Pennsylvania, the region had long been at odds with the state legislature in Richmond.[22]

The Confederate government was growing increasingly concerned about sentiment gaining strength in Western Virginia toward separation from the Commonwealth, as well as the likelihood that federal forces building in Ohio, under the command of Major General George B. McClellan, would soon advance into the region. Confederate colonel George A. Porterfield was ordered to Grafton on 4 May, for the purpose of mustering troops and preparing the region for defense. What Colonel Porterfield found disturbed him. "There is great disaffection in this and the adjoining counties," he advised Colonel Robert S. Garnett, adjutant general of Virginia state forces, on 14 May, "and opposition to the lawful action of the State authorities is certainly contemplated." Richmond looked on with alarm as delegates met in Wheeling on the 13th, pledging allegiance to the Union, and proposing a plan to carve their own state out of Virginia's western counties.[23]

Porterfield had little success recruiting soldiers. On 3 June, his disorganized force of about 775 Rebels was surprised and routed at Philippi, by a federal force numbering close to 3,000 troops. As Porterfield's forces hastily pulled back toward Beverly, Northern newspapers trumpeted the minor affair. Dubbing the one-sided clash as the "Philippi Races," the Union press inflated the minor encounter into a major federal victory.[24]

---

[21] W. Hunter Lesser, *Rebels at the Gate: Lee and McClellan on the Front Line of a Nation Divided* (Napierville IL: Sourcebooks, Inc., 2004) 6–7.

[22] Ibid., 2.

[23] US War Department, comp., *The War of the Rebellion: A Compilation of the Official Records of the Union and Confederate Armies*, 128 vols. (Washington DC: Government Printing Office, 1880–1901) (hereafter cited as *OR*) ser. 1, vol. 2, pt. 1, p. 843.

[24] Clayton R. Newell, *Lee vs. McClellan: The First Campaign* (Washington: Regnery Publishing, Inc., 1996) 87–88.

Promoted to brigadier general, Robert Seldon Garnett was ordered to the region on 8 June, charged with reorganizing the Confederate forces and to plan for a more substantial defense. Born in 1816 to a distinguished Virginia family, Garnett graduated from the United States Military Academy at West Point in 1841. Serving with distinction in Mexico under General Zachary Taylor, he was brevetted a major. After holding the post of commandant of cadets at West Point for a time, Garnett was sent to the northwestern corner of the United States to battle Indians. Devastated after losing his wife and child to disease, Garnett applied for extended leave, returning to the army just as Virginia seceded from the Union. Going with his state, he resigned his commission of major with the 9th US Infantry, and offered his services to Virginia. Continued grief over the loss of his family left Garnett prone to dark moods. "They have sent me to my death," he confided to an associate before leaving Richmond to take up his new command.[25]

Upon Garnett's arrival in the Trans-Allegheny region, he immediately began to consolidate the scattered troops. Studying the rugged terrain, he decided to fortify two mountain passes. West of Beverly at Rich Mountain, where the Staunton-Parkersburg Turnpike cut through the mountains, Garnett stationed the 25th Virginia, under the command of Lieutenant Colonel Jonathan M. Heck. The general felt this post would be the most easily defended. The position was christened "Camp Garnett" in his honor. He next placed the bulk of his forces at Laurel Hill, near Belington, believing this was the most likely position to be threatened. From there he could cover the Beverly-Fairmont Road, which ran from north to south, connecting the Northwestern and Staunton-Parkersburg turnpikes. Making his headquarters at Laurel Hill, Garnett wired the capital, requesting more troops to bolster his small force, now styled the "Army of the Northwest."[26]

Richmond responded to Garnett's request by sending three Virginia regiments: the 23rd, under Colonel William B. Taliaferro; the 37th, commanded by Colonel Samuel V. Fulkerson; and seven companies of the 20th, led by Major Nat Tyler. On 7 June, the office of the adjutant and inspector general issued orders for Colonel Ramsey's 1st Georgia

[25] Ezra J. Warner, *Generals in Gray* (Baton Rouge: Louisiana State University Press, 1959) 100; Douglas Southall Freeman, *Lee's Lieutenants*, 3 vols. (New York: Charles Scribner's Sons, 1942: 1970 ed.) 1:24–25.

[26] Lesser, *Rebels at the Gate*, 85–86; Newell, *Lee vs. McClellan*, 112.

Volunteers to proceed to Staunton, from there to report for duty to General Garnett.[27]

Colonel Ramsey read the orders to his cheering troops. "The announcement seemed to electrify the regiment and the vast assemblage of spectators," reported a Savannah newspaper.[28] The eagerly awaited contact with the hated Yankees seemed to be at hand. Gear was hastily packed into wagons, and the soldiers carefully checked their weapons. "Each man in the regiment," wrote one correspondent, "in addition to the ordinary arms, is provided with a bowie knife and a repeater, and they leave with the confident expectation of driving the enemy into the Ohio river."[29]

They Were Not Only Soldiers, but Gentlemen

Gripped with enthusiasm, the troops of the 1st Georgia once again boarded train cars for the first leg of their journey. Stopping in Waynesboro, the regiment was greeted by tables groaning with food. Reporting to the *Central Georgian,* Sergeant Medlock wrote, "We all partook freely of the good things set before us, gave three hearty cheers for Waynesboro—but especially for the ladies—bade them farewell, and went on our way rejoicing."[30] Villagers at another stop also arranged for a lavish supper for the regiment, but there was confusion about the regiment's railroad schedule. The 1st was actually supposed to pass through the following night; as a result, the troops failed to show up for the carefully prepared meal. Determined not to let the soldiers miss their feast, several ladies made arrangements to convey the food to the Georgians' camp in Staunton.[31]

Passing into the Shenandoah Valley, the Georgians marveled at the thriving farms, healthy livestock and fields of thriving crops. "Virginia is a beautiful country," wrote Lieutenant Fleming,

---

[27] Lesser, *Rebels at the Gate*, 86–87; *OR*, ser. 1, vol. 2, pt. 1, p. 255; US War Department, *Special Orders of the Adjutant and Inspector General's Office, Confederate States*, 5 vols., National Archives and Records Administration (Washington DC: Government Printing Office n.d.) 1:31.

[28] Anonymous, "Virginia Correspondence," *Savannah Republican*, 13 June 1861.

[29] Ibid.

[30] J. M. G. Medlock, letter to the editor, *Sandersville Central Georgian*, 3 July 1861.

[31] Ibid.

> her mountains & valleys make up a magnificent picture. Wheat, Rye, clover &c cover the valleys & hill sides & these grow so luxuriously that it a perfect feast for the eyes to behold. Fat horses & cows can be seen grazing through the fields.... Fresh butter, sweet milk, butter milk, strawberries &c you can buy at a...song—besides more substantial food. I never heard of things so cheap. Our Company & so fare as I can hear the whole regiment are delighted with the change—All are in high spirits and anxious to come in sight of the enemy.[32]

The regiment arrived in Staunton on 10 June. The Georgians impressed the citizens, with the local newspaper lauding their military skills and conduct: "The manner in which they drilled showed that they had been properly taught the exercise of the soldier, and the manner in which they comported themselves in society showed that they were not only soldiers, but *gentlemen*."[33]

Staunton's residents could not do enough to provide for the regiment's members. "Scarcely an hour in the day passed without something being sent to the camp for our comfort," wrote Sergeant Medlock, who told of a woman who stuffed his haversack to overflowing.[34] Children from the Asylum for the Blind performed for the troops, singing "patriotic Southern airs."[35]

While in Staunton, the regiment received their army pay. "We got $21. for 6 mo's clothing," wrote Private William Miller of the Oglethorpe Infantry, "$16.50 for 1 1/2 months wages." Miller was not happy with the small amount. "They would not pay us all they owed us," he grumbled.

Orders arrived to lighten up for the march ahead. "We were allowed to bring no clothes with we could bring in our knapsacks," continued Private

---

[32] William O. Fleming to his wife, 12 June 1861, in the William Oliver Fleming Papers, #2292-z, Southern Historical Collection, the Wilson Library, University of North Carolina at Chapel Hill (hereafter cited as Fleming Papers). Quoted with permission of William Fleming, descendent.

[33] Anonymous, "The 1st Georgia Regiment," *Staunton (VA) Spectator and General Advisor*, 18 June 1861.

[34] J. M. G. Medlock, letter to the editor, *Sandersville Central Georgian*, 3 July 1861.

[35] Walter A. Clark, *Under the Stars and Bars: Or Memories of Four Years Service with the Oglethorpes, of Augusta, Georgia* (Augusta GA: The Chronicle Printer, 1900) 13.

Miller. He and his comrades schemed to lessen the load further. "We hired an extra wagon to bring our knapsacks for us. We stored all of our extra baggage away in Staunton so as we could get it if we should stay in one place any length of time which would pay us for sending for it or when we passed through Staunton on our way home."[36]

The regiment remained in Staunton until the 14th and then began its march toward the mountains of Western Virginia. Along the way, local townsfolk feted the Georgians. They had traveled only a short distance before they were met by another group of well-wishers providing an abundance of food and cold spring water. Setting out once again, the regiment proceeded just a few miles further, then stopped to make camp at Buffalo Gap, a mere ten miles from their day's starting point. Here, again, the residents provided the troops with refreshment. "At Buffalo Gap," recalled Private Cantrell, "ten miles from Staunton, the citizens gave the whole regiment a dinner of buttermilk and bread—after which the boys gave it the name of Buttermilk Gap; one gentleman furnished one hundred gallons."[37]

Men dropped out of ranks to imbibe at taverns and inns along the road, sometimes with tragic consequences. On 16 June, after the regiment bivouacked for the evening near Shaw's Pass, several members of the Quitman Guards slipped out of camp, returning with a small keg of whiskey. Wanting more, Private James Stokes attempted to sneak out past the sentries. Discovered and stopped by the pickets, the intoxicated and fuming Stokes returned to his tent, snatching up his musket. Trying again to get past the guards with no luck, the enraged soldier raised his weapon and shot Private Bernard H. Meyer. Meyer, who had joined the Newnan Guards just over two weeks earlier, fell mortally wounded, the ball entering his thigh and exiting next to his lower spine. He lingered barely fifteen minutes before dying. Stokes was promptly arrested for murder.

The slaying was the regiment's first death by gunfire, and it unsettled the entire group. Colonel Ramsey composed a heartfelt letter of consolation to Meyer's parents. "Dear Sir and Madam: It becomes my painful duty, as Commander of the 1st Regiment, to inform you of the death of your son. He

---

[36] William Miller to his mother, 13 June 1861, in the A. J. Miller Papers, #510-z, Southern Historical Collection, The Wilson Library, University of North Carolina at Chapel Hill (hereafter cited as Miller Papers).

[37] Fairman, *Chronicles of the Old Guard of the Gate City Guard*, 206–207; Cantrell, *Sketches of the First Regiment Georgia Vols.*, 6.

was shot last night, while in the faithful discharge of his duty, as one of my sentinels. From the information I have been enabled to pick up in reference to the affair, your son was shot without any cause—simply for doing his duty. I will see that justice is done the offender."

"I know this news will come with crushing effect upon your feelings," Ramsey continued, "but console yourselves with the reflection that he fell at his post, and had conducted himself so as to merit and receive the high approval of his officers. I saw him soon after he was wounded; his sufferings were short. I send him back to you for burial, hoping God may give you fortitude to bear this heavy affliction. It is the great sacrifice you have made for your country. Respectfully, J. N. Ramsey, Col. Commanding 1st Reg. Ga. Vol."[38]

Newnan Guard privates Solomon Haas, Andrew J. Stallings, and Winston B. Wood were detailed to escort Meyer's body back to Coweta County. Stokes was lodged in a Staunton jail. Newspapers across Georgia condemned the senseless crime.[39]

I Intend to Kill an Enemy

The march over the mountains began to take its toll. A soldier of the Walker Light Infantry wrote his sister, "I have just travelled the longest road I ever undertook on foot. We left Staunton on Saturday last and reached this place yesterday, having travelled 105 miles in seven days, over the roughest road imaginable—over mountains all the way. We stood the march very well, with the exception of blistered feet and excessive fatigue."[40] Once more Private William Miller displayed his exasperation as he declared to his mother, "I intend to kill an enemy for every ten miles they made me walk after them, besides what I will kill in battle."[41]

For Georgians recently removed from the flat terrain of the Florida panhandle, the scenic vistas they now encountered were mesmerizing. "The country that we are traveling over is very mountainous," reported a member

---

[38] John H. Woods, ed., "Soldier and Prisoner, Two Confederate Memoirs by Robert H. Little," unpublished typescript (University of Chicago, 2000) 18; "A Melancholy Affair," *Atlanta Daily Intelligencer*, 23 June 1861; Anonymous, "Melancholy," *Atlanta Southern Confederacy*, 23 June 1861.

[39] Anonymous, "Melancholy," *Atlanta Southern Confederacy*, 23 June 1861.

[40] Anonymous, "Letter from the Walker Light Infantry," *Augusta Daily Constitutionalist*, 29 June 1861.

[41] William Miller to his mother, 13 June 1861, Miller Papers.

of the Gate City Guard, "although a great many beautiful vallies are to be met with on the route. Last night we camped upon the summit of the Alleghany Mountains. The place of our encampment, I am told, is the highest peak of the Alleghanies in the State. This, I can assure you was a pretty *lofty perch*. The climate in this section of country is delightful; the nights, however, are sometimes very cool."[42]

Passing through the unfamiliar terrain of the Allegheny Mountains, the Georgians found themselves contending with a different sort of foe—rattlesnakes. Making camp near Cheat Mountain on the evening of 19 June the soldiers found the area teeming with serpents. "There are a great many rattlesnakes in the mountains," wrote Lieutenant Fleming to his wife. "Two or three have been killed in & around our camp ground. One snake with six rattles was actually killed in one of the tents. The tent I suppose was pitched over it."[43]

Later in the evening, the troops were delighted when a local woman visited the camp to entertain them. Bringing "a melodeon accompaniment," she sang a medley of Southern songs. Several of the soldiers joined in.[44]

Rumors spread along the column of ravages committed by Union troops. "The Lincolnites are committing great depredations at Phillippa and the surrounding country," wrote a member of the Gate City Guard. "There are several families in this and the adjoining county, who were driven from their peaceful homes at Phillippa owing to their Southern proclivities.—Rumor says that there are eight or ten thousand federal troops at Phillippa, and that they are daily receiving reinforcements." Such reports fueled the Georgians' desire to get at the enemy. The writer concluded "that they are anxiously awaiting to revenge the blood of the noble Virginians who have already fallen in protecting their homes and firesides."[45]

Incidences of weary and hungry soldiers falling out of ranks began to increase. Men were dropping out so often along the trail that officers were forced to station guards in front of each dwelling the regiment passed. "If it was not done they would be in every part of the house in the twinkling of an eye looking for some thing to eat," wrote Lieutenant Fleming, blaming the behavior on sparse rations. "Hard biscuits & fresh beef & not enough of that is all we have to eat. What is drawn at night for a whole day is eaten up at

---

[42] "F.," letter to the editor, *Atlanta Southern Confederacy*, 27 June 1861.
[43] William O. Fleming to his wife, 19 June 1861, Fleming Papers.
[44] Clark, *Under the Stars and Bars*, 14.
[45] "F.," letter to the editor, *Atlanta Southern Confederacy*, 27 June 1861.

supper & breakfast & very few have any thing to eat when we stop to rest about noon on the march. This will account for the bad conduct of some of the Soldiers on the road."[46] One elderly woman claimed several Newnan Guards stole milk from her house. Colonel Ramsey offered a reward of ten dollars for the culprits, but apparently they were never caught.[47]

Welcoming crowds dwindled as the troops continued westward. Private John Pillsbury and the other soldiers noticed a definite change of attitude toward the Confederates. Pillsbury wrote, "Passing along the turnpike on the march the large numbers of citizens that gathered to view our passage through, were cool and distant. We failed to receive that good cheer and Godspeed that we had been led to expect, plainly indicating by actions and manners their want of heart in the cause we represented—coolly polite, but never discourteous. No sign of encouragement or sympathy was given, so different from that which we had received up to the time of taking up the line of march."[48]

Immediately after marching into Beverly on the 21st, several soldiers planted a Confederate flag on top of the courthouse. "This, I suppose is the first Southern flag raised here," mused Sergeant Medlock.[49]

Ramsey expected to make contact with General Garnett the next day, but the Allegheny Mountains were about to give the regiment a taste of their frequent and unpredictable weather changes. Heavy clouds began to build as the soldiers bedded down for the night. Around midnight the storm broke, with howling winds and pounding rain. The Georgians scrambled to keep their shelters upright. "I began to think that soldiers and tents would be blown away," recalled Private Cantrell.[50] "We had to hold on to our tent poles to keep the tent from falling," wrote Lieutenant Fleming, "but at last one of the tent poles broke & down came the tent on us. Every thing was already soaking wet so the tent falling made very little difference. I never

---

[46] William O. Fleming to his wife, 22 June 1861, Fleming Papers; Lavender R. Ray to his mother, 18 November 1861, in the personal papers of Lavender R. Ray, box 2, accession 1949 0012M, Georgia Department of Archives and History, Morrow GA.

[47] Lavender R. Ray, personal papers, box 2, accession 1949 0012M, Georgia Department of Archives and History, Morrow GA.

[48] John B. Pillsbury, "Garnett's Retreat After Rich Mountain," *Atlanta (GA) Journal*, 25 May 1901.

[49] J. M. G. Medlock, letter to the editor, *Sandersville Central Georgian*, 3 July 1861.

[50] Cantrell, *Sketches of the First Regiment Georgia Vols.*, 7.

got from under the canvas until breakfast time." Fleming and many other soldiers finally gave up and just tried to get some sleep. "I wrapped my self in a blanket & actually slept soundly in the wet bed clothing…."[51]

Because everything—tents, blankets, clothing, and weapons—was soaked, the planned march for that day was cancelled. As the troops worked to clean up the mess, Lieutenant Fleming mused about the changes campaign life had wrought. "It is surprising what men can stand when they are put to the test. Ordinarily it would be considered death to go through what we are now."[52]

Here Our Holiday Soldiering Ended

On the 24th, after a taxing tramp of 120-plus miles, the 1st arrived outside Laurel Hill. With the regimental band blaring forth, the troops dressed ranks in order to make a good show. Just outside the fortifications, the regiment was halted while the officers went on ahead to find out where to set up camp. While the Georgians waited, a good-natured banter commenced with soldiers of the 37th Virginia. "They began to guy us for stopping in such a place as the country there presented," recalled Lieutenant A. C. Hagy of the Virginia regiment. "Why did we not go on and seek better ground? If they went to sleep there, they would roll off their pallets down the hill and break their necks. They were not going to stop here, but farther on, and invited us to pull up and go with them."

The Virginians heckled the Georgians right back. "We advised them that they would do well to stop awhile with us and consider the matter. We knew that they would run without rolling off their pallets. We also told them that we had some dear friends up the road whom we thought of visiting soon and that if they were aiming to do the same it would be best for us all to go together."[53]

Colonel William Booth Taliaferro (pronounced TOL-i-ver) of the 23rd Virginia, looking on as the Georgians filed into the fortifications, took note of the regiment's musicians and resplendent uniforms:

> The appearance of this little regiment created a great sensation in our little command. It was a very full regiment, the companies of

---

[51] William O. Fleming to his wife, 22 June 1861, Fleming Papers.

[52] William O. Fleming to his wife, 22 June 1861, Fleming Papers.

[53] P. S. Hagy, "The Laurel Hill Retreat in 1861," *Confederate Veteran* 24/4 (April 1916): 171.

> which were old volunteer companies, called by their original distinctive name, such as 'Gate City Guards', etc. They were beautifully equipped, and the material, composed of young and active men, handsomely uniformed, was superb. The regiment was proceded by a full drum corps, and the clangor of their kettle-drums and screams of their fifes were unsubdued by the shouts and loud cries of welcome with which they were saluted.

The martial display did not impress Taliaferro with the Georgians' abilities as fighting men, however. "They were fancy volunteers of the cities," he recalled after the war,

> and had left their homes apparently rather for a gay holiday than for real war. All the paraphernalia of a volunteer summer encampment accompanied them. Cards, wines, liquors and potted luxuries, as well as "red gold for the winning," abounded. Discipline was their only want, but in that they were sadly deficient. The field officers, as well as company officers, had been elected directly by the men. Promotions were to be made by a like suffrage, and discipline and consequent efficiency were impossible. These men, possessing all the elements of good soldiers, but careless, reckless, and uncontrolled, became a terror to the country in which they were encamped. Unrestrained by their officers and far from homes and the influence of social life and public opinion, they abandoned themselves to all manners of deviltry, more, however from the life of excitement than from any really evil intent.[54]

The addition of the 1st Georgia, along with the three Virginia regiments, brought Garnett's strength to about 4,500 soldiers. With these reinforcements at hand, he ordered Lieutenant Colonel John Pegram, recently arrived with the remaining companies of the 20th Virginia, to proceed to Rich Mountain to augment the troops there. Because his Confederate Army commission ranked Colonel Heck's militia grade, Pegram assumed command of Camp Garnett.

The Georgians quickly set about putting up their tents, though some were not at all pleased with their campsite. The Oglethorpe Infantry was

[54] William B. Taliaferro, "Annals of the War. Chapters of Unwritten History. Garnett in West Virginia...," typescript from the *Philadelphia Weekly Times*, 11 March 1882, p. 7. Personal collection of W. Hunter Lesser.

situated on a particularly distasteful plot, as Private William Miller described: "When we got to our alotted part of the camping Ground we (the O.I.s) found that we had to pitch our tents on a piece of ground which had been used as a cowpen for many years judging by the appearance and smell of the place. But as our camp was larger than the pen and Burts tent and mine being even numbers (4&6) we got grassy spots on the outside."[55]

Back in Georgia, enrolling officers were busy signing up men to replace those lost through sickness or other reasons. Though in his mother's eyes one soldier in the army was quite enough, Lavender Ray finally convinced his parents to allow him to join his brother John in the Newnan Guards. In Washington County, Isaac Hermann felt compelled to enlist. Approaching the local recruiter, he exclaimed, "I, a Frenchman, wish to fight like an American!" With twenty other new soldiers, Hermann set out for Western Virginia to join the Washington Rifles.[56]

Garnett remained uneasy, feeling his small army was still inadequate for the task expected of it. Repeated requests to Richmond for more men brought a message from Brigadier General Robert E. Lee: three more regiments, one each from Georgia, Virginia, and North Carolina, were enroute. Unfortunately, these reinforcements would arrive too late. A new storm, not of nature's making, was about to break upon the Army of the Northwest. Recalled Private Simeon Speer of the Newnan Guards, "Here our holiday soldiering ended. Now the stern realities of a soldier's life was entered upon."[57]

---

[55] William Miller to his mother, 24 June 1861, Miller Papers.

[56] David N. Wiggins, *Georgia's Confederate Sons, Volume I* (Carrollton GA: University of West Georgia Press, 2007) 14; Ella Mitchell, *History of Washington County* (Atlanta GA: Byrd Press, 1924) 135–36.

[57] Letter from Simeon F. Speer to unknown recipient, n.d., in the George M. Hanvey papers, Ms 494, Hargrett Rare Book and Manuscript Library, University of Georgia Libraries, Athens GA (hereafter cited as Hanvey Papers).

5

LAUREL HILL

"At Phillippi a gallant Georgian band,
Led on by Ramsey, took a fearless stand;
Foiled thrice their numbers, captured all their camp,
And made the boasters take the backward tramp."[1]

I Believe We Could Resist an Attack

The regiment was itching for a fight, ready to sally forth against the Federals. To their dismay, they were immediately put to work on the fortifications at Laurel Hill. "We have been kept quite busy," wrote Lieutenant Fleming, "The General in command, Garnett, is having the woods cut down all around the Brigade encampment & erecting two batteries on hills commanding the road from Phillippi." Digging trenches and felling trees was a disagreeable reminder of their hard labor at Pensacola, and caused much grumbling. They had come to fight, not to shovel dirt. "Our officers are outraged," continued Fleming, "at the idea of fortifying ourselves at this distance from the enemy. They think, and doubtless rightly, that we should be advancing & driving the enemy from their fortifications & not preparing against an attack from them."[2]

Like it or not, the Georgians were put to work alongside Garnett's other troops, toiling with pick, shovel, and axe to build up the defensive stronghold on Laurel Hill. The works were extensive: "The trenches for the infantry start from the woods on the right," read one description.

---

[1] John H. Hewitt, *War: A poem, with copious notes, founded on the Revolution of 1861–62 (up to the Battles before Richmond, Inclusive)* (Richmond VA: West and Johnson, 1862) 27.

[2] William O. Fleming to his wife, 27 June 1861, in the William Oliver Fleming Papers, #2292-z, Southern Historical Collection, the Wilson Library, University of North Carolina at Chapel Hill (hereafter cited as Fleming Papers). Quoted with permission of William Fleming, descendent.

> This line of earth-works is about half a mile long, and the forest in the ravine in front of it having been cut away, they command the approach from Beelington for nearly three quarters of a mile. In the rear of the entrenchments, on the left, was a strong fortification, with embrasures in the front and salients for artillery. A similar breastwork was thrown up on the summit of the hill on the right. They were not only strongly, but handsomely constructed, of logs fastened by piles, strengthened by stone and earth thrown up in front, neatly turfed, and partially concealed by brush.
>
> These formed the first line of defense. The second line was on the left of the road, on the slope of Laurel Hill. A large area had been cleared away, and trenches dug not only along the side of the pike, but close to the woods, the latter forming an arch, the ends of which came down to the pike and were strengthened by well-constructed piers. If driven from their first line, they could retire to the second, and by holding it render it unsafe for an assaulting party to retain the first position without driving them from the second; and in that event they had the woods in the rear to fall back upon, and make good their retreat over the mountains, and out on the Beverly pike.[3]

Sergeant Medlock did not believe the Union Army would be foolish enough to assault the Confederate works. "I doubt very much our ever being attacked here," he wrote on 3 July, "yet others think there is a probability of such a thing. To be in readiness for any emergency, Gen. Garnett has caused this place to be put in proper condition for a defense, and I believe we could successfully resist an attack from double our numbers.... These hills...are well situated (as well as any near here) for the repulsion of the enemy, should the cowardly hirelings ever pay us a visit."[4]

While he was convinced their earthworks were impregnable from attack, Medlock was unhappy with the location. "This is by no means a desirable place for an encampment. Water is scarce, and very poor when we get it," he wrote.[5] As in Pensacola, excavations were begun to find water. "Every two companies of the Regiment are engaged in digging a well

---

[3] Anonymous, "Accounts of the Battle at Laurel Hill," *Cincinnati (OH) Commercial*, as related in the *Augusta Chronicle and Sentinel*, 23 July 1861.

[4] J. M. G. Medlock, letter to the editor, *Sandersville Central Georgian*, 19 July 1861.

[5] Ibid.

between them," wrote a member of the Oglethorpe Infantry, "and it would tickle you to see some of our fancy young men lay off their hat, coat, shoes and socks, roll up their pants, go down into a dirty, muddy well and go to digging. But every one of us has got it to do—and there is no getting out of it, either."[6]

New recruits continued to arrive, swelling the regiment's numbers. Isaac Hermann and his party from Sandersville came into camp about 30 June, joining the Washington Rifles. Hermann attracted quite a bit of attention with his foreign accent. Hopping onto a stump, the newcomer addressed the curious soldiers: "Gentlemen, it seems that I am eliciting a great deal of curiosity; now all of you will know me as Isaac Hermann, a native Frenchmen, who came to assist you to fight the Yankees." Hermann then mingled with the troops and later wrote, "and thus in a short time I knew every man in the Regiment."[7]

Lavender Ray arrived from Newnan a few days later, bringing with him "Dick," his personal servant. Dick, who had been the Ray family's carriage driver, was immediately pressed into service as cook for Ray's mess of eleven men.[8]

There Is Much Wickedness in Camp

The cold and frequent precipitation high in the Alleghenies discomfited the Georgians, most of who were not used to such weather conditions, especially in the summer. "Our company had suffered," recalled Lieutenant Austin Leyden of the Gate City Guard, "like all new troops, from the different camp diseases and the great change of climate from Florida to the mountains of Virginia. We had almost constant rains, keeping the men wet for weeks at a time."[9]

Frosts prompted another officer to write: "We cannot stay up here later than September. It is too cold now, and then it will be intolerable."[10]

---

[6] Ibid.; Anonymous, "Letter from the Oglethorpes," *Augusta Daily Constitutionalist*, 7 July 1861.

[7] Isaac Hermann, *Memoirs of a Confederate Veteran 1861–1865* (Atlanta GA: Byrd Printing Company, 1911) 14–15.

[8] Mary G. Jones and Lily Reynolds, eds., *Coweta County Chronicles for One Hundred Years* (Atlanta GA: The Stein Printing Company, 1928) 374.

[9] Henry Clay Fairman, *Chronicles of the Old Guard of the Gate City Guard, Atlanta, Georgia, 1858–1915* (Atlanta GA: Byrd Printing Company, 1915) 28.

[10] Anonymous, "Suffering among the Washington Rifles," Sandersville Central Georgian, 10 July 1861.

Soldiers little used to such temperatures shook as they crowded campfires. "This climate we find rather too cool for such clothing as we brought with us," wrote Sergeant Medlock. "It may seem a little incredulous to you in Georgia, to hear that today, the third of July, we find thick clothing and warm fires indispensable to our comfort. But it is even so. Last night I, with others, sat around a log fire and some of the men were shivering even at that."[11]

"Today has been very cold here," wrote Lieutenant Fleming to his wife on 2 July. "This morning I had to go to bed to keep warm. Tomorrow morning there will doubtless be some frost." Fleming pondered on how the troops would tolerate winter weather if it was so cold in summer: "We could not stand it, I know. The citizens say that the ground is most of the time covered with snow. My hands are so cold now that I write with difficulty."[12]

Intermittent showers kept everything saturated. During a short respite from drizzle, one Georgian inquired of a local if he thought there might be a drought. When the incredulous man wanted to know why, the wag answered, "Because we haven't had any rain for about three hours."[13]

The rain interfered with all aspects of camp life. James Campbell had to dodge raindrops to perform his Chaplain's duties. "The rain ceased yesterday afternoon," he wrote to his brother, "and we had servis in camp. I was standing on the ground, a camp stool by my side and my books on it. And a large crowd gathered around me, after having preached about twenty minutes the rain began to fall and I stopped short and said you are dismissed, and all went to their tents." Campbell was hopeful he would still be able to get in a sermon that evening: "We will have prayer meeting tonight. There is much wickedness in camp for which I reprove them boldly."[14]

---

[11] J. M. G. Medlock, letter to the editor, *Sandersville Central Georgian*, 19 July 1861.

[12] William O. Fleming to his wife, 2 July 1861, Fleming Papers.

[13] Joseph Tyrone Derry, *Story of the Confederate States: Or, History of the War for Southern Independence* (Richmond VA: B. F. Johnson Publishing Company, 1895) 119.

[14] James McDonald Campbell to his brother, 30 June 1861 in Edmond Lee Rice, ed. "Compiled Civil War Letters of James McDonald Campbell of the 47th Alabama Infantry Regiment with a Brief Sketch of His Life," facsimile copy of unpublished typescript, 197-, p. 41, Alabama Department of Archives and History, Montgomery AL.

The uniforms that had so impressed Colonel Taliaferro were suffering as well. An officer of the Washington Rifles described his company's straits in a letter on 10 July. He wrote,

> On the march the men divested themselves of all the clothing but what was indispensable. Many brought but one suit. This they have worn all the time, rain or shine, in sleeping as well as waking hours. They have worn considerably. Men who pride themselves on neatness at home, go about in almost tatters and rags, and it is impossible to get clothes here for any price. When we were at home we intended and did order a new uniform made; but some of our citizens persuaded us that they would do that for us and make the clothes and send them on at their expense. I regret that I yielded to this—for we will wait till suffering come in on the men, if we wait till they raise the money to buy the cloth by taxing the county. [15]

The officer begged for a shipment of new uniforms.

Other necessities were solicited in addition to uniforms. "WANTED," read an advertisement in the *Sandersville Central Georgian*, "200 PAIRS HOME-KNIT SOCKS, for the Washington Rifles. They will be gratefully received by the Ladies Volunteer Aid Association, as donations from the patriotic ladies at Washington County, by leaving them at the store of Youngblood, Newman & Co.."[16]

Food was plentiful, though not always to the taste of the troops, especially after the feasting they had enjoyed on the journey from Richmond. "Our eating is the worst feature," wrote Chaplain Campbell to his brother, "we have plenty and that would be good if prepared right. Our biscuits are very different from those we were raised on. I do not know what I would give for a dinner at home. It makes me hungry to think of *clean* milk and butter and well baked bread even if there was not even salt in it. Do not believe that I am suffering for quanity *but the quality*."[17]

---

[15] "Suffering Among the Washington Rifles," *Sandersville Central Georgian*, 10 July 1861.

[16] Advertisement, *Sandersville Central Georgian*, 10 July 1861.

[17] James McDonald Campbell to his brother, 30 June 1861 in Rice, "Compiled Civil War Letters of James McDonald Campbell," 40.

The men appreciated any amusement, especially music. The soldiers of the Walker Light Infantry enjoyed listening to the harmonica of their black drummer, Henry Hill.[18]

Despite the fact the regiment had been in service for three months, the 1st had not seen actual combat since forming in Macon. Even though the Georgians were eager to fight, their enthusiasm was tempered by the knowledge that the enemy was close at hand. Nervous pickets were under orders to fire on anyone approaching their lines who failed to answer a challenge. One soldier supposed it would be great fun to sneak up to his bunkmate, posted on a section of the picket line commanded by First Lieutenant James H. Colbert of the Bainbridge Independents. Caught by surprise, the sentry shot and killed his friend.[19]

Skirmishes between the Confederates' outlying picket posts and federal reconnaissance parties alerted General Garnett of danger approaching from the west. General McClellan, with roughly 20,000 troops under his command, was advancing from Ohio toward Garnett's position in two columns: one, under Brigadier General William S. Rosecrans, moved toward Rich Mountain; the other, under Brigadier General Thomas Morris, advanced on Laurel Hill.

General Morris's column of approximately 8,000 Indiana and Ohio troops, marching from their encampment at Phillipi, arrived outside Belington on 7 July. Morris's instructions from McClellan were not to bring on a general engagement, but rather "to do all in your power to hold the enemy in check in their present position, and to induce them to believe that you will make the main attack; the object being to cut them off at Beverly."[20]

By the end of the first week of July, Garnett listed as present for duty 3,351 officers and men at Laurel Hill, 859 at Rich Mountain, and another 375 at his supply depot at Beverly, giving him a total force of just under

---

[18] Florence Fleming Corley, *Confederate City: Augusta, Georgia, 1860–1865* (Columbia: University of South Carolina Press, 1960) 108.

[19] William O. Fleming to his wife, 2 July 1861, Fleming Papers; James McDonald Campbell to his brother, 30 June 1861 in Rice, "Compiled Civil War Letters of James McDonald Campbell," 40.

[20] US War Department, comp., *The War of the Rebellion: A Compilation of the Official Records of the Union and Confederate Armies*, 128 vols. (Washington DC: Government Printing Office, 1880–1901) (hereafter cited as *OR*) ser. 1, vol. 2, pt. 1, pp. 210, 293.

4,600. McClellan and Garnett each misunderstood his opponent's strength and positions. McClellan believed the main force of the Confederates was holding Rich Mountain, while Morris's feints toward Laurel Hill led Garnett to conclude that the majority of the Federals were before him. The mistakes would work to McClellan's advantage.[21]

Remember You Are Georgians

In front of the Confederate works rose several hills. Shortly before sunrise on the morning of Sunday, 7 July, Lieutenant Leyden had just relieved Lieutenants H. M. Wylie and Chester Stone of the Gate City Guards from command of a picket post, located on one of the rises overlooking the Beverly-Fairmont Road. Suddenly, scattered gunshots were heard from a distance, followed by the rapid retreat of several cavalry scouts. Sergeant Gaines Chisholm reported, "we could see the wagons of the enemy in the distance, and a large body of their troops with their bayonets glistening brightly in the sun."[22] Federal skirmishers began peppering the Confederate pickets, though most of their shots thudded high in the trees. The Georgians derided the Union soldiers for their poor aim: "Some of them hallooed at them to try it over, and Henry Mitchell asked for a match to light his pipe."[23] Sergeant Chisholm waved a brandy bottle toward the Yankees, remarking "the damn fools couldn't hit the hillside."[24] Chisholm then passed the bottle around his contingent, each man "taking something."[25]

General Garnett directed Colonel Ramsey to advance the 1st to the relief of the pickets. Ramsey selected four companies, reportedly saying, "Boys, clean them up with your bayonet." The soldiers, who were busily eating their breakfast, tossed away their meal and bounded into ranks. Within ten minutes the Walker Light Infantry, Dahlonega Volunteers, Quitman Guards, and Bainbridge Independents were rushing forward under the command of Lieutenant Colonel Clarke, eager to close with the enemy.

---

[21] Martin K. Fleming, "The Northwestern Virginia Campaign of 1861," *Blue & Gray Magazine* 10/6 (August 1993): 48–49.

[22] Fairman, *Chronicles of the Old Guard of the Gate City Guard*, 28.

[23] Gaines Chisholm, "News from The Gate-City Guards," *Atlanta Southern Confederacy*, 17 July 1861.

[24] Stephen Turner to J. N. Langston, 4 August 1901, Civil War Miscellany, Personal Papers, drawer 283, reel 42, Georgia Department of Archives and History, Morrow GA.

[25] Gaines Chisholm, "News from The Gate-City Guards," *Atlanta Southern Confederacy*, 17 July 1861.

They marched with an air of confidence and pride, "feeling highly complimented by this order from the General, to first advance and meet the enemy, although several *crack regiments* were on the ground from Eastern Virginia and around about Richmond."[26]

Ramsey, with the remaining five companies, set out for the Confederate left to investigate reports of another Union force coming up on the flank. In their haste to assemble, the Washington Rifles suffered a tragic, meaningless casualty—Private William Clay's musket discharged accidentally, killing the young soldier.[27]

The Gate City Guards were throwing a rapid fire toward the enemy as they held their position on the hill. To their right was another rise, its crest dominating the Beverly-Fairmont Road. Soldiers of the 9th Indiana and 14th Ohio began moving up this hill, intending to flank the Guardsmen.[28]

Clarke's detachment came pounding up the road toward their beleaguered comrades. As they neared the scene of action, they received warning of the Union flanking movement. Sending the Quitman Guards and Bainbridge Independents further up the road to guard the flank, Clarke formed the Dahlonega Volunteers and Walker Light Infantry into line of battle. Drawing his sword, Clarke pointed toward the slope, crying, "To the top of the hill, boys! To the top of the hill! And remember you are Georgians!" Rushing forward at the double-quick, the two companies swept toward the Yankees.[29]

Colliding at the crest, Yankees and Rebels struggled for possession of the hill. Catching a glimpse of an Indiana soldier reloading his weapon behind a tree, Private George Tanner of the Walker Light Infantry took a

---

[26] Untitled article, *Charleston (SC) Courier*, as related in the *Augusta Chronicle and Sentinel*, 31 July 1861; "G.," "Special Correspondence of the Constitutionalist," *Augusta Daily Constitutionalist*, 17 July 1861.

[27] Jesse W. Rankin, "Letter from Virginia," *Augusta Daily Constitutionalist*, 31 July 1861; Anonymous, "The Fight at Laurel Hill," *Columbus Daily Sun*, 18 July 1861; Lillian Henderson, ed., *Roster of the Confederate Soldiers of Georgia, 1861–1865*, 6 vols. (Hapeville GA: Longing & Porter, Inc., 1959–1964) 1:256.

[28] Jesse W. Rankin, "Letter from Virginia," *Augusta Daily Constitutionalist*, 31 July 1861; J. V. H. Allen, "From Lieut. Allen," *Augusta Chronicle and Sentinel*, 16 July 1861; Clayton R. Newell, *Lee vs. McClellan: The First Campaign* (Washington: Regnery Publishing, Inc., 1996) 124.

[29] "G.," "Special Correspondence of the Constitutionalist," *Augusta Daily Constitutionalist*, 17 July 1861; George C. Tanner, "From a Member of the Walker Light Infantry," *Augusta Chronicle and Sentinel*, 16 July 1861.

bead with his musket, then pulled trigger. His buck-and-ball shot flew dead on, for the Yankee "threw up his hand and fell." Another Federal hiding behind the same tree bolted. "George Williams took after him with an empty gun," reported Tanner, "and scared him so that he ran about twice as far as I ever saw a man run in the same space of time."[30]

Seeing no sign of federal soldiers anywhere near their position, the Quitman Guards and Bainbridge Independents charged up the rise in support of the other companies. The added weight proved too much for the Yankees; they withdrew back down the hill toward their commands, "under cover of six cannons and about 5,000 infantry in ambush."[31] The musketry had been furious, but only one of the Georgians was wounded. Private George Washington Allen of the Walker Light Infantry was hit in the thigh by a musket ball caroming off a tree. Allen thus became the regiment's first combat casualty.[32]

Back in the camp, Gate City Guard Captain William L. Ezzard's Native-American cook made up his mind to join the fray. Gathering several black cooks from the camp, he led them toward the fighting. They had not gone far before musket balls began to whistle past them. Losing heart, the group "threw down their guns and "skedadled" to camp."[33]

With the action over and the enemy in retreat, Private Tanner resolved to retrieve the weapon of the soldier he had killed.

> I started down the hill to my man that I had shot. Lieut. Russell stopped me and said that I should not go there to get my brains blowed out. I went back and thought I would wait till he turned his back on me and I would slip off and go any how, for I wanted his gun and I thought I would take his scalp. I watched my opportunity and got a chance to slip off. By that time they had stationed guards around us. One of our Sergeants stopped me and said I should not go; I told

---

[30] George C. Tanner, "From a Member of the Walker Light Infantry," *Augusta Chronicle and Sentinel*, 16 July 1861. A buck-and-ball load consisted of three or more buckshot along with one large, round ball.

[31] "G.," "Special Correspondence of the Constitutionalist," *Augusta Daily Constitutionalist*, 17 July 1861.

[32] H. G. Hammond, "Virginia Correspondence," *Atlanta Daily Intelligencer*, 19 July 1861.

[33] Stephen Turner to J. N. Langston, 4 August 1901, Civil War Miscellany, Personal Papers, drawer 283, reel 42, Georgia Department of Archives and History, Morrow GA.

> him I would. Mr. Pugh then stepped up and urged me not to go, but I kept on as though I did not hear him. They saw I was determined to go, and they accompanied me.[34]

Tanner was taken aback by the effect of his shot. "When I got to him, he was lying at full length on the ground with three buckshot in his face and one large bullet. I never stopped take to his scalp and thought I was doing well to get his gun, for the sight was enough for me."[35]

Seeing the bodies of men killed in combat for the first time was unnerving to the Georgians. "They left one dead man on the ground," wrote Lieutenant J. V. H. Allen of the Oglethorpe Infantry to his wife, "whom I saw with my own eyes, and a horrid sight it was. Our men report that several others were carried off by the running scamps, dead." The ghastly sight did not keep the young officer from investigating the slain soldier's personal effects, though. "In the dead man's pocket was found a paper of pins, one of which I enclose you in this, and you must keep it."[36]

Colonel Ramsey, having found no sign of Federals in his search of the Confederate left flank, now ordered his men toward the hill held by Clarke's detachment. With the regiment consolidated, the 1st continued to exchange fire with the Federals until mid-afternoon. Around 3:30 P.M., Ramsey noticed the fire coming from the Union lines appeared to be slackening. Sensing an opportunity, the colonel dispatched an urgent request to General Garnett, asking the 1st be allowed to attack. Garnett refused, saying he did not wish "to expose the Georgia Reg't unnecessarily and needlessly, as he placed great dependence on them." The general seemed to have developed a fondness for the Georgians—when informed of their success in driving the Yankees back, he supposedly remarked, "God bless the boys—that's a feat worthy of veteran soldiers."[37]

The Shells Stirred Them Up Lively

Sometime mid or late Sunday afternoon, Colonel Taliaferro's 23rd Virginia relieved the 1st. The Virginians took up position slightly in

---

[34] George C. Tanner, "From a Member of the Walker Light Infantry," *Augusta Chronicle and Sentinel*, 16 July 1861.

[35] Ibid.

[36] J. V. H. Allen, "From Laurel Hill—Letters from the Augusta Volunteers," *Augusta Chronicle and Sentinel*, 16 July 1861.

[37] See, e.g., ibid.; Anonymous, untitled article, *Charleston Courier*, as related in the *Augusta Chronicle and Sentinel*, 31 July 1861.

advance of the Georgians and immediately began exchanging fire with the Yankees. One company of Taliaferro's regiment possessed rifled muskets, which allowed them to duel with the Federals with much greater accuracy. The famished Georgians, having had no chance to eat all day, returned to camp "to get our breakfast, dinner, and supper, all in one."[38]

Later that evening, the 37th Virginia, under Colonel Fulkerson, replaced the 23rd. At daybreak of 8 July, the 1st returned to the firing line, "who, until a late hour in the day, kept up a continual fire upon them, and succeeded in killing six of the Yankees and taking a Lieutenant prisoner. The number of them wounded of course cannot be ascertained. The Georgians left the ground in the afternoon, with not a man killed or even a scratch." Over the next few days, different regiments rotated out to the post.[39]

On the 9th, four companies were sent to occupy another hill adjacent to where the skirmish had taken place. Lieutenant Allen chafed as his company made ready to leave. Allen was the designated "Officer of the Day," the duties of which required him stay and oversee the camp operations. Going to Colonel Ramsey, the lieutenant asked to be released from his assignment so he could go with the Oglethorpes. Ramsey refused. Undeterred, Allen determined to try another course. "I could not be satisfied; and finding a Lieutenant of another company who was willing to serve for me as officer of the day, I put out with the boys."[40]

The Georgians exchanged fire with federal skirmishers until afternoon, when a heavy rainstorm soaked the troops for two hours. Once the storm passed, the action resumed—with the Yankees upping the ante. "After the rain held up," wrote Lieutenant Allen, "all at once we heard the report of a cannon, and looking up, I saw the ball strike some distance to our right. Pretty soon another followed, accompanied with a sharp whizzing sound, and followed by a tremendous report over our position. A bomb-shell! Our

---

[38] Jesse W. Rankin, "Letter from Virginia," *Augusta Daily Constitutionalist*, 31 July 1861. Differing reports had the Virginians relieving the 1st as early as 2:00 P.M., and as late at 8:00 P.M.

[39] "Ned," "Fight Near Laurel Hill, Additional Particulars," *Richmond (VA) Daily Dispatch*, 15 July 1861.

[40] J. V. H. Allen, "From Laurel Hill...Letter from the Augusta Volunteers," *Augusta Chronicle and Sentinel*, as reported in the *Columbus Daily Times*, 18 July 1861.

men at once sheltered themselves, and took it easy. As shell followed shell, we became used to them, and amused ourselves counting them."[41]

The lack of accuracy from their old muskets frustrated the Georgians. "They have a decided advantage of us in weapons," wrote Corporal Horace Clarke of the Oglethorpes, "we being furnished with the common smooth bore gun, while they have the Minie musket, which shoots with considerable accuracy 500 yards."[42] Private Tanner put his captured rifle to work. "To-day, I fired at, and hit a house, in which there were several of the enemy. I suppose it went in at the window, for some of them ran out, and one of our men shot at them, but they were not in range of our muskets. I had the gun which I took from the Indiana Yankee that will kill at 1,000 yards."[43]

For the next few days, the Confederate and Union forces exchanged musket and artillery fire. On 10 July the Federals overran a hill close to the Garnett's lines, on which Union artillerymen quickly went into battery. Now within easy range of the Confederate camps, the gunners let loose a barrage. A Northern newspaper reported, "The shell and balls fell near enough to drive them out of their entrenchments into the woods in the rear, and stirred them up lively."[44] Unnerved by the Union shells crashing around them, the Georgians moved their tents to the far side of the ridge.[45]

Performing guard duty in the "ditches" forward of the camp was disconcerting, to say the least. While inspecting the guard posts, Lieutenant Colonel Clarke came upon Isaac Hermann, who was understandably nervous about being fired upon by cannon so soon after leaving home. "Colonel," said Hermann, "am I placed here as a target to be shot at by those fellows yonder? One of their shots came rather close for comfort." Clarke instructed the private to watch for the puff of smoke when an artillery piece fired, then duck down into the trench. Hermann followed Clarke's advice. "For nearly two hours, until relieved, I kept close watch for the smoke of their gun, which I approximated was about a mile distant, and there I learned

---

[41] See, e.g., ibid.

[42] Horace P. Clarke, "From Laurel Hill—Letters from the Augusta Volunteers," *Augusta Chronicle and Sentinel*, 16 July 1861.

[43] George C. Tanner, "From a Member of the Walker Light Infantry," *Augusta Chronicle and Sentinel*, 16 July 1861.

[44] Anonymous, untitled article, *Cincinnati Commercial*, as reported in the *Columbus Daily Enquirer*, 13 July 1861.

[45] W. Hunter Lesser, *Rebels at the Gate: Lee and McClellan on the Front Line of a Nation Divided* (Napierville IL: Sourcebooks, Inc., 2004) 95.

that it took the report of the cannon eight seconds to reach me after seeing the smoke, and the whiz of the missel four seconds later still; this gave me about twelve seconds to dodge the ball." Hermann was exceedingly thankful when his relief arrived.[46]

Tents in the Confederate camp became riddled with holes. "In the afternoon," recalled Hermann, "minnie balls became rather multipherous, were hissing among the boys in camp, but up to that time no damage was done."[47] A musket ball zipped through Major Thompson's shelter, but fortunately did not find a mark. Once again trying to escape enemy fire, many of the Georgians abandoned their unsafe camps, laying their blankets among the trees.[48]

Musketry and shellfire made cooking an adventure, if not downright dangerous; the smoke from the campfires allowed Yankee gunners to zero in on troops cooking their meals.[49] The Georgians, though, made light of the danger as they learned to dodge the missiles: "A man would place on the fire a frying-pan containing bacon or flap-jacks. At the sound of a whistling shell he would run behind some large rock for protection; then after the shell had burst, hurrying to the pan he would gather its contents, replenish it, and again take refuge from an approaching bomb. All the while the men were laughing and joking, as if no danger were nigh."[50]

Officers were not immune to the distractive effects of the federal ordnance whirring overhead. Two shells hit near General Garnett's tent, one of which showered the general with dirt as he ate supper. Pouring the soil from his cup, he asked his servant to bring more coffee, then calmly returned to his meal. The troops marveled at Garnett's air of nonchalance.[51]

---

[46] Hermann, *Memoirs of a Confederate Veteran*, 16–17.

[47] Ibid., 17.

[48] H. G. Hammond, "Virginia Correspondence," *Atlanta Daily Intelligencer*, 19 July 1861; Homer Floyd Fansler, *A History of Tucker County, West Virginia* (Parsons WV: McClain Printing Company, 1962) 151.

[49] Derry, *Story of the Confederate States*, 120.

[50] Ibid., 120–21.

[51] "P.," "Accounts of the Battle at Laurel Hill," *Cincinnati Commercial*, as related in the *Augusta Chronicle and Sentinel*, 23 July 1861; Douglas Southall Freeman, *Lee's Lieutenants*, 3 vols. (New York: Charles Scribner's Sons, 1942: 1970 ed.) 1:32–33.

This Is a "Strategic" Movement

The soldiers at Laurel Hill were convinced they could hold their position against any number of Union troops. Events taking place to the south at Rich Mountain, however, would soon diminish their confidence. Rather than commit his troops to a full-scale attack, General Morris continued to "amuse" the forces in his front, holding them in place as a diversion while McClellan, with the bulk of his army, planned an assault on Rich Mountain. Morris had done his job well. Garnett, believing the main federal thrust was toward Laurel Hill, remained in position, awaiting an assault that was never to materialize.

On 11 July General Rosecrans, acting on information provided by a local Northern sympathizer, maneuvered his column around Lieutenant Colonel Pegram's position in an attempt to attack the Confederate left flank. Learning the Federals were moving against him, Pegram hastened most of his forces to his right, in the mistaken belief the danger was there. To cover his left, Pegram posted a small contingent consisting of one artillery piece and about 300 infantrymen. Caught by surprise, the vastly outnumbered defenders fought gallantly but were overwhelmed by superior federal numbers. Some of the Rebels managed to escape. Pegram, however, surrendered with 553 men on 13 July, after having wandered for two days lost in the tangled forests north of Beverly.[52]

The devastating news of Pegram's defeat arrived at Garnett's tent the evening of 11 July. With Rich Mountain in federal hands, the door was open into Garnett's rear. The general was forced to admit his position at Laurel Hill had instantly become untenable. With few choices left to him, Garnett decided to evacuate and retreat toward Beverly, his supply depot. There he would join other troops and make a stand.

The camp erupted in a frenzy of activity as wagons were hastily loaded and the troops prepared for the march. Showers continued to plague the Southerners. "Two days rations were ordered to be issued, which owing to the drenching rain, &c, were mainly lost, being uncooked," recalled one soldier.[53] Soldiers on the picket lines had little if any time to prepare. Corporal Nathan Pugh of the Walker Light Infantry, who was on sentry duty, recorded in his diary: "[O]n returning to camp at night, we packed up,

---

[52] Newell, *Lee vs. McClellan*, 128, 133.

[53] Anonymous, "Retreat of Gen. Garnett's Command in North-Western Virginia," *Richmond (VA) Examiner*, 23 July 1861.

and prepared to leave, not having time to eat supper, and notwithstanding many of us had nothing to eat during the day."[54] The consequences of lack of food or time to eat what there was would became sadly apparent over the following days.

Attempting to mislead the Federals in order to gain time for his escape, Garnett ordered the tents to remain standing and campfires left burning. With darkness descending quickly under angry, rain-swollen clouds, the troops pulled out of their entrenchments. "Early in the night the Confederate forces were drawn out of their line of works," recalled Private John B. Pillsbury of the Gate City Guards, "and placed in order of march on the Staunton pike. For hours the troops were kept standing in line on the pike to rest. After midnight the order of march were given, and pursued quietly and orderly, no panic, or nothing of a demoralizing nature whatever exhibited, but halting often."[55]

Garnett ordered the column southwards down the Beverly-Fairmont Road. Mystified as to the reason for the retreat, a soldier in Oscar Cantrell's company inquired of Colonel Ramsey "why we marched in the night and the weather so inclement?" Ramsey gave the question a thought, then answered, "This is a 'strategic' movement."[56]

Twenty men from the Gate City Guard were almost left behind. Through some mistake, a contingent under Lieutenant Leyden did not receive notice to withdraw from the picket lines. Returning to their camp at 2:00 A.M., they found it deserted. Hurriedly they made their way after the army, not catching up with the regiment until eight hours later. By this time, General Garnett's plans were beginning to unravel. Instead of escape, the road followed by the Army of the Northwest was drawing it closer to disaster.[57]

---

[54] Nathan S. Pugh, "Letter from Western Virginia," *Augusta Daily Constitutionalist*, 9 August 1861.

[55] John B. Pillsbury, "Garnett's Retreat After Rich Mountain, *Atlanta Journal*, 25 May 1901.

[56] Oscar A. Cantrell, *Sketches of the First Regiment Georgia Vols.: Together with the History of the 56th Regiment Georgia Vols., to January 1, 1864* (Atlanta GA: Intelligencer Steam Power Presses, 1864) 7.

[57] Fairman, *Chronicles of the Old Guard of the Gate City Guard*, 29.

6

Retreat to Corricks Ford

"I never felt prouder of our old State and her sons, than at the time the bullets were falling thick and fast around the boys, and they as firm as a rock to their place, and at every discharge you could count somebody among the enemy killed or wounded."—Private John W. Rigsby, Oglethorpe Infantry, to a friend in Augusta[1]

They Had Packed Off in a Desperate Hurry

"They're gone, all gone!" shouted the sergeant as he burst into General Morris's headquarters. "There's no one in their camp!" It was 7:00 A.M. on 12 July, and Morris was enraged. Garnett had stolen a march on him, right from under his nose. Determined to bag the retreating Confederates, the general fired off orders to the colonels of the 7th and 9th Indiana and 14th Ohio infantry regiments, along with two guns of the 1st Ohio Artillery, to make ready to track them down. Morris tapped Captain Henry W. Benham, his chief of engineers, to command the chase. Making all haste to depart, it was still after noon before Benham's force of roughly 1,800 troops set out in pursuit. Putting the rest of his command in motion, Morris followed several hours later.[2]

Union soldiers cautiously entered the deserted Confederate fortifycations. A correspondent for the *Cincinnati Commercial* described the sight:

> It was a scene of indescribable confusion when I visited it—a miscellany of tents thrown down and torn in pieces, tent poles, some half burned; camp kettles, mess pans, plates, spoons, knives and forks, and all the utensils common to camps; camp stools, cots,

---

[1] John W. Rigsby, "Letter from Virginia," *Augusta Daily Constitutionalist*, 31 July 1861.

[2] Homer Floyd Fansler, *A History of Tucker County, West Virginia* (Parsons WV: McClain Printing Company, 1962) 160; W. Hunter Lesser, *Rebels at the Gate: Lee and McClellan on the Front Line of a Nation Divided* (Napierville IL: Sourcebooks, Inc., 2004) 110. Benham's regular army commission ranked him above the volunteer regimental officers.

> blankets; champagne baskets and bottles, flasks, decanters, wagons; hospital stores, bandages, lint, litters, stretchers; seedy boots and shoes, "old clo's," stockings; and an endless litter of papers, letters, boxes, barrels, &c. They had packed off in a desperate hurry.—Many valuable camp equipages had been tied up, but they could not load them or had no time.—Fifty barrels of flour, as many of had biscuit, and a quantity of corn in the ear, were found in one place; in another, whole bundles of stockings, pants, coats, and blankets, which they had not the leisure to destroy; and in a pasture close by were seventy-five or a hundred sheep which they had "impressed."

In one corner of the encampment, the newspaperman came upon a grave with a wooden marker, upon which was carved the single word "Colonel." He speculated it might hold the body of Colonel Ramsey.[3]

Very much alive, though ailing, Ramsey and his regiment were slogging southward at the head of the retreating Army of the Northwest. By the time General Morris's sergeant was delivering his report, Garnett's army was within three miles of Beverly. There the general received grave news: Union soldiers were in the town. Compounding Garnett's bad luck, barricades had been thrown across the road ahead.

Not knowing the scouts were mistaken (the troops they had seen were actually Confederate) and with time slipping away, Garnett weighed his rapidly disintegrating options. Colonel Ramsey argued in favor of the army continuing on to Beverly, fighting its way into the town if necessary. Rejecting this plan, Garnett ordered his column to reverse course. Their only remaining avenue of escape was north toward St. George, crossing into the tip of Maryland near Red House, then turning southward across the Alleghenies and eventually reaching Monterey, Virginia. The soldiers about-faced, heading back toward Leadsville (present-day Elkins). The 1st Georgia, which had been the lead regiment, now found itself bringing up the rear of the army.[4]

The sun made a brief appearance from among the rain clouds, increasing the heat and humidity, to the discomfort of the Georgians. "The

---

[3] "P.," "Accounts of the Battle at Laurel Hill," *Cincinnati Commercial*, as reported in the *Augusta Chronicle and Sentinel*, 23 July 1861.

[4] W. Hunter Lesser, *Battle at Corricks Ford, Confederate Disaster and Loss of A Leader* (Parsons WV: McClain Printing Company, Inc., 1993) 7; Jesse W. Rankin, "Letter from Virginia," *Augusta Daily Constitutionalist*, 31 July 1861.

day was extremely hot," wrote Private Oscar Cantrell, "and the soldiers began to throw their clothing from their knapsacks, and during the day I was scarcely out of sight of clothing which was thrown away, the bushes on either side the road were strewn with them."[5]

Retracing their course past Leadsville to the tiny village of New Interest (present-day Kerens), the army turned eastward onto a narrow road that ascended a series of ridges. Passing alongside the steep slopes of Pheasant Mountain, the trace was barely wide enough for single wagons to make their way without dropping off the side into deep ravines. Adding to the misery, the skies once more darkened. As the rain fell in torrents, the road became a muddy morass, churned up by dozens of wheels and hundreds of feet. Heavily laden wagons bogged down, and soldiers sank knee deep in the mire. Teamsters jettisoned equipment from the wagons, desperately trying to lighten them so they could keep going. Teams veering too close to the edge slid off, their loads crashing down into the abyss. Several wagons ended up hanging upside down in trees. One of the wagons carried the flag of the Gate City Guards, so proudly presented to the company only a few months before. The banner of the Southern Guard met a similar fate.[6]

Our Brave Boys Stood the Storm

Shavers Fork of the Cheat River flows lazily through the Alleghenies, carving its way through flood-plain valleys bordered by steep mountains. The river flows northward, giving it the unusual distinction of having upstream being south and downstream being north. Curving like a snake from one side of the basin to the other, the stream butts up against steep rises before turning to cross the valley again. Travelers moving along the Shavers Fork Valley were forced to cross the river over and over again at numerous fords.

Alongside the narrow trail followed by Garnett's sodden army coursed a meandering stream known as Pleasant Run, flowing through the hills towards Shavers Fork. Nearing exhaustion, the straggling command approached Kalers Ford around midnight, near the location where Pleasant

---

[5] Oscar A. Cantrell, *Sketches of the First Regiment Georgia Vols.: Together with the History of the 56th Regiment Georgia Vols., to January 1, 1864* (Atlanta GA: Intelligencer Steam Power Presses, 1864) 8.

[6] Henry Clay Fairman, *Chronicles of the Old Guard of the Gate City Guard, Atlanta, Georgia, 1858–1915* (Atlanta GA: Byrd Printing Company, 1915) 32.

Run empties into Shavers Fork. Garnett called a halt, ordering the army into bivouac to give his trailing soldiers a chance to catch up. "The point where Garnett's command encamped on the night of the 12th," recalled Private John B. Pillsbury, "was a tract of open land, some under cultivation. On the opposite side of the river and left of the ford, crossed the night before, there was a small mountain spur, the river flowed along its base and the road running down on the side upon which the Confederates had been encamped, to a large mountain, and then turning to the right and recrossing the river at another ford."[7] The "mountain spur" was a low plateau on the eastern side of the Shavers Fork watershed, its nearly perpendicular face rising roughly forty to fifty feet above the valley floor. The 1st Georgia continued across Kalers before stopping for the night.[8]

Meanwhile, Captain Benham's pursuit force was gaining ground on its quarry. Benham's troops had no trouble finding the route taken by the retreating Confederates—they simply followed the trail of discarded equipment and churned-up mud. A correspondent traveling with the Federals wrote, "[E]very few rods we found stacks of tent poles, tents, blankets, and other camp equipages, which they had thrown out of their wagons and off their shoulders, to lighten their burdens and facilitate their retreat. Several wagons had got off the track, and were found upside down in the gorges of the mountains."[9] Garnett's men had felled trees along the path to block pursuit, and Confederate axmen exchanged sporadic shots with federal skirmishers, but the mud proved to be more of an obstruction to the Yankee advance. Even so, the Union soldiers were eager to close with the Rebels.[10]

Around 8:00 A.M. on 13 July the Confederates resumed their retreat, with the 1st Georgia, Colonel Taliaferro's 23rd Virginia, and Lieutenant Adolphus C. Lanier's section of the Danville Artillery forming the rear guard. It took two hours for the train of men to navigate the crossing at Kalers. Following a sunken trail hugging the east bank of the river, the wagons moved down the valley toward the next crossing.

---

[7] John B. Pillsbury, "Garnett's Retreat After Rich Mountain, *Atlanta Journal*, 25 May 1901.

[8] Ibid.

[9] "P.," "Accounts of the Battle at Laurel Hill," *Cincinnati Commercial*, as reported in the *Augusta Chronicle and Sentinel*, 23 July 1861.

[10] Lesser, *Rebels at the Gate*, 112.

The slow progress gave the federal pursuers time to close with their prey. Benham's advance, having stopped for only a few hours to rest during the night, was fast approaching Kalers. The supply train was still crossing Shavers Fork when scouts from Captain George Jackson's cavalry squadron reported Federals coming up behind them.

Colonel Ramsey, perhaps in a scheme to catch the Yankees in a crossfire, directed Major Thompson to position six companies in ambush. Thompson ordered his men to secrete themselves in a thick cornfield near (or possibly on) the plateau. Finding several logs lying between the cornstalks, the Georgians quickly piled them up into a makeshift breastwork. Thompson's position was ideal, just a short distance from the river path at the narrowest part of the valley, located to make best use of his short-range muskets and the longer carrying distance of the Gate City Guard's rifles. From here, the major's men could easily take the Federals in flank when they passed in line of battle.[11]

Benham, spotting Garnett's train stopped on the far side of Kalers Ford, prepared to attack as soon as more troops came up. Before he was ready, however, a musket fired by accident alerted the Confederates to the enemy's near presence.[12] Rebel teamsters immediately lashed their animals into motion. Ramsey sent a dispatch to alert General Garnett of the situation, then formed the remainder of his regiment in line of battle.[13] "We had reached another ford of the Cheat river," wrote Private James N. Bass of the Newnan Guards, "it making there a horse-shoe-bend, when seven [actually six] of our companies were stationed on the same side of the river with the enemy, at the foot of a Mountain about two hundred yards from the road while the remaining three [four] companies crossed the river."[14] Colonel Taliaferro positioned the 23rd Virginia to defend the wagons.[15]

---

[11] Isaac Hermann, *Memoirs of a Confederate Veteran 1861–1865* (Atlanta GA: Byrd Printing Company, 1911) 20–21. It is not certain whether Thompson's position was at the base or on top of the plateau.

[12] US War Department, comp., *The War of the Rebellion: A Compilation of the Official Records of the Union and Confederate Armies*, 128 vols. (Washington DC: Government Printing Office, 1880–1901) (hereafter cited as *OR*) ser. 1, vol. 2, pt. 1, p. 222.

[13] Cantrell, *Sketches of the First Regiment Georgia Vols.*, 8.

[14] James N. Bass, "The Retreat from Laurel Hill—The Sufferings of the First Georgia Regiment," *Atlanta Southern Confederacy*, 2 August 1861. Various accounts give from four to seven as the number of companies in Thompson's detachment. The most common number is six, which is corroborated in Ramsey's

Colonel Ramsey led his remaining section of the 1st forward, giving the order to open fire. "A galling fire was poured into the advancing foe," Ramsey recalled.[16] His attempt to catch the Federals in flank with his hidden troops miscarried, however. Expecting the Union soldiers to form line of battle, he was surprised when they remained in column of fours, following the wagon path and moving directly toward Taliaferro's Virginians and the Confederate train. This unexpected maneuver kept the Federals out of range of the smoothbore muskets of Thompson's concealed companies, effectively isolating his men from the rest of the regiment.

The 23rd Virginia fired several volleys, then fell back. As the Virginians retired, Ramsey directed his four companies to right-face, placing them across the road between the Union troops and the wagon train. "Now the battle commenced," wrote Private Bass, "the enemy pouring into our midst a volley of musketry of at least two thousand shots together with a shower of grape shot. Our brave boys stood the storm of bullets without flinching, and quickly returned the fire, taking as deliberate aim as if they were shooting squirrels. The combat raged, balls hissed past us as thick as hail but without effecting any damage exciting any fear in the hearts of Georgia's brave sons."[17]

Colonel Ramsey later wrote,

> The four companies who were making the desperate stand, being almost enveloped by the heavy masses of the enemy, having received no supports, and having entirely despaired of receiving assistance from the six companies who were cut off, and there being but about two hundred of these noble Georgians to contend against the whole Yankee army, who were pouring a hot fire of artillery and musketry into our ranks from every point, were ordered to fall back. In this encounter, the regiment lost twenty men, mostly captured by the enemy.[18]

---

own account of the action in James Madison Folsom, *Heroes and Martyrs of Georgia: Georgia's Record in the Revolution of 1861* (Macon GA: Burke, Boykin & Co., 1864; Baltimore MD: Butternut and Blue, 1995).

[15] W. H. Renroe, untitled article, *Sandersville Central Georgian*, 31 July 1861.

[16] Folsom, *Heroes and Martyrs of Georgia*, 7.

[17] James N. Bass, "The Retreat from Laurel Hill—The Sufferings of the First Georgia Regiment," *Atlanta Southern Confederacy*, 2 and 3 August 1861.

[18] Folsom, *Heroes and Martyrs of Georgia*, 7–8.

It was now about 11:30 A.M. His small battle line nearly surrounded and raked by artillery and increasing small arms fire, Ramsey gave the order to retreat. His remaining companies fell back in disarray across the second ford. Thompson's companies, too far away to hear the order, remained concealed in the cornfield. The Federals crossed the river in hot pursuit, surging past several abandoned wagons. A soldier of the 9th Indiana, finding the battle flag of the Washington Rifles in one wagon, drew it out and waved it in triumph.[19]

About three-fourths of a mile ahead, the 23rd Virginia and Lanier's artillery were formed in a position selected by Garnett's adjutant general, Captain James L. Corley. The Virginians allowed the 1st to pass through their lines, then commenced firing at the Union skirmishers. Advised by Corley the 1st had been reformed some distance in their rear, Taliaferro withdrew the 23rd. Bypassing the Georgians, Taliaferro's men moved rearward a short distance, then formed line of battle again. This leapfrogging of the two regiments continued for more than three and a half miles as they backpedaled toward the next set of crossings—Corricks Ford.[20]

Swollen by heavy rains, the river was difficult to cross. While navigating the upper ford of the two crossings that made up Corricks, the wheels of several wagons became wedged among rocks in the river bottom. While the Confederates desperately tried to extricate the wagons, Benham's advance caught up once again. Abandoning most of their remaining wagons to the enemy, Garnett's teamsters fled.[21]

As an unrelenting rain continued to fall, Colonel Taliaferro posted his Virginians on a bluff overlooking the upper ford, along with remnants of the 1st Georgia. Three pieces of artillery from Lanier's battery supported the Confederates. When the Federals appeared in the woods opposite his position, Taliaferro held his fire for a moment, thinking they might be Thompson's missing Georgians. But when it was discovered they were Union soldiers charging toward the river, the Virginians let out a cheer for President Davis, then poured down an intense fire on the Yankees, driving them to cover.

---

[19] Lesser, *Rebels at the Gate*, 114.

[20] *OR*, ser. 1, vol. 2, pt. 1, 286; Clement A. Evans, ed., *Virginia*, vol. 3 of *Confederate Military History*, 12 vols. (Atlanta: Confederate Publishing Company, 1890) 54–55.

[21] Lesser, *Rebels at the Gate*, 112.

Attempts to turn the Confederates' flank were obstructed by dense laurel thickets surrounding the crossing. For half an hour a vicious firefight raged. Finally, his ammunition nearly gone and one gun disabled, Taliaferro ordered his men to retreat.[22]

We Have Suffered Awfully

The supply wagons of the Army of the Northwest lay abandoned, scattered along the approaches and in the river below the bluff vacated by the Confederates. Along with the tents, camp equipment, and food deserted by the Rebel teamsters were several sick soldiers. One, Private G. D. Badger of the Gate City Guards, lay in a wagon standing in the middle of the stream. Badger was taken prisoner, cared for by the Federals, and released on parole eleven days later.[23]

Meanwhile, the other Virginia regiments had reached Job's Ford, three miles in advance.[24] Receiving word of the fight going on back at Corricks Ford, Garnett rode back toward the sound of the firing. As he galloped toward the scene of action, the general began to encounter disorganized remnants of the shattered 1st. Coming upon Captain Hanvey of the Newnan Guards, he demanded to know what was happening. "I don't know," answered Hanvey; "It is a damned shame."[25] Continuing on, Garnett met Colonel Ramsey. "Where is your regiment?" challenged the general. With several hundred men missing and presumed captured, the ailing colonel could only reply, "I don't know." Stunned by this answer, Garnett ordered Ramsey to collect what men he could and follow the general back to the ford.[26]

Arriving at the lower crossing of Corricks, Garnett conferred with Colonel Taliaferro as the rear guard streamed across Shavers Fork. Spying a pile of driftwood next to the riverbank, Garnett called for a squad of sharpshooters from the 23rd Virginia to conceal themselves, to hold up the

---

[22] Lesser, *Battle at Corricks Ford*, 13–15.

[23] J. M. Blackewell, "The Sufferings of the Gate-City Guards," *Atlanta Southern Confederacy*, 28 July 1861; Lillian Henderson, ed., *Roster of the Confederate Soldiers of Georgia, 1861–1865*, 6 vols. (Hapeville GA: Longing & Porter, Inc., 1959–1964) 1:266.

[24] Fansler, *A History of Tucker County, West Virginia*, 163.

[25] John H. Woods, ed., "Soldier and Prisoner, Two Confederate Memoirs by Robert H. Little," unpublished typescript (University of Chicago, 2000) 19.

[26] Robert R. Howison, "History of the War," *Southern Literary Messenger* 37/3 (March 1864): 136.

Federals when they reached the river. Ordering Taliaferro and the remaining troops to pull back, he stayed to direct the riflemen. The colonel protested, stating the general should not remain. Unmoved by Taliaferro's arguments, Garnett ordered the colonel to retire with his regiment.[27]

From across the stream, the officers could hear the cries of a wounded Georgia soldier. Receiving permission to attempt a rescue, aide-de-camp Samuel M. Gaines splashed across. The man was horribly injured; a ball had gone through both cheeks, breaking his jaws and severing a large portion of his tongue. Supporting the Georgian, Gaines made his way back across the ford. The soldier was carried to a nearby house.[28]

When Union skirmishers came into view across the river, the sharpshooters' fire brought them up short, but only for a few minutes. As more Yankee troops came up, they pressed forward toward the little band of Confederates. Garnett gave the order for the skirmishers to retreat. As he turned, a minie ball struck him in the back, knocking him from his saddle. The general lingered only a few minutes, breathing his last as the Union soldiers reached him.[29]

Garnett's death threw the issue of command into turmoil. "The head of the army had perished," recalled Taliaferro after the war, "and we had no information of the whereabouts of the next officer in rank, Colonel Ramsey, or of his knowledge of this succession to the command."[30] Captain Corley

---

[27] Lesser, *Rebels at the Gate*, 114.

[28] Fansler, *A History of Tucker County, West Virginia*, 163–65. The soldier could possibly have been Pvt. William P. S. Poole of the Walker Light Infantry. The Atlanta *Southern Confederacy* reported that Poole was left at a farmhouse after being wounded. Once the armies had moved on, the family returned to the house to find the terrified Georgian cowering under a bed. Given a drink of milk, liquid poured out through the holes in his cheeks. Neighbors cared him for the next two weeks, after which he was transported to Franklin and other points. About a year later, Gaines was himself a hospital patient at Amelia Court House, tended by a male nurse who communicated by means of a slate, being unable to speak due to terrible wounds. It was the same Georgia soldier that Gaines had rescued. (Martin K. Fleming, "The Northwestern Virginia Campaign of 1861," *Blue & Gray Magazine* 10/6 [August 1993]: 60; "From the First Regiment," *Atlanta Southern Confederacy*, 26 July 1861.)

[29] Lesser, *Rebels at the Gate*, 114–15.

[30] William B. Taliaferro, "Annals of the War. Chapters of Unwritten History. Garnett in West Virginia…," typescript from the *Philadelphia Weekly Times*, 11 March 1882, p. 7. Personal collection of W. Hunter Lesser. Even though Taliaferro had arrived with his regiment at Laurel Hill before the 1st Georgia, Ramsey's

was sent ahead to advise Ramsey of Garnett's death and request reinforcements, while Taliaferro's regiment, along with the remaining troops of the 1st Georgia, continued their retreat. Accompanied by Colonel William L. Jackson's 31st Virginia, Corley returned to inform Taliaferro that Ramsey was ill, and command of the army was now in the hands of the Virginian.[31]

Taliaferro's retreating troops continued to retire toward Job's Ford, where they found the other Virginia regiments drawn up in line of battle, ready to repel any Federals who might still be following. With the army reunited, Colonel Taliaferro positioned the 23rd and 37th Virginia as rear guard, along with an artillery battery, with instructions to "protect the trains at all hazards."[32]

Unbeknownst to Ramsey and Taliaferro, Benham had discontinued his pursuit, allowing his winded men a much-needed respite, while waiting for General Morris to catch up with the rest of his brigade. The Confederates, fearful of more attacks, continued to push on. Their path took them northeast into the tip of Maryland near the small village of Red House, on the Northwestern Turnpike. The column struggled to stay united as the fatigued troops staggered forward. "It was distressing beyond anything I ever witnessed," wrote a soldier of the 23rd Virginia. "They would drop from the ranks by the score utterly exhausted, and we had no means of transporting them. By this means, we have lost many men, though we hope to see them again as the enemy were not near enough to capture them. Some have already come in and we hope for more. All our baggage was lost; and neither officers nor men have a change of clothes."[33]

Still more river crossings lay ahead to be navigated. Several men had to be rescued from drowning while crossing the rain-swollen Cheat River at Neville's Ford. Fatigued horses could barely pull the few remaining wagons, leading teamsters to continue dumping supplies along the road. Tents and blankets were used to fill potholes. Weapons, ammunition, clothing, medicine, and even food were discarded. Weakened soldiers began to climb

---

colonel's commission predated Taliaferro's, as well as all the other regimental commanders. By army protocol, Ramsey was senior officer, making him second in command.

[31] Ibid.

[32] "P.," "Retreat of Gen. Garnett's Command in North-Western Virginia," *Richmond Examiner*, 23 July 1861, as reported in the *Columbus Weekly Times*, 29 July 1861.

[33] See, e.g., ibid.

into the now-empty wagons, causing spent horses to break down under the added weight. Drivers unhitched their exhausted teams, then smashed the wheels, rendering the conveyances useless to the enemy. Unfortunately, this also blocked wagons coming up from behind, forcing their abandonment also.[34]

Reeling from illness, Colonel Ramsey was barely able to remain in his saddle. Panicky soldiers imagined Union troops were all around them, preparing to strike and devour the remnants of Garnett's command. Several times they formed to receive an attack, only to realize there were no Yankees near. Reaching Red House about 2:00 A.M. on 14 July, the column shuddered to a halt. "There our men were rested a few hours," recalled the Virginian, "and had about two crackers issued to each man—being all that most of the men had received since Thursday night. Such suffering from hunger and fatigue was never witnessed."[35]

McClellan had positioned several regiments of Ohio militia at Grafton, under Brigadier General Charles W. Hill, to protect the Baltimore and Ohio Railroad. At 11:00 A.M. on 13 July, Hill received an urgent telegraph message: "General McClellan, having just learned that the rebel forces abandoned their positions at Laurel Hill last night, and are now making for Eastern Virginia, via Louisville and Saint. George pike, directs that you take the field at once, with all the force you can make available, to cut off their retreat."[36] Hill ordered Colonel J. Irvine with his 16th Ohio, who was supposed to be on the St. George Road, to intercept the Confederates heading in his direction. Relying on faulty intelligence, Irvine occupied the town of West Union, supposing it to be at the junction of the Northwestern Pike and St. George Road, which was actually some miles east. Discovering his error around 6:00 A.M. on 14 July, Irvine immediately marched toward Red House. Reaching the town about an hour later, he discovered the last of the Rebels had passed through only two hours before.[37]

With the realization Union troops were within striking distance, the army resumed its retreat at 5:00 A.M. Turning back into Virginia, the demoralized troops made their way slowly south. Colonel Ramsey's health

---

[34] Fansler, *A History of Tucker County, West Virginia*, 166–68.

[35] Ibid., 169; Robert R. Howison, "History of the War," *Southern Literary Messenger* 37/3 (March 1864): 137; "P.," "Retreat of Gen. Garnett's Command in North-Western Virginia," *Richmond Examiner*, 23 July 1861.

[36] *OR*, ser. 1, vol. 2, pt. 1, pp. 224, 229–230.

[37] Hermann, *Memoirs of a Confederate Veteran*, 140–41.

had improved enough for him to assume command by the time the army reached Greenland.[38] As the battered column passed through Petersburg on 16 July, the colonel sent a desperate message to Brigadier General Henry Roote Jackson's headquarters at Monterey, advising his plans to march to Harrisonburg and bemoaning the army's condition. "We have suffered awfully," he said. "Not many men were killed by the enemy, but there are hundreds missing. We were near starvation. The cavalry scouts still hang on our rear, but I do not think they are pursuing in force. What is left of this army will not be fit for service in a month."[39]

I Never before Knew What It Was to Suffer

Major Thompson's six companies were not the only ones cut off when the 1st retreated at Kalers Ford. Dozens of soldiers became separated from the regiment during the withdrawal. Private Oscar Cantrell, taking shelter behind a large tree, did not hear the order to retire. By the time he realized his Newnan Guards had pulled back, the Federals were between him and his company. Cantrell remained hidden until nightfall, watching the Union troops pass by as the rain poured. Once it was dark enough, he began to work his way on his hands and knees up a nearby hillside. Having crawled far enough to be satisfied he was out of sight of the enemy, he rose to his feet, continuing over the hill. On the other side, Cantrell encountered Captain Francis Wilkins of the Southern Guard, along with nineteen of his company. Hungry and exhausted, the soldiers camped for the night. The next morning the little group stumbled onto a Union picket post. Frightened out of their wits when Wilkins and his men charged out of the underbrush, the sentries fled. "One left his gun and blanket," Cantrell wrote later. "We took the blanket, but left the gun, as each of us had a gun, and no one of us was willing to carry another."[40]

The soldiers continued on through the forest and stumbled upon the camp of an unknown outfit. Wilkins asked who they were. "We are Ohio troops," said one of the men. "Who are you and where are you bound?" Thinking fast, the captain answered they belonged to an independent

---

[38] William B. Taliaferro, "Annals of the War," 18.

[39] *OR*, ser. 1, vol. 2, pt. 1, p. 253. See Folsom, *Heroes and Martyrs of Georgia*, 8, for Ramsey's account, in which the colonel states he assumed command of the army while it was at Job's Ford.

[40] Oscar A. Cantrell, "The Retreat from Laurel Hill—The Sufferings of the First Georgia Regiment," *Atlanta Southern Confederacy*, 3 August 1861.

Pennsylvania regiment and had gotten separated. "And are darned hungry," Wilkins added for emphasis. The Ohio soldier told him he had better hurry up and find his regiment, advising him to steal provisions from houses in the area. Wilkins's men hurriedly moved on. "As soon as we got out of sight," wrote Cantrell, "we took the woods and traveled in the mountains, wandering about for three or four days, with but little to eat. I never before knew what it was to suffer."[41]

Another Georgian to lose his way was James P. Crockett of the Gate City Guards, who left his company early on the 13th to find something to eat. Unable to rejoin his comrades once the federal attack began, Crockett fell in with the Newnan Guards, remaining with them during the staged retreat towards Corricks Ford. During one stop, Crockett was detailed with nine other men to go out on the company's flank to watch for any movement. Positioned farthest out, Crockett waited for three hours. "I called to the man on the next post, and received no answer. I called again with the same result. I then crept down to the road, and found that our men were gone, and the enemy's Cavalry were riding the road."[42] The forsaken solder plunged into the forest and evaded the Union horsemen. Crockett wandered in the woods for the rest of that evening, then again after waking in the morning. Coming onto a road, he followed it a short distance. Crockett described the incident for the *Atlanta Daily Intelligencer*: "I came to a bend in the road, and just as I turned this bend, I heard a voice hail me, and at the same time I heard the cock of a gun. I then saw four men, with their guns leveled at me. Of course I caved and gave up my gun."[43] Taken as a prisoner of war, Crockett was marched from Union camp to camp, then put on a train to Grafton, where he was paroled on 24 July. "While in custody I was threatened to be sent to prison," Crockett reported, "and be tried for treason and hung, but I remained unflexible."[44]

Relatives and friends of soldiers in the 1st Georgia waited anxiously for news of the events in Virginia. Reports were rushed into print, many based on pure speculation. "GALLANT CONDUCT OF THE GEORGIA REGIMENT," proclaimed the *Savannah Republican*, "Four Georgia

---

[41] See, e.g., ibid.; "Captain Wilkins and the Ohioans," *Columbus Daily Sun*, 31 July 1861.

[42] J. P. Crockett, "Mr. J. P. Crockett," *Atlanta Daily Intelligencer*, 9 August 1861.

[43] Ibid.

[44] Ibid.

Companies Captured."[45] The *Columbus Daily Enquirer* also reported the surrender of four companies, stating, "[T]he entire number of prisoners surrendered is six hundred."[46] Many newspapers ran articles lifted directly from Northern periodicals, such as a piece in the *Cincinnati Gazette* reporting "[F]our Georgia Captains and Lieutenants were taken among the prisoners."[47]

A correspondent for the *Atlanta Southern Confederacy*, stationed in Richmond, reported he had

> called at the War office, the Telegraph office, and at the various newspaper establishments and hotels, with the hope of hearing something that would allay the great anxiety that must be felt in Georgia in relations to Col. Ramsey's regiment; but nowhere have I been able to obtain anything definite. It is believed here however, that the regiment is safe, and that it has suffered no such casualties as those reported by the Northern telegraph correspondents, indeed, it is the general impression in well informed circles, that the disaster to our arms beyond the mountains has been exaggerated on both sides, and that our loss has not been as great as first reported.[48]

The *Sandersville Central Georgian* warned its subscribers about the multitude of mistaken reports, advising them to be patient and wait for accurate information. "FALSE NEWS" blazed the headline:

> We deem it our duty to caution our readers against the innumerable trashy, sensation dispatches which disgrace the columns of the daily newspapers. There are 120 gallant soldiers from this town and county in the 1st Georgia Regiment, and last week there was many an aching heart and sleepless eye in our midst, occasioned by news of the character we have mentioned. It will not do to believe everything the telegraph reports. In due course of time the truth will

[45] Anonymous, "Telegraphic," *Savannah Republican*, 19 July 1861.

[46] Anonymous, "The Fight at Laurel Hill," *Columbus Daily Enquirer*, 20 July 1861.

[47] Anonymous, "The Battle at Laurel Hill," *Raleigh North Carolina Standard*, 24 July 1861.

[48] Anonymous, "Exaggerated reports about the disasters in the West," *Atlanta Southern Confederacy*, 25 July 1861.

> come through the mails, and until then let us not distress ourselves about uncertainties and improbabilities.[49]

Slowly, better news began to emerge. Mayor Robert H. May of Augusta received a letter from the mayor of Staunton, Nicholas K. Trout, written 19 July: "Seven companies were cut off in the retreat. They have not been heard from, but it is believed they are in the mountains, and will work their way out. The Walker Light Infantry are of the number. Ten of the Oglethorpe Infantry are missing. It is feared about 7 are killed. The whole number killed in the Georgia Regiment is thought to be about 35. Some 20 of the Regiment are here: The others are looked for at head-quarters at Monterey to night." Trout paid tribute to the valor of the Georgians. "The Federal General McClelland announced the three fights made in the retreat by Garnett as very gallant. Your Regiment fought gloriously. We feel a deep interest in its fate. Can't you send us more such men?"[50]

Finally having time to write, the soldiers began penning letters home to their anxious relations. Private William H. Jones scribbled out a letter to his father while stopped briefly in Petersburg. "I have walked three days without shoes, and my feet are badly swollen. Have lost every rag of clothing, every blanket that we had, and in fact, everything. I have now no shoes, stockings, shorts or blankets. We walked three days and two nights through the mountains without anything to eat. So you see I am in a bad condition."[51]

Private Thomas J. Tutt of the Oglethorpes wrote later to his mother "from Thursday night until Sunday morning we had not a mouthful to eat. Sunday we received two crackers only. That evening they gave us a small piece of beef without bread, and nothing to cook it in. That is all that I had. After this, we came into a better disposed country, and we could get a sufficiency to sustain life along the road."[52]

---

[49] Anonymous, "False News," *Sandersville Central Georgian*, 24 July 1861.

[50] "W. A.," [N. K.], "Late from Staunton," *Augusta Chronicle and Sentinel*, 20 July 1861.

[51] William H. Jones, "Letters from Augusta Volunteers," *Augusta Chronicle and Sentinel*, 25 June 1861.

[52] Thomas J. Tutt, "Letter from Monterey," *Augusta Daily Constitutionalist*, 23 July 1861.

Our Journey Has Been a Hard One

Brigadier General Henry Rootes Jackson waited anxiously in Monterey for news from the remnants of Garnett's command. Jackson, a former newspaperman, judge and minister to Austria, had assisted Governor Brown in arranging the surrender of the Augusta Arsenal. Jackson had been dispatched to Monterey along with reinforcements for Garnett. When news of the disaster began filtering through to Richmond, the brigadier was instructed to take command of all forces in the region. Colonel Ramsey's message advising of his movement toward Harrisonburg startled Jackson, who had expected the retreating troops to head toward his concentration point. Jackson immediately forwarded a dispatch to Ramsey directing the colonel to bring his troops to Monterey.[53]

After seven days of marching through nearly continuous downpours, Ramsey's weary army straggled into the relative safety of Monterey. Jackson was shocked at the terrible state of the regiments: "The condition of Colonel Ramsey's command, the larger portion of which has arrived in camp, is in truth pitiable. Officers and men are absolutely stripped of everything—tents, clothing, cooking utensils, shoes—and I am sorry to believe that many have thrown away their arms."[54] Concerned their appearance would demoralize new regiments being ordered to the area, Jackson ordered the troops to McDowell, about twelve miles away to rest, refit, and recruit.

Private James Bass wrote home to his family about his ordeal: "Our journey has been a hard one; no set of troops ever experienced a harder time than we—worn out of fatigue, and foot-sore from our long march. There is not a soldier who was with us but whose feet are blistered—bleeding—and whose limbs are so worn out that they can only walk with great pain."[55]

Newspaper editors looked for ways to put a positive spin on the retreat. "It will take its place in the pages of history with the retreat of the ten thousand," declared the *Columbus Daily Times*. "Such scenes I hope never again to witness, and the soldiers of this command may rest assured that war has no terrors superior to those they have already undergone…[H]ad our

---

[53] *OR*, ser. 1, vol. 2, pt. 1, p. 253.

[54] James N. Bass, "The Retreat from Laurel Hill—The Sufferings of the First Georgia Regiment," *Atlanta Southern Confederacy*, 2 August 1861.

[55] "P.," "Retreat of Gen. Garnett's Command in North-Western Virginia," *Columbus Daily Times*, 27 July 1861.

men been fed, we would have accomplished the retreat with a loss of less than thirty men. Officers and men alike bore up, and all felt that they could make no sacrifice too great for the cause in which they were engaged."[56]

"If we have lost brave men," reported a correspondent for the *Atlanta Southern Confederacy*, "their country will reap the benefits of their deaths. All accounts concur in the assurance that they taught the enemy in North-Western Virginia that, before they conquer this land blood will flow like water."[57]

"It is the general impression that we will be sent to the mountains and have a chance to slay a few more Lincolnites," wrote Private Walter A. Wiley to his father, "and have revenge for the loss of our baggage, and the terrible long run they gave us. After all it was a victory for us, for we had them whipped before we left, but there was too many for us, for they would very soon have sent part of their force in front, then they would have had us all prisoners. As it was, we had to retreat. Their force was 13,000, ours 2,200. Gen. Garnett, just before he was killed, remarked that he had never seen a more gallant set of men than those Georgians."[58]

Criticism of Garnett's strategy began to appear. A reporter for the *Southern Confederacy* opined,

> The effect of this affair in North-Western Virginia will be unfortunate. It will encourage the Tories, to whose services upon the field and as spies, Gen. McClellan is indebted for no small part of his success, and will have a tendency to protract and embitter the contest in the disaffected counties. Its effect at the North will be equally pernicious. The sensation papers in New York will magnify it into the huge proportions of a great battle, in which the "rebels" were routed and driven back with great slaughter across the mountains and out of Western Virginia. Our regrets will be diminished, however, if the disaster shall but open the eyes of our own people to the now

---

[56] Anonymous, "The First Georgia Regiment," *Atlanta Southern Confederacy*, 27 July 1861.

[57] Walter A. Wiley, "From Staunton," *Atlanta Daily Intelligencer*, 6 August 1861.

[58] Anonymous, untitled article, *Atlanta Southern Confederacy*, 25 July 1861.

> established fact, that we are entering upon a great war, and have a stupendous work to perform.[59]

Sergeant Medlock blamed Richmond for the disaster:

> I must say that our Government should never have sent a handful of men into those mountains, filled with tories, and so near the Baltimore and Ohio Railroad that thousands of Northern troops could be concentrated there in a few days, when it requires at least a week for troops to come to our assistance. Little did we think that that would be our situation when we left Richmond feeling certain of victory. Instead of victory we were compelled to retreat, and to night, instead of sleeping in those nice large tents brought with them from Georgia, our men are exposed to all kinds of weather. Not a change of clothing or anything of the kind. But if by this means we can gain the independence of our beloved South, we are ready to make the sacrifice.[60]

To Private James Kinmon of the Washington Rifles, the army's defeat was the result of something more sinister: "When we left camp for Corinth at Laurel Hill," he wrote,

> we never expected to be whipped and then perish but so it was. Old General Garnett tried to sell our little army to his enemy but something prevented and although we retreated we killed the most men. One great deed that was done was the killing of General Garnett. The whole army rejoiced, but the General of the other side wept like a child when he saw him dead upon the field. The two Generals were old classmates at school, and it is natural to suppose they wished not to fight each other. We have got brave men but treacherous commanders. We can never be victors while this is the case.[61]

---

[59] Anonymous, "Exagerated [*sic*] Reports about the Disasters in the West," *Atlanta Southern Confederacy*, 25 July 1861.

[60] J. M. G. Medlock, letter to the editor, *Sandersville Central Georgian*, 31 July 1861.

[61] "An Incomplete Letter from James Kinmon, July 1861," in Mills Lane, ed., *"Dear Mother: Don't grieve about me. If I get killed, I'll only be dead.," Letters from Georgia Soldiers in the Civil War* (Savannah GA: The Beehive Press, 1977) 26.

Exhausted in both body and spirit, the troops set up camp at McDowell with what little equipment they had left. Over the next several days men straggled into the bivouac, singly or in small groups. Apprehensive of the fate of the six companies under Major Thompson, the Georgians looked back toward the mountains, wondering what had become of them. As commissary sergeant, Medlock had been with the army's advance units when his company, the Washington Rifles, was cut off. He wrote, "No one can imagine the anguish I felt when told positively that the regiment was cut to pieces, and that the Washington Rifles were in the hands of the enemy. May I be spared ever experiencing such feelings again. I thought of that noble band of men, (the regiment), second to none in the service, now as I supposed, nearly all prisoners or killed. The thought was sickening."[62]

---

[62] J. M. G. Medlock, letter to the editor, *Sandersville Central Georgian*, 31 July 1861.

7

LOST IN THE WILDERNESS

"Thus began a dreary march of three days and four nights in a perfect wilderness, soaked to the bone and nothing to eat, cutting our way through the heavy growth of laurel bushes."—Private Isaac Hermann, Washington Rifles[1]

The Enemy Had Not Seen Us

Waiting for the enemy to show themselves, Major George H. Thompson and his four hundred Georgians hunkered down behind their makeshift breastwork near Kalers Ford. They hid in the cornfield and watched intently as a column of soldiers hurried down the Shavers Fork Valley. Several soldiers leveled their muskets in preparation to fire on a battery of artillery as it passed less than a hundred yards in front of them. Major Thompson, either believing the troops were Confederate or not wanting to expose his position, instructed his men to hold their fire. "Had he given orders to fire and charge," recalled Isaac Hermann bitterly, "we could have been on them before they could possibly have formed themselves into battery, captured their guns, killed and captured many of their men, and would have turned into victory what proved to have become a disastrous defeat." [2] The guns were soon to be turned on Colonel Ramsey's four companies, hastening their departure.

From their cover, Thompson's detachment watched helplessly as the Yankees remained in column along the river side of the valley, out of range of the Georgians' old smoothbores. With the Federals now between them and the rest of their regiment, Thompson's troops remained concealed while Benham's force continued to cross Shavers Fork in pursuit of Garnett's retreating Confederates. "We were now cut off from our men, but the enemy had not seen us," wrote Private James Kinmon.[3] Trapped against the

---

[1] Isaac Hermann, *Memoirs of a Confederate Veteran 1861–1865* (Atlanta GA: Byrd Printing Company, 1911) 21.

[2] Ibid., 20–21.

[3] "An Incomplete Letter from James Kinmon, July 1861," in Mills Lane, ed., *"Dear Mother: Don't grieve about me. If I get killed, I'll only be dead.," Letters*

mountains as the column of Union troops passed close by, Thompson and his anxious officers weighed their situation. Vastly outnumbered and with all chance of support from the rest of the army gone, it was too risky to remain where they were. Wrote Kinmon, "We had no road to go out on, so our only chance was either to give ourselves up to the enemy or try to make our way through the mountains of which we knew nothing. We chose the latter."[4]

Once the Federals had moved on, Major Thompson flung away his horse's saddle and bridle, then released the animal. The Georgians crossed the plateau and began scaling the steep slope of Fork Mountain, traveling in single file through the dense underbrush. Because falling rock might give them away to the federal burial parties coming up, only a few men at a time were permitted to climb. Once all the soldiers reached the top, the officers huddled, trying to determine what course to take. Their options were few: they could work their way through the mountains to link up with the army, fight their way through the federal lines, or surrender.[5] Corporal Nathan S. Pugh recorded the meeting in his diary: "It was here determined to make our way across the mountains, through the wilderness, in search of the turn-pike leading to Staunton—Capt. Crump and Lieut. Russell, of the Walker Light Infantry, only, voting to return and fight our way through a desperate foe to our boys, being ignorant of their fate."[6]

Night was quickly descending, making the climb even more treacherous. Reaching a mountain hollow, the exhausted soldiers sank to the ground. Hunger gnawed at their stomachs. Most of the men had not eaten since their hasty departure from Laurel Hill. With little or no cover, they shivered through the night, catching scant bits of sleep while a cold drizzle continued to fall.[7]

Anxious to make General Garnett and Colonel Ramsey aware of their predicament, Major Thompson detailed Lieutenant Fleming and three men to make their way over the mountains, find the army, and report the troops

---

from Georgia Soldiers in the Civil War (Savannah GA: The Beehive Press, 1977) 24.

[4] Ibid.

[5] Louise Frederick Hays, *History of Macon County* (Atlanta GA: Stein Printing Company, 1933) 333.

[6] Nathan S. Pugh, "Letter from Western Virginia," *Augusta Daily Constitutionalist*, 9 August 1861.

[7] See, e.g., ibid.

situation to the general. For two days, the foursome crossed mountains and waded rivers. Coming to a house on top of a ridge, they were given food by the woman living within. She warned them not to stay, so they made camp on a nearby hill. At sunrise they returned to the house for breakfast, then continued on their way. After coming close enough to Union camps to hear their drums, Fleming's party reached Franklin, where they found sixteen other men also separated from the regiment.[8]

Rising next morning from their fitful slumbers, Thompson's Georgians continued on, snaking their way over McGowan Mountain. The farther they went, the thicker the undergrowth became. "On Sunday morning we started again," wrote Kinmon, "[the] fourth day without eating, up the chalk mountain. We got to the top and commenced going down. Here the laurel bushes were so thick we had to cut our way with bowie knives, making about a mile in two hours. We went on in this way all Sunday, and at night we found ourselves at the foot and by a small river, which ran through large flat rocks. On these rocks, 400 famished men made their bed."[9]

Starving men chewed strips of birch bark to slake their hunger. Others sliced off their shoe soles, sucking on the old leather. One soldier found a small chunk of biscuit while rooting through his knapsack. Spotting the tiny morsel, another man immediately offered him five dollars for it. The soldier refused.[10]

Captain S. A. H. Jones of the Washington Rifles had two sons in his company. "Father," begged Stephen B. Jones, age eighteen, "Please give me something to eat. I am starving!" Captain Jones shook a few slivers of hardtack from his haversack. "Take this, my dear boy," he told his son, "Eat it slowly; and may God save your life!" For his other son, Weaver, Jones produced a tallow candle. The youngster would not take it, insisting his father consume it. Watching from aside, Isaac Hermann reached for the

[8] William O. Fleming to his wife, 18 July 1861, in the William Oliver Fleming Papers, #2292-z, Southern Historical Collection, the Wilson Library, University of North Carolina at Chapel Hill (hereafter cited as Fleming Papers). Quoted with permission of William Fleming, descendent.

[9] "An Incomplete Letter from James Kinmon, July 1861," in Lane, *"Dear Mother: Don't grieve about me,"* 24–25.

[10] Anonymous, "A Great Company—A Running Sketch of the Gate City Guard," *Constitution*, 18 January 1889; S. B. Jones, "Extracts from Letters Written by Capt. S. B. Jones to His wife 1861—1865," Civil War Miscellany Files, Personal Papers, drawer 283, reel 30, Georgia Department of Archives and History, Morrow GA.

candle, splitting it with his knife. Giving the halves to father and son, Hermann licked the blade. "It was the first taste of anything the writer had had in four days," he recalled later.[11]

The harrowing conditions weakened men's spirits and preyed on their minds. Lieutenant Austin Leyden of the Gate City Guard worried about the mental and physical state of his soldiers. "Numbers of the men broke down and declared they could go no further. Some became delirious, and had to be watched."[12]

There Was No Prospect of Escape

As the miserable soldiers made their way through the dense forest, small groups became separated from the column. Thirteen men, led by Lieutenant Evan. P. Howell, somehow found themselves cut off and on their own. They followed a small stream with hopes it would lead toward civilization. Spotting an otter sunning itself on a rock, Howell shot the animal, dividing the meat by lot among the men. Sometime after nightfall, a soldier on guard duty ran excitedly into camp, exclaiming he had heard the jingle of a cowbell close by. Deriding the sentry for hearing things, the weary men fell back to sleep. Too hungry for skepticism, the soldiers set out in search and discovered cattle grazing nearby. With shaking hands, one soldier took a shot. He missed, and the errant shot scattered the animals. Determined to get meat, they followed the cattle trail to a cabin. A sympathetic woman there offered to let them slaughter one of her sheep. The next day, after another full meal, Howell and his companions hired wagons to take them to Monterey.[13]

Brooding skies, continual rain, and wild terrain conspired against the Georgians. "Our condition on the fourth morning was extremely wretched," Lieutenant Leyden recorded. "Many of the men could not move, and there was no prospect of escape for those remaining on their feet."[14]

---

[11] See, e.g., S. B. Jones, "Extracts from Letters Written by Capt. S. B. Jones to His wife 1861—1865," 21–22.

[12] Henry Clay Fairman, *Chronicles of the Old Guard of the Gate City Guard, Atlanta, Georgia, 1858–1915* (Atlanta GA: Byrd Printing Company, 1915) 31.

[13] E. C. Bruffey, "Lost Gate City Guard of Georgia Resembled Lost Battalion of A.E.F.," *Atlanta (GA) Journal*, n.d. 1918, in Robert L. Rodgers Collection, Civil War Miscellany Files, Personal Papers, drawer 283, reel 58, Georgia Department of Archives and History, Morrow GA.

[14] Fairman, *Chronicles of the Old Guard of the Gate City Guard*, 31.

Desperation was growing among the famished, exhausted soldiers. A few of the men, either through starvation or delirium, entertained thoughts of cannibalism.[15]

The column struggled down Otter Creek. "We commenced going down this river," wrote Kinmon, "sometimes wading and at others leaping from rock to rock over deep chasms and down precipices at all times in danger of falling and killing ourselves. After going in this way for a mile, we quit the river and commenced going up another mountain."[16]

Fighting their way through the almost impenetrable laurel forest drained the soldiers' stamina. A constant rotation of men was kept working, hacking at the brush. "Those who were able were sent to the front with knives to continue to cut the way," wrote Leyden, "As soon as one would give out another would take his place."[17]

Private Kinmon could not stand much more. "I resolved to follow our men until 12 o'clock and, if [we] did not come to something to eat or to a road, to take the back track, go to the enemy and give myself up as a prisoner of war. I considered this preferable to perishing in a mountain where neither beast [n]or beards ever lived."[18]

"This was the first time that *starvation stared me in the face*," wrote Frank W. Farrar of the Gate City Guards. "Oh! God, what a thought! I cannot describe to you my feelings at this juncture. My system was so shattered for want of food, that I really felt very little like eating, but had a greater desire to sleep. I had scarcely closed my eyes, until I heard a brother-in-arms cry out, 'pilot, *pilot*.'"[19]

It was now about 10:00 A.M. Excited whispers passed from man to man along the column. A glimmer of hope began to stir. They had been located by someone—a mountain man, some said—a pilot who might guide them out of this labyrinth.

---

[15] "A Great Company—A Running Sketch of the Gate City Guard," *Atlanta Constitution*, 18 January 1889.

[16] "An Incomplete Letter from James Kinmon, July 1861," in Lane, *"Dear Mother: Don't grieve about me,"* 25.

[17] Fairman, *Chronicles of the Old Guard of the Gate City Guard*, 31.

[18] "An Incomplete Letter from James Kinmon, July 1861," in Lane, *"Dear Mother: Don't grieve about me,"* 25.

[19] Frank W. Farror, "The Retreat from Laurel Hill—The Sufferings of the First Georgia Regiment," *Atlanta Southern Confederacy*, 3 August 1861.

You Would All Perish to Death

James Rust Parsons, known locally as "Tanner Jim" for a tannery he once ran from his home, owned a 450-acre farm on Shavers Fork in Tucker County. Learning of the soldiers' plight, he decided to attempt a rescue.[20]

Parsons was an unlikely angel of deliverance, described by Isaac Hermann as "a man of about fifty years, rather ungainly as to looks, and somewhat cross-eyed."[21] Parson's arrival raised the spirits of most of the soldiers. A few feared, however, this visitor could be a Union sympathizer, planning to lead them into a trap.

Major Thompson asked Parsons how he had located them. "Sunday evening two men came to my house for something to eat," replied Parsons. "In talking with them I found they belonged to the 1st Georgia regiment and had been cut off the day before at Cheat river. They also told me that you men, about four hundred in number, were still in these mountains hoping to make your way across to the valley. I found out from them what direction you were going in when they had left you, and I have come to lead you out."[22]

Thompson voiced his suspicion that the stranger was a Yankee spy. "Gentlemen," said Parsons, "I am in your power; the country through which you propose to travel is not habitable, I have been raised in these regions, and there is not a living soul within forty miles in the direction you propose to go, and at the rate you are compelled to advance, you would all perish to death, and your carcasses left for food to the wild beasts of the forest."[23]

"Go on," replied the major, "take us out of this wilderness and we will reward you—but betray us, and I will blow your brains out with my own hand at the first sight of the enemy." Thompson had the mountain man disarmed, and assigned a guard to watch him closely.[24]

Parsons directed the Georgians to turn about. Many were too sick or injured to move any further. "Those that were able started on the trail of the

---

[20] Homer Floyd Fansler, *A History of Tucker County, West Virginia* (Parsons WV: McClain Printing Company, 1962) 165. Several soldiers from different companies claimed to be the ones who found Parsons.

[21] Hermann, *Memoirs of a Confederate Veteran*, 23.

[22] J. W. Stokes, "The Retreat from Laurel Hill, West Virginia," *Southern Bivouac* 3/10 (October 1884): 62.

[23] Hermann, *Memoirs of a Confederate Veteran*, 25.

[24] Anonymous, "A Great Company—A Running Sketch of the Gate City Guard," *Atlanta Constitution*, 18 January 1889.

hunter," wrote Lieutenant Leyden, "leaving their disabled companions lying along the path where they gave out, and others to take care of them until relief could be sent back."[25]

"Thus we retraced our steps," wrote Private Kinmon, "following our leaders, when after about three miles march we struck a mountain stream, in the bed of which we waded for nine miles, the water varying from knee to waist deep, running very rapidly over mossy, slippery rocks, and through gorges as if the mountains were cut in twain and hewn down. In some places, the walls were so high, affording a narrow dark passage, I don't believe God's sun ever shone down there."[26]

Several officers still harbored a deep distrust of the stranger. "Many times during the day halts are made by different Captains and Lieutenants," recorded Corporal Pugh, "who almost determine to return with their commands; declaring Mr. Parsons and young Irons to be traitors, taking us into the hands of the enemy. Some said they had suspicioned them from the time we were overtaken in the morning, and now, late in the afternoon, their suspicions are confirmed by their conduct and conversation—that we will be taken by traitors to the enemy's camp and annihilated." Captain Samuel H. Crump defended Parsons, urging the rest of the men to believe in him.[27]

The column followed Parsons back along Otter Creek to a small valley at the stream's confluence with Dry Fork. While the Georgians set about building fires to warm themselves, Parsons left to find food. Lacking matches or other dry materials to start fires, the soldiers improvised. "Happily some of the men had paper that escaped humidity," wrote Isaac Hermann. "Loading a musket with wadding, they fired into a rotten stump, setting it on fire, and by persistent blowing, produced a bright little flame, which soon developed into a large camp fire, around which the boys dried themselves."[28]

---

[25] Fairman, *Chronicles of the Old Guard of the Gate City Guard*, 32.

[26] "An Incomplete Letter from James Kinmon, July 1861," in Lane, *"Dear Mother: Don't grieve about me,"* 25.

[27] Nathan S. Pugh, "Letter from Western Virginia," *Augusta Daily Constitutionalist*, 9 August 1861. Two sources tell of another man with Parsons. In Isaac Hermann's *Memoirs of a Confederate Veteran*, he states Parsons was accompanied by a son. Corp. Nathan Pugh's diary identifies the second man as John B. Irons. Out a wealth of information available about the trek of Thompson's detachment, only these two accounts have been found to date that mention a second guide.

[28] Hermann, *Memoirs of a Confederate Veteran*, 27.

Parsons returned with a supply of cornbread, which was quickly devoured. Captain Crump was offered one of the first pieces, but even though he had been without any nourishment for days, he refused. "I will not eat a mouthful until my company are supplied with food," Crump declared. "If my men eat nothing, I will eat nothing myself." Some of the soldiers had been without food for so long they had difficulty getting it down. "The first I got into my mouth choked me so that I could scarcely swallow it," recalled Private Kinmon.[29]

Next morning, the men were overjoyed when Parsons drove several head of cattle into camp. The cattle were swiftly butchered, with much of the meat gobbled down before reaching a cook fire. "To get rations was a quick performance," wrote Hermann. "The meat was devoured before it had time to get any of the animal heat out of it." Parsons also provided meal for baking bread. Some were still too weak to eat. "Many of the men were so far gone," wrote Lieutenant Leyden, "that they could not be gotten up to take their meat, but had to be served by stronger companions."[30]

Parties were sent back along the trail to bring in those left behind. The remainder of the soldiers reached the valley by the end of the day. There they stayed for another day, resting and regaining their strength.[31]

Laughter and Tears Greeted Them

Thursday morning, refreshed and with full bellies, the Georgians filled their haversacks and prepared to set out once more. Parsons resumed guiding them toward safety. "We then started down the river to a small path that led across the mountains," Private Kinmon wrote, "To another turnpike and which carried us below the enemy, traveling at the rate of one mile for hour. When we got to the path we travelled a little faster, but on account of weakness we still went slow."[32]

Signs of civilization slowly began to appear. "The next day we come to a few miserable huts on the mountains," noted Private Kinmon, "and in a

---

[29] "Letter from Western Virginia," *Augusta Daily Constitutionalist*, 9 August 1861; "An Incomplete Letter from James Kinmon, July 1861," in Lane, *"Dear Mother: Don't grieve about me,"* 25.

[30] Hermann, *Memoirs of a Confederate Veteran*, 29; Fairman, *Chronicles of the Old Guard of the Gate City Guard*, 32.

[31] See, e.g., Fairman, *Chronicles of the Old Guard of the Gate City Guard*, 32.

[32] "An Incomplete Letter from James Kinmon, July 1861," in Lane, *"Dear Mother: Don't grieve about me,"* 25.

few days we got into a country very well settled by very poor people. Here we got bread and milk to eat."[33]

Kinmon, along with several of the men, still feeble from their exertions, found shelter at homes and farms along the way. "I became so weak that I could not travel, so [I] stopped behind the army and threw myself on the mercy of settlers...I found myself among friends who gave me food and lodging without pay."[34]

A young woman at one house provided Isaac Hermann with milk and enough meal to cook a large "hoe-cake." Unable to find a skillet, Hermann employed an old shovel to bake the bread in a fireplace. Joined later by two comrades, he spent the night "under shelter in a warm room, a luxury not enjoyed in some time."[35]

Traveling past the mouth of Seneca Creek, where it flows into the North Fork of the Potomac River (near present-day Seneca Rocks), the column worked its way south into Crab Bottom Valley (present-day Bluegrass Valley). With straggling becoming an increasing problem, Major Thompson decided to split up the troops, allowing groups to strike off on their own with orders to converge on Monterey as quickly as possible.[36]

On 20 July, a full week after being cut off at Kalers Ford, the ragged columns reached Monterey. The rest of the Army of the Northwest had made its way into camp there only the day before. "Laughter and tears greeted them with hearty hand-shakes or embraces," wrote Joseph T. Derry of Company D. Jubilation erupted at the reunion.[37]

Incredibly, once all the stragglers came in and were accounted for, not a single man had been lost. Communications were fired off to jubilant relatives. Mayor Robert H. May of Augusta received a wire from E. H. Hall of Staunton: "The Oglethorpe Infantry and Walker Light Infantry are all safe, except two killed, Messr. Roll and Cloyd, and one who died in camp."

Their trial in the mountains had taken an enormous toll on the Georgians, both physically and psychologically. Lieutenant Leyden recalled, "A great many of those who had suffered so much died of fevers and other

---

[33] Ibid., 24–25.

[34] Ibid., 26.

[35] Hermann, *Memoirs of a Confederate Veteran*, 31–34.

[36] Lillian Henderson, ed., *Roster of the Confederate Soldiers of Georgia, 1861–1865,* 6 vols. (Hapeville GA: Longing & Porter, Inc., 1959–1964) 1:282; Stokes, "The Retreat from Laurel Hill," 66.

[37] Fairman, *Chronicles of the Old Guard of the Gate City Guard*, 209.

ailments in a few months. Most of those who had become crazy, recovered for a time, but either died soon afterward or become permanently deranged."[38] Private James W. Stokes of the Gate City Guards reported, "Some fifteen of the men died soon after we reached Monterey.... Several of them were deranged for two or three weeks. Two were sent to the insane asylum, one (Jessie T.) was only little better than an idiot till the day of his death, which occurred some years later."[39]

The day after the six companies staggered into Monterey, a low rumbling noise was heard to the east, not unlike the sound of thunder over distant mountaintops. The mysterious sound was the remote boom of artillery, some 120 miles away, near the banks of a meandering stream known as Bull Run. Northwest of Richmond, Confederates under the command of Brigadier Generals Joseph E. Johnston and P.G.T. Beauregard were engaged with the federal army of Brigadier General Irvin McDowell. When details of the clash reached Monterey, the troops cheered the decisive Confederate victory.[40]

Several days later, William Fleming received a letter from his father. The contents stunned him. "My dear and only Son," wrote the elder Fleming. "My gallant boy your noble brother has fallen in battle. God grant us grace sufficient to our day and sanctify this affliction to our spiritual and eternal good. We are in great affliction and I cannot write more."[41]

The momentous Battle of Manassas Junction, which had been heard by the troops in Monterey, had included the 8th Georgia Infantry. In Company B of the 8th, the Oglethorpe Light Infantry, was John M. Fleming, William's younger brother. Their father's grief poured from the short letter, as well as his fear for William's well-being in the last few lines he had managed to scribble. "We are in great distress about you—if you can send us a letter it will be a great comfort in our afflictions. God help and protect my only boy and return him to us in his own good time in health and

---

[38] Ibid., 32.

[39] Stokes, *The Retreat from Laurel Hill*, 66.

[40] Fairman, *Chronicles of the Old Guard of the Gate City Guard*, 32.

[41] William Bennett Fleming to William O. Fleming, 26 June 1861, in the William Oliver Fleming Papers, #2292-z, Southern Historical Collection, the Wilson Library, University of North Carolina at Chapel Hill (hereafter cited as Fleming Papers). Quoted with permission of William Fleming, descendent.

safety."[42] Fleming set about to obtain a furlough so he could go to his despairing parents.

We Were Entirely without Tents

Encamped at McDowell, the 1st Georgia was in terrible condition. Almost all of their equipment—tents, blankets, cook pots, and more—had been lost during the retreat from Laurel Hill. Uniforms were in tatters, and clothing of any description was desperately needed. Shelter of any kind was scarce—even to the point of having no lockup for prisoners. Private Richard Deshaser of the Southern Guards was arrested for stealing, but there was nothing even remotely resembling a guardhouse in which to imprison him. With no place to hold the thief until he could be court-martialed, the company voted to have Deshaser drummed out of camp.[43]

Shortly after he reached McDowell, an unexpected delivery arrived for Colonel Ramsey. Unwrapping a package sent through the Union lines, Ramsey discovered to his astonishment his watch, lost during the retreat from Laurel Hill. The timepiece had been packed in the colonel's trunk, which was among those unceremoniously dumped from wagons. In a gallant gesture, General McClellan had returned the watch to its owner. Such chivalrous behavior would soon become a very rare thing.[44]

Concerned with the health of his command, Ramsey issued verbal orders to his company commanders allowing their men to take refuge among civilians in the surrounding countryside. "Col. Ramsey," reported Sergeant Medlock,

> seeing the condition of his men after our arrival at McDowell—fatigued, sick, worn down and greatly in need of rest—with his usual kindness of heart, relieved them all restraint, as far as was consistent with military law, and gave them ten days to recruit in.... [W]e were entirely without tents, and had but few blankets in the regiment. Rain was falling almost every day, and the men were without protection from it. Seeing this, Col. R. gave them permission to find shelter where best they could in the neighborhood of McDowell.[45]

---

[42] Ibid.

[43] Henderson, *Roster of the Confederate Soldiers of Georgia*, 1:228.

[44] J. M. G. Medlock, letter to the editor, *Sandersville Central Georgian*, 7 August 1861.

[45] Ibid., 21 August 1861.

Ramsey provided written orders for selected officers from each company to travel to Richmond, for the purpose of obtaining desperately needed clothing and equipment for their men.

Colonel Taliaferro, formerly major general of Virginia state troops and very much a stern disciplinarian, watched with dismay at the flood of soldiers from the 1st Georgia camps. In a request to General Jackson, Taliaferro asked that his regiment be "placed under my exclusive control." Confounded by the appeal, Jackson asked for an explanation. "I have the honor frankly to Say," replied Taliaferro,

> that I made the application because I was unwilling, Should it not conflict with your views, to be placed under the command of Col Ramsey, 1st Geo Regt, who was my ranking officer. I had witnessed with mortification the almost total disintegration of his regiment in the march from Laurel Hill to this place, & I feared that the relaxation of discipline which had been exhibited by him on the march when in command of the troops of Genl Garnetts command, would characterize his conduct at McDowell. And as any general orders touching discipline & police would apply to the whole command, I desired to have An opportunity of keeping my regiment under my exclusive control, that I might apply rules of more rigid discipline than I believed would be required by Col Ramsey.[46]

"More rigid discipline," in the form of a new commanding general, was about to arrive.

---

[46] Col. William B. Taliaferro to Gen. Henry R. Jackson, 13 August 1861, in the Robert Edward Lee Papers, Mss3L515b, Virginia Historical Society, Richmond VA.

8

THE FAILURE OF GENERAL LEE

"General R. E. Lee, rode up one day, and we were ordered in line for inspection, he was riding a dapple gray horse. He looked every inch a soldier. His countenance had a very paternal and kind expression. He was clean shaven, with the exception of a heavy iron gray mustache. He complimented us for our soldiery bearing. He told Captain Jones that he never saw a finer set of men."—Private Isaac Hermann of the Washington Rifles[1]

I Have Ordered the Arrest of Colonel Ramsey

A soldier since youth, William Wing Loring was a stickler for obedience and order. Born in North Carolina, Loring and his family moved to Florida while he was young. He battled Seminoles as a second lieutenant in the Florida militia, then later served in the state government. When war with Mexico broke out in 1846, he was appointed captain in the Regiment of Mounted Rifles. Brevetted twice for valor, Loring took a wound at Chapultapec serious enough to require the amputation of his left arm. The severity of the injury, however, was not enough to keep the determined young officer out of the service. By the time his state left the Union, he held the distinction of being the youngest full colonel in a field command.[2]

Loring arrived in Richmond after the Confederate victory at Manassas and received orders directing him to proceed to Western Virginia and assume command of the Army of the Northwest with the rank of brigadier general. Reaching Staunton on 23 July, Loring was infuriated to encounter scores of soldiers from the 1st Georgia scattered throughout the countryside. Immediately canceling all leaves, he set to work reassembling his command. In a dispatch to the assistant adjutant general, Colonel George Deas, he wrote,

---

[1] Isaac Hermann, *Memoirs of a Confederate Veteran 1861–1865* (Atlanta GA: Byrd Printing Company, 1911) 39.

[2] Ezra J. Warner, *Generals in Gray* (Baton Rouge: Louisiana State University Press, 1959) 193–92; Sifakis, *Who Was Who in the Civil War*, 395.

> Upon my arrival at Staunton, day before yesterday, I there found a large number of officers and several hundred men belonging to Colonel Ramsey's and to other regiments, with leaves of absence to visit Georgia and other places. I immediately countermanded all of the furloughs, and ordered a competent officer stationed there to take charge of them, and to permit neither officer nor man to leave without authority from me. *En route* from Staunton I passed large numbers on the road, and was told that the farm houses on the road were filled with them. This is in consequence of Colonel Ramsey—stationed by General Jackson some ten miles below this point—having given his entire regiment leaves of absence. I have directed that every effort be made to concentrate them, but it may now be impossible to do so. I have ordered the arrest of Colonel Ramsey.[3]

Shocked by the colonel's arrest, soldiers and home-folk alike rose to his defense. "But for the fatherly feeling of Col. Ramsey toward his men in thus providing shelter for them from the pelting rain," wrote Sergeant Medlock, "and relieving their minds of the usual restraint of camp life, many a brave man that is now able and ready to march to the battle field would lie silent in the grave. The 1st Georgia Regiment owes their Colonel a lasting debt of gratitude."[4] The editors of the *Columbus Daily Sun* offered their support:

> Prompted by sympathy with the men under his command who have suffered more hardships perhaps than any other regiment in Virginia, he granted them furloughs to recruit their exhausted health and energies and thereby to enable them the better to encounter others incident to the perilous service in which they are engaged. This may not be compatible with the stern, hard rules of military discipline as viewed by the martinet, but it will be conceded that his course was

---

[3] US War Department, comp., *The War of the Rebellion: A Compilation of the Official Records of the Union and Confederate Armies*, 128 vols. (Washington DC: Government Printing Office, 1880–1901) (hereafter cited as *OR*) ser. 1, vol. 2, pt. 1, p. 999.

[4] J. M. G. Medlock, letter to the editor, Sandersville Central Georgian, 21 August 1861.

> perfectly consistent with the dictates of wisdom, and reflects credit upon a spirit as brave as it is kind and generous.[5]

Loring also suspected General Jackson of allowing the wholesale exodus from camp. In his defense, Jackson quizzed the 1st's company captains about Ramsey's orders. "In compliance with your request that I shall communicate in writing any knowledge I may have in regard to granting furloughs to any of my Officers & men by yourself," responded Captain Hanvey of the Newnan Guards. He wrote, "I can only say that I went to Richmond under a special order signed by yourself for the purpose of obtaining Clothing, Camp & Garrison Equippage &c for my men, but that I am certainly ignorant of a single furlough granted by you, and that my men were suffered as I learn from them generally to go at large for ten days into the Country, and else where-ever they saw fit, by permission from Col. J. N. Ramsey."[6]

Captain Jones of the Washington Rifles replied,

> I have simply to state that upon our arrival at this place on our late retreat I understood from Col Ramsey & others that in view of our extreme destitute condition one commissioned Officer (or other member) would be allowed to go on furlough to Staunton or other place for the purpose of procuring supplies for our new companies. In accordance with that understanding after the Regiment had gone forward to Mc Dowell I applied to you and obtained permission for a private in my company to go upon that business. I know of no other nor do I believe that any other furlough was granted by you to any other member of my company. Upon my arrival at Mc Dowell I received a verbal order from Col Ramsey to grant at my discretion permits for ten days. He gave permits to my officers for a much longer time.[7]

---

[5] Anonymous, "Col. James N. Ramsey," *Columbus Daily Sun*, 20 August 1861.

[6] Capt. George M. Hanvey to Gen. Henry R. Jackson, 12 August 1861, in the Robert Edward Lee Papers, Mss3L515b, Virginia Historical Society, Richmond VA.

[7] Capt. S. A. H. Jones to Gen. Henry R. Jackson, 12 August 1861, in the Robert Edward Lee Papers, Mss3L515b, Virginia Historical Society, Richmond VA.

At General Loring's direction, Lieutenant Colonel Clarke placed notices in several Georgia newspapers, instructing absent soldiers to return to their commands. The *Columbus Daily Enquirer* ran one such notice: "Commissioned, non-commissioned officers, and privates, of the 1st Regiment of Georgia Volunteers, are hereby ordered to report themselves at these Headquarters, without delay, excepting those who have leave of absence granted by Gen. Henry R. Jackson. All leaves of absence granted by Col. James N. Ramsey are hereby revoked by general order. By order of General Loring."[8]

Is Not This Awful to Contemplate

Loring next set to work preparing to retake the ground lost by Garnett's defeat. Union forces now occupied Cheat Mountain Pass on the Staunton-Parkersburg Turnpike. General Jackson had sent the recently arrived 12th Georgia, under Colonel Edward Johnson, to hold the Greenbrier Pass on Allegheny Mountain, supported by the 3rd Arkansas, Colonel Albert Rust; and the 52nd Virginia, Colonel John B. Baldwin. Loring agreed with Jackson that the Yankee position at Cheat Pass was too strong to take by direct assault. The best plan, he thought, was to dash up the Huntersville road towards Huttonsville. If carried out quickly enough, the maneuver could put the Confederates squarely on the flank of Cheat Mountain, cutting it off. Loring established his headquarters at Huntersville on 30 July. There he began to build up supplies in preparation for going back on the offensive. Reinforcements including regiments from North Carolina, Tennessee, and Virginia continued to arrive, swelling the ranks of the Army of the Northwest.[9]

Back in Georgia, relief efforts were underway to provide essentials for the regiment. "The women of Georgia are bearing a noble part in this contest," reported Sergeant Medlock. "For several days past, box after box, and package after package of clothing and blankets have been coming in to the different companies of this regiment—principally the work of the ladies

---

[8] James O. Clarke, "Important to the Officers and Members of the First Georgia Regiment," *Columbus Daily Enquirer*, 9 August 1861.

[9] W. Hunter Lesser, *Rebels at the Gate: Lee and McClellan on the Front Line of a Nation Divided* (Napierville IL: Sourcebooks, Inc., 2004) 144; Hermann, *Memoirs of a Confederate Veteran*, 175–76.

of our beloved State. No State in the Confederacy can boast of more patriotic women than Georgia."[10]

In Atlanta's city hall, several ladies were put to work making and mending trousers for the Gate City Guards. The women were assembled in small groups, each given a bundle labeled with the name of a particular soldier. Sallie Clayton, along with four others, was given a package addressed to "Quill Orme." After completing one pair of pants, one of the women placed a note to Orme in the pocket, "telling him how much pleasure it had given us to make the garment for him."[11] The other ladies decided to sign the note as well, after which it was deposited back in the pocket, along with several coins. The pocket was then sewn closed to keep the contents safe. Unfortunately, the sentiment was for naught. Miss Clayton confessed years afterward: "[W]e learned later that after all our enthusiasm over those clothes Mr. Orme never saw the bundle or heard of it until we told him long afterwards."[12]

The Confederate defeats at Rich Mountain and Corricks Ford had emboldened a separatist assembly calling itself the "legitimate government of Virginia" as they pursued plans to carve a loyal Union state from the Old Dominion's western counties. Following the departure of McClellan for Washington, General Rosecrans was promoted to the command of the Union Department of Western Virginia and was busy building up his army and constructing fortifications. Federal troops were building a fort overlooking the pass at Cheat Mountain. Yankees also dug in at the Tygart River Valley town of Elkwater, located where the Staunton-Parkersburg Turnpike crossed the Huntersville Turnpike, which ran northward from Huntersville to Huttonsville. Fortifications at these locations effectively blocked any Confederate effort to reestablish control of Western Virginia.

President Davis considered the situation dire enough to dispatch his most trusted adviser to the area. Brigadier General Robert E. Lee left Richmond on 28 July, bound by rail for Staunton. His orders were vague—he was to coordinate the various forces in Western Virginia in an attempt to

---

[10] J. M. G. Medlock, letter to the editor, *Sandersville Central Georgian*, 21 August 1861.

[11] Sarah "Sallie" Conley Clayton, *Requiem for a Lost City: A Memoir of Civil War Atlanta and the Old South*, ed. Robert Scott Davis, Jr. (Macon GA: Mercer University Press, 1999) 83. The soldier was Aquilla J. Orme, Sr.

[12] Ibid.

retrieve their losses, but his status as to actual command was not expressly spelled out.

Lee left Staunton the next morning, accompanied by two officers and two servants, enroute to General Jackson's headquarters at Monterey. After a brief consultation, Lee proceeded to General Loring's headquarters in Huntersville. Loring was not particularly happy to see the general, having outranked Lee in the pre-war regular army. He had only recently taken command on Lee's order, and now here was that officer himself to oversee Loring's operations.[13]

Lee stayed at Huntersville for several days, gently urging Loring to unite his forces and advance on the enemy stronghold at Cheat Mountain. Loring, however, seemed to be content to continue building up supplies at his depot. Finally, on 8 August Lee rode forward to Valley Mountain, making his own personal reconnaissance. Loring joined him on the 12th.[14]

Lieutenant Fleming returned from leave on 16 August (having discovered to his profound relief that his brother was not dead, though wounded severely) and encountered Colonel Ramsey at Stribling Springs, a health resort located some thirteen miles northwest of Staunton. Ramsey invited the lieutenant to stay the night at his lodgings, then ride with him to Monterey the next day in his carriage. Fleming gladly accepted. The next day, the two officers discussed Ramsey's arrest. The colonel informed Fleming of his restoration to command, without undergoing court martial proceedings. "I believe the only charge preferred against him," Fleming informed his wife, "was that of granting too many furloughs & on examination into the matter it was found that he had not granted as many furloughs as at first supposed."[15]

Ramsey and Fleming arrived at Monterey to find illness rampant among the soldiers. The shocking mortality rate alarmed Fleming:

> There have been as many as ten buried here in one day—scarcely a day passes that there is not from three to four deaths. There are three graveyards & the Dr says at this principal one there is an average of

[13] Lesser, *Rebels at the Gate*, 159–61

[14] Ibid., 161, 167.

[15] William O. Fleming to his wife, 17 August 1861, in the William Oliver Fleming Papers, #2292-z, Southern Historical Collection, the Wilson Library, University of North Carolina at Chapel Hill (hereafter cited as Fleming Papers). Quoted with permission of William Fleming, descendent.

> three burials a day. Is not this awful to contemplate. The report is that at Huntersville & our station on the Allegany there are even more deaths among the soldiers than at this point. I believe I have already stated that the diseases that are so prevalent as typhoid fever & pneumonia. If Col Ramsey had not permitted his regiment to find quarters in the country as he did there is no doubt but a great many more would have died.[16]

Unremitting rains had inundated the Alleghenies since early July, making a quagmire of the roads. Nothing could move. Sickness continued to scour the camps. Lee bemoaned the conditions in a letter to his daughters on 29 August:

> It rains here all the time, literally. There has not been sunshine enough since my arrival to dry my clothes.... But the worst of the rain is, that the ground has become so saturated with water that the constant travel on the roads have made them almost impassable, so that I cannot get up sufficent supplies for the troops to move. It is raining now. Has been all day, last night, day before & day before that, &c. But we must be patient. It is quite cool, too. I have on all my winter clothes & am writing in my overcoat. All the clouds seem to concentrate over this ridge of mountains, & by whatever wind they are driven, give us rain.... There has been much sickness among the men, measles, &c.[17]

In addition to dealing with Mother Nature, Lee's patience was also tried by squabbling between Brigadier Generals John B. Floyd at Lewisburg and Henry A. Wise at White Sulphur Springs. The two officers, both former governors of Virginia, loathed each other with more passion than their hatred for the Yankees. Lee urged collaboration, but each continued to operate independently, sniping at one another in dispatches. Even Lee's 31 August promotion to full general had little effect on the two warring officers.

On 30 August, as the 1st prepared to move to a new camp on the Greenbrier River, Lieutenant Fleming wrote home of the horrible conditions

---

[16] See, e.g., ibid.

[17] Robert E. Lee to his daughters, 29 August 1861, in *The Wartime Papers of R. E. Lee*, ed. Clifford Dowdey and Louis H. Manarin (Boston: Little Brown and Company, 1961) 67.

at Monterey. "If the regiment had left to day as was expected I could not have gone with it," he wrote. "I am more than half sick.—can hardly walk a hundred yards without resting. It is surprising that the whole regiment is not down. It is raining all the time & the mud, this black mud is right up to our very tent door. And there the stench arising from decaying mud & about the camps is enough to give one yellow fever."[18]

The sun finally emerged from the clouds on the last day of August. Rapidly drying roads no longer impeded the flow of supplies into the camps. Morale improved, sickness declined, and the troops actually began to look forward to having another chance to pit themselves against the Yankees. Lavender Ray and his compatriots entertained themselves with imaginative methods: "Joe Keller and the boys are playing the banjo and dancing around a large fire from where I have just come. We have a nice time here at nights singing 'Old Cabin Home,' 'Home Again' and other songs. We also amuse ourselves with Mock trials. We tried Joe Welch for larceny last week, but found him not guilty. We have tried others for slander, misdemeanor, &c."[19]

Drills and religious meetings provided additional distractions for the troops. "i went to meating twist last sunday," wrote Dahlonega Volunteers Private James M. Norrell. "we have preaching twist every sunday it seams more like home than anything else it seames mity od too to pickup agun and go and drill and then come in and go to meating last sunday morning we was marcht out in the field on revew and inspection of arms and then we went back to camps and some went to playing cards some marble and some went to preaching."[20]

In preparation for the resumption of offensive operations, General Jackson was directed to have his brigade take up new positions closer to Cheat Mountain. Wagons rolled out of Monterey on 7 September carrying the 1st Georgia's resupplied equipment and baggage to its new position. Named Camp Bartow in honor of Colonel Francis Bartow of Georgia, who was killed at the Battle of Manassas, the encampment was located near the point where the Staunton-Parkersburg Turnpike crossed the East Fork of the

---

[18] William O. Fleming to his wife, 30 August 1861, Fleming Papers.

[19] Lavender Ray to his mother, 6 September 1861. Ruby Felder Ray Thomas, comp., *Letters and Diary of Lieut. Lavender R. Ray, 1861–1865, comp. and ed. by his daughter Ruby Felder Ray (Mrs. Eli. A. Thomas)* (Atlanta GA: n.p., 1949), typed manuscript (Morrow GA: Georgia Department of Archives and History) 4.

[20] James M. Norrell to his wife, 29 August 1861, in the Madeleine Anthony Collection, box 7, folder 10, Lumpkin County Library, Dahlonega GA.

Greenbrier River. Travelers Repose, a tavern that had welcomed stagecoach passengers for many years, stood near the river crossing. Andrew Yeager, the owner, watched his valley became a military camp.[21]

The regiment welcomed the change of location. A soldier of the Newnan Guards reported the improvement in the men's spirits to the *Atlanta Southern Confederacy*: "The move from Monterey has had a salutary effect. Our boys, many of whom had become tired of lying around that camp with no duty to perform except that of guarding a few commissary stores, and who had become rather low-spirited, in consequence of the great monotony of the times around there, have, since the move, and now that there is a prospect of their getting into a fight soon, become merrier and are now in finer spirits than they have been since the five days of excitement at laurel Hill."[22] In a similar vein, Lieutenant Fleming informed his wife of his improving health. "I was very weak when I left Monterey, but before I reached this place I felt considerably stronger. Now I am all right & fit for duty."[23]

Chaplain Campbell was moved by the region's beauty: "We are encamped in a valley which is only a few hundred yards wide. Through this valley flows a beautiful stream called the Green Brier River. The scenery surrounding is romantic and some of it sublime. In preaching in these mountains I have but to point out the green clad mountains and clouds that rest as heavenly drapery and carrossals on their side and tops—to the murmuring streams and rustling breases. I sometime catch the inspiration."[24]

You Are Killing Your Own Friends

Lee and Loring now set about to reorganize the Army of the Northwest. Loring's Order Number 10, issued on 8 September, assigned the 1st to General Daniel Smith Donelson's 3rd Brigade. For undetermined reasons, the Georgians remained with General Jackson's 1st Brigade at Camp

---

[21] Lesser, *Rebels at the Gate*, 223–24.

[22] J. M. B., "Our Special Western Virginia Correspondence—from the Newnan Guards," *Atlanta Southern Confederacy*, 19 September 1861.

[23] William O. Fleming to his wife, 30 August 1861, Fleming Papers.

[24] James McDonald Campbell to Sister Lizzie, 8 September 1861 in Edmond Lee Rice, ed. "Compiled Civil War Letters of James McDonald Campbell of the 47th Alabama Infantry Regiment with a Brief Sketch of His Life," facsimile copy of unpublished typescript, 197-, p. 47, Alabama Department of Archives and History, Montgomery AL.

Bartow. Loring retained command of the troops at Huntersville, while Jackson was in charge of the regiments on the Monterey line.[25]

With the weather improving, Lee saw an opportunity to concentrate the Confederates for a strike against the federal army's fortified position at Elkwater. The general was preparing orders for an advance by Jackson's and Loring's divisions, when Colonel Albert Rust of the 3rd Arkansas reported he had discovered a route into the enemy's rear while scouting the Union position on Cheat Mountain. Rust convinced General Jackson and General Loring that the Union strongholds on Cheat Mountain and at Elkwater could be taken together by a three-pronged attack. Though Lee was hesitant to change his plans, Rust's enthusiasm swayed him to make the attempt. The orders were altered to have Loring attack Elkwater, while Jackson's division drove for Cheat Pass. A third column would work its way along the route scouted by Rust, coming up on the federal rear.[26]

The troops designated to pass around behind the enemy position were Rust's 3rd Arkansas, Colonel Taliaferro's 23rd Virginia, the 31st Virginia under Lieutenant Colonel William L. Jackson, Colonel Samuel Fulkerson's 37th Virginia, and Major George Hansborough's 9th Virginia Battalion. Colonel Rust requested Lee give him the honor of leading the attack. Taliaferro and Fulkerson, though senior to Rust, relinquished the command. The assignment of such an inexperienced officer would have unfortunate consequences.

Late in the afternoon of 11 September, word circulated around the camp of the 1st Georgia to ready their weapons and cook two days rations. Around 9:00 P.M., strips of white cloth were passed out to the men to attach to their uniforms for identification.[27]

Grateful for another chance to redeem their fortunes against the Yankees, the 1st and other regiments were certain this time they would

---

[25] *OR*, ser. 1, vol. 51, pt. 2, p. 283. No explanation has been found for this confusing order. The 12th Georgia was assigned to Jackson's brigade, while the 14th Georgia was placed with Donelson. The 1st Georgia continued to serve with Jackson's (later Taliaferro's) Brigade until they were ordered to Tennessee in February 1862.

[26] Garnett Andrews, "A Battle Planned But Not Fought," *Confederate Veteran* 5/11 (June 1897): 294.

[27] "The Attack upon Cheat Mountain and Death of Tom Brown," n.d., in the personal papers of Lavender Ray, box 2, accession 1949 0012M, Georgia Department of Archives and History, Morrow GA (hereafter cited as Lavender Ray Letters).

emerge victors. Lieutenant Fleming fairly brimmed with confidence: "So you see things are coming to a focus very soon in this position of the State. Before you receive this, no doubt you will have read in the papers of a Confederate victory or defeat—I think the former.…The men are, I believe, all in good spirits & congratulate themselves on *at last* the prospect of having the yankee's in the lead."[28]

Even while assuring his wife, Fleming cautioned her against listening to wild rumors, writing, "Let me beg that you will pay no attention to anything you may hear concerning myself unless it be from Dr Hines or one of our commissioned officers, who will, if I am killed or wounded, give you notice in the shortest possible time."[29]

Not everyone was "in good spirits." Rufus McPherson Felder, one of four Felder brothers in the Southern Rights Guard, was gripped by a sense of impending doom. One of his brothers, Lawrence, had died of disease just that morning. Another sibling, Lieutenant John R. Felder, had perished at McDowell on 24 August. As the 1st marched out of their camp, the depressed McPherson confided to his messmates his conviction he would not survive the coming fight.[30]

Starting early because he had the longest distance to cover, Colonel Rust set out toward the Union rear on 9 September with 1,600 soldiers. As other Confederate columns began their marches the heavens reopened, soaking men, arms, and equipment.[31]

Into the night marched the regiments as they set out for their designated assault positions. Lavender Ray struggled to keep moving, but the route through the mountains made for hard going. He wrote, "We then traveled about eight miles up and down mountains through cold rain, mud, branches, creeks and rivers without waiting to cross on logs or find dry places."[32] Stumbling through the tangled landscape in the darkness and rain, with lightning flashing across the sky, was enough to unnerve the strongest of

[28] William O. Fleming to his wife, 11 September 1861, Fleming Papers.

[29] See, e.g., ibid.

[30] Walter A. Clark, *Under the Stars and Bars: Or Memories of Four Years Service with the Oglethorpes, of Augusta, Georgia* (Augusta GA: The Chronicle Printer, 1900) 27.

[31] Jack Zinn, *R. E. Lee's Cheat Mountain Campaign* (Parsons WV: McClain Printing Company, 1974) 146.

[32] Lavender R. Ray to his mother, 18 September 1861, in Thomas, *Letters and Diary of Lieut. Lavender R. Ray*, 9–10.

men. Runoff from the rains caused rivers to swell. Reaching the fog shrouded bank of Shavers Fork, the Georgians struggled to cross the icy torrent. Off in the distance the soldiers could hear the screams of a wild panther. Many of the Georgians feared the cries were manmade, a warning to the Yankee camps.[33]

By early morning of the 12th, the weary, soaked brigades arrived at their positions. General Jackson's brigade, with the 1st Georgia, held the Staunton-Parkersburg Turnpike east of Cheat Mountain, while General Samuel R. Anderson's brigade of Tennesseans was on the Turnpike west of Cheat. A third brigade, under General Donelson, was between Anderson and the Union encampment at Elkwater. General Loring, with the remainder of the Army of the Northwest, took up position south of Elkwater. The Federals were encircled. Lee expected a decisive victory.

Shortly before dawn, a scouting party made up of five soldiers from each company of the 1st and 12th Georgia, under the command of Lieutenant Samuel Dawson of the 12th, worked their way close to the federal pickets. Their orders were to silence the federal sentries. Rainwater made a slippery mess of the hillsides as they climbed. Fixing bayonets, the soldiers drove the points into the earth, using the muskets to pull themselves up the slope.[34]

Up ahead was a picket post, manned by soldiers of the 14th Indiana. Quietly moving into position, Dawson's small command had the Federals nearly surrounded when they opened fire. Caught by surprise, the sentries fled towards the fort, leaving behind the bodies of a lieutenant and private. Another Yankee lay on the ground, playing dead until the Confederates passed. The ruse worked, and the Federal made good his escape.[35]

With a local resident guiding them, the soldiers crept closer to Cheat Summit Fort. From within, they could hear a regimental band playing airs such as "Annie Laurie." The Georgians were settling into position when they were startled by the discharge of a musket. One of the men had fallen asleep and accidentally triggered his weapon. "Every thing was then as still as death for about ten minutes," recalled Lieutenant Fleming. Drawn by the sound, a Union sergeant came down the road to investigate. "About five

---

[33] "The Attack upon Cheat Mountain and Death of Tom Brown," n.d., Lavender Ray Letters.

[34] Henry Clay Fairman, *Chronicles of the Old Guard of the Gate City Guard, Atlanta, Georgia, 1858–1915* (Atlanta GA: Byrd Printing Company, 1915) 210.

[35] Zinn, *R. E. Lee's Cheat Mountain Campaign*, 161–62.

guns now fired from our ambush," wrote Fleming, "and he fell dead without a groan. In a few minutes the whole picket about 15 or 20 strong came marching down the road. When about opposite where I stood they discovered us & their officer ordered them, with an oath, to charge."[36]

The Federals fired a wild volley toward the Georgians with little effect, though one ball nicked a tree barely three inches above Fleming's head. Dawson ordered his detachment to charge, scattering the Yankees. The survivors ran back toward their entrenchments while the Confederates rifled the picket camp, carrying off blankets, a coffee pot, and other "trophies."[37]

Dawson was concerned it was now too dangerous for the party to remain so close to the Federals and decided it was time to return to the Confederate lines. As they made their way through the mist hanging low in the dense laurel, the small band suddenly observed dim figures approaching from out of the fog. Fearing the men were Yankees, a few of Dawson's troops panicked and opened fire. The approaching column was actually the main body of the 1st and 12th Regiments, led by Colonel Johnson of the 12th and Colonel Ramsey. Having already experienced brief fights with other Union pickets, the soldiers deployed into the trees and commenced returning fire. The Georgians blazed away at each other through the fog for several minutes before some of Dawson's men realized who they were shooting at. The astonished detachment ceased fire and began to yell "Hurrah for Jeff Davis!" and "Georgians! Georgians!"[38]

Colonel Johnson spurred his horse to the head of the column. "They are liars, boys!" he roared. "Pop it to 'em! Pop it to 'em!"[39]

"It is a damned Yankee trick," bellowed Ramsey, "Give them hell, boys!" The 1st and 12th stepped up their fire, while the men in Dawson's detachment continued to cry out they were friends. Sergeant William Dent of the Newnan Guards, blood pouring from a gash on his forehead, dashed through the whizzing balls toward his company. "Great Gods," he screamed, "you are killing your own friends!"[40]

---

[36] Ibid., 165; William O. Fleming to his wife, n.d., Fleming Papers.

[37] See, e.g., William O. Fleming to his wife, n.d., Fleming Papers.

[38] "The Attack upon Cheat Mountain and Death of Tom Brown," n.d., Lavender Ray Letters.

[39] Clark, *Under the Stars and Bars*, 24–25.

[40] Ibid., 26–27; "The Attack upon Cheat Mountain and Death of Tom Brown," n.d., Lavender Ray Letters.

Spotting the white badges on their uniforms, the Georgians ceased fire, finally convinced they were shooting at their own men. Dazed and bewildered, the soldiers emerged from the trees, mingling as they tried to assess the damage. Tom Brown of the Newnan Guards was shot through the bowels and died several days later. In addition to Sergeant Dent, Private William Welch of the Southern Guard received a wound. Rufus McPherson Felder lay dead, his premonition fulfilled by a ball through his heart. The 12th Georgia lost one soldier. Collecting their wits and their casualties, the Georgians continued on to their jump off point.[41]

Why Don't He Attack?

Notwithstanding everything from rain to collisions with isolated federal units, the Southern brigades somehow all managed to reach their appointed positions on time. Lee's forces had the Union positions in a vice. Only an incredible turn of bad luck would prevent the Confederates from achieving a significant victory.

Lee's carefully laid plans now began to unravel. Rain continued to pour down during the night. The general came upon General Donelson's brigade before sunrise, finding them cold, wet and tired from lack of sleep. Many were armed with old flintlock muskets, and the racket created by drawing loads and firing blanks to dry weapons worried Lee. Certainly the element of surprise had evaporated. The noise and sorry condition of the men convinced him to pull the brigade back at 10:00 A.M.[42]

The plan was for Colonel Rust to launch his attack early on the morning of the 12th. The sounds of his assault would be the signal for the rest of the brigades to move forward. Throughout the day they waited…and waited. Ears strained for sounds of attack. But there was none. "On every side was continuously heard 'What has become of Rust…. Why don't he attack?'" recalled Major A. L. Long of Loring's staff. Anderson's command

---

[41] See, e.g., "The Attack upon Cheat Mountain and Death of Tom Brown," n.d., Lavender Ray Letters; Clark, *Under the Stars and Bars*, 27; Hermann, *Memoirs of a Confederate Veteran*, 53; "Nestor," letter to the editor, *Atlanta Southern Confederacy*, 25 September 1861.

[42] Lesser, *Rebels at the Gate*, 194–96.

skirmished with Ohio and Indiana troops. Day passed into night with no word from Rust—and no attack.[43]

Jackson's Brigade deployed in line of battle about a mile and a half from the federal lines. Offering themselves as a diversion to cover Rust's assault, the brigade spread out across an open field, inviting the Yankees to attack. By about 4:00 P.M., with no sound from Rust and no sign of a Union foray against them, the brigade withdrew. They had not gone far, though, before the order came to "Counter march by file left." Close to exhaustion, Private Ray was dismayed by the command: "It was almost like a death neal to me. I was broken down with fatigue, my feet ached and my shoulders and hips were sore from carrying a heavy cartridge box and haversack packed with food for two days and a large shell and canteen full of water the idea of going back miles to fight seemed like death, but I hurried up determined to go as long as I could."[44]

Not a fight, but a new campsite was the destination. Ray was grateful for the chance to get warm and eat: "We made a large fire and I warmed some coffee I had in my canteen (having brought it as it was good to quench thirst when cold) and eat a cracker then wrapped my shell around me and threw myself upon the grass to catch a few hours sleep in the open air with my accoutrements around me and my gun by my side not knowing at what moment I should be aroused."[45]

The next morning, (Friday the 13th—a harbinger of events to come) the brigade was roused and ordered to make ready to move forward again. To prevent idlers from claiming illness and leaving the ranks (which had occurred frequently the previous day), General Jackson declared "if any soldier went back to camp on the plea of sickness and when examined was not sick his life should not be spared by his mercy."[46]

While Jackson warned his brigade against slacking, Generals Lee and Loring were meeting to assess the situation. No word had been received

---

[43] Ibid., 197–98; A. L. Long, "Lee's West Virginia Campaign," in *Annals of the War*, edited by Alexander K. McClure (Edison NJ: Blue & Grey Press, 1996) 90.

[44] "Nestor," letter to the editor, *Atlanta Southern Confederacy*, 25 September 1861; Lavender R. Ray to his mother, 18 September 1861, in Thomas, *Letters and Diary of Lieut. Lavender R. Ray*, 12.

[45] Lavender R. Ray to his mother, 18 September 1861, in Thomas, *Letters and Diary of Lieut. Lavender R. Ray*, 12–13.

[46] Ibid., 13.

from Rust, and the advantage of surprise was gone. Loring urged an immediate attack on the federal camp at Elkwater. Lee disagreed, certain such a frontal assault would prove futile. He set about to find another way to land a blow against the Federals, sending out reconnaissance parties led by Colonel John Augustine Washington, his aide-de-camp, along with Major William Henry Fitzhugh "Rooney" Lee, the general's son.[47]

Jackson was in a better mood as the 1st moved forward once again, offering compliments to the regiment. One wag suggested the general put the 12th Georgia out in front this time. Jackson responded "he had more confidence in the 1st Ga. and always gave us this post of honor."[48] Two hundred men were selected from the various regiments to be sent forward in an attempt to lure the Federals into emerging from their earthworks. The troops "performed every manner of movement that could be conceived in order to induce the Yankees to come out from behind their fortifications, and to decoy them into our ambuscade. But if one may judge from indications, the enemy felt by no means safe in their entrencements, and had no idea of coming out to give us a fair fight."[49] By late afternoon, with the ruse proving unsuccessful, the brigade withdrew once more.

General Jackson finally received a message from Colonel Rust on Friday morning. The dispatch revealed Rust had been unable to attack as planned due to the strength of the Union fortifications. Union prisoners convinced the colonel he was greatly outnumbered, and extensive rows of abatis gave him pause. A discussion with his officers led to the conclusion that attacking the works would be suicide. Rust decided to retire without a shot fired toward the fort.

Jackson sent back a hasty note ordering Rust to return to Camp Bartow, and once there to write a report to General Loring, giving reasons for his failure. Rust's guide lost his way in the forest, and his troops stumbled along for a full day before reaching camp. The colonel's report, written at 10:00 P.M., contended the Yankees had between 4,000 and 5,000 men in the fort

---

[47] Lesser, *Rebels at the Gate*, 199.

[48] Lavender R. Ray to his mother, 18 September 1861, in Thomas, *Letters and Diary of Lieut. Lavender R. Ray*, 13–14.

[49] "Nestor," letter to the editor, *Atlanta Southern Confederacy*, 25 September 1861.

on Cheat Mountain. (Their actual strength was closer to 3,000—some reports claimed only 300.)[50]

A personal blow was next to strike Lee—Colonel Washington, his aide, had been killed while on his scouting trip with Major Fitzhugh Lee. Washington was the great-grandnephew of President George Washington and a close friend of the general. The loss of his friend and the close call of his son shook Lee to his very soul.[51]

They Never Expected to See Us Again

As Jackson's Brigade retired to their blankets Friday evening, a guard consisting of one hundred men, six from each company, was selected from the two Georgia regiments. Placed under the command of the 12th's Lieutenant Dawson, they were to guard the road leading toward the enemy's lines. Nervous at being so close to the Yankees, the soldiers spent a restless night. Early the next morning, Dawson decided to advance his guard closer to the Union fortifications. A jumpy Private Ray was certain they would be overrun at any moment: "Lieut. Dawson who is a very brave man with little judgement carried our guard half a mile closer to the Enemy and farther than anyone had gone when the whole enemy was near. We expected every moment the enemy to fire upon us from ambush or rush in overwhelming numbers upon our little band but we marched on and found blankets and guns which the Enemy's Pickets had thrown away when they heard us coming."[52] Dawson then withdrew his little detachment, much to the relief of the soldiers: "We then went back to the old field and were welcomed by our company who said they never expected to see us again."[53]

Saturday morning found only the 1st Georgia ordered forward, again for the purpose of drawing the enemy out. Riding up to the regiment, General Jackson told the soldiers he believed the chances were good for a fight, especially if the Yankees saw how small the approaching force was. "He stated that for this reason he had determined to bring us out alone," reported correspondent "Nestor" to the *Atlanta Southern Confederacy*, "that

---

[50] *OR*, ser. 1, vol. 5, pt. 1, pp. 191–92; A. C. Jones, "The Mountain Campaign Failure," *Confederate Veteran* 22 (July 1914): 306; Zinn, *R. E. Lee's Cheat Mountain Campaign*, 174; Lesser, *Rebels at the Gate*, 191.

[51] Lesser, *Rebels at the Gate*, 200–202.

[52] Lavender R. Ray to his mother, 18 September 1861, in Thomas, *Letters and Diary of Lieut. Lavender R. Ray*, 14–15.

[53] Ibid.

he had the utmost confidence in our skill and bravery, and felt confident that with the position he would assign us we could whip any force the enemy might bring against us."[54]

Jackson continued to shower the regiment with praise. As "Nestor" reported,

> He further stated that he had a conversation with President Davis, not long since, who, when speaking of the Regiments that would form his brigade, said, "You will have at least one Regiment upon which you may depend under any and every circumstance. It is composed of the flower of the land of the intelligent, patriotic men, who knowing their rights will dare maintain them, even at the bayonet's point or cannon's mouth. I have watched the 1st Ga. Reg't closely since it first enlisted in the Southern cause, and am confident it is the best Regiment in the Confederate service."—Gen. Jackson remarked that our conduct since we were placed under his command showed him conclusively that we merited the praise given us by President Davis.[55]

Jackson's expectations of battle were dashed once more—the Yankees would not come out and fight. After another day of maneuvering with no success, the 1st retired again. No excursions were sent out the following day. Sunday was spent quietly in camp. The only activity was the periodic changing of sentries.[56]

With the Northerners fully aroused to the Confederates' presence and with the various commands in disarray and suffering from exposure, Lee had ordered the army to withdraw on the 14th. The general tried to put the best light on the failure, referring to the campaign as a "forced reconnaissance." "The Army of the Northwest," he directed, "will resume its former position at such time and in such manner as General Loring shall direct, and continue its preparations for further operations."[57]

---

[54] "Nestor," letter to the editor, *Atlanta Southern Confederacy*, 25 September 1861.

[55] Ibid.

[56] Lavender R. Ray to his mother, 18 September 1861, in Thomas, *Letters and Diary of Lieut. Lavender R. Ray*, 15.

[57] *OR*, ser. 1, vol. 5, pt. 1, pp. 192–93.

General Jackson's brigade was now the only Confederate force left in front of the federal lines. On Monday, 16 September, having not received Lee's recall order, Jackson ordered his regiments forward once more—this time with instructions to erect earthworks in a field and adjacent hill within a mile and a half of the Union lines. Gun emplacements were well underway when the general received an urgent dispatch from Lee. Jackson was ordered to cease work on his fortifications and immediately return to Camp Bartow.[58]

Lee's grand plan was in shambles. The general expressed his chagrin in a letter to Governor Letcher: "It is a grievous disappointment to me, I assure you. But for the rainstorm, I have no doubt it would have succeeded. This, Governor, is for your own eye. Please do not speak of it; we must try again."[59]

As the bedraggled Army of the Northwest filed back into its camps, Lee's attention was drawn to another front. Some miles south at Gauley Bridge, General Floyd's forces had been attacked on the 12th by the Union army of General Rosecrans. Floyd's troops had held their own, but without support from General Wise's nearby Legion. If the Confederates stayed put, they would most likely be overrun when Rosecrans attacked with his superior numbers the next day. Floyd, realizing his position was untenable, retreated toward Sewell's Mountain and a linkup with General Wise.

Lee headed south on 20 September to try to resolve the conflict between Generals Wise and Floyd. It was a forlorn hope, for the enmity of the two ex-politicians toward each other blinded them to the necessity for cooperation against the common enemy, shattering all hopes of defeating the Federals. By late October, Lee's scheme to destroy General Rosecrans's army by letting him batter his regiments against impregnable Confederate positions failed. Unable to coexist with the equally vain Floyd, Wise had been recalled to Richmond. Lee left Western Virginia on 30 October, his reputation in tatters, having failed in his efforts to drive back the Union armies in Western Virginia and to stop the creation of a new loyalist state. Criticism of Lee's tactics abounded in Richmond. Much had been expected of him, but now his ability was being openly questioned. "Granny Lee" was the phrase heard often in Richmond. The general was reassigned to

[58] "Nestor," letter to the editor, *Atlanta Southern Confederacy*, 25 September 1861; "S.," "From Jackson's Brigade," *Savannah Republican*, 1 October 1861.

[59] Robert E. Lee to Governor John Letcher, 17 September 1861, in Clifford Dowdey and Louis H. Manarin, eds., *Wartime Papers of R. E. Lee*, 75.

command the district covering the coasts of Georgia and South Carolina. The only thing Lee had to show for his efforts in Western Virginia was a beard as gray as his uniform, and a horse, purchased from a local farmer, which Lee named "Traveler."[60]

[60] Zinn, *R. E. Lee's Cheat Mountain Campaign*, 201–203; Lesser, *Rebels at the Gate*, 216.

9

Battle On The Greenbrier

"It is said that when the Yankees saw a Regiment drawn out in battle array asked who they were and being told they were the first Ga. immediately said, 'Good Godd this won't do us, let's travel,' and being ordered to charge said, 'Oh no, Col. those are Georgians over there go anywhere else.'" Lavender Ray, Newnan Guards.[1]

We Would Like to Receive Our Yankee Friends

On 24 September, General Lee instructed General Loring to lead five regiments—two from Virginia and three from Tennessee—from the Huntersville line south as reinforcements for Generals Floyd and Wise. While Loring was gone, General Jackson was to remain at Camp Bartow to keep watch over the Federals on Cheat Mountain.[2]

Throwing up works against Union probes began in earnest in the camps around Yeager's tavern. Correspondent "Nestor" reported to the *Atlanta Southern Confederacy*:

> There is considerable activity among the officers and soldiers here. Fortifications are being constructed as rapidly as if the hands of magic were engaged in the work.—in a few days this encampment will be so strongly fortified that the force now here could resist successfully an attack of 10,000 of the enemy; at any rate, we would like to receive a *call* from that number of our Yankee *friends* in our fortifications. We would be willing to risk *all* in the result of the *conference* that would ensue at such a meeting.—That our officer expect an attack here soon is evident from present indications. We are preparing to meet it. How

---

[1] Lavender R. Ray to his sister, 11 October 1861, in Ruby Felder Ray Thomas, comp., *Letters and Diary of Lieut. Lavender R. Ray, 1861–1865, comp. and ed. by his daughter Ruby Felder Ray (Mrs. Eli. A. Thomas)* (Atlanta GA: n.p., 1949), typed manuscript (Morrow GA: Georgia Department of Archives and History) 26.

[2] James W. Raab, *W. W. Loring: Florida's Forgotten General* (Manhattan KS: Sunflower University Press, 1996) 47; Isaac Hermann, *Memoirs of a Confederate Veteran 1861–1865* (Atlanta GA: Byrd Printing Company, 1911) 234.

soon it may take place, or whether an engagement will be had here at all or not, I can't tell; but, be assured, we will ever be ready to welcome the ruthless invaders of our soil "with bloody hands to hospitable graves."[3]

Private Lavender Ray and the other Georgians were kept busy with axe and spade. He wrote, "We have been fortifying our encampment here ever since we came from Cheat mountain, an account of which I wrote Pa a week ago, by digging entrenchments around our camps, cutting down trees and sharpening the limbs by which means we made a complete wall of fallen trees on the left flank and rear of our camp to prevent the Enemy attacking us on those sides and building batteries for our cannon."[4]

Intermittent rain kept Camp Bartow in a constant state of sogginess. "Our camp is in a very low place," reported a member of the Quitman Guards, "and every time it rains, which is almost ever twenty-fours, in our tent it is as damp and as wet as if there were no tents at all." The soldier noted that out of 112 Guardsmen, only 60 were fit for duty. Colonel Ramsey, ill once again, was spending a few days at Stribling Springs to recuperate.[5]

In the Confederate capital, the reverse at Cheat Mountain filled newspapers with questions of competence, from General Lee on down through the officer corps. The *Richmond Examiner* implied that it was General Jackson, not Colonel Rust, who had scouted the federal positions, and that the flanking force was under Jackson's immediate command. Rust's involvement was not mentioned. "The column of Gen. Jackson was withdrawn in the face of the likelihood of much wholesale slaughter of his force," read the article, "and the movements of Gen. Lee, which were intended to be simultaneous in their results with the attack, entirely disconcerted."[6]

Taking offense with these erroneous statements, Jackson replied with a scathing letter to the *Examiner*. After explaining he could not give an exact description of the events due to military security, he wrote, "Assuredly,

---

[3] "Nestor," letter to the editor, *Atlanta Southern Confederacy*, 6 October 1861.

[4] Lavender R. Ray to his sister, 4 October 1861, in Thomas, *Letters and Diary of Lieut. Lavender R. Ray*, 23.

[5] "S.," "From Jackson's Brigade," *Savannah Republican*, 1 October 1861.

[6] "The Cheat Mountain Affair—Letter from Gen. Jackson," *Richmond Examiner*, 28 September 1861.

however, it cannot be contemplated presentations, wholly false to history, should go uncontradicted to the world…." Jackson continued by refuting the charges point by point.[7]

Not wanting to impugn the honor of a fellow officer, Jackson chose not to mention Rust in his letter. He concluded by declaring that "editors should, in common justice, be cautious of inflicting an undeserved stab upon the humblest reputation, knowing, as all men must, that in the rapid movement of events, when the attention of the public is from moment to moment diverted to some new think of excitement, a name once dragged in the mire may be hopelessly sullied."[8]

In its defense, the newspaper retorted that "the statements of the Examiner were derived from the official accounts of the affair, the justice, impartiality, or even truth of which, were not subjects of any interference or judgment on our part in a relation of facts, information of which was obtained under all the usual circumstances of authenticity in the news department of our paper."[9]

While Jackson was setting things straight with the Richmond papers, his troops in Camp Bartow were preoccupied with staying warm and dry. Signs of fall and oncoming winter were slowly appearing across the Alleghenies. The changes entranced Private Walter Clark of the Oglethorpes: "The foliage of the forest growth, alchemized by the autumn frost had changed its hues to gold and crimson and with its blended tints forming to the eye an immense boquet, the picture was worthy an artist's brush."[10]

Even the nature of the ever-present precipitation was changing. On 27 September, a cold rain began to spatter on the tents. "On Friday last the rain commenced falling early in the morning," wrote Corporal Nathan Pugh,

> and continued without intermission throughout the day, almost submerging our camp in water. Early in the afternoon, a dreary, cold wind commenced blowing, and a storm of rain and wind prevailed until night, prostrating camp tents, trees, limbs, &c., and causing a

---

[7] Ibid.

[8] Ibid.

[9] See, e.g., ibid.

[10] Walter A. Clark, *Under the Stars and Bars: Or Memories of Four Years Service with the Oglethorpes, of Augusta, Georgia* (Augusta GA: The Chronicle Printer, 1900) 28.

> general confusion of matters and things in general throughout this vicinity, and rendering camp life quite uncomfortable for the time being. The hovering clouds having disappeared during the night, on Saturday morning we were greeted by that time-honored and venerable personage, jack frost, who made his first appearance for the season on this occasion, in his usual costume of glittering white.[11]

"We don't like the idea of having to quarter in these Mountains during the coming winter," wrote another soldier, "which will necessarily be the case unless we succeed in expelling the Hessians from Western Virginia."[12] One of the Quitman Guards feared for his life if the regiment did not retire soon to winter quarters. He begged for those at home to use whatever influence they might possess to have the troops transferred.[13]

Your Regiment Have the Post of Danger

While Lee struggled to mediate between the bickering Wise and Floyd, the federal command on Cheat Summit was not idle. Union General Joseph Reynolds was preparing to attack Jackson's fortifications at Traveler's Repose. Reynolds first attempt on 26 September was stopped by a severe ice storm. Shortly after midnight on the night of 2–3 October, he tried once more. Nine infantry regiments, three companies of cavalry and thirteen cannon, some five thousand men in all, began snaking their way down from their lofty perch in the darkness.[14]

Colonel Ramsey, having returned to Camp Bartow after recovering from his most recent bout of illness, was the post's Officer of the Day, in charge of guard positions around the camp. About an hour before sunrise on the 3rd, Ramsey was out inspecting the picket lines covering the western approaches to the camp. Suddenly, the report of a musket was heard close

---

[11] Nathan S. Pugh, letter to the editor, *Augusta Daily Constitutionalist*, 8 October 1861.

[12] "Nestor," letter to the editor, *Atlanta Southern Confederacy*, 6 October 1861.

[13] "S.," "From Jackson's Brigade," *Savannah Republican*, 1 October 1861.

[14] Hermann, *Memoirs of a Confederate Veteran*, 245; US War Department, comp., *The War of the Rebellion: A Compilation of the Official Records of the Union and Confederate Armies*, 128 vols. (Washington DC: Government Printing Office, 1880–1901) (hereafter cited as *OR*) ser. 1, vol. 5, pt. 1, p. 220; W. Hunter Lesser, *Rebels at the Gate: Lee and McClellan on the Front Line of a Nation Divided* (Napierville IL: Sourcebooks, Inc., 2004) 228.

by. The accidental misfire of an enemy weapon alerted the sentries to the presence of Reynolds's skirmish line, made up of some 350 men from the 9th Indiana. Immediately the pickets commenced firing on the Union troops.[15]

Dismounting and tying his horse to a tree, Ramsey took command of the picket line, directing a desperate resistance. Three times the Federals hurled themselves against the stubborn defenders; each time they were driven back. As the firing intensified, Private David Beck of the Dahlonega Volunteers dropped as a minie ball tore into his groin.[16]

Loading and firing their single-shot muzzleloaders as quickly as they could, the pickets were soon in danger of being overwhelmed by superior numbers. The Indianans were now supported by artillery, and, as they prepared for a fourth rush, Ramsey ordered his soldiers to "take to the bushes and secrete themselves."[17] The anxious pickets called for him "to come in, as he was in a very dangerous position."[18] Searching for some of his men, Ramsey disappeared from view as the Federals swirled past his position. The remaining Georgians ran for the rear. Private Beck, unable to get away, was taken prisoner.[19]

While Ramsey's pickets fought their delaying action, Colonel Edward Johnson patched together an advance guard of some one hundred men, throwing together soldiers from the 1st and 12th Georgia, along with some Virginians. Moving to the aide of the pickets, Johnson's small force was about a mile from the main fortifications when it was struck by the Federals about 7:00 A.M. A vicious firefight commenced as the Union skirmishers tried to push Johnson's small band out of the way. John A. Bankston of the Gate City Guard claimed to have brought down a federal officer at about six hundred yards. Losing a horse in the melee, Colonel Johnson finally ordered

---

[15] "HUD," "Western Virginia Correspondence," *Atlanta Daily Intelligencer*, 17 October 1861; "Nestor," letter to the editor, *Atlanta Southern Confederacy*, 17 October 1861; *OR*, ser. 1, vol. 5, p. 220.

[16] "Nestor," letter to the editor, *Atlanta Southern Confederacy*, 17 October 1861; "George," letter to the editor, *Augusta Chronicle and Sentinel*, 11 October 1861; "HUD," "Western Virginia Correspondence," *Atlanta Daily Intelligencer*, 17 October 1861.

[17] "George," letter to the editor, *Augusta Chronicle and Sentinel*, 11 October 1861.

[18] Ibid.

[19] "HUD," "Western Virginia Correspondence," *Atlanta Daily Intelligencer*, 17 October 1861.

his detachment to retire after the Yankees began to threaten his flanks and rake his position with artillery fire. Another member of the Gate City Guards, Private David W. Brown, was ramming down his twenty-ninth round when he heard the order to fall back. "I will give them one more shot before I leave," he declared, saying he "wanted to kill one more." Moments later, a ball pierced Brown's chest near his heart.[20]

Concerned about his incomplete earthworks, especially on the right flank and rear, General Jackson feared Reynolds might turn his position if the federal general was able to maneuver troops along the mountains to the north. To protect against this likelihood, Jackson held the 1st Georgia in reserve on the army's right, ready to block any such flanking movement. Jackson rode up to Major Thompson, commanding the regiment in the absence of Colonel Ramsey and Lieutenant Colonel Clarke, who was on detached duty in Staunton. "Major," he called out, "your regiment have the post of danger, and I hold you and them responsible for this part of the field."[21]

Greenbrier River turns to the northeast near Traveler's Repose, then about four hundred yards along makes a sudden forty-five-degree swing to the east. The 12th Georgia was positioned along the river near the angle. Major Thompson ordered the 1st to fix bayonets, then posted seven companies some five hundred yards to the right of the 12th. The remaining companies, under Captain John A. Houser of the Southern Rights Guard, were located about three hundred yards behind. Adjutant James Anderson warned the men to be prepared for an advance. "[W]hen the order is given to charge double-quick," he cautioned, "keep cool, men, and keep your places." Shortly thereafter, the Georgians were ordered to lie down, so as not to provide easy targets for the federal artillery. The 12th Georgia used a shallow millrace as a natural trench. "We took shelter," wrote a soldier of

---

[20] "George," letter to the editor, *Augusta Chronicle and Sentinel*, 11 October 1861; *OR*, ser. 1, vol. 5, pt. 1, p. 228.

[21] *OR*, ser. 1, vol. 5, pt. 1, p. 225; Anonymous, "The Battle of Greenbrier River," *Augusta Daily Constitutionalist*, 11 October 1861; Clement A. Evans, ed., *Georgia*, vol. 6 of *Confederate Military History*, 12 vols. (Atlanta: Confederate Publishing Company, 1890) 72.

the 12th, "as well as we were able, in a ditch partially filled with mud and water."[22]

Soldiers from the overrun picket posts continued to straggle into the fortifications, singly and in small groups. Concern mounted for the missing Colonel Ramsey, especially when his horse, spattered with blood, bolted into the camp. "We all thought he had been killed," wrote one Georgian, "and it was reported during the afternoon that he had been wounded and taken prisoner."[23]

Jackson next sent a dispatch to Colonel John B. Baldwin, stationed on Allegheny Mountain with his 52nd Virginia, to bring his regiment up to the rear of Camp Bartow, in order to head off any federal movement in that area. As the Federals pushed the advance guard back, Jackson sent what few cavalrymen he had available out beyond the 1st Georgia to watch for any movement in that quarter. With the Georgians posted to his right, Colonel Taliaferro's Virginians holding his center, and the 3rd Arkansas of Colonel Rust on his left, Jackson awaited the federal onslaught.[24]

He Didn't Intend to Die

Jackson did not have long to wait. Colonel Johnson's small force was scrambling toward the safety of the earthworks. The advanced guard had bought precious time for Jackson's division, managing to hold up the Yankees for almost an hour and give the army time to bolt its breakfast and form for battle. Jackson directed Johnson to take command of his "right wing," which consisted of the two Georgia regiments.

It was close to 8:00 A.M. when the federal artillery dropped trail some eight hundred yards from Jackson's works and opened fire with a tremendous roar. The batteries of Confederate Captains Lindsey Shumaker and William Rice, along with a gun from Captain P. B. Anderson's battery, returned the fire. Union musicians were forced to scatter when several rounds landed uncomfortably close. "The Yankees came down 'gallantly' with the 'stars and stripes' proudly waving and the brass band 'discoursing

---

[22] George, letter to the editor, *Augusta Chronicle and Sentinel*, 11 October 1861; "Nestor," letter to the editor, *Atlanta Southern Confederacy*, 17 October 1861; "R. T. D.," "The Greenbrier Fight," *Savannah Republican*, 15 October 1861.

[23] G. W. Cooper, letter to the editor, *Columbus Daily Sun*, 12 October 1861; "George," letter to the editor, *Augusta Chronicle and Sentinel*, 11 October 1861.

[24] *OR*, ser. 1, vol. 5, pt. 1, p. 225.

eloquent music,' but a few shots from our batteries abruptly silenced the music," wrote Chaplain Campbell.[25]

A nearly four-hour titanic artillery duel followed. The air between the two armies was alive with flying projectiles. "With an almost deafening roar the fight commenced between the Artilleries," wrote Private Ray:

> The balls flew in quick succession through the air making a curious hissing noise which could be heard for miles. We had eight cannon and the Enemy eight or more, ones a great deal larger than ours. But all the pieces belched forth their iron hail through the skies with a roar which almost shook the earth. We could see the balls hitting in front of us and in the rear and shells bursting among the horses causing them to run away with their wagons, others falling among the cowardly wagoners who would instantly cut loose their horses and jumping upon them ride in haste to the woods.[26]

Infuriated at the teamsters' lack of courage, General Jackson ordered his son and aide Henry to "Go up there and shoot the first wagoner who cuts a trace or leave his team!"[27]

Colonel Taliaferro's regiments in the center received the brunt of the bombardment. Hunkered down in a ditch behind an embankment with shot and shell screaming over their heads, the Virginians miraculously sustained only light casualties. At 9:30, a column of Union infantry crossed the shallow Greenbrier River toward the Confederate left, moving toward a wooded area in an attempt to turn Jackson's flank. Colonel Rust's 3rd Arkansas poured several volleys into the Federals and drove them back. Two Union guns turned to fire on the Arkansans, but Rust's regiment took few injuries due to the protection of the trees.[28]

---

[25] Lesser, *Rebels at the Gate*, 228; James McDonald Campbell to Bro Joe, 14 October 1861 in Edmond Lee Rice, ed. "Compiled Civil War Letters of James McDonald Campbell of the 47th Alabama Infantry Regiment with a Brief Sketch of His Life," facsimile copy of unpublished typescript, 197-, p. 49, Alabama Department of Archives and History, Montgomery AL.

[26] Lavender R. Ray to his Sister, 4 October 1861, in the personal papers of Lavender Ray, box 2, accession 1949 0012M, Georgia Department of Archives and History, Morrow GA.

[27] "Nestor," letter to the editor, *Atlanta Southern Confederacy*, 17 October 1861; Clark, *Under the Stars and Bars*, 31.

[28] Lesser, *Rebels at the Gate*, 230.

The Rebel artillerymen were not so fortunate. The superior firepower and accuracy of the Union cannon were exacting a toll on the gunners and their weapons. One by one, the Confederate guns were taken out of action. Captain Rice was down, his left foot severed by federal shot. Shumaker ordered several of his cannoneers to cease fire so to clean and cool their pieces.[29]

Reynolds, under pressure by his commanders to launch an attack, ordered four regiments to probe the Confederate right flank. As the soldiers from Indiana and Ohio moved through the brush, they were spotted by the 12th Georgia. The Georgians taunted the Yankees, calling out that "they would not fire on them until they could get in the open field."[30]

"[O]ne of the Yankees hailed to us," wrote Corporal James T. Smith of the Southern Guard, "and asked us what Regiment that was, and upon one of our boys telling him it was the 1st Georgia, he sung out to his comrades, 'let's leave here,' and they did leave, and in about as big a hurry as ever I saw men leave."[31]

Captain Shumaker swung his remaining two guns toward this new threat, unleashing a deadly hail of canister. The artillery fire stopped the Federals in their tracks. Union officers railed at their men to reform and push forward, but could not prod them to advance.[32] "Distinctly could their officers be heard," reported General Jackson, "with words of mingled command, remonstrance, and entreaty, attempting to rally their battalions into line and to bring them to the charge; but they could not be induced to reform their broken ranks nor to emerge from the cover of the woods in the direction of our fire."[33] The federal troops withdrew before the 12th Georgia, advancing toward the river to contest a crossing, could make contact.[34]

It was now close to 1:00 P.M. Peering through his field glasses, General Reynolds could see troops approaching from beyond the Confederate

---

[29] "HUD," "Western Virginia Correspondence," *Atlanta Daily Intelligencer*, 17 October 1861.

[30] Anonymous, "The Battle of Greenbrier River," *Richmond Daily Dispatch*, 12 October 1861.

[31] James T. Smith, "From Western Virginia," *Columbus Daily Times*, 16 October 1861.

[32] Lesser, *Rebels at the Gate*, 230.

[33] *OR*, ser. 1, vol. 5, pt. 1, p. 227.

[34] "R. T. D.," letter to the editor, *Savannah Republican*, 15 October 1861.

fortifications, most likely Colonel Baldwin's 52nd Virginia.[35] "The enemy's force was about 9,000, and we distinctly saw heavy reinforcements of infantry and artillery arrive while we were in front of the works," wrote Reynolds in his after-action report.[36] Fearing his brigade would become quickly outnumbered, Reynolds ordered a retreat. Leaving a trail of equipment and arms behind, the exhausted federal regiments fell back to their stronghold on Cheat Mountain.[37]

Private Beck of the Dahlonega Volunteers, wounded and taken captive earlier that day on the picket line, found himself once again left behind. "As the Union troops passed him again on their return," recalled Private Walter Clark, "a surgeon was asked as to the propriety of taking him along as a prisoner. 'No,' said he. 'Give him a canteen of water. He'll be dead in a few hours.' The wounded man looked up at him, and quoting, as Dr. McIntyre would say, very liberally from profane history, told him he didn't intend to die." After being recovered from the field early next morning, Confederate surgeons told Beck he would most likely die from his wounds. "He dissented very strongly from their opinions, was sent to the hospital, and came out a well man."[38]

The hospital was in bad shape. No less than twenty-eight shells had passed through its walls during the battle, even though both a yellow hospital standard and a white flag were flown over it. Dr. H. K. Green, Jackson's surgeon general, marveled that no one was killed: "Two of the conical shells burst in my office, wounding one of my sick men, though, God be thanked, none of my people were killed. How we escaped death, heaven alone can tell."[39]

The army's animals had suffered as well. "There was about 20 horses killed," reported Corporal Smith, "and a good many wounded, some of them

---

[35] Boyd B. Stutler, *West Virginia in the Civil War* (Charleston WV: Education Foundation, Inc., 1966) 113.

[36] *OR*, ser. 1, vol. 5, pt. 1, p. 221.

[37] Ibid.

[38] Clark, *Under the Stars and Bars*, 32–33. Clark mistakenly identifies Beck as being from the Bainbridge Independents. Clark may have been thinking of Pvt. Patrick H. C. Beck of the Independents, who died in Winchester on 21 December 1861. See Lillian Henderson, ed., *Roster of the Confederate Soldiers of Georgia, 1861–1865*, 6 vols. (Hapeville GA: Longing & Porter, Inc., 1959–1964) 1:283.

[39] H. K. Green, "The Greenbriar Fight," *Columbus Daily Times*, 15 October 1861.

going about with their noses shot off, some with a leg off, other their entrails hanging out."[40]

With the Yankees gone, members of the 1st wandered about the field, assessing the damage and collecting souvenirs. An Augusta soldier reported the devastation to the *Chronicle and Sentinel*: "The ground is plowed up in every direction by our balls, and the track of their artillery. The dead and wounded have all been carried off. The ground around where their cannon were placed, is stained with blood; and in every fence corner and behind every bush were left camps, canteens, haversacks filled with provisions, &c., showing the haste with which they took their departure. I found an excellent canteen, cup and haversack, and many of our boys have been over there this morning supplying themselves."[41]

Searchers came upon Private David Brown's body, leaning against a small tree at the scene of Colonel Johnson's stand. Brown's lifeless fingers were clutching his musket as if taking aim. The firearm had been discharged—Brown had managed to fire that "one more shot."[42]

"Many trophies were picked up on the field," wrote Corporal Pugh, "among which was a beautiful and mammoth federal Flag, made of the finest silk, which was borne in triumph to the camp of the 1st Georgia regiment by a member of the Quitman Guards, amid the deafening shouts of our whole army."[43]

Found leaning against a tree, the banner belonged to the 7th Indiana Infantry. Upon reaching the battlefield, the 7th had been ordered to lie down. Exhausted from the overnight march, the color-bearer set his flag against the tree, then fell fast asleep. When the order was given to rise, the groggy soldier dashed ahead with his regiment, completely forgetting the colors. The 7th Indiana was known as the "Banner Regiment" from that time forward.[44]

---

[40] James T. Smith, "From Western Virginia," *Columbus Daily Times*, 16 October 1861.

[41] "Nestor," letter to the editor, *Augusta Chronicle and Sentinel*, 11 October 1861.

[42] Henry Clay Fairman, *Chronicles of the Old Guard of the Gate City Guard, Atlanta, Georgia, 1858–1915* (Atlanta GA: Byrd Printing Company, 1915) 33.

[43] Nathan S. Pugh, letter to the editor, *Augusta Daily Constitutionalist*, 15 October 1861.

[44] Catharine Merrill, *The Soldier of Indiana in the War for the Union*, 2 vols. (Indianapolis: Merrill and Company, 1866) 1:94.

As they presented the flag to General Jackson, the Georgians undoubtedly savored a moment of sweet revenge for the loss of their own banners during the Laurel Hill retreat. Jackson promised to send it to Richmond "as a trophy from the 1st Georgia Regiment."[45]

Just before dark, Colonel Ramsey made his way back to camp, "to the great rejoicing of the regiment," wrote Private Hermann, "for we all loved him."[46] Once the federal tide had swept past him, Ramsey worked his way up one of the adjoining mountains. From this vantage point, he had watched the battle unfold. Ramsey reported to General Jackson "that they carried off at least twenty wagons loaded with their dead."[47]

General Jackson Is Every Inch a Man

Ramsey was a bit overenthusiastic in his account. Amazingly, even with the tons of ordnance expended by either side, there were few casualties. In his report of the battle, Jackson reported six killed (one in the 1st Georgia), thirty-three wounded (one in the 1st) and thirteen missing. General Reynolds advised his superiors that his brigade sustained eight killed, thirty-five wounded. Nevertheless, the Battle of Greenbrier River was ferociously fought. The victory gave the Confederates a much needed morale boost. Secretary of War Judah P. Benjamin wired General Jackson:. "I congratulate both yourself and the officers and men under your command for your brilliant conduct on this occasion."[48]

Gratified by the victory, and proud of his soldiers, Jackson issued an address to be read at evening parade:

> SOLDIERS: After a campaign to you of peculiar hardships, the enemy, descending from his mountain fastness, has afforded to you the long coveted opportunity of testing your efficiency in action. Confident in his greater numbers, his superior arms, and the comparative weakness of our position, he came, with his wagon trains in anticipation of an easy victory, and a permanent enjoyment of it profits. But gallantly and well have you maintained your place,

---

[45] "George," letter to the editor, *Augusta Chronicle and Sentinel*, 11 October 1861.

[46] Hermann, *Memoirs of a Confederate Veteran*, 49–50.

[47] Hermann, *Memoirs of a Confederate Veteran*, 49–50; Anonymous, "the Battle of Greenbrier River," *Augusta Daily Constitutionalist*, 11 October 1861.

[48] *OR*, ser. 1, vol. 5, pt. 1, pp. 223, 229, 231–232.

> in line with your brethren of the army of Northwestern Virginia—meeting his earlier grievances with striking exhibitions of individual daring, receiving his concentrated fire for more than four hours with the coolness of veterans, and, then, when he supposed your spirit to be shaken, with a calm determination indicating to him what his fate would be should he attempt to carry out further his original designs have you repulsed his first efforts to charge and break your lines.
>
> Though you were not in force to pursue him and to realize the full fruits of your triumph, retreating he left behind him the unmistakable evidence of his rout, in the bodies of his dead, too numerous to be carried with him, the abandonment of arms and accoutrements, even to the colors which, in the morning, he had flaunted so insolently in your front. Soldiers! With pride, I congratulate you![49]

For the next month and a half, the Army of the Northwest settled into their camps, busily improving their breastworks, for they expected that another Union attack might come at any time. "Nestor," correspondent for the *Southern Confederacy*, boasted of the army's progress to his newspaper: "Gen. Jackson's command occupies the same position now that it did prior to the battle of 3d inst. Since that time we have labored very hard in strengthening our old fortifications and in constructing new ones. The result of this work is, that we are now more than twice as able to repulse an attack from the enemy as we were on the day of the recent battle at this place, with the same arms and force we then had."

"Nestor" noted the confidence of the troops in their ability to beat off any further assault. "With...the strong position we now occupy, I dare say we can repulse the efforts of at least 15,000 Hessians to break through our lines; indeed, some are of opinion that with the force we now have here, our position is impregnable against an attack of 20,000."[50]

In the battle's aftermath, the troops of General Jackson's division had developed a great fondness and faith in their commander. "Gen. Jackson's action yesterday won the affection and confidence of his entire command,"

---

[49] Anonymous, "The Victory in Western Virginia," *Sandersville Central Georgian*, 16 October 1861.

[50] "Nestor," letter to the editor, *Atlanta Southern Confederacy*, 25 October 1861.

wrote one soldier.[51] Captain S. A. H. Jones expressed his admiration for the officer: "[O]ur General Jackson is every inch a man, either as a gentleman or an officer."[52]

Far away in Georgia, family and friends breathed sighs of relief at the light casualty counts. Lieutenant Fleming's family was exuberant when they learned he had survived the battle unscathed. "After more than two weeks of great anxiety on your account," wrote his father, "[I am] some what relieved by the fact that your name did not appear among the killed and wounded as published in the papers we at last heard from you direct. Yesterday three letters arrived from you one dated after the battle and we were relieved from all doubt as to your fate. We have great reasons to thank God that so far your life has been spared. May He continue to guard and protect you and in his own good time return you to us unimpaired in health."[53]

Fleming was growing increasingly worried about his family back in Bainbridge. He longed to see his wife, now six months pregnant, and his daughter, Lila. In a letter sent shortly after the battle, the lieutenant had asked his father's opinion as to the wisdom of resigning and coming home. The elder Fleming replied on 16 October:

> I hardly feel comfortable to advise you. I am afraid that if you resign just now you will hardly ever get over it. As you state in your letter this is now the time for active military operations and whatever you may do in the future I am sure you will injure yourself by resigning now. And even after you go into winter quarters I should suppose that your might obtain a furlough long enough to arrange your business to your satisfaction. In this matter you must judge for yourself but as you have asked my advice I give it as above. At least don't resign until military operations have ceased for the winter and even then consider well if a furlough would not as well suit your purposes. Your term of enlistment will expire in five months—it is not long to wait especially if in the mean while you can obtain a

---

[51] James T. Smith, "From Western Virginia," *Columbus Daily Times*, 16 October 1861.

[52] S. A. H. Jones, "The Greenbriar Battle—A Letter from Capt. Jones," *Sandersville Central Georgian*, 16 October 1861.

[53] William B. F. Fleming to William O. Fleming, 16 October 1861, in the William Oliver Fleming Papers, #2292-z, Southern Historical Collection, the Wilson Library, University of North Carolina at Chapel Hill (hereafter cited as Fleming Papers). Quoted with permission of William Fleming, descendent.

> furlough. I need not say how much I would be pleased to have you at home again but I would blame myself very much if you should injure yourself in the future by reason of any advice I may give you.[54]

Both sides continued to send out raiding parties, trying to keep each other off balance and on edge, as well as to collect intelligence. The 12th's Lieutenant Dawson was detailed once again to take a scouting party out to determine the location of the Union pickets. With one hundred men selected from both the 1st and 12th, Dawson's expedition left camp around midnight of 15 October. Dawson was to approach as close as possible to the Federals. By 10:00 A.M. the Georgians had managed to creep to within three miles of the Union lines before being discovered and fired upon. Dawson's men replied with a scattering of shots, then beat a hasty retreat before being surrounded by the Yankees. "We made," reported a soldier from the Oglethorpe Infantry, "I can assure you a very narrow escape. If we had not discovered their force so soon, we should all have been compelled to surrender."[55] Retiring toward Camp Bartow, Dawson's men were fired on by Confederate pickets, who mistook the Georgians for enemy troops. Fortunately, none of the shots found a mark.[56]

Private James Norrell reported to his wife that "we have some rite lively stampedes with the yankeys but tha have not made anything of us yet and we don't intend that tha shel." Any report of Federals approaching Camp Bartow brought the garrison to arms. "Yesterday between twelve & one o'clock the whole camp was in great commotion," wrote Lieutenant Fleming on 16 October. "The long roll was at once beat & on every hand you could hear the command "*fall in*" company A. = "*fall in*" Company B. &c &c."[57]

Fleming described another foray on the 21st; "Last evening about dark the enemy again attacked our picket at the bridge who were obliged again to fall back to the next post.... The report is that three yankees were left dead on the field."[58]

---

[54] See ibid.

[55] "I.," "From Western Virginia," *Augusta Daily Constitutionalist*, 24 October 1861.

[56] Ibid.

[57] James M. Norrell to his wife, 27 October 1861, in the Madeleine Anthony Collection, box 7, folder 10, Lumpkin County Library, Dahlonega GA; William O. Fleming to his wife, 16 October 1861, Fleming Papers.

[58] William O. Fleming to his wife, 21 October 1861, Fleming Papers.

Late on the night of the 26th, pickets again reported federal troops near their outpost. Two companies each from the 1st and 12th Georgia, along with the 37th Virginia, were roused from their slumbers to investigate. Colonel Taliaferro led the column out into the no-mans-land between the armies. Coming up to the bank of the Greenbrier River, the soldiers created a bridge by running wagons into the stream, then arranging planks from end to end. Blinded by the glare of torches while crossing, Private Isaac Hermann took a misstep and plunged into the icy water.[59]

A few miles further on, the column reached a switchback in the road. One of the leading soldiers stepped on a twig, snapping it with enough volume to sound like the cocking of a musket hammer. Nervous troops began sidling to the side of the road, creating a cascade of noise that, by the time it reached the rear of the line, resembled the sound of galloping horses. Made even more jumpy by the clatter, a few of the rear troops mistook the men passing above them for enemy soldiers, and opened fire. Once again, the soldiers were lucky, as the friendly fire went wide. "[F]ortunately there were no casualties," recorded Private Clark, "save a few skinned noses from too sudden contact with the undergrowth that walled in the road." Finding no Federals, the column turned back for camp. Clark angrily observed that the Yankees "probably never existed except in the perverted vision of a nervous picket."[60]

The Snow Is over a Foot Deep

Increasingly cold weather soon brought these excursions to a halt. In both the Union and Confederate camps, the troops prepared for winter. The soldiers set to work making their camp as comfortable as possible. "In our tent we are quite comfortable, having a fireplace," bragged a member of the Walker Light Infantry. "It is made by digging a trench which is covered with rock, one end being in the tent, in which we build a fire, a barrel with both heads knocked out is our chimney."[61]

The Georgians did have to be careful about one thing; rolling out of their tents. "The place where the 1st Georgia Regiment is encamped," groaned one soldier, "is on of the highest spots I ever saw. It is on the side

[59] Hermann, *Memoirs of a Confederate Veteran*, 50–51.

[60] Clark, *Under the Stars and Bars*, 34–36.

[61] "W.," "From a Member of the Walker Light Infantry," *Augusta Chronicle and Sentinel*, 24 November 1861.

of a steep hill—so steep, that if you lay down and go to sleep on its side, you will be apt to find yourself at the bottom when you wake up."[62]

Many in the regiment were still without shelter, and snow was beginning to fall. Those with tents were the lucky ones, though canvas was scant protection from the cold. A member of the Oglethorpe Infantry wrote home on 16 November saying the "snow is about six inches deep, perhaps in some places fully a foot deep. We are still staying in tents, which is not quite so comfortable as staying at home in a pleasant house."[63]

Waking one morning after another night with only his blanket for cover, Private Hermann rose to find a layer of white covering the encampment. "Not a man was to seen," he recalled, "the hillocks of snow, however, showed where they lay, so I hollowed, 'look at the snow.' Like jumping out of the graves, the men pounced up in a jiffy, they were wrestling and snowballing and rubbing each other with it."[64]

Unused as they were to such weather extremes, the suffering of the Georgians was acute as winter descended on the mountains of Western Virginia. As Lavender Ray wrote, "The snow is over a foot deep and several of the tents have been broken in from its weight. We keep large fires burning during the day but there is no peace nor comfort in standing near it for the wind changes so often that it blows both blaze and smoke in one's face which almost puts his eyes out."[65]

"It is now about one o'clock & the icicles hanging from the eaves of the houses are over three feet by measure & as large as your arm," wrote Lieutenant Fleming on 15 November.[66]

Even in the frigid conditions the troops still found ways to have fun. Heaving snowballs became a favorite pastime. "[F]ew in our regiment have ever seen such cold weather," wrote one soldier, "but the boys enjoy it and suffer no one to pass, not even the Colonel, without pelting the passer with snow balls. Colonel Clark and our Surgeon are enjoying themselves with

---

[62] "T.," "From Western Virginia," *Augusta Daily Constitutionalist*, 10 November 1861.

[63] "Incidents of Camp Life," *Augusta Daily Constitutionalist*, 27 November 1861.

[64] Hermann, *Memoirs of a Confederate Veteran*, 54–55.

[65] Lavender Ray to his mother, 18 November 1861, in Thomas, *Letters and Diary of Lieut. Lavender R. Ray*, 34.

[66] William O. Fleming to his wife, 15 November 1861, Fleming Papers.

this pleasant sport."[67] Lieutenant Colonel Clarke was quite fond of the game. When a snowball fight erupted between members of the 1st and 12th Georgia on 17 November, Clarke mustered the entire regiment, attacking not only the 12th but a battery as well. Neither side in the icy conflict was able to claim victory.[68]

Sutlers provided liquid warmth to the soldiers in the form of whiskey and other spirits. Schemes abounded as enterprising soldiers found ways to "liberate" liquor from the merchants. "Our sutler received a fresh supply of whisky," wrote an amused Oscar Cantrell,

> and one of the soldiers concluded that he would cheat the old gentleman out of a quart. The soldier had two black bottles of the same s[tyle] he filled one with water, and placed one in each pocket, (then) went to the sutler in the night and handed him his empty bottle to be filled with whisky; after the bottle was filled, and the soldier had placed it back in his pocket, he remarked to the sutler, (well knowing that he sold his whisky only for cash) that he would settle with him in a few days. The sutler replied that he must pay the money immediately, or return the whisky. The soldier handed him the bottle of water, telling him to empty it quick, as he was in a great hurry and wanted his bottle. The trick succeeded, and the soldier returned to his quarters plus a quart of whisky, thinking how well the suttlers whisky was watered, and how easily the trick was played.[69]

Winter quarters were on the minds of everyone in Camp Bartow. James Norrell wrote, "we have had some varry cold wether hear and some snow and i think we will go somewhare to winter quartes before long but i do not no whare we will go too yet."[70] "We hear a great many conflicting reports concerning our quarters for the winter," Private Ray advised his father. "One report says that we will go to Charlottesville at the University of Virginia,

---

[67] "W.," "From a Member of the Walker Light Infantry," *Augusta Chronicle and Sentinel*, 24 November 1861.

[68] Ibid., Clark, *Under the Stars and Bars*, 37.

[69] Oscar A. Cantrell, *Sketches of the First Regiment Georgia Vols.: Together with the History of the 56th Regiment Georgia Vols., to January 1, 1864* (Atlanta GA: Intelligencer Steam Power Presses, 1864) 13.

[70] James M. Norrell to his wife, 27 October 1861, in the Madeleine Anthony Collection, box 7, folder 10, Lumpkin County Library, Dahlonega GA.

another on the coast at Norfolk or Brunswick, others Staunton, Scribling Springs, Allegany mountains, Kanawah valley, or Kentucky."[71]

Lieutenant Fleming feared the high command might have other plans for them:

> I should not wonder myself if our destination is Winchester to join Stonewall Jackson's command. If so it will have a depressing effect upon the spirits of our men. It will be as cold and bleak a climate as that we have just left & the country in no wise better so far as the business of life were concerned on account of the vast numbers of troops that have been quartered there. It is true we could get nothing more than the commissary contained in the way of supplies if we go to Manassas but there we would feel more as if we had gotten into the army & the constant expectations of getting into a great battle would have a tendency to keep us alive.[72]

In a 21 October letter to his brother, Private Elijah W. Blissit of the Quitman Guards expressed his hope of soon heading to warmer climates. "[W]e will move in 3 or 4 weeks so our leading men thinks to the coast of Georgia." He added wryly, "[W]e are building winter quarters 10 miles in our rear in top Alleggany Mountains as soon as we finish building winter quarters & fortifying we will move some where I care not how soon for I am sick & tired of thise mountains."[73]

Every man in the camp with carpentry experience was ordered to the summit of Allegheny Mountain to construct huts. "All the carpenters brickmasons &c are detailed from our Reg. to build cabins for the soldiers on the Allegany nine miles from here, but I think the Virginians will occupy them," wrote Private Ray with a degree of hopefulness.[74]

On 21 November General Jackson ordered the evacuation of Camp Bartow.[75] As the troops collected their gear and made ready to move out,

---

[71] Lavender Ray to his father, 27 October 1861, in Thomas, *Letters and Diary of Lieut. Lavender R. Ray*, 31.

[72] William O. Fleming to his wife, 25 November 1861, Fleming Papers.

[73] E. W. Blissit to his brother, 16 October 1861, Blissit Family Papers, Accession 1977–0365M, Georgia Department of Archives and History, Morrow GA.

[74] Lavender Ray to his father, 27 October 1861, in Thomas, *Letters and Diary of Lieut. Lavender R. Ray*, 31.

[75] Clement A. Evans, ed., *Virginia*, vol. 3 of *Confederate Military History*, 12 vols. (Atlanta: Confederate Publishing Company, 1890) 172.

gossip abounded of possible transfers to warmer stations. One story held that the 1st and 12th Regiments were to be sent back to Georgia to be included in a brigade commanded by Jackson. Private Walter Clark recalled, "For some weeks rumors, or 'grape vine' bulletins, as they were called, had been afloat in camp that our regiment was to be transferred to coast service. To boys reared in the milder climate of Georgia the taste we were having of a Virginia winter rendered these rumors very palatable."[76] Those who were convinced they were leaving the mountains built great bonfires of clothing and blankets to reduce the amount they would have to carry. They would come to regret that decision.[77]

[76] Clark, *Under the Stars and Bars*, 38.
[77] Lesser, *Rebels at the Gate*, 245–46.

10

To the Valley

"If, upon consideration of affairs on this line, you should desire the proposed campaign to be prosecuted, be assured that I shall enter into it with a spirit to succeed, and will be seconded by a command as ardent in the cause as any in the country, and who will cheerfully endure all the hardships incident to a winter campaign." —General William Wing Loring to Secretary of War Judah P. Benjamin, regarding a possible move to support General Thomas J. Jackson[1]

We Disliked to Leave Them

Roused from their slumber at 3:00 A.M., Jackson's division collapsed their tents and other shelters, then loaded their camp equipage onto the wagons. The 1st waited for the order to march, optimistic that their destination would be Georgia. "[W]hen, on Nov. 21, orders came to break came we felt rather confident that we were bidding a long farewell to 'Travelers Repose' and Northwest Virginia, and were off for Georgia," wrote Private Walter Clark. "The baggage wagons, of which the 1st Ga. had at that stage of the war, enough, in Gen. Loring's opinion, to equip a division, were loaded and went on their way." Some unknown hitch kept the regiment stalled, however. Clark and his bunkmate were forced to spend a frigid night in their old campsite without cover. Clark recalled, "All the afternoon we lay around the dismantled camp awaiting order to 'follow pursuit,' as a friend of mine once said, but they failed to come. Night settled down cold and cheerless, with our tents and blankets ten miles away, and we had to make the best of it. My bedfellow and I slept on an oilcloth, covered with an overcoat, and tied our four feet up together in a flannel shirt."[2]

---

[1] US War Department, comp., *The War of the Rebellion: A Compilation of the Official Records of the Union and Confederate Armies*, 128 vols. (Washington DC: Government Printing Office, 1880–1901) (hereafter cited as *OR*) ser. 1, vol. 5, pt. 1, p. 984.

[2] Walter A. Clark, *Under the Stars and Bars: Or Memories of Four Years Service with the Oglethorpes, of Augusta, Georgia* (Augusta GA: The Chronicle Printer, 1900) 37.

Next morning, the column started eastward, heading for the recently completed camp on Allegheny Mountain. The march was reminiscent of the Laurel Hill retreat, as rain and melting snow combined with feet, hooves, and wagon wheels to turn dirt roads into a mucky mess. Private Lavender Ray wrote that "the road from Greenbriar to the top of Alleghany was horrible being choked up with mud. The wagoners were forced to throw out tents, blankets &c. all of which were burnt, they also abandoned broken waggons and horses who would step off the road and roll many feet down the mountain. But our regiment succeeded in bring all their things away."[3]

Upon reaching Camp Allegheny, General Jackson issued General Orders Number 21, reorganizing his division. Colonel William B. Taliaferro would take charge of the Monterey Line, in command of a brigade to include the 1st Georgia, 3rd Arkansas, and 23rd and 37th Virginia. Colonel Edward Johnson was given another brigade, which included his own 12th Georgia, and was assigned the post on Allegheny Mountain. The soldiers of the 1st were saddened to lose their fellow Georgians' companionship, a camaraderie forged in the fire of battle on Cheat Mountain and at Greenbrier River. "The next morning we left the top of Alle and started down the mountain in a heavy snowstorm," wrote Private Ray, "leaving the 12th Ga. and four Va. Regiments there under the command of Col. Johnson. The 12th Ga. hated very much to be sepperated from us, and we disliked to leave them knowing how much they would suffer upon that bleak mountain."[4]

The trek down from Camp Allegheny was almost as difficult as the ascent. Many soldiers wished they had not been in such a rush to burn their blankets. Wrote Private Ray, "We traveled two days from Alleghany to Monterey through snow & rain, up and down ice mountains which we could scarcely climb as our feet would often slip and perhaps throw us upon the hard ice. In crossing my thoughts often ran back to the time when I first read of Hannibal and Napoleon crossing the Alps, little dreaming then I would undergo or experience their trials and sufferings. It was really an impressive

---

[3] Lavender Ray to his father, 7 December 1861, in Ruby Felder Ray Thomas, comp., *Letters and Diary of Lieut. Lavender R. Ray, 1861–1865, comp. and ed. by his daughter Ruby Felder Ray (Mrs. Eli. A. Thomas)* (Atlanta GA: n.p., 1949), typed manuscript (Morrow GA: Georgia Department of Archives and History) 38.

[4] *OR*, ser. 1, vol. 51, pt. 2, p. 388; Lavender Ray to his father, 7 December 1861, in Thomas, *Letters and Diary of Lieut. Lavender R. Ray*, 38.

sight to look miles behind and see the long trains of wagons and men winding round and through the tall mountains."[5]

The usual straggling and foraging plagued the march. Passing through Crab Bottom Valley, several Newnan Guards happened across a still, with predictable results. In camp that evening, a Virginia soldier peddling apples visited the inebriated men. Unknown to the Virginian, the Georgians had just purchased apples at twenty cents a dozen. When the peddler offered his fruit at fifty cents per dozen, the drunken Guardsmen became incensed. "One of the boys took the sack and struck him over the head with it," wrote Oscar Cantrell. "The sack was rotten, and it tore almost to strings. The apples fell in every direction. The whole crowd began to pelt the Virginian with the apples; he began to beg, but they only pelted him the harder; he then began to run, and the crowd pursued until they ran him out of camps."[6]

Having been offered the rank of major general in Governor Brown's state army, Henry R. Jackson departed Monterey for Staunton on 25 November, enroute to Georgia by way of Richmond. Colonel Ramsey, whose health was reported to be "quite feeble," traveled with Jackson as far as Richmond.[7]

Taliaferro's Brigade was not to remain at Monterey for long. In and around Washington, General George B. McClellan, the supposed victor at Rich Mountain, devoted his energies toward building the largest military force on the American continent. Nervous over federal intentions, Jefferson Davis and Secretary of War Judah P. Benjamin were once again concentrating troops near Richmond. On the same day General Jackson left for the capital, orders arrived in Monterey directing him to forward four regiments to Staunton, in preparation for being sent to Manassas. Having been instructed by Jackson to open any dispatches addressed to the general, Taliaferro answered the next day that he would start his brigade on Wednesday, 27 November. In preparation for the march, the colonel

---

[5] Lavender Ray to his father, 7 December 1861, in Thomas, *Letters and Diary of Lieut. Lavender R. Ray*, 38.

[6] Oscar A. Cantrell, *Sketches of the First Regiment Georgia Vols.: Together with the History of the 56th Regiment Georgia Vols., to January 1, 1864* (Atlanta GA: Intelligencer Steam Power Presses, 1864) 13–14.

[7] *OR*, ser. 1, vol. 51, pt. 2, p. 390; Anonymous, untitled article, *Richmond Daily Dispatch*, 30 November 1861; Anonymous, "Col. Ramsey's Regiment," *Columbus Daily Sun*, 27 November 1861.

directed that all sick and convalescents in the camp hospitals be sent immediately to Staunton.[8]

Chaplain Campbell was serving as a nurse when he was informed of his regiment's imminent departure. Campbell accompanied the ill soldiers to Staunton, but he had no intention of letting the 1st go in harm's way without his services: "At this point, an officer came into my room and tells me that the 1st Geo, 3rd Ark and two Va regiments will be at Buffalo Gap tomorrow evening and have orders to go directly to Manassas and that a battle is expected to commence at that place today covering an extent of country some sixty miles in extent and perhaps will last several days. If my regiment goes to Manassas and there is a prospect of a battle, I will go with it…I will not leave my regiment while they have the prospect of an engagement."[9]

Lieutenant Colonel Clarke Is in Arrest

The directive ordering the four regiments to Manassas set off a confusing sequence of events. General Loring received a copy of Jackson's orders on the 26 November, the same day Taliaferro made his reply. Loring's adjutant general, Carter L. Stevenson, wrote to Taliaferro the next day, informing the colonel to delay his departure until he received additional instructions. The order arrived too late, for the brigade had already marched early that morning. Fearing rightly he might have missed Taliaferro's departure, Loring sent another dispatch, ordering the colonel to remain in Monterey, or having left, to stop wherever he might be pending further orders. This letter caught up with Taliaferro that evening in McDowell, where the Virginian obediently halted.[10]

While he waited for more word from Loring, Taliaferro took steps to tighten discipline in his brigade and to retrieve missing soldiers. Informing Adjutant General Stevenson of his efforts, the colonel wrote, "I have forwarded to Staunton the names of all those who have left since I assumed the command of the regiments to Colonel Barton, acting assistant adjutant-general, and requested him to arrest them and have them imprisoned until

---

[8] *OR*, ser. 1, vol. 51, pt. 2, p. 390.

[9] James McDonald Campbell to Bro Joe, 28 November 1861, in Edmond Lee Rice, ed. "Compiled Civil War Letters of James McDonald Campbell of the 47th Alabama Infantry Regiment with a Brief Sketch of His Life," facsimile copy of unpublished typescript, 197-, p. 51, Alabama Department of Archives and History, Montgomery AL.

[10] *OR*, ser. 1, vol. 51, pt. 2, pp. 390, 392–94.

we should reach that place, or returned to their regiments should our march be arrested."[11] Taliaferro blamed the lack of order on absent officers: "I have adopted measures which I hope will correct this disgrace in future, and I shall use every exertion to increase the discipline of the command, but the number of field officers is entirely inadequate. Colonel Ramsey, 1st Georgia, is absent on leave. Colonel Rust is attending the session of Congress; Colonel Scott, the convention; Colonel Fulkerson is in arrest; Lieutenant-Colonel Clarke is in arrest and has tendered his resignation; Lieutenant-Colonel Hubard is absent sick, as is Lieutenant-Colonel Taliaferro."[12]

The charges against Lieutenant Colonels Clarke and Fulkerson evidently had been preferred by Colonel Edward Johnson, though the reason why remains obscure. Clarke may have been placed under arrest for reasons relating to the officer's penchant for fun—possibly a result of his recent snowball attack on Johnson's 12th Georgia. Whatever the reason, Clarke resigned his commission and went home to Augusta.[13]

Lieutenant Fleming decided that it was time he, too, should submit his resignation, but he was to be disappointed. "My resignation has been returned to me by the War Department not accepted," he informed his wife sadly. "It is very hard that I should be compelled to make such a sacrifice of my interests & the interests of others but I will have to submit to the stern fact of military law."[14]

On 28 November, Adjutant and Inspector General Samuel Cooper sent a wire to Lieutenant Colonel M. G. Harman, General Jackson's adjutant in Staunton. The message directed Colonel Taliaferro to proceed to the closest point on the Manassas Gap Railroad, where he would meet transportation to Manassas Junction. Harman redirected the communication to Lieutenant Colonel Seth M. Barton, Taliaferro's acting assistant adjutant general.

---

[11] Ibid., 395.

[12] Ibid.

[13] Col. William B. Taliaferro to Lt. Col. Carter L. Stevenson, Roll 241, William B. Taliaferro service record, Compiled Service Records of Confederate General and Staff Officers and Non-Regimental Enlisted Men, National Archives Microfilm Publication M331, Georgia Department of Archives and History, Morrow GA.

[14] William O. Fleming to his wife, 2 December 1861, in the William Oliver Fleming Papers, #2292-z, Southern Historical Collection, the Wilson Library, University of North Carolina at Chapel Hill (hereafter cited as Fleming Papers). Quoted with permission of William Fleming, descendent.

Barton in turn forwarded the communication, which the colonel received the next morning. Taliaferro had barely broken the seal on this dispatch when orders arrived from Loring to march to Staunton.[15]

The colonel was in a quandary. Although General Loring had given him a direct order to proceed southeast to Staunton, Taliaferro felt he should defer to Cooper's higher rank. (Cooper was the Confederacy's senior full general at this time, outranking Joseph E. Johnston and Robert E. Lee.) Thus, Taliaferro's brigade left McDowell on Friday, 29 November, and headed northeast for Mount Jackson where he would meet transportation to Manassas. After sending a dispatch to Loring giving his reasons for leaving McDowell, Taliaferro marched as far as Shaw's Pass, where his command bivouacked for the night. That evening, another message arrived from Loring, once again directing the colonel to take his brigade to Staunton. Taliaferro, fretting over the conflicting instructions, wrote Barton: "I expressed to General Loring the telegram from General Cooper to me, and have just received an order from him to proceed to Staunton with my command, and await his further instructions or his arrival. This is directly opposed to the order from Richmond, and I wish you would telegraph the fact to Richmond, so that I can be relieved from all blame."[16]

Loring was ignorant of Cooper's orders when he directed Taliaferro to proceed to Staunton. Arriving there two days later, the quick-tempered Loring was furious to find his regiments absent. The general wrote to Secretary Benjamin, his irritation apparent: "I came here to-day to carry into effect the proposed campaign, and find a telegram sending four regiments to Manassas. It is proper to state that, in consequence of movements made, in which I have been endeavoring to carry out your instructions, officers at a distance from my headquarters have been telegraphing without my authority to Richmond, the result of which has been a conflict of orders. One of the objects I had in bringing the regiments to Staunton was that they should not only be on the spot for the contemplated movement, but should be in readiness for any emergency."[17]

Cooper wired Loring on 4 December: "Your letter of 1st instant received, Use your discretion about all the regiments sent from your command, and countermand, if you think proper, the order sending the four

[15] *OR*, ser. 1, vol. 51, pt. 2, pp. 392–93, 397–98.
[16] Ibid., 397–401.
[17] *OR*, ser. 1, vol. 5, pt. 1, p. 975.

regiments to Manassas."[18] Loring immediately requested clarification from Major R. G. Cole, Cooper's assistant, writing, "Ask whether I can stop the four regiments under Taliaferro now marching to Strasburg. Reply immediately, so that I can do so, as they reach the railroad to-morrow at Mount Jackson." Cooper answered simply: "Direct the four regiments under Colonel Taliaferro to proceed to Winchester." Loring immediately fired off a dispatch to Taliaferro: "COLONEL: You will upon receipt of this take your command upon the cars to Strasburg, and there await further orders. I have received instructions from the War Department to this effect."[19]

General Loring had his reasons for wanting Taliaferro's regiments in Winchester, though the situation was not to his liking. Major General Thomas J. Jackson, the hero of Manassas, was now in command of the Valley District of Virginia. General Jackson had been lobbying for the transfer of the Army of the Northwest from the Alleghenies since he was assigned to the Valley on 5 November. Pressure had been brought to bear on Loring from several quarters to send troops.

I Have Proposed an Arduous Undertaking

"Stonewall" Jackson was a study in contradictions. A deeply religious man, he seemed to glory in battle. Though he would never write a letter that would be in transit on a Sunday, fate decreed that most of his major battles were fought on the Lord's Day. Jackson would never use pepper in his food, and he seldom consumed liquor, for he feared he liked it too much.[20] He frequently kept one arm raised, allegedly to keep his body balanced (a habit that resulted in a finger wound at the Battle of First Manassas).[21] Jackson rarely confided his plans to his staff or officers, and this secrecy would have repercussions in the upcoming campaign.

Charged with defending the Shenandoah Valley, Jackson immediately called for more troops. His old command, the Stonewall Brigade, was dispatched from Richmond. The general's goal was to drive the federal army away from the Baltimore and Ohio Railroad. If he could block the rail

---

[18] Ibid., 979–80.

[19] Ibid., p. 979–80; *OR*, ser. 1, vol. 51, pt. 2, p. 405.

[20] James I. Robertson, *Stonewall Jackson: The Man, the Soldier, the Legend* (New York: MacMillan Publishing, 1997) 299.

[21] John Bowers, *Stonewall Jackson: Portrait of a Soldier* (New York: William Morrow and Company, 1989)71. While Jackson was holding his hand aloft during the battle, a flying shell fragment broke one of his fingers.

lines, he could deprive Union troops of necessary supplies. The small town of Romney, located on the northwestern Virginia turnpike, was Jackson's target. From there he could guard the railroad and prevent northern forces from joining near Martinsburg.[22]

Jackson would have preferred a chance at retaking Western Virginia, land of his birth. He hoped that the capture of Romney might lead to a campaign to push the Federals from their strongholds on Cheat Mountain and Elkwater.[23] Corresponding with Secretary Benjamin on 20 November, Jackson wrote,

> I deem it of very great importance that Northwestern Virginia be occupied by Confederate troops this winter. At present it is to be presumed that the enemy are not expecting an attack there, and the resources of that region necessary for the subsistence of our troops are in greater abundance than in almost any other season of the year. Postpone the occupation of that section until spring, and we may expect to find the enemy prepared for us and the resources to which I have referred greatly exhausted. I know that what I have proposed will be an arduous undertaking and cannot be accomplished without the sacrifice of much personal comfort; but I feel that the troops will be prepared to make this sacrifice when animated by the prospects of important results to our cause and distinction to themselves.[24]

Another possible effect of Jackson securing Romney would be to draw McClellan's army out of the Washington defenses. If his movements could tempt "Little Mac" to attack General Joseph E. Johnston's forces near Manassas, Jackson could force-march his little army to combine with Johnston. Once McClellan was defeated, Jackson's force would return to the Valley. Jackson continued, "The attack on Romney would probably induce McClellan to believe that the Army of the Potomac had been so weakened as to justify him in making an advance on Centreville; but should this not induce him to advance, I do not believe anything will during the present winter. Should the Army of the Potomac be attacked, I would be at once prepared to re-enforce it with my present volunteer force, increased by

---

[22] Robert G. Tanner, *Stonewall in the Valley: Thomas J. "Stonewall" Jackson's Shenandoah Valley Campaign, Spring 1862* (Garden City NY: Doubleday and Company, 1976) 43–44.

[23] Ibid.

[24] *OR*, ser. 1, vol. 5, pt. 1, pp. 965–66.

General Loring's."[25] Once McClellan was defeated, Jackson's force would return to the Shenandoah Valley.[26]

Jackson wanted Richmond to order all of Loring's men to the valley. Loring, however, was not happy about sending troops, and certainly not the entire army, especially after listening to persuasive arguments from Colonel Edward Johnson. Johnson felt his brigade should remain on Allegheny Mountain, in case the Federals ensconced on Cheat Mountain should try something. Johnson was proven right—his 1,200 men were attacked early on the morning of 13 December. Leaping out of bed when the assault began, Johnson snatched up his coat and pulled it over his nightclothes. Wielding an oak club, he yelled "Give 'em hell, boys," and drove the Union troops back. The colonel was known as "Allegheny" Johnson from that moment on.[27]

Convinced that Loring had excessive soldiers to guard the Allegheny passes, Jackson continued lobbying to have the one-armed general's troops sent to Winchester. In apparent agreement, Secretary Benjamin wrote Loring on 24 November:

> I have for several weeks been impressed with the conviction that a sudden and well-concealed movement of your entire command up the valley towards Romney, combined with a movement of General Jackson from Winchester, would result in the entire destruction, and perhaps capture, of the enemy's whole force at Romney, and that a continuation of the movement westward, threatening the Cheat River Bridge and the depot at Grafton, would cause a general retreat of the whole forces of the enemy from the Greenbrier region to avoid being cut off from their supplies; or if the farther movement west was found impracticable, a severe blow might be dealt by the seizure of Cumberland.[28]

To mollify Loring's anger at being overruled, Benjamin held out an olive branch. "We do not desire," he wrote, "under such a state of things, to direct the movement above described without leaving you a discretion, and

---

[25] Ibid. Jackson refers to the *Confederate* Army of the Potomac, under the command of Gen. Joseph E. Johnston.

[26] See, e.g., ibid.

[27] W. Hunter Lesser, *Rebels at the Gate: Lee and McClellan on the Front Line of a Nation Divided* (Napierville IL: Sourcebooks, Inc., 2004) 249–50, 253–57, 260.

[28] *OR*, ser. 1, vol. 5, pt. 1, pp. 968–69.

the President wishes you to exercise that discretion. If, upon full consideration, you think the proposed movement objectionable and too hazardous, you will decline to make it, and so inform the Department. If, on the contrary, you approve it, then proceed to execute it as promptly and secretly as possible, disguising your purpose as well as you can, and forwarding to me by express an explanation of your proposed action, to be communicated to General Jackson."[29]

Loring reluctantly agreed to send three brigades, but advised Benjamin that a quick transfer to the valley was not possible. Writing on 29 November, Loring ticked off his reasons: "Owing to the difficulty of procuring means of transportation and to the present state of the roads, it will require, with every exertion, two, possibly three, weeks to remove to the rear the troops, a large sick report, and a considerable amount of munitions not needed on the campaign."[30]

Loring made it plain that he did not intend to hurry:

> It appears that General Jackson anticipates a sudden movement of this command. With the utmost exertion on our part it is impossible to effect it in less time than that heretofore stated. There is a large quantity of ammunition, and from two hundred and fifty to two hundred and sixty thousand pounds of subsistence stores at this depot, a reserve of ammunition at Warm Springs, and a large number of sick in hospital at the springs between this and the railroad. All of these must be transferred to Staunton, and transportations collected here, before the movement can be made.[31]

General Cooper sent a terse message to Loring on 5 December. "The exigency requires the arrival of your entire command as rapidly as possible at Winchester."[32] Reports of a possible attack on the Valley Army by troops under Union Major General Nathaniel P. Banks were causing anxiety in the Confederate War Department. General Jackson received a nervous message from Secretary Benjamin:

> I am led, by what I deem reliable information, to conclude that a movement is contemplated by the enemy for an attack on you by a

[29] Ibid.
[30] Ibid., 984
[31] Ibid.
[32] *OR*, ser. 1, vol. 5, pt. 1, pp. 982.

> rapid concentration of Banks' division, combined with an advance of the forces at Romney, which latter are being partially re-enforced.... This may not be true, but prudence requiring that no time shall be lost, I have telegraphed General Loring to-day to move his whole force to Winchester as rapidly as possible, and if successful in joining you promptly you may be able to turn the tables handsomely on the enemy by anticipating his purpose.[33]

We Had a Splendid Camp

Receiving orders to continue on to Winchester, Taliaferro's Brigade left Strasburg on 7 December. Marching on improved roads made for much easier progress. "The road we traveled over yesterday & today is better than you ever saw," wrote Lieutenant Fleming. "It is all Macadamized from Staunton to Romney—over one hundred miles & passes right through what is called the Valley of Virginia. I can not describe to you the beautiful scenery, rich lands &c &c—my time & paper would not permit."[34]

The beauty of the countryside they were traversing once again captivated the troops. Happy to be out of the mountains, Fleming was charmed: "This shall be my subject of conversation around the hearthstone when I return home—then you shall, if it pleases you to listen, pass with me over every foot of ground that I have marched as a soldier & see with the minds eye every rugged mountain & beautiful place. I wish you could have been with me this evening after we got to camp to enjoy the picture that held me enraptured so long."[35]

"Having for several months past been shut up in the mountains where we could view Nature in her pristine glory," reported a correspondent for the *Atlanta Southern Confederacy*,

> and enjoying the sublimity of the wild and picturesque scenery, it was really refreshing and imposing to get where once again we could view a scene in which both Nature and Art were presented. On the East in the distance arose the majestic range of mountains known as the Blue Ridge, and on the West and still further off, the lofty and towering summits of the Alleghenies lifted up their snow-clad peaks and bathed them in the clouds, while the plain between these ranges

---

[33] Ibid., 983.
[34] William O. Fleming to his wife, 8 December 1861, Fleming Papers.
[35] Ibid.

> was dotted with the beautiful white cottages and magnificent brick mansions of Virginia farmers. Beautiful and flourishing villages and towns loomed up in every direction at not very great distances from each other.[36]

Lavender Ray likewise found many enjoyable distractions along the road. He wrote, "[W]e have passed through one of the prettiest countries I have ever seen and met with the kindest people. One town in particular I shall not soon forget which is Bridgwater. It was snowing when we arrived there still the ladies met us with milk bread &c. which they gave us. We camped near here during the night and I went up town and eat supper at a very nice lady's house indeed and formed the acquaintance of her two daughters with whom I spent a nice time."[37]

The 1st Georgia arrived in Winchester on 8 December with 918 men and officers present for duty under the command of Major Thompson. Colonel Ramsey was still absent. The regiment first bivouacked about five miles beyond Winchester, but after three days they were moved just two miles to Camp Mason, named in honor of local resident James M. Mason, Confederate commissioner to Great Britain and France. Private Ray wasted little time searching out pleasant diversions. "Please tell Ma to send me a towel," he implored his sister, "a good pair of boots which Painter can make, a pair of shoes for dick and a pot, also two Blankets & a nice flannel shirt to wear outside if she can get it. I have formed the acquaintance of several young ladies here and like to have something nice to wear sometimes."[38]

Certain they would be spending the winter at Camp Mason, the troops quickly set to work erecting shelters. The Washington Rifles were quite satisfied with their quarters. "[W]e had a splendid camp about a mile to the left of the city," recalled Isaac Hermann. "The weather had greatly moderated and the snow was melting. The regiment had received tents to

---

[36] "Nestor," letter to the editor, *Atlanta Southern Confederacy*, 29 December 1861.

[37] Lavender Ray to his father, 7 December 1861, in Thomas, *Letters and Diary of Lieut. Lavender R. Ray*, 39.

[38] *OR*, ser. 1, vol. 5, pt. 1, p. 1005; Thomas M. Rankin, *Stonewall Jackson's Romney Campaign, January 1–20 February 1862* (Lynchburg VA: H. E. Howard, Inc., 1994) 70; Lavender Ray to his sister, 13 December 1861, in Thomas, *Letters and Diary of Lieut. Lavender R. Ray*, 40; William S. Smedlund, *Camp Fires of Georgia's Troops, 1861–1865* (Marietta GA: Kennesaw Mountain Press, 1994) 199.

which we built chimneys with flat rocks that were abundant all around us. The flour barrels served as chimney stacks, and we were comfortable; rations were also good and plentiful."[39]

Shortly after setting up camp outside Winchester, the Oglethorpe Infantry took delivery of a wagonload of blankets donated by the citizens of Augusta. Private Elmore Dunbar received "a handsome crumb-cloth, which like Joseph's coat, was of many colors, red and green being the prevailing tints." An accommodating tailor in Winchester fashioned a coat and pants out of the material, using the remnants to produce a hat. Parading around in the garish outfit, Dunbar "had an innumerable company of gamins, white and black, following in his wake all over the town."[40]

With the regiment encamped, it was time to turn attention to filling open offices. On 11 December, an election was held to pick a new lieutenant colonel to replace James O. Clarke. Major George H. Thompson, running against Captain George M. Hanvey of the Newnan Guards, won promotion. Adjutant James W. Anderson became major, and First Lieutenant Joseph Palmer of the Newnan Guards was selected to be the new regimental adjutant. Shortly thereafter, Second Lieutenant Chester A. Stone was elected to replace Captain William L. Ezzard of the Gate City Guards, who resigned on 18 December.[41]

Other losses were remembered with sadness. A meeting of the Oglethorpe Infantry was called on 12 December to honor those who were gone. Chaired by Lieutenant J. V. H. Allen, and with Corporal Samuel H. Shepard acting as secretary, the company assembled to remember their dead. In a communiqué forwarded by Lieutenant Allen to the *Atlanta Southern Confederacy*, they wrote, "Whereas, Death has visited us, and taken from our midst, Privates Dillard Adams, on the 8th of July last, at Laurel Hill, Charles M. Goodrich, at Monterey, on the 13th of August last, William J. Miller, on the 22d of August last, at home in Augusta, Ga., and James J. Lamar, at Monterey, Va., on the 19th of November last, it is now the desire of the whole Company to express at one time their deep sorrow

---

[39] Hermann, *Memoirs of a Confederate Veteran*, 65–66.

[40] Clark, *Under the Stars and Bars*, 39.

[41] Lavender Ray to his sister, 13 December 1861, in Thomas, *Letters and Diary of Lieut. Lavender R. Ray*, 40; "Nestor," letter to the editor, *Atlanta Southern Confederacy*, 29 December 1861.

and affection for those with whom they have been so intimately associated in Camp."[42]

Death in other forms continued to touch the ranks. Brothers Archibald and Sylvester Norwood both succumbed to disease on 16 December. They had traveled from their native Houston County to enlist together and had joined the ranks of the Southern Rights Guards on 1 September.[43]

Drills were reinstated to bring the regiment back to fighting trim. "The fields adjoining our camp present a lively and beautiful spectacle every morning and evening," reported one correspondent. "At these times all the troops, except the sick and those on duty, repair to these fields as their drill ground, where their commanders cause them to perform every manner of evolution laid down in tactics. Our brigade is very expert in drilling—understand tactics well—it makes a beautiful show whilst manoeuvering over the field."

As in Camp Oglethorpe, the maneuvers attracted the attention of the local townsfolk—especially the women, to the great enjoyment of the soldiers. Correspondent "Nestor" of the *Atlanta Southern Confederacy* boasted to his editors that the damsels seemed to be especially drawn to the Georgians: "Many young ladies come out from the city almost every evening to witness the drill and dress parade. Our regiment never fails to attract the special attention of the ladies. Whether it is in consequence of the fact that most of the members composing it are young unmarried men, most of whom are handsome, or because we have a good brass band attached to it, I can not speak certainly, but am inclined to think both are influential in attracting them, as the ladies are partial to music and beauty."[44]

Ever solicitous of female attention, Private Lavender Ray also enjoyed the ladies' visits, especially those who brought food to the camp:

> Our camps are daily filled with market women who come in two wheeled cars from the country bringing pies, bread, cakes butter lard chickens and turkeys both alive and cooked. They sometimes bring their daughters too with whom we often have a nice time. Our Reg. is the most popular among these women, their daughters and the town

---

[42] J. V. H. Allen, "Communicated," *Augusta Daily Constitutionalist*, 30 December 1861.

[43] Lillian Henderson, ed., *Roster of the Confederate Soldiers of Georgia, 1861–1865*, 6 vols. (Hapeville GA: Longing & Porter, Inc., 1959–1964) 1:238.

[44] "Nestor," letter to the editor, *Atlanta Southern Confederacy*, 5 January 1862.

ladies because, I suppose, we pay for all we get, treat them politely & and are a better looking set of men than the others. The town ladies often come out to hear our band perform. Some come in carriages, some in buggies and others on horseback.[45]

I Can See You All Now

Everything was not bliss. The soldiers of the 1st bridled under Colonel Taliaferro's harsh discipline. During the march from Camp Bartow, he had issued a series of orders that baffled as well as irritated the Georgians, such as instructing his men to display their eating utensils and plates to the officer of the day, both before and after each meal.[46]

"Taliaferro is the strictest general we have ever been under," complained Lavender Ray.

> He makes a perfect goose of himself. all the regiments dislike him & he hates our Reg. & the Ark. because he can't make us obey him like negroes as his own Va. Reg. does. When we were on the march our surgeon left some sick men at a house on the road, but he went back and sent them on saying that this God d—— hell roaring first Ga. Reg. were scattered from there to hell. At another time one of our sentries had orders not to permit anyone from another Reg. to visit a certain place and while on post Talliaferro came there, when the sentinel immediately ordered him away which made T——— mad and he asked him what he meant the sentinel answered and said, "that it was his orders not to let any one visit that place." Talliaferro then asked if he did not make any difference between officers and privates, he answered no he did not. Talliaferro then swore that "if this 1st Ga. Reg. didn't show him more respect he would have them all shot," and left.[47]

The threat did not sit well with Ray and his comrades. As Ray explained in a letter, "But if he does have one shot he will be killed in the

---

[45] Lavender Ray to his mother, 16 December 1861, in Thomas, *Letters and Diary of Lieut. Lavender R. Ray*, 41–42.

[46] John Bowers, *Stonewall Jackson: Portrait of a Soldier* (New York: William Morrow and Company, 1989) 146.

[47] Lavender Ray to his mother, 16 December 1861, in Thomas, *Letters and Diary of Lieut. Lavender R. Ray*, 42–43.

first battle. I think there are some in both the 1st Ga. and Ark. Reg. who will shoot him anyhow at the first good chance."[48]

One of the Southern Guards, drunk and in a foul mood, happened upon Taliaferro and proceeded to take out his wrath on the colonel by giving him a beating. The soldier was arrested and put in the guardhouse. Shortly thereafter the prisoner climbed a wall and escaped, never to be seen again. "I am glad he made his escape," mused Private Ray, "for I think he would have been shot had he remained."[49]

Taliaferro was also aggravated by the unexpected mid-month return of Colonel Ramsey, whom he mistakenly assumed had left the army permanently. The Virginian was concerned that Ramsey, his superior officer due to earlier commission date, might take control of his brigade. On 16 December, Taliaferro directed an anxious letter to Lieutenant Colonel J. T. L. Preston, Jackson's adjutant general:

> At the period of the assignment of one of the regiments, the 1st Ga. Vols., I was informed that the Colonel had returned to Georgia on sick leave, and would probably not return. I have now to state that Col Ramsay has returned, and that his commission is of earlier date than my own, and if he reports for duty I can not give him an order.
>
> I have moreover to state that Col Ramsay, whilst he superintended the drill of his regt on yesterday, did not intimate his intention or disposition to assume any command, and that he is not quartered with his regiment.[50]

Jackson did not see a problem. Three days later, Taliaferro received a response from Preston: "Majr. Gen Jackson directs me to say to you in reply to your letter of the 16th inst. that until Col. Ramsay reports for duty, no

---

[48] Ibid.

[49] Lavender Ray to his sister, 13 December 1861, in Thomas, *Letters and Diary of Lieut. Lavender R. Ray*, 41; Bowers, *Stonewall Jackson: Portrait of a Soldier*,146.

[50] William B. Taliaferro to Lt. Col. J. T. L. Preston, 16 December 1861, Roll 241, William B. Taliaferro service record, Compiled Service Records of Confederate General and Staff Officers and Non-Regimental Enlisted Men, National Archives Microfilm Publication M331, Georgia Department of Archives and History, Morrow GA.

action as to the subject matter of your communication is necessary on the part of the Commanding General."[51]

This reply must have reassured Taliaferro, for he left on a brief furlough shortly before Christmas. Ramsey found himself in command of the brigade.[52]

Rumors about Jackson's intentions filled the air of Camp Mason. In a report to the *Southern Confederacy*, correspondent "Nestor" wrote,

> The point which it was rumored we would attack is Romney, Hampshire county, forty miles northeast from this place. Gen. Anderson's Brigade, composed mostly of regiments from Tennessee, a part of Gen. Loring's former command, is now on the Valley turnpike, near Strasburg. Whether it will come hither, or go to Manassas, or some other point, I can't tell. Some are of opinion that we are only awaiting the arrival of that brigade before marching against Romney, while others believe that we will not make an advance against that place before the great battle, which is now pending on the Potomac, shall have come off.[53]

---

[51] See, e.g., ibid. Col. Taliaferro believed that Ramsey had gone home to Georgia and was much surprised when he returned in mid-December. See Appendix D for further discussion of when Ramsey and Clarke left the regiment.

[52] William Booth Taliaferro to his wife, 27 November and 6 December 1861, in the William Booth Taliaferro Papers, Special Collections Research Center, Earl Gregg Swem Library, College of William and Mary, Williamsburg VA; Lavender Ray to his mother, 25 December 1861, in Thomas, *Letters and Diary of Lieut. Lavender R. Ray*, 45; "Nestor," letter to the editor, *Atlanta Southern Confederacy*, 29 December 1861, 5 and 12 January 1862; Anonymous, untitled article, *Atlanta Daily Intelligencer*, 3 January 1862; Anonymous, "First Georgia Regiment," *Columbus Daily Sun*, 31 December 1861. While nothing stating definitively that Taliaferro was absent has been located, there is much circumstantial evidence to indicate that he was gone on leave. The colonel mentioned his requests for leave in letters. In his letter of 27 November, Taliaferro says he had requested his leave to begin on 10 December. Accounts from the Atlanta *Atlanta Southern Confederacy* of 17 and 26 December 1861, the *Atlanta Daily Intelligencer*, the *Columbus Daily Sun*, and in Pvt. Ray's letter of 25 December all state that Ramsey was in command of the brigade. The correspondent for the *Atlanta Southern Confederacy* mentions "Col. Taliaferro's (formerly Col. Ramsey's) brigade" in a report dated 10 January 1862.

[53] "Nestor," letter to the editor, *Atlanta Southern Confederacy*, 5 January 1862.

General Jackson, eager to assail the Yankees, was frustrated by Loring's dalliance. He reported to Secretary Benjamin that he believed Romney, under the command of Brigadier General Benjamin F. Kelley, now held some 7,000 Union troops. Jackson expressed his anxiety about the consequences if Loring did not arrive soon: "If General Loring's entire command were here I would, with God's blessing, soon expect to see General Kelley's army, or a large portion of it, in our possession; but if General Loring is not here speedily my command may be a retreating instead of a victorious one."[54]

Impatient to make some strike toward the enemy and unwilling to wait for Loring's arrival to take action, Jackson decided to send an expedition to destroy two dams on the Potomac River. A detachment sent out on 7 December had little success. The general determined to try again, so on 17 December Jackson put the Stonewall Brigade on the road toward Martinsburg. The next day the Virginians marched fourteen more miles and were then set to work trying to destroy the dams. They achieved only marginal success, and Jackson's troops returned to their camps on 23 December. What he discovered on his arrival angered him further. Loring had still not reached Winchester with the remainder of his brigades.[55]

The same day of Jackson's return, a fierce storm pummeled Camp Mason. Lavender Ray had great difficulty keeping his tent upright:

> The wind commenced blowing about sundown and continued until next day. Almost every tent in the Brigade was blown down and a great many were burnt by the sparks which flew from the camp-fires. We succeeded in making our [tent] so fast to the ground that it stood through the night but it received some awful wrenches and several times during the night we had to rise and remove the sparks of fire from our tent and re-nail our pegs. Some of the boys had their hats blown away. Some their tin pans, cups &c. All say it was a more sever blow than they had at Beverleys.[56]

As Christmas approached, the Georgians wrapped their blankets close around, stared into their campfires and longed for home. Lieutenant Fleming sat imagining the scene at his house, as his family celebrated the holiday:

---

[54] *OR*, ser. 1, vol. 5, pt. 1, pp. 988–89.

[55] Robertson, *Stonewall Jackson: The Man, the Soldier, the Legend*, 297–99.

[56] Lavender Ray to his mother, 25 December 1861, in Thomas, *Letters and Diary of Lieut. Lavender R. Ray*, 45.

> This is christmas eve & I was thinking this afternoon of what would probably be the conversation around the hearth to night. I can see you all now, in my imagination, seated around a nice, blazing *Georgia* christmas Eve fire. The usual egg nog for the evening is discussed & all are ready to do their part towards getting up a nice one. The children are all aglow in anticipation of the visit Santa Claus will certainly make down the chimney & the nice presents that will fill their stockings in the morning, bestowed by *his* bountiful hand, is the all absorbing topic with them. I wonder if my little Lila's sock wont hang in the chimney to night—no doubt Cassie will see to it that her little cousin is not neglected. I wish I were their to put something in it.[57]

The next morning Fleming was overjoyed to receive a cherished Christmas present—a letter from his wife, Georgia.

Private Ray likewise reflected on being so far from loved ones. "It is now Christmas and the boys having been accustomed to celebrate this day with fun, mirth, the bold &c. from their infancy seem not to have forgotten that this is the day for pleasure; although being seperated by many miles from the home of their kindred and friends and in camps where everything is so difficult to be obtained, all seem to be in good health and spirits." Still, Ray and his tent mates found ways to celebrate. "Our Mess succeeded in purchasing several dozen of eggs, some brandy, sugar &c. and enjoyed ourselves last night and this morning over a large bold of egg-nog."[58]

General Jackson spent Christmas Eve planning his strike against the Federals. "I have given the subject much thought," he wrote that day, "and as the enemy appears to be continually receiving accessions, and as I may receive no more, it appears to me that my best plan is to attack him at the earliest practicable moment, and accordingly, as soon as the inspection of General Loring's forces shall be finished and the necessary munitions of war procured, I expect to march on the enemy, unless I receive orders to the contrary."[59]

General Loring's other two brigades, under Brigadier General Samuel R. Anderson and Colonel William Gilham, finally reached Winchester on 26

---

[57] William O. Fleming to his wife, 24 December 1861, Fleming Papers.

[58] Lavender Ray to his mother, 25 December 1861, in Thomas, *Letters and Diary of Lieut. Lavender R. Ray*, 44.

[59] *OR*, ser. 1, vol. 5, pt. 1, p. 1005.

December. With roughly 8,500 men, Jackson now felt he had troops enough to proceed with his plans. He intended to move north, drive the Union troops out of Bath, then turn and capture Romney. Several days of fair weather persuaded him that the time was ripe for an advance, so he issued orders for the army to move on 1 January.[60]

Jackson's troops were instructed to prepare rations for five days—a sure sign that some kind of movement was about commence. The Bainbridge Independents would find themselves short one officer, though. Lieutenant William O. Fleming had received the news he had been anxiously awaiting. Fleming's resignation had finally been accepted, and he was going home to Bainbridge to be with his wife as they waited for the birth of their child.[61]

Lavender Ray penciled a quick note to his father as he collected his gear that New Year's morning. "We leave here today," he wrote, "I do not know where we will go but I suppose towards Romney. Some say to the Baltimore and Ohio Rail Road which we will destroy. But Dr. Calhoun can inform you as he will remain until we leave. He can also tell you the news from this section. Every one is busy preparing for the march. We leave in an hour. I am on the advance guard today & suppose we will go about fifteen miles. But I must closse as I am in a great hurry."[62]

After months of enduring rain, snow and ice high in the Alleghenies, the Georgians reveled in the unusually mild mid-winter weather. Ray and his comrades probably anticipated an easy march in the balmy conditions. Unseen over the horizon, however, winter storm clouds were building. The most severe test yet of the 1st Georgia was about to begin.

---

[60] Rankin, *Stonewall Jackson's Romney Campaign*, 79; Sauers, *The Devastating Hand of War*, 24.

[61] Henderson, *Roster of the Confederate Soldiers of Georgia*, 1:272.

[62] Rankin, *Stonewall Jackson's Romney Campaign*, 80; Lavender Ray to his father, 1 January 1862, in Thomas, *Letters and Diary of Lieut. Lavender R. Ray*, 46–47.

11

DEATH IN THE SNOW

"I had thought that in the retreat from Laurel Hill we had seen the worst phase of a soldier's life, but I think I only express the feelings of a majority of our men when I say that I would rather take two such trips as that than go through the exposure and hardships of the last two weeks."—1st Georgia soldier, writing to the Savannah Republican *from Winchester*[1]

This Is the Damnedest Outrage Ever Perpetrated

The first day of 1862 dawned bright and warm. General Jackson's lead element, the Stonewall Brigade, left Winchester at 6:00 A.M. Other commands were not as prompt. Colonel Taliaferro, back from his leave, was unable to start the 1st Georgia and his other regiments until almost noon. A column of militia did not get underway until nearly 6:00 P.M. With the temperature reaching an unseasonable fifty degrees, the sweating troops jettisoned their greatcoats, piling them in company wagons or tossing them along the road. Certain they were marching directly for Romney, the troops were surprised when after seven miles Jackson turned the head of the column northward. Bewildered officers could only guess the reason; as usual, the commanding general was keeping his own counsel.[2]

A frigid wind began to gust from the north. By late afternoon, the temperatures were plunging. Soldiers shivered as freezing winds pierced their jackets. With their wagons now far behind, the troops cursed themselves for discarding their coats. The weather worsened as the army forced its way through the building snow. By that evening, the strung out

---

[1] Anonymous, "Severe Sufferings of Jackson's Men," *Savannah Republican*, as reported in the *Richmond Daily Dispatch*, 28 January 1862.

[2] Thomas M. Rankin, *Stonewall Jackson's Romney Campaign, January 1–20 February 1862* (Lynchburg VA: H. E. Howard, Inc., 1994) 81; James I. Robertson, *Stonewall Jackson: The Man, the Soldier, the Legend* (New York: MacMillan Publishing, 1997) 304. Colonel Taliaferro returned from leave shortly before the march began.

column staggered to a halt near Pughtown (present day Gainesboro), barely eight miles from their starting point.[3]

Little progress was made the next day. In the face of howling winds and below freezing temperatures, the troops struggled toward the small crossroads community of Unger's Store, another eight miles ahead. Loring halted his troops as darkness fell, intending to allow his men to bivouac, but just as the men were building fires for warmth and cooking, the general received an order from Jackson: his men had to continue their march.[4] Loring was furious. "By God, sir," he cried, "this is the damnedest outrage ever perpetrated in the annals of history, keeping my men out here in the cold without food!"[5] Nevertheless, Loring ordered his command back into column before they had time to fix their rations.[6]

Famished, and suffering terribly from the cold, the troops managed to stagger along. Regiments became intermingled as they struggled through marshy terrain. "At last darkness came on and with it the greatest confusion," wrote Private Lavender Ray to his brothers.

> Our road or path now lay through a swamp & here was the greatest confusion. Men from every company, regiment and Brigade were mixted up together. And as we marched along no one knew where we were to camp. So, Col Thompson determined to camp at the first good place he arrived at But we could not find one so we marched on slowly through this swamp and the greatest confusion. No one scarcely knew where his Capt. company or friends were. Now and then you could see a poor fellow worn out with fatigue, hunger cold and want of sleep drop out on the roadside by a fire and fall asleep leaning against a tree.[7]

---

[3] Robert G. Tanner, *Stonewall in the Valley: Thomas J. "Stonewall" Jackson's Shenandoah Valley Campaign, Spring 1862* (Garden City NY: Doubleday and Company, 1976) 69.

[4] Rankin, *Stonewall Jackson's Romney Campaign*, 81–84.

[5] US War Department, comp., *The War of the Rebellion: A Compilation of the Official Records of the Union and Confederate Armies*, 128 vols. (Washington DC: Government Printing Office, 1880–1901) (hereafter cited as *OR*) ser. 1, vol. 5, pt. 1, p. 1066.

[6] Rankin, *Stonewall Jackson's Romney Campaign*, 81–84.

[7] Ibid., 70; Lavender Ray to his brothers, 12 January 1862, in Ruby Felder Ray Thomas, comp., *Letters and Diary of Lieut. Lavender R. Ray, 1861–1865, comp. and ed. by his daughter Ruby Felder Ray (Mrs. Eli. A. Thomas)* (Atlanta GA: n.p.,

Unable to go any further, the soldiers fell out of ranks, kindling fires wherever they had halted.[8] "At last Capt. Wilkins Co. B swore," continued Ray, "that his men should go no farther and the other Capts. determined to stop also. So we were ordered to fall out on the roadside and build fires which we did. And here we remained all night in the cold without a blanket or anything to eat. Virginians, Georgians, Tennesseans were all mixed up around fires made of trash and pieces of dead wood as had no ax to cut with."[9]

Early on the morning of the 3rd, Jackson directed Loring to halt so his men could eat. With his supply wagons three miles behind, Taliaferro decided to march back through the bog. There his men finally received rations. Two hours later, they traversed the swamp once more on their way to Unger's Store.[10]

Jackson's intent had been to attack the resort town of Bath (present day Berkeley Springs) that morning and capture the Union garrison, which comprised some 1,400 soldiers of the 39th Illinois and 84th Pennsylvania and was supported by a section of the 4th US Artillery. By afternoon, however, the struggling troops were still some three miles from the village. Instructions were sent to General Loring to quickly bring his brigades forward; Jackson planned to have Loring's troops make the assault. A column of Virginia militia was sent to the west; their objective was to approach Bath from that side and prevent a federal escape. Twice encountering Union pickets who fired and fell back, the militiamen encamped on the far slope of Warm Springs Ridge, a range of heights just west of the town.[11]

After a skirmish between the 21st Virginia of Colonel William Gilham's brigade and federal pickets, Jackson ordered Gilham to press forward into Bath. Loring, fuming that Jackson expected exhausted and frozen soldiers to make an attack, instead directed his command to bivouac. The two officers exchanged heated words. Loring, frustrated at being kept in

---

1949), typed manuscript (Morrow GA: Georgia Department of Archives and History) 48–49.

[8] Ibid.

[9] Lavender Ray to his brothers, 12 January 1862, in Thomas, *Letters and Diary of Lieut. Lavender R. Ray*, 48–49.

[10] Tanner, *Stonewall in the Valley*, 71.

[11] Robertson, *Stonewall Jackson: The Man, the Soldier, the Legend*, 306–307; Rankin, *Stonewall Jackson's Romney Campaign*, 87–88.

the dark as to Jackson's plans, finally exclaimed that if Jackson were to be killed, "I would find myself in command of an army of the object of whose movement I know nothing!" Giving no response to Loring's outburst, Jackson turned, mounted his horse, and rode away.[12]

Relations between Jackson and Loring soured further with this incident. The animosity began to affect the two officers' commands. Cries of "Tom Fool" and "Lunatic" erupted from Loring's ranks whenever Jackson ventured near. The veterans of the Stonewall Brigade mocked the Army of the Northwest's slow progress. In a letter home, a private in the 4th Virginia jeered that his brigade could easily outmarch the Northwesterners.[13]

Jackson aimed to take Bath the next day, 4 January, regardless of difficulty. The 1st Georgia, along with the 21st and 23rd Virginia, was placed on the main road into the town. To the east, along Horse Ridge, moved the 42nd and 48th Virginia regiments. Colonel Gilham, with the 1st and 7th Tennessee, 3rd Arkansas, and 37th Virginia, moved toward Bath along the base of Warm Spring Ridge. Bringing up the rear as reserve was the Stonewall Brigade.[14]

Alerted by the clash with Jackson's skirmishers, the Federals had taken defensive positions on Warm Spring Ridge. As Gilham moved toward Bath, fire from the ridge brought his brigade to a halt. For some reason, Gilham did not press forward but stopped where he was. Jackson, his frustration mounting, took matters into his own hands. He ordered the 1st Tennessee to charge the guns. The Tennesseans rushed forward with a yell, driving back the Federals.[15]

Meanwhile, Jackson's inspector general, Lieutenant Colonel William S. H. Baylor, encountered a detachment of Confederate cavalry retreating in disarray. Rallying the horsemen, Baylor charged into Bath, followed closely by General Jackson himself. The Georgians and Virginians coming up the main road were ordered forward. Lavender Ray and his comrades in the

---

[12] Tanner, *Stonewall in the Valley*, 73; Rankin, *Stonewall Jackson's Romney Campaign*, 84, 87; Elihu S. Riley, *"Stonewall Jackson": A Thesaurus of Anecdotes of and Incidents in the Life of Lieut. General Jonathan Jackson, CSA* (Annapolis MD, self-published, 1920) 123.

[13] Robertson, *Stonewall Jackson: The Man, the Soldier, the Legend*, 306–307; Tanner, *Stonewall in the Valley*, 79.

[14] Rankin, *Stonewall Jackson's Romney Campaign*, 90–91.

[15] Ibid., 86, 90–91; Robertson, *Stonewall Jackson: The Man, the Soldier, the Legend*, 307.

Newnan Guards were eager to advance: "Soon we heard a roar of musketry on our left and then the joyful news came that the Enemy was retreating. Then we receaved the order 'forward double quick time march.' Everyone gave three cheers and said 'Remember Laurel Hill' and off we put with more than double quick time determined to run them as hard as they ran us from Laurel Hill."[16]

Outnumbered and nearly surrounded, the Federals beat a hasty retreat northward, pausing briefly to set up a defensive line at the rail depot of Sir John's Run. Low on ammunition, they continued retreating toward Hancock, Maryland, just across the Potomac River. Jackson's Virginia militia had been sent to the opposite side of Warm Spring Ridge to block the Yankees' escape route, but they were scattered by a single volley fired by retreating Union troops.[17]

They Had Died at Their Post of Duty

Anxious to overtake and capture the Federals before they could escape across the Potomac, Jackson immediately ordered the army to push on toward Hancock. The 1st Georgia and 23rd Virginia continued northward out of Bath, behind cavalry led by Colonel Turner Ashby. Jackson directed Colonel Rust to quickly march his 3rd Arkansas and the 37th Virginia west to the Great Cacapon River, near its confluence with the Potomac, to burn the Baltimore and Ohio Railroad bridge. Loring was to advance with his brigades toward Hancock, while the Stonewall Brigade remained in Bath to secure the town. Leaving the 1st Tennessee to clean up any remaining federal resistance on Warm Springs Ridge, Jackson and his staff followed after Ashby and the two infantry regiments. Once more, Loring's troops were slow in coming up. In his after-action report, Jackson wrote, "So prematurely and repeatedly had General Loring permitted the head of the column to halt, that even his skirmishers were not kept within continuous sight of the enemy."[18]

After several skirmishes with Union rearguard soldiers, Jackson arrived at Alpine Station that evening, on the Potomac River opposite Hancock.

---

[16] Robertson, *Stonewall Jackson: The Man, the Soldier, the Legend*, 307–308; Lavender Ray to his brothers, 12 January 1862, in Thomas, *Letters and Diary of Lieut. Lavender R. Ray*, 50.

[17] Robertson, *Stonewall Jackson: The Man, the Soldier, the Legend*, 307.

[18] Rankin, *Stonewall Jackson's Romney Campaign*, 92–93; *OR*, ser. 1, vol. 5, pt. 1, p. 391.

Sighting a detachment of Union cavalry, the general sent two companies of horsemen charging after the Federals. Running into an ambush, the Confederates retreated, their horses frantically clawing for a foothold on the ice. Jackson next ordered up the Rockbridge artillery, which threw shells across the river into Hancock.[19]

A building full of supplies discovered in Alpine Station was ransacked by the Georgians and Virginians. "We arrived before Hancock Saturday night, 4th inst.," wrote a soldier of the 1st, "and captured a Commissary and Quartermaster's store, containing many articles of value. The articles were taken out of the depot, and the house burnt. Most of our boys have some trophy of the war."[20] Wiley M. Leatherwood of the Gate City Guard reveled in the abundance of material: "Almost every man got something, such as overcoats, clothing, knapsacks, canteens, &c. I took a canteen, carpet bag, a quantity of letters, ambrotypes, a pipe, some tobacco, a portfolio, and a quantity of envelopes, two of which I send you herewith."[21]

By 9:00 P.M. General Loring's troops were reaching the Potomac riverbank. Jackson posted the regiments along wooded bluffs overlooking the river, after having artillery fire into the trees to drive out any remaining Federals. The cannon fire startled Private Walter Clark. He wrote, "[W]e were standing in the road awaiting orders when a sudden flash illuminated the heavens and the regiment sank as one man into the snow. We thought we had struck a masked battery, but it was our own guns throwing grape shot into the woods in front."[22]

With the temperatures well below freezing and still dropping, the chilled soldiers began to kindle fires for warmth. General Jackson ordered all fires out, so as not to give away his deployments, much to the anger of men struggling to ward off the bitter cold. "We were not allowed to build fires," reported a member of the Oglethorpe Infantry, "lest the enemy should shell us. Men walked up and down, to and fro, to keep warm. Now and then

---

[19] Rankin, *Stonewall Jackson's Romney Campaign*, 95; Robertson, *Stonewall Jackson: The Man, the Soldier, the Legend*, 308.

[20] Anonymous, letter to the editor, *Atlanta Southern Confederacy*, 12 January 1862.

[21] Wiley M. Leatherwood, "Highly Interesting from the Gate-City Guards," *Atlanta Southern Confederacy*, 23 January 1862.

[22] Walter A. Clark, *Under the Stars and Bars: Or Memories of Four Years Service with the Oglethorpes, of Augusta, Georgia* (Augusta GA: The Chronicle Printer, 1900) 45.

we could see a little blaze started—somebody disobeying orders—and then an order 'put out that fire'—'wait until the General has his fire, then you can have yours.'—Here we stood shivering and hungry."[23]

Before returning to Bath sometime after 1:00 A.M., Jackson relented and allowed his troops to bivouac behind the bluffs and start fires. With supply wagons far behind, the men faced a harrowing night in the snowy forest with no tents and little food. An Oglethorpe described the harrowing conditions in a letter home: "About four o'clock next morning, we were ordered to the woods on the bank of the river, with the privilege of building fires, but without a tent or blanket, snow six to eight inches deep, and still falling—our wagons twelve miles behind and stalling on the bad roads. I had two or three ears of corn, which our company devoured as quick as a setting hen could have done it."[24]

Private Clark tried to stay as comfortable as possible by keeping himself above the ice. "After standing for an hour or so in the snow without fire," he wrote, "we bivouacked and I slept, or tried to sleep, on three rails with their ends resting on a stump. We had built a fire of rails, a favorite army fuel in those days. I do not remember from what species of timber they were made, but I do recall the fact that it was a popping variety when subjected to heat." Desperate for warmth, the men crowded near the flames. Sleeping so close to the fires was risky: "All through the night our sleep was disturbed by the necessity of rising at frequent intervals to extinguish our burning blankets, and one man had his cap nearly burned from his head before it awoke him."[25]

Captain Samuel H. Crump's Walker Light Infantry huddled around their campfires. The captain had just settled down for the night when orders arrived to select a picket detail. With thirty soldiers, Crump trudged through the darkness to the designated position, a wooded area on one of the bluffs overlooking the Potomac. Due to the nearness of the enemy, no fires were permitted on the picket line. With the temperature close to zero and wind chills dangerously low, the Georgians tried marching in place and running in

---

[23] "J.," "Interesting Letter from the Oglethorpe Infantry," *Augusta Daily Constitutionalist*, 23 January 1862.

[24] See, e.g., ibid.

[25] Clark, *Under the Stars and Bars*, 45.

circles to keep from freezing. Death by hypothermia hovered over the troops.[26]

Sometime early Sunday morning, a party of soldiers from the 1st Tennessee was sent out to relieve one of the 1st Georgia's picket posts near Sir John's Run. What they found upon reaching the sentry camp horrified them. "I cannot tell the facts as I desire to," recorded Private Sam Watkins in his memoirs.

> In fact, my hand trembles so, and my feelings are so overcome, that it is hard for me to write at all. But we went to the place that we were ordered to go to, and when we arrived there we found the guard sure enough. If I remember correctly, there were just eleven of them. Some were sitting down and some were lying down; but each and every one was as cold and as hard frozen as the icicles that hung from their hands and faces and clothing—dead! They had died at their post of duty. Two of them, a little in advance of the others, were standing with their guns in their hands, as cold and as hard frozen as a monument of marble—standing sentinel with loaded guns in their frozen hands![27]

---

[26] Samuel H. Crump, "From the Augusta Constitutionalist," *Sandersville Central Georgian*, 29 January 1862.

[27] Sam Watkins, *1861 vs. 1882: "CO. AYTCH," Maury Grays 1st Tennessee Regiment or a Sideshow of the Big Show* (Nashville TN: Cumberland Presbyterian Publishing House, 1882; (Dayton OH: Press of Morningside Bookshop, 1992) 30, 163. In his memoirs, Watkins says his detachment was to relieve elements of the 3rd Arkansas and 14th Georgia; later in the book he talks about meeting the parents of one of the dead Georgians, whom he also identifies as being from the 14th Georgia. Thomas Rankin, mentioning the account in *Stonewall Jackson's Romney Campaign*, relates in an endnote that as the 14th Georgia was not with Jackson during the Romney Campaign, Watkins's memory was probably faulty on the regimental designation, though it was unlikely that he imagined such an extraordinary episode. Ray Dewberry, in his *History of the 14th Georgia Infantry Regiment*, places the 14th near Richmond as part of Wade Hampton's Brigade of the Confederate Army of the Potomac, as does the *OR*. Likewise, the frozen soldiers could not be from the 3rd Arkansas, as that regiment had returned to camps northwest of Bath just that evening, after attempting to destroy the Great Cacapon railroad bridge. See Rankin, *Stonewall Jackson's Romney Campaign*, 163 n. 64; Ray Dewberry, *History of the 14th Georgia Infantry Regiment* (Westminster MD: Heritage Books, Inc., 2004) 9–10; *OR*, ser. 1, vol. 5, pt. 1, p. 1035.

Captain Crump's pickets shivered as "the coldest night we ever expect to spend on earth" mercifully came to an end.[28] As dawn slowly approached, Crump received word from one of his sentries that there were Yankees close by. Quickly forming a defensive line, the captain waited for the sight of blue uniforms. Several anxious minutes passed with no sign of Federals. The captain decided to see for himself what was in his front and crept forward. Wrote Crump, "We formed, ready to receive him, and after waiting some time and no one appearing, I advanced to the sentinel, who showed me a military encampment not sixty yards from our position! I had stationed my guard in a Yankee camp in the night time, it being dark, without knowing it. It was a company camp stationed on this side of the river who fled upon our approach, leaving, in their hurry, everything behind them, even their supper, which they had prepared."[29]

The Walker Light soldiers pounced on these "spoils of war." As one writer recalled, "We took formal possession, capturing seven very fine Sibley tents, camp equipage, and their baggage, official and personal. We came out ahead on the Laurel Hill sensation. The tents are very capacious, and will accommodate easily fifteen men, which is quite an important item with us, as we are sadly deficient in good tents. These are as comfortable as a house; besides, we captured any quantity of wearing apparel, jewelry, &c. I have been presented with one of the tents for my Company, which will render my command now independent as regards, bad weather."[30]

Crump was able to outfit himself quite splendidly as well:

> I have also some very superior military works, not to be procured at this time, two magnificent blankets, oil cloth to lay under them, officers' canteens, miniatures, &c. These things were the Captain's, whose name is Hunnewell, hailing from Chicago, Ill. From an inspection of the Captain's effects, they show him to be a gentleman of rare taste; and I don't know any more whom I would rather select, than him from whom to purchase an officer's outfit. He is, no doubt, a fast young gentleman at home; he had two daguerrotypes, one of

---

[28] Samuel H. Crump, "From the Augusta Constitutionalist," *Sandersville Central Georgian*, 29 January 1862.

[29] Ibid.

[30] Ibid.

which is his wife's, which I have; besides his private letters, which I myself shall not read, and shall return, if the opportunity offers.[31]

There Was but Little Sleeping Done that Night

Once again, General Jackson found himself breaking the Sabbath with acts of war. Returning from Bath, Jackson ordered Loring to assist Colonel Rust, who had met opposition in his task to destroy the Great Cacapon trestle. The bridge and adjacent depot were burned, and several miles of Baltimore and Ohio track were ripped up. Jackson next dispatched Lieutenant Colonel Turner across the Potomac under a flag of truce with a message for the federal commander. If the town were not surrendered, the communication read, then Jackson would open with his batteries. "Colonel Ashby," replied General Frederick Lander, "give my compliments to General Jackson and tell him to bombard and be damned!"[32]

While Ashby and Lander were having their parlay, Private Lavender Ray and several of his comrades decided to go down along the river and "reconoiter on my own hook." Investigating several small homes, the Georgians came across more belongings abandoned by the Federals. Ray described their discoveries to his brother: "The Yankees were quartered in the private houses for the winter and had everything fixed comfortable. Some of our soldiers got a great many things such as fine blue overcoats, new jackets, pants, knapsacks, plates, minie rifles, cups, shoes &c. We had a good deal of fun reading love letters, looking at Yankee books, letters &c. ambrotypes &c."[33]

Rebuffed by the Union commander, Jackson gave the order for his artillery to open fire on Hancock at 2:00 P.M. For most of the next hour, shells rained down on the Union troops. Fortunately, most of the civilian population had already fled the town. Though property was damaged, there were no injuries from the bombardment.

Meanwhile, the 14th Tennessee regiment was given the task of bridging the Potomac about two miles upstream. The water was frigid, so progress

---

[31] Ibid.

[32] Rankin, *Stonewall Jackson's Romney Campaign*, 100.

[33] Lavender Ray to his brothers, 12 January 1862, in Thomas, *Letters and Diary of Lieut. Lavender R. Ray*, 51.

was painfully slow. Chopping down trees in the sub-freezing temperatures quickly exhausted the soldiers.[34]

Darkness once more began to descend on the Virginia mountains, and with it came the prospect of another night without shelter. More wintry precipitation blanketed the forests along the Potomac bluffs. One soldier described the difficult conditions: "Sunday night a heavy snow fell covering *terra firma* with a white carpet at least three inches thick. Our wagon train being several miles in our rear, we had to remain in this snow storm without tents or provision, and but one blanket to shield us from that slow-falling, flaky offspring of dew and frost. Of course there was but little sleeping done that night by our boys. Occasionally one, worn down of fatigue, would sink into a disturbed slumber as he sat near the camp fire."[35]

Wiley Leatherwood dubbed the Georgian's encampment "Camp Despair." "It is the hardest camp you ever saw," he wrote, "on the side of a mountain, so cussed steep you have to pull up by bushes. It has snowed, and it is now deep, and here we are, camped in the woods, and do not know where we will go, or what we will do."[36]

Jackson intended to resume operations against Hancock on Monday morning, 6 January, but several factors conspired to upset his plans. Union troops began firing at the Confederates that morning. The Confederates had to seek shelter, but there was little damage. "The next day the Yankees discovered our possition and shelled us for several hours," wrote Private Ray, "but we left our fires and sat under the bottom of the hill and watch their shells which would fly over us and burst in the air without doing any harm." Ray's servant, Dick, arrived with food only moments before the federal gunners touched off their pieces. "Just before they commenced shelling us Dick brought me something to eat and a blanket or two from the wagon. But the balls commenced whizzing so that Dick thought that he had better leave so away he went back to the wagon which was a mile distant."[37]

---

[34] *OR*, ser. 1, vol. 5, pt. 1, p. 392; Rankin, *Stonewall Jackson's Romney Campaign*, 100–101.

[35] Anonymous, "Our Special Correspondence from North-Western Virginia," *Atlanta Southern Confederacy*, 12 January 1862.

[36] Wiley M. Leatherwood, "Highly Interesting from the Gate-City Guards," *Atlanta Southern Confederacy*, 23 January 1862.

[37] Lavender Ray to his brothers, 12 January 1862, in Thomas, *Letters and Diary of Lieut. Lavender R. Ray*, 53.

Federal General Lander was receiving reinforcements, and it would take more than forty-eight hours for the Tennesseans to complete their bridge. Jackson, conceding his chance to secure Hancock had passed, reluctantly decided to pull the army back to Unger's Store. "On the 6th the enemy was re-enforced," the general recorded, "to such an extent as to induce me to believe that my object could not be accomplished without a sacrifice of life, which I felt unwilling to make, as Romney, the great object of the expedition, might require for its recovery, and especially for the capture of the troops in and near there, all the force at my disposal."[38] Jackson would withdraw his troops the next morning. That evening a freezing wind blew through the camps, but fortunately the army's wagons had finally caught up. For the first night since leaving Winchester, the 1st Georgia slept in its tents and blankets.[39]

Throughout the day of 7 January the Confederate troops broke camp and headed back down the road through Bath toward Unger's Store. The wagon trains started first that morning, followed by the different brigades of the Army of the Northwest. Colonel Taliaferro's brigade, including the 1st Georgia, brought up the rear, putting the Potomac River to their backs around noon. Taliaferro reached Bath after dark.[40]

As they passed through Bath, several Georgians left behind notes, taunting the Union soldiers they knew would be following. Illinois troops reentering the town found such messages:

> We are about to leave you, and our comfortable quarters to your tender mercies. If you should happen to pick up anything lying around here, I expect that you will want to keep it as a slight token of our regard, or send it home. How much better it would be for the "liberty boys" if they would go home themselves and leave us poor rebels to enjoy freedom in their own way.
>
> —Company G, 1st Reg't Georgia Vol's
>
> P.S. We are poor rebels and cannot offer a more valuable keepsake, but hope you will prize it for the spirit in which it is given.
>
> —Col. J. W. Ramsey, 1st Georgia Vol's

---

[38] *OR*, ser. 1, vol. 5, pt. 1, p. 392.
[39] Rankin, *Stonewall Jackson's Romney Campaign*, 105.
[40] Ibid., 106.

P.S. Go home, boys! Go Home! We owe you no ill will further than results from your efforts to conquer the Freeman of the South. We will go home gladly when we have effectually defended our borders.

—Company G.[41]

The column continued the march well into the night, straining to keep upright in the treacherous footing. The snowstorms of the past several days had deposited a thick layer. Thousands of feet compressed the snow and turned the roadbed into a sheet of ice. Men, animals, wagons, and cannon slid on the frozen surface.

Taliaferro's regiments, exhausted from the constant effort to keep upright in subzero temperatures, went into bivouac near midnight. Once again, the Georgians and others suffered from the lack of shelter—this time their wagons were too far ahead of the brigade.[42]

For the next two days, the column labored, fighting to move every few feet in the ice and snow. This march would be remembered long afterwards by the veterans of the 1st Georgia as the worst ordeal suffered by the troops—far worse than the retreat following Laurel Hill and Corricks Ford. With temperatures plummeting and snow flying, men and animals crashed to the frozen ground again and again. General Loring barely avoided being crushed when his mount lost its footing and collapsed. The general escaped with only painful bruises.[43]

Private Ray related the conditions to his brother: "The roads were covered with solid ice and the horses would slip upon level ground and almost break their necks. The wagons would slide sideways down a hill sometimes and we would have to pull it up hill and hold it back going down as the horses could scarcely carry themselves up. You can't imagine how we have suffered, a great many say it beats the Laurel Hill retreat." Blood froze in icicles from horses' mangled knees. Jackson himself joined soldiers struggling to move a wagon.[44]

---

[41] Ibid., 108; Charles M. Clarke, *The History of the Thirty-Ninth Regiment Illinois Volunteer Veteran Infantry (Yates Phalanx) in the War of the Rebellion, 1861–1865* (Chicago: Veteran Association of the Regiment, 1889) 48–49.

[42] Rankin, *Stonewall Jackson's Romney Campaign*, 107.

[43] Tanner, *Stonewall in the Valley*, 76; "Ned," "Special Correspondence of the Dispatch," *Richmond Daily Dispatch*, 15 January 1862.

[44] Lavender Ray to his brothers, 12 January 1862, in Thomas, *Letters and Diary of Lieut. Lavender R. Ray*, 54; Tanner, *Stonewall in the Valley*, 76.

Colonel R Says It Is Cruelty and Murder

Taliaferro's Brigade arrived at Unger's Store on 8 January, but it was 10 January before all of Jackson's troops reached the encampment. The general set about to reorganize and regenerate his frazzled command. Horses were roughshod for better footing on the ice, and the soldiers were directed to bathe. Officers, such as Colonel Gilham of the 21st Virginia, who had failed to live up to the general's expectations were reassigned to other duties away from the army. Jackson also fretted over what the federal army might be doing. A week earlier, he had heard rumors that Romney had been reinforced to more than 18,000 men. The rout of seven hundred Virginia militia at Hanging Rock, just a few miles south of his position, only served to increase Jackson's anxiety. He feared that while he was stalled at Unger's Store, Union forces might drive for Winchester and the Shenandoah Valley. A further worry was that Romney would receive additional reinforcements, making the town too strongly held for him to attack.[45]

Scores of sick men had dropped out of the column during the march to Bath and Hancock and made their way back to the hospitals in Winchester. Upon reaching Unger's Store, the flow of ill and injured soldiers became a flood. "I heard that there were a hundred cases of pneumonia in the Arkansas Regt.," reported Private Ray, "about two hundred of our Regt. has been sent to Winchester sick. George Ware came and carried Favor to Winchester he had a bad cold and sore foot. Most of the boys have had colds."[46]

Unable to comprehend what they had endured over the previous week, officers and soldiers alike were openly questioning both Jackson's strategy and sanity. A letter from one of the Oglethorpe Infantry, printed in the *Augusta Daily Constitutionalist*, fairly seethed with resentment: "In writing home two or three days ago to you and to ——, the tone was as cheerful as possible. Now, you shall hear the real state of affairs. I have hitherto written cheerfully, so as not to cause uneasiness at home."

The writer blamed Jackson for the army's woes. "The late trip to Hancock is the most disastrous thing that has yet happened to this Regiment.

---

[45] Rankin, *Stonewall Jackson's Romney Campaign*, 108; *OR*, ser. 1, vol. 5, pt. 1, p. 1018; Robertson, *Stonewall Jackson: The Man, the Soldier, the Legend*, 309–11; Tanner, *Stonewall in the Valley*, 77.

[46] Lavender Ray to his brothers, 12 January 1862, in Thomas, *Letters and Diary of Lieut. Lavender R. Ray*, 54.

This is not the opinion of myself alone; others high in command so express themselves.—Colonel R [Ramsey], says it is cruelty and murder. General L. [Loring] expresses himself as opposed to this winter operation. Our Brigade commander, Colonel T. [Taliaferro], says it is horrible, and that he has done all he could to get his command out of it."[47]

While the general cleanup was in progress, Jackson received a report that galvanized him. The Union army had withdrawn from Romney, most likely from fear of what Jackson might do next and mistaken perceptions of his strength. Turner Ashby's cavalry was holding the town. By the 13th, the Valley Army was again on the march. Once again, the elements conspired to impede the army's progress. Melting snow turned the road into bottomless mud. Later in the day sleet and snow coated the men as they struggled forward. Footwear fell to pieces under such severe conditions. "In the bleak climate of North Western Virginia," wrote Second Lieutenant Evan P. Howell of the Washington Rifles, "the ground covered one foot deep with snow, with the meager protection of a common tent and half the time not even that, traveling in the day over the rough frozen road, some men with their bare feet on the ground. This is no exaggerated picture, we see it every day. I marched day before yesterday seven miles with my toes on the icy road, having worn out the second pair of shoes since I left Winchester." The Stonewall Brigade entered Romney on the 15th, followed two days later by General Loring's straggling command.[48]

The scene that greeted the Confederates as they approached Romney was sobering. Robert L. Dabney, who would later become Jackson's chief of staff, wrote in his biography of the general:

> Nearly every dwelling, mill, and factory, between that place and Romney, was consumed; the tanneries were destroyed, and the unfinished hides slit into ribbons; the roadside was strewed with the carcasses of milk-kine, oxen, and other domestic animals, shot down in mere wantonness. As they came in view of the town, lately smiling in the midst of rural beauty, scarcely anything appeared, by which it could be recognized by its own children, save the everlasting hills which surround it. Gardens, orchards, and out-buildings, with their

---

[47] "J.," "Interesting Letter from the Oglethorpe Infantry," *Augusta Daily Constitutionalist*, 23 January 1862.

[48] Tanner, *Stonewall in the Valley*, 78; Evan P. Howell, Untitled article, *Sandersville Central Georgian,* 5 February 1862.

> enclosures, were swept away; the lawns were trampled by cavalry horses into mire; many of the dwellings were converted into stables, and the blinds and wainscot torn down for fuel; and every church, save one, which the federal commander reserved for the pious uses of his own chaplains, was foully desecrated.[49]

Jackson now had the prize he had long coveted, but he was not satisfied. He wanted to continue forward, to try to secure a section of the Baltimore and Ohio Railroad by destroying the New Creek Railroad Bridge, some twenty miles away near Cumberland, Maryland. Jackson also believed there might be large amounts of provisions stored there, including much needed medical supplies. He therefore made up orders for another advance, selecting his Stonewall Brigade and that of Colonel Taliaferro.[50]

The officers and soldiers of the Army of the Northwest would have none of it. Most of Taliaferro's regiments were decimated by sickness and injuries. Jackson's other units, including the Stonewall Brigade, were not in much better condition. Forced to recognize the demoralized and destitute state of Loring's brigades, Jackson gave up on the idea:

> On last Friday night I designed moving rapidly with my old brigade and one of General Loring's, for the purpose of destroying one of the railroad bridges across the North Branch of the Potomac west of Cumberland and thus cut off their supplies from the west, and consequently force them to reduce their army in front of me; but as General Loring's leading brigade, commanded by Colonel Taliaferro, was not in a condition to move, the enterprise had to be abandoned. Since leaving Winchester, on the 1st instant, the troops have suffered greatly, and General Loring has not a single brigade in a condition for active operations, though in a few days I expect they will be much improved, and will, if placed in winter quarters, be able to hold this important portion of the valley.[51]

Believing the Army of the Northwest was "very much demoralized,"[52] Jackson instructed Loring to have his brigades encamp in Romney, along

---

[49] R. L. Dabney, *Life and Campaigns of Lieut.-Gen. Thomas J. Jackson (Stonewall Jackson)* (New York: Blelock and Co., 1866) 270.

[50] *OR*, ser. 1, vol. 5, pt. 1, p. 1033.

[51] Ibid., 1039, 393.

[52] Ibid., 1039.

with three cavalry companies and thirteen cannon.[53] Jackson's motive for leaving Loring's entire command (three brigades) in Romney, while returning to Winchester with a single brigade may have been intended to give the Northwesterners time to recuperate. Jackson wrote later that this disposition "enabled me to avoid dividing his command."[54] Unfortunately, the general's continued failure to involve Loring in his planning, or even to explain his reasoning, gave rise to a belief that the Army of the Northwest was being left to fend for itself in an exposed, worthless position. Certain that "Tom Fool" was pulling his "pets" back to enjoy warm quarters in Winchester, Loring's troops seethed.

On 23 January, Jackson left for Winchester. As the Stonewall Brigade formed ranks to leave Romney, they let out a loud cheer. "Jackson's Lambs!" yelled back Loring's incensed soldiers as they watched the Virginians march away.[55]

It Would Move the Heart

The 1st, along with Loring's other regiments, settled in as best they could, but a stench permeated the air. Before the Federals evacuated Romney, they filled the courthouse with piles of garbage and rotting meat.[56] "We pitched camp near the town, where we remained over two weeks," recalled Lieutenant Howell, "during which time we never saw the sun, owing to the awful weather of rain, snow and sleet alternately, and frequently all at the same time. The roads were knee-deep in muddy slush and ice making picket duty an almost unbearable hardship. The men got the blues and became discontented and began to inquire of each other, 'What are we here for, anyhow?' Both officers and men were on the verge of mutiny."[57] "This is the worst camping place we ever had," wrote Private David Young of the Gate City Guards, "on the side of a mountain and raining nearly all the time."[58]

---

[53] Ibid., 393.

[54] Ibid.

[55] Tanner, *Stonewall in the Valley*, 81.

[56] Ibid.

[57] Evan P. Howell, "Old Stonewall and the Boys," *Atlanta Constitution*, as quoted in the *Cumberland (MD) Evening Times*, 12 October 1905.

[58] "The Sufferings and Privations of the Gate City Guards and the 1st Ga. Regt," *Atlanta Southern Confederacy*, 16 February 1862.

Union garrisons had denuded the area around Romney of forage. Loring dispatched wagons to the nearby town of Moorefield in search of supplies. Deciding after the fact that the train might be exposed to attack by federal cavalry, Loring ordered Captain John A. Houser of the Southern Rights Guard to take a detachment out to guard the wagons. Houser's squad, selected from several companies, left late that night, making their way through deep snow and freezing temperatures. When they reached a creek, debate broke out whether to ford the deep water or turn back. "Some spoke of returning to camp," wrote Private Oscar Cantrell of the Newnan Guards, "and some said that it was too cold to wade, while others said they would follow the captain wherever he went. The captain led the way, and the whole party followed, and in a short time the dread was over; but they had scarcely traveled a hundred yards before the water on their clothes was frozen to ice. They soon got some fire, and took a complete thawing." Meeting up with the wagons, Houser's patrol escorted them back to town.[59]

The rigors of the past few weeks had ravaged the 1st Georgia. Some companies were barely at squad strength. "Our Regiment left Winchester with seven hundred men," complained Howell to his uncle, "and brought to Romney only two hundred and forty men. The Washington Rifles left Winchester with sixty-two men and now have twenty-five. Two-thirds of our Regiment are now sick enough to be in the Hospital.... It would move the heart of any one who is not in the army (for all of us are used to it,) to go through this camp and hear the terrible coughing—some coughing until they vomit. Yet we have no Hospital for our sick. Few men at home have any idea what we are undergoing, nor is it possible to tell all we have stood."[60]

Officers were not spared from the rampant illness. Lieutenant Colonel Thompson, along with Captain Hanvey and Lieutenant Thomas Swint of the Newnan Guard, was sick in Winchester. Captain Horton B. Adams of the Oglethorpe Infantry was absent, and Captain Wilkins of the Southern Guard was on his way home to Georgia after receiving leave "to recruit his health." While passing through Richmond, Wilkins called on Colonel Ramsey,

---

[59] Richard A. Sauers, *The Devastating Hand of War: Romney, West Virginia, during the Civil War* (Glen Ferris WV: Gauley Mount Press, 2000) 30; Oscar A. Cantrell, *Sketches of the First Regiment Georgia Vols.: Together with the History of the 56th Regiment Georgia Vols., to January 1, 1864* (Atlanta GA: Intelligencer Steam Power Presses, 1864) 15.

[60] Evan P. Howell, untitled article, *Sandersville Central Georgian*, 5 February 1862.

confined to a bed and "prostrated by sickness." Command of the regiment devolved on Major James Anderson.[61]

Lieutenant J. V. H. Allen reported the decimated condition of his company to headquarters: "As commanding officer of the Oglethorpe Infantry, I returned twenty men and two commissioned officers present, said officers being Lieut. Foreman and myself." Allen was appalled at the state of the other companies:

> The Walker Light Infantry reported eight men and two officers, Capt. Crump and Lieut. Russell. The Newnan Guards had eighteen men, the Quitman Guards about twenty, these two companies being the largest in the 1st Georgia regiment. The Gate City Guards reported about the same number. The Dahlonega Volunteers had left about twelve or fifteen men. The Bainbridge Independents about a like number, and so with all our companies, making a total of about two hundred rank and file left in the Regiment, and all of these were really unfit for duty, from fatigue and exposure to the extreme cold weather. The balance of our regiment had been sent back to Winchester on the sick list after our trip to Hancock.[62]

With the hospitals in Winchester overflowing with dangerously ill soldiers, many citizens accepted the sick into their homes. A family took in Isaac Hermann, calling in their doctor to care for him. "Mr. Mandelbawm sent their family physician," recalled Hermann with gratitude, "who prescribed for me. He prounounced me very sick, he did not know how it might terminate. It took all his efforts and my determination to get well after three weeks struggling to accomplish this end."[63]

---

[61] Lavender Ray to his father, 29 January 1862, in Thomas, *Letters and Diary of Lieut. Lavender R. Ray*, 57; "Return of Capt. Wilkins," *Columbus Daily Sun*, 7 February 1862.

[62] "The Oglethorpe Infantry and the Late Expedition to Hancock and Romney," *Augusta Daily Constitutionalist*, 28 January 1862. Some of these shocking numbers can be attributed to shirkers. Dr. Hunter McGuire, Jackson's chief surgeon, declared that he arrested "hundreds of Loring's men who claimed to be sick, had them examined by the surgeons and returned to duty unless they were sick enough to stay in the hospital." McGuire maintained later that he sent a thousand men back to Romney. See Robertson, *Stonewall Jackson: The Man, the Soldier, the Legend*, 315.

[63] Isaac Hermann, *Memoirs of a Confederate Veteran 1861–1865* (Atlanta GA: Byrd Printing Company, 1911) 68–69.

Lavender Ray and several members of the Newnan Guards were accepted into another home. "I am now staying at a private house where I get very good fare. Tim and Chug Mitchell, Will and Bob Barnes, Clements, Sol Hass & Chas. McKinley are staying here also, Chug Mitchell is very sick indeed with the pneumonia. Bob Barnes and Clements are also sick but dangerous, the others have bad colds diarrhea &c."[64] Though most of Ray's comrades would return to duty, Clements would be discharged on 8 February.

Illness claimed the lives of many 1st Georgia soldiers. Richard and Samuel Hines of the Washington Rifles both succumbed to pneumonia, Richard on 24 January, and Samuel on the 29th. Determined to be incapable of returning to service, Isaac Hermann was discharged late in January.[65]

Rampant sickness and the filthy conditions, coupled with officers seething at being abandoned in what they considered to be an exposed and worthless post, fed a growing bitterness among the troops. Without realizing it, "Stonewall" had left behind in Romney a smoldering resentment that soon would flare into a crisis of command.

---

[64] Lavender Ray to his mother, 18 January 1862, in Thomas, *Letters and Diary of Lieut. Lavender R. Ray*, 56.

[65] Hermann, *Memoirs of a Confederate Veteran*, 68; Lillian Henderson, ed., *Roster of the Confederate Soldiers of Georgia, 1861–1865*, 6 vols. (Hapeville GA: Longing & Porter, Inc., 1959–1964) 1:259.

12

Mutiny...and Then Home

"Our company should remember their departed brothers. This community should revere their names. This whole nation should rise up and call their memory blest. If our cause is lost; if our freedom and independence are wrested from our grasp; if devastation and ruin spread their pall over our beloved Southland, our brothers will be free from the blight which may fall in our land. They did all they could do to save us from threatening ruin. If our all is lost it will not be their fault."—Resolution of the Southern Rights Guard after their return to Houston County, 22 March 1862[1]

It's Nothing Less than Mutiny

As discontent continued to simmer in Romney, a meeting of several brigades was called. The agenda centered on the drafting of a petition of protest, spelling out the soldiers' opposition to a "continuation of the campaign."[2] The letter recommended that Romney be evacuated, and the soldiers be returned to Winchester. Captain Samuel Crump and Lieutenant Evan Howell were selected as part of a committee to deliver the letter to General Jackson. As the nervous officers headed for Jackson's headquarters in Winchester, Crump turned to Howell, his voice full of anxiety, "Evan, do you know that this thing means death to this whole blamed committee, for it's nothing less than mutiny!" Howell replied with an air of resignation. "Oh, well, but we've got to go and see the general all the same."

Shaking with trepidation as they climbed the stairs to Jackson's room, the officers presented their letter to the general. In a voice quavering with fear, Howell read the petition. "During this scene," recalled Howell after the war, "General Jackson's face never changed from its unusual mild

---

[1] Warren Grice, ed. *A History of Houston County, Georgia* (Perry GA: n.p., 1934) 157.

[2] Evan P. Howell, "Old Stonewall and the Boys," *Atlanta Constitution*, as quoted in the *Cumberland Evening Times*, 12 October 1905.

expression. When the reading of the resolutions was over you could have 'heard a pin drop.'"[3]

Fearing the worst, Howell and the other officers waited uneasily for Jackson's response. "The general assumed an attitude of deep thought for a moment—a moment when each committeeman's knees smote each other—and then said in a rather weary voice, 'You can return to your commands, gentlemen, and should I need your advice I will send for you.'"[4]

The officers removed themselves from the general's presence as quickly as they could go, "the most relieved set of men you ever saw," wrote Howell.[5]

News of the troops' discontent filtered back to Winchester. From his sickbed, Lavender Ray wrote to his mother:

> There is a great deal of dissatisfaction in the army about Jackson making his men suffer so. There is a about two hundred men with our Reg. now and twenty with the Co. Every Church hospital and a great many private houses are filled with sick soldiers. Capt. Hanvey is sick at a private house here, but the most of our boys have gone to some springs six miles below here. I have never seen an army so completely disorganized as Jackson's is in my life. It was one of the finest in the service when it started out but now is almost disbanded by sickness. There is hundreds of men who will die from exposure of the campaign. All say the Laurel Hill is not to be compared with this.[6]

As if to add insult to the horrible conditions in Romney, the 1st received word of trouble brewing in Richmond. The government, citing Colonel John H. Forney's 16 April 1861 order from Pensacola that mustered the regiment into Confederate service, deemed that the Georgians' term of enlistment would continue until that date in 1862. The news came as a shock to the regiment, which considered its term of service as having commenced on 18 March. To exhausted soldiers weary of war and homesick for their loved ones, the suggestion that they might be held in the army for an

---

[3] Ibid.

[4] Ibid.

[5] Ibid.

[6] Lavender Ray to his mother, 18 January 1862, in Ruby Felder Ray Thomas, comp., *Letters and Diary of Lieut. Lavender R. Ray, 1861–1865, comp. and ed. by his daughter Ruby Felder Ray (Mrs. Eli. A. Thomas)* (Atlanta GA: n.p., 1949), typed manuscript (Morrow GA: Georgia Department of Archives and History) 56–57.

additional month was sickening. Officers from every company (except the Southern Guard) met on 21 January to compose a letter to Governor Brown decrying this outrage: "Sir: We a portion of the officers of the 1st Regt. of Ga. Vol. Now in the midst of the most intolerable sufferings that soldiers ever encountered desire to address to your Excellency in behalf of ourselves and associates in arms a petition for the exercise of your Executive influence touching the time of discharge of this command from service."[7]

Declaring it was not their fault that the Confederate government took so long to muster the regiment into service, the officers insisted that they had been paid by the government for "services commencing on the 18th day of March 1861," and that as such, "such service must have its limitation the 18th day of March 1862."[8]

The Georgians stated flatly they could not be made to serve beyond 18 March. "We deny the *right* of the Confederate Government to any military service from this Regt. after the 18th day of March 1862—as founded in any just interpretation of our contract—and assert that the Government is estopped from any other construction than that we put on that contract by every fair implication from its act & deed in the payment of men and officers."[9] Nineteen officers signed the letter, which was forwarded to Governor Brown on 23 January by regimental adjutant Joseph Palmer.

Brown did not receive the petition until 17 February. Three days later he wrote to Secretary of War Benjamin requesting the regiment be discharged:

> I respectfully request that you will take the case into consideration, and order the discharge of the Regiment on the 18th of March—a measure in my judgement demanded by every principle of right and justice. You will not understand me as being opposed to the re-enlistment of this or any other Georgia Regiments for all reasonable efforts are made on my part to secure their re-enlistment. But decimated as the 1st Regt has been by disease and death, and believing that few if any of the remnant will consent to continue in the service, I regard it not only right, but politic on the part of the

---

[7] Officers of the 1st Georgia Regiment to Gov. Joseph E. Brown, 21 January 1862, typewritten transcript, personal papers of Barry Colbaugh, Lula GA.

[8] Ibid.

[9] Ibid.

Government this remnant, after all their privations and hardships, should have awarded them the justice which they claim.[10]

As Brown's letter was posted, however, matters had already come to a head. The 1st Georgia was no longer in Romney.

This Place Is of No Importance

Morale continued to plummet in the squalid atmosphere of Romney. Whether justified or not, the officers of the Army of the Northwest had convinced themselves there was no strategic or tactical reason that would justify keeping troops in what they perceived as such an exposed location. General Loring requested his chief engineer, Colonel Seth M. Barton, make a survey of the defenses. Barton's conclusion bolstered Loring's opinion: "For a small force this point is indefensible. For a large one (say 20,000), it could be made a strong position."[11]

Colonel Samuel Fulkerson of the 37th Virginia fulminated against the army's plight in a letter to an influential friend, Confederate congressman Walter R. Staples, written 23 January. "This place is of no importance," Fulkerson explained to Staples, "in a strategical point of view; the country around it has been exhausted by the enemy, and its proximity to the enemy and the Baltimore and Ohio Railroad will wear us away (already greatly reduced) by heavy picket and guard duty. Besides this, there is no suitable ground and not sufficient wood here upon and by which men can be made comfortable. We have not been in as uncomfortable a place since we entered the service."[12]

Before mailing the letter, Fulkerson showed it to Colonel Taliaferro, who added an endorsement: "I take the liberty with an old friend, which I know you will pardon, to state that every word and every idea conveyed by Colonel F. in his letter to you is strictly and most unfortunately true. The best army I ever saw of its strength has been destroyed by bad marches and

---

[10] Joseph E. Brown to Judah P. Benjamin, 20 February 1862, *Letters Received by the Confederate Adjutant and Inspector General 1861–1865*, record group 109, M474, roll 20, National Archives Microfilm Publication, National Archives, Washington DC.

[11] US War Department, comp., *The War of the Rebellion: A Compilation of the Official Records of the Union and Confederate Armies*, 128 vols. (Washington DC: Government Printing Office, 1880–1901) (hereafter cited as *OR*) ser. 1, vol. 5, pt. 1, pp. 1055–56.

[12] Ibid., 1041.

bad management. It is ridiculous to hold this place; it can do no good, and will subject our troops to great annoyance and exposed or picket duty, which will destroy them. Not one will re-enlist, not one of the whole army. It will be suicidal in the Government to keep this command here." With the term of many regiments expiring soon, Taliaferro feared it would be impossible to reenlist the disgruntled soldiers. The colonel finished by imploring Staples to help get the Army of the Northwest out of Romney. "For Heaven's sake urge the withdrawal of the troops, or we will not [have] a man of this army for the spring campaign."[13]

Meeting on 25 January, several officers drafted a letter to General Loring, in which they expounded on the hardships their commands had endured. "The terrible exposure and suffering of this expedition can never be known to those who did not participate in it," they wrote. "We regard Romney as a place difficult to hold, and of no strategical importance after it is held. Besides, the country around it for some distance has already been by the enemy exhausted of its supplies." In the absence of Colonel Ramsey and Lieutenant Colonel Thompson, Major Anderson signed this so-called "Romney Petition" as commanding officer of the 1st Georgia.[14]

Loring added a postscript. "As this is a respectful communication, and presents for the consideration of the honorable Secretary of War the true condition of this army, and coming from so high a source, expressing the united feeling of the army, I deem it proper to respectfully forward it for his information. I am most anxious to re-enlist this fine army, equal to any I ever saw, and am satisfied if something is not done to relieve it, it will be found impossible to induce the army to do so, but with some regard for its comfort, a large portion, if not the whole, may be prevailed upon." Loring then sent the letter along through channels. The next person to read it was General Jackson.[15]

Jackson's exasperation with Loring and his troops doubtless worsened as he examined the document. Nevertheless, he passed the letter to his immediate superior, General Joseph E. Johnston, to be sent on to Secretary of War Benjamin. Jackson added his own endorsement, "Respectfully forwarded, but disapproved."[16]

---

[13] Ibid., 1042.
[14] Ibid., 1046–47.
[15] Ibid., 1048.
[16] See, e.g., ibid.

Taliaferro next went over Jackson's head, taking his cause directly to Richmond. Obtaining leave, he presented his case in person to Vice President Alexander Stephens, Secretary Benjamin and President Jefferson Davis. The politicking, bolstered by the officers' petition and rumors of a push by Federal general Nathaniel P. Banks, had the desired effect. Fearing the Army of the Northwest was unnecessarily exposed, President Davis instructed Benjamin to have Loring's men recalled.[17] The secretary fired off a short but direct order to Jackson on 30 January: "Our news indicates that a movement is being made to cut off General Loring's command. Order him back to Winchester immediately."[18]

Stunned by the dispatch, Jackson issued the necessary orders to return the Army of the Northwest to Winchester. Angry at government interference negating his accomplishments, Jackson next forwarded a terse dispatch to Secretary Benjamin in which he complained of the government's interference with his command and asked to be reassigned to the Virginia Military Institute. "If this could not be done," he continued, "I respectfully request that the President will accept my resignation from the Army."[19]

The soldiers of the Army of the Northwest were euphoric when the orders arrived to withdraw to Winchester. Supplies that could not be carried were destroyed. "In the streets of Romney were a great many wagons," wrote Private Oscar Cantrell, "mired to their axletrees, which we burnt, to keep them from the enemy."[20]

Sunday evening, 2 February, supply wagons began pulling out of Romney with the remainder of Loring's brigades beginning their march around midnight. Snow began to fall near dawn, hampering the column's progress. "We braved the fury of the storm," reported correspondent "Nestor" of the *Atlanta Southern Confederacy*, "waded through the snow 6 or 8 inches deep, and marched to Hanging Rock, a distance of 16 miles, by 10 o'clock Monday night."[21] "We traveled all day and night," recalled

---

[17] James I. Robertson, *Stonewall Jackson: The Man, the Soldier, the Legend* (New York: MacMillan Publishing, 1997) 311.

[18] *OR*, ser. 1, vol. 5, pt. 1, p. 1053.

[19] Ibid.

[20] Oscar A. Cantrell, *Sketches of the First Regiment Georgia Vols.: Together with the History of the 56th Regiment Georgia Vols., to January 1, 1864* (Atlanta GA: Intelligencer Steam Power Presses, 1864) 15.

[21] "Nestor," letter to the editor, *Atlanta Southern Confederacy*, 20 February 1862.

Private Cantrell, "wading a great many creeks, after which, in a few minutes, our clothes would be frozen stiff with ice; all the rails near the road were burnt; there was a large rail fence about every ten steps."[22]

Arriving outside Winchester on 6 and 7 February, the Army of the Northwest was kept outside of town to prevent fights with the Stonewall Brigade. News of Jackson's resignation was received by the Georgians and other Northwesterners with glee. Lavender Ray continued to question Jackson's leadership. "Ther is a great deal of trouble among the Citizens and Jackson's Brigade about Gen. Jackson's reported resignation," he wrote. "They seem to think there is no other General in the Confederacy, but I have a very poor opinion of him, he does not know anything about managing a large army. His trip to Bath verifies that. I suppose the cause of his resignation was that him and Loring has had several quarrels and all the officers in Loring's and our Brigades are displeased with him for showing so much partiality to his Brigade."[23]

The Georgians bridled at newspaper accounts that claimed that reports of illness during the campaign were overstated. "Nestor" scolded the editors of the *Southern Confederacy* for just such a piece, writing, "I noticed in your telegraphic column of the 4th instant, a dispatch from Richmond, to the effect, that the Winchester 'Republican' had stated that the reports concerning the many deaths and vast amount of sickness resulting from the hardships and exposure of the recent campaign in this section, have been 'grossly exaggerated.' With due deference to the Editor of that journal, I would state, that he was wrongly informed, and that instead of these reports being 'grossly exaggerated,' the *half* was never told."[24]

After much persuasion by Governor Letcher, General Johnston, and several friends, Jackson withdrew his resignation. The general quickly filed charges against General Loring for neglect of duty and other offences. Loring wrote to Secretary Benjamin, refuting the charges one by one in a scathing rebuttal.[25]

---

[22] Cantrell, *Sketches of the First Regiment Georgia Vols.*, 15.

[23] Robert G. Tanner, *Stonewall in the Valley: Thomas J. "Stonewall" Jackson's Shenandoah Valley Campaign, Spring 1862* (Garden City NY: Doubleday and Company, 1976) 86; Lavender Ray to his mother, 3 February 1862, in Thomas, *Letters and Diary of Lieut. Lavender R. Ray*, 59.

[24] "Nestor," letter to the editor, *Atlanta Southern Confederacy*, 20 February 1862.

[25] *OR*, ser. 1, vol. 5, pt. 1, p. 1066.

To President Davis and Secretary Benjamin, it had become painfully obvious that the clash of personalities between Loring and Jackson had become unmanageable. On 9 February, "for the good of the service," Benjamin directed Jackson to dispatch the 1st Georgia to Knoxville, along with all the Tennessee Regiments from Loring's army, there to join the command of General Albert Sidney Johnston. Loring himself was promoted to major general and ordered to Georgia.[26]

Colonel Ramsey, still recuperating in Richmond, received orders on 19 February directing him to proceed to Knoxville to rejoin his regiment. That same day, the 1st left Winchester for Strasburg, where they would board rail cars to take them to Knoxville.[27]

Before the train traveled very far, however, landslides and a wreck on the rail line ahead forced the regiment to stop at Lynchburg. With the end of the regiment's term of enlistment rapidly approaching, it was decided to cancel their deployment to Tennessee and start them toward Georgia. Orders directed them to Augusta to be mustered out of service.[28]

The soldiers hastily posted letters to let families and friends know of the regiment's imminent return. "We will be home in a few days I suppose," wrote Lavender Ray to his parents, "as we are ordered to deliver all our arms & Government property up tomorrow and receive transpotation to Georgia. Some think we will go to Macon to be disbanded but I do not know that this is true." Ray did not forget to advise his servant's beloved that Dick was coming home, too, writing, "Tell Henrietta that Dick will be there soon to see her with enough money to burn up a wet dog and enough pans, ovens, kittles, plates, blankets and clothes to go to housekeeping anew. He is fat and well & I weigh 9 pounds more than I did on entering the servis."[29]

---

[26] Ibid., 1070–71.

[27] US War Department, *Special Orders of the Adjutant and Inspector General's Office, Confederate States*, 5 vols., National Archives and Records Administration (Washington DC: Government Printing Office n.d.) 2:68; Lavender Ray to his brother, 2 March 1862, in Thomas, *Letters and Diary of Lieut. Lavender R. Ray*, 60.

[28] Possibly as a result of Gov. Brown's 20 February letter to Secretary of War Benjamin.

[29] Lavender Ray to his brother, 2 March 1862, in Thomas, *Letters and Diary of Lieut. Lavender R. Ray*, 62–63.

On 3 March the Georgians turned their weapons and accoutrements over to troops of General E. Kirby Smith, then packed for their final journey as the 1st Georgia Regiment.[30]

A Hearty Welcome Home

For the families and friends in Georgia, the news that their men were returning was cause for elation, and they rushed to plan lavish homecomings. A writer to the *Columbus Daily Sun*, signing himself as "Suggester," proposed a joyous welcome for the Southern Guard:

> I see it stated, that the 1st Georgia Regiment will soon return to their homes, to be mustered out of service. It seems to me a fitting occasion to extend "a warm and cheerful welcome" to our brave defenders. Perhaps no regiment has done more service and undergone more exposure than this regiment. Columbus is honored with one company under command of Captain Wilkins in this regiment. I respectfully suggest, that on their arrival, our citizens tender them a public dinner worthy of the occasion, and the brave soldiers who compose Capt. Wilkins command.—Will our fair women take this matter in hand, and arrange for their reception in a body, and escort to proper quarters until the hour of dining?[31]

It was a circuitous route home. From Lynchburg, the regiment traveled to Petersburg, just south of Richmond, then through Wilmington, North Carolina. They arrived at Kingsville, South Carolina, outside of Columbia, on 8 March. The owner of the local hotel saw an opportunity to make some money from the influx of soldiers. Unfortunately, the Dutch tavern keeper was unprepared for the hungry and unruly Georgians. "They agreed to set supper for us," recalled Private Cantrell, "[but] there was only room at the table for about fifty persons to sit; a great many members of the regiment had taken a little more than an average supply of whisky, and while supper was preparing several fights took place in the passage near the dining-room door."

Complete chaos erupted when the food was served. "As soon as supper was announced," wrote Cantrell, "there was a general rush made for the dining-room. The door-keeper, who tried to keep order, was soon knocked

[30] Cantrell, *Sketches of the First Regiment Georgia Vols.*, 16.
[31] "Suggester," "Honor the Brave!" *Columbus Daily Sun*, 7 March 1862.

down and run over. Finding that getting in at the door was a very slow process, they soon began to leap in at the windows, and in a few minutes the dining-room was crowded, and in the shortest time imaginable everything was taken off the table; all was 'broken loose,' and every man was for himself."[32]

Soldiers who so recently had been starving could not be restrained. Cantrell continued,

> Some had sugar-dishes, filling their pockets with sugar, and some had coffee-pots turned almost upside down, drinking coffee out of the spouts, while others were drinking coffee out of plates; one soldier took a ball of butter from the table, and meeting with another who had a loaf of bread, he soon effected an exchange of half the butter for half the bread; he pulled the butter apart with his hands; the remaining half of the butter he spread on his bread with his right hand, which reminded me of a mason spreading mortar on his bricks with a trowel. I visited the kitchen, and a crowd of soldiers were standing around the stove busily engaged in eating a half-cooked tripe. Everything was in a perfect uproar, and a great many dishes were broken before supper was over. The old Dutch lady, with her peculiar way of talking, was all the time abusing us. The old Dutchman was very much frightened, and he did not collect a cent out of the regiment.[33]

The citizens of Augusta were preparing a lavish welcome for the 1st. The railroad depot had been decrated with flags and boughs of evergreens. Over the station's entrance was an arch with the words, "A Hearty Welcome Home."[34] A short distance up the street from the depot was a wreath, hung from more evergreens stretched from one side of the street to the other.[35]

The regiment was expected to arrive around 10:00 A.M. on 9 March, but the train was early and pulled into Augusta as the sun was rising. As a result, there were few people at the depot when the soldiers disembarked. Once the citizens realized the regiment had arrived, they rushed out to greet the troops. Private Cantrell was overwhelmed by the enthusiastic welcome. "The ladies in large numbers favored us with their presence," he wrote.

---

[32] Cantrell, *Sketches of the First Regiment Georgia Vols.*, 16–17.

[33] See, e.g., ibid.

[34] Anonymous, "Arrival and Discharge of the First Georgia," *Augusta Chronicle and Sentinel*, 10 March 1862.

[35] Ibid.

"The regiment was marched to the different hotels, two companies stopping together. We had the best fare the city afforded, free of charge."[36]

The next day, the regiment marched from the depot to the city bell tower, where they were formed into a square beneath "Big Steve." Colonel Ramsey gave a short speech in which he "returned thanks to the officers and men for the patience and zeal which had always marked their career, for the strict discipline they had maintained, for their kindness and affection to each other."[37] Ramsey challenged the men, saying "after they had returned to their homes and recuperated their energies, to return once more to the service, to vindicate the homes and name of Georgia, and add new glories to the First Regiment."[38]

Former lieutenant colonel James O. Clarke also appeared, coming out to address the regiment. After the speakers finished, three cheers rose from the ranks. Adjutant Joseph Palmer read the order of discharge, mustering the regiment out of Confederate service. The gallant soldiers of the 1st Georgia Infantry were private citizens once more.[39]

Many of the ex-soldiers scattered back into town—some to sleep, others to eat, but the majority to make arrangements for their return home. Remaining in ranks, the Oglethorpe Infantry marched to the city cemetery, where they held a brief prayer vigil over the graves of William Holmes and William Miller. Afterward the Oglethorpes escorted another local company, the Augusta Guards, to a presentation to receive a new flag.[40]

Over the next few days the men left Augusta, spreading across the state to their homes and families. Editor Joseph Medlock welcomed the Washington Rifles back to Sandersville: "[T]he train from Augusta Monday evening last, brought back to their anxious friends, our brave boys of the Washington Rifles. The joy that was felt can only be realized by those who participated in it."

Medlock then laid bare his personal sorrow.

---

[36] Cantrell, *Sketches of the First Regiment Georgia Vols.*, 17.

[37] Anonymous, "Arrival and Discharge of the First Georgia," *Augusta Chronicle and Sentinel*, 10 March 1862.

[38] Anonymous, "The First Georgia Regiment," *Augusta Daily Constitutionalist*, 11 March 1862. The officially recorded date of the regiment's muster has been recorded as either 15 or 18 March 1862.

[39] Ibid.

[40] See, e.g., ibid.

> [B]ut we mourn a brother dead. For weeks and months had we looked forward to the return of the Rifles, for then HE would once again gladden our hearts by his presence. But the hand of disease fell heavily upon him. When the Regiment left Winchester he was confined to the hospital. He now sleeps his last sleep in that far off land. Yes EUGENE is dead! If we only knew that some friend was with him in his last moments to hear his last request; but if so we know not who that friend was, as the company were far on their way homeward. But he has given up his life in a noble cause, and we try to say 'thy will be done.'[41]

Atlanta also welcomed home its soldiers. "The 'Gate City Guards' of this city," reported the *Intelligencer*,

> or at least most of them, have already reached their homes. We have had the pleasure of shaking hands with a number of them and cordially welcome them all home.... We hope that promotion will follow all the field officers of the regiment—and especially that it will soon overtake Lieut. Col. Thompson of this city, than whom none more deserves it, and but few as well qualified to lead a regiment in the field. The service cannot now well spare such men, and those in authority ought to see to it that they be tendered positions to which they are entitled, and in which their military capacity and gallantry may be made useful to the South.[42]

As the men came home, they were mindful of those who did not return with them. In the Southern Rights Guard of Perry, three brothers out of the Felder clan had perished: John R., Lawrence, and Rufus McPherson. Their mother, though grieving, declared "that if she had more sons to give, she would gladly offer them for her country's defense."[43]

Meeting shortly after arriving home, the Guard passed a series of declarations in memory of those lost during the past year. A "resolutions committee," consisting of Sergeant Samuel D. Killen, Sergeant Minor W. Havis, and Private John M. Giles, wrote,

---

[41] J. M. G. Medlock, "Welcome Home," *Sandersville Central Georgian*, 12 March 1862.

[42] Anonymous, "The First Georgia Regiment of Volunteers," *Atlanta Daily Intelligencer*, 13 March 1862.

[43] Grice, *A History of Houston County, Georgia*, 157.

Our joy is mingled with sorrow. We rejoice that we are at home once more. Here is rest and comfort for the weary, way-worn. We have found joyous smiles and bright beaming eyes and warm hearted welcome, but we see sad faces. We are touched by the fact that our return which brings gladness to many hearts but opens afresh the bleeding wounds of others. Our coming but too quickly and vividly brings back recollection of those who went away with us but who have not returned with us, who alas will never return. We admire as heroes those who fall on the battle field facing the foe. Are not these our brothers also heroes worthy of honor who fell victims to disease contracted on the march or in camp? Their names may not be recorded on the pages of history; monuments may not be reared to commemorate their death but we owe them lasting honor and respect. We should cherish their memory in our hearts as sacredly as if their epitaphs were carved in marble in capitals of gold. They gave their lives to their country's cause. Who could give more?[44]

Around It Cling a Thousand Memories

By chance, the 1st became the only one-year regiment from the state of Georgia to be mustered out of service at the end of its tour of duty. The Confederate Conscription Act of 1862 forced all other men to remain in the army, but they were allowed to change their branch of service if they chose. To their credit, most the men of Ramsey's 1st reenlisted in Confederate service. Four companies reenlisted as a body to form the 12th Battalion Georgia Light Artillery. The men of Company C also elected to convert to artillery, forming the Southern Rights Battery. Reorganizing under the same name, the Quitman Guards became part of the 53rd Georgia Infantry. Most of the remaining soldiers joined other commands, going on to serve in nearly every theater of the war.

Just over three bloody years later, the American Civil War ended with Robert E. Lee's surrender at Appomattox, and Joseph E. Johnston's capitulation near Durham, North Carolina. With the conflict over, the soldiers of the 1st Georgia Regiment went about making new lives for themselves and their families. Evan P. Howell of the Washington Rifles was elected mayor of Atlanta and became owner of the *Atlanta Constitution*. Several veterans were successful attorneys, among them Captain Thomas B.

[44] Ibid., 157–158.

Cabiness of the Dahlonega Volunteers and Clinton C. Duncan of the Southern Rights Guard. Simeon F. Speer of the Newnan Guards opened a hotel. Francis Wilkins of the Southern Guard was elected mayor of Columbus. Joseph T. Derry of the Oglethorpe Infantry would write several histories of the war.

Though once again citizens of the United States, few of these men regretted their service to the Confederacy. John W. Tench wrote with pride to a former comrade, "I believed that I was right and so believing tried to do my duty, tried to kill every foe who confronted me, and even at this late day have no desire to go into any repentance meeting with any organizations, either North or South. To all who are willing to let me take my place as a Georgian and citizen of the American Union of the States, without putting me through any political catechism, I say here's your friend, to all others, here's your foe."[45]

Decades passed. Some members of the 1st kept in touch, but there was no concerted effort to assemble the survivors of the regiment. Two veterans, Charles A. Lilly of the Dahlonega Volunteers and Philip M. Sitton of the Gate City Guards (now a resident of Dahlonega), decided it was time to bring the 1st Georgia back together again. The two old soldiers began making arrangements for survivors of the regiment to meet, and on 4 July 1883, 176 veterans of the 1st descended on Gainesville, Georgia. Every company except the Columbus Southern Guard was represented. Major James W. Anderson was selected to be chairman of the meeting, and Evan P. Howell was chosen to act as secretary. The soldiers voted to create a committee whose purpose was to establish a permanent veteran's organization.[46]

Members of the 1st gave several speeches. The frayed battle flag of the Quitman Guards was unfurled. Archibald H. Sneed of the same company came forward, wearing his old uniform. A correspondent for the *Atlanta Constitution* described it as "faded and rusty of course, but around it cling a thousand memories that stirred the hearts of the old veterans as they gazed upon it. The torn and tattered pants, frayed around the feet, told of weary dragging steps on many a march, and the stains and rents in the old gray coat told of many a night when it had served as the robe de noit of its gallant

---

[45] John W. Tench to Young Thompson, 11 August 1885, in the George M. Hanvey papers, Ms 494, Hargrett Rare Book and Manuscript Library, University of Georgia Libraries, Athens GA (hereafter cited as Hanvey Papers).

[46] "H. W. J. H.," "The First Georgia," *Atlanta Constitution*, 5 July 1883.

owner while he had the earth for his bed and pillowed his aching head upon some friendly stone."[47]

That afternoon, the results of the organization committee were read. A permanent 1st Georgia Survivors Association was created. Officers were elected, and a series of resolutions were passed. Resolutions 1, 2 and 3 thanked the organizers, hosts, and the railroad, which had provided transportation to and from the reunion. Additional resolutions remembered those who had not survived the war:

> Resolved 4. That we hold sacred the memory of our dead comrades, who have left us forever, and who will never meet us again. While they died in a cause that was unsuccessful, they were as gallant and true soldiers as ever fought in battle, and we doubt not had they survived, as we have, they would have obeyed the parting injunction of our gallant soldier, General Robert E. Lee, who told us to return to our homes and make as good citizens as we had made soldiers.
>
> Resolved 5. That we are gratified that we have met so many of our comrades who have survived the many changes that have taken place since our first meeting, and that we find them in such fine health and spirits, and so cheerful and prosperous."
>
> Resolved 6. That we respectfully request every member of our gallant old regiment to meet us at our next reunion.[48]

The meeting ended with a stirring speech by Evan Howell, who evoked memories of the veterans' trials while serving in the 1st Georgia. The *Constitution's* reporter was as moved by the address as were the old soldiers, and he wrote, "It was soldier talking to soldier—a man who had fought without bread talking to men who had suffered, marched and camped with gaunt hunger gnawing at their vitals. Was it any wonder that as he poured forth the impassioned story that men whose cheeks never blanched at the cannon's roar, found the tears coursing down their furrowed faces? It is not for outsiders to contemplate such a scene. I draw the veil."[49]

---

[47] "H. W. J. H.," "Reunion Echoes," *Atlanta Constitution*, 6 July 1883. The article identifies Sneed as a member of the Newnan Guards, but he was in the Quitman Guards.

[48] "The First Georgia," *Atlanta Constitution*, 5 July 1883.

[49] See, e.g., ibid.

With the gathering at an end, the veterans mingled before returning to their homes. They would see each other again; Lilly and Sitton's plan had succeeded. The regiment continued to hold reunions for many years. But as time passed, fewer survivors were able to make the trip. The 1898 reunion announcement contained a somber plea: "All members are earnestly requested to be present, as this may be the last reunion of the regiment for a large number of us. We are all growing old and we want to meet once more and talk of old times."[50]

Finally, the reunions ended. The soldiers continued to grow old and pass away. Incredibly, some veterans lived into the twentieth century. The last recorded death of a 1st Georgia soldier was of Private Thomas Marshall, who served in the Dahlonega Volunteers. Born on 25 March 1843, Marshall died on 8 October 1928, at age 85.[51]

William Henry Norwood, who had written to the *Atlanta Constitution* pleading for his comrades to come to the 1883 reunion, concluded his letter with these words: "All who can and feel disposed will have opportunity to spend ten days in that delightful climate and go back in memory to Pensacola, Richmond, Staunton, Blue Ridge, Alleghany and Cheat Mounts, Green Brier river, McDowell; and all along the lines, around the camp fires, through the snows, mud and rivers, and wake up again at reveille and roll call. Don't forget the day."[52]

---

[50] "First Georgia to Hold Reunion," *Atlanta Constitution*, 5 June 1898.

[51] O. Lee Sturkey, compiler, "Gravesites of Georgia Civil War Soldiers," personal research, McCormick SC: n.p., n.d. (in the author's possession).

[52] William H. Norwood, "The First Georgia Volunteers," *Atlanta Constitution*, 20 June 1883.

13

Requiem

When home their footsteps our sad soldiers turned,
This thought, we say, within their bosoms burned:
"All has been lost except an honored name."
No shouting throngs now cheered them as they came;
Yet soon they found, they were not quite bereft
Of ev'ry good, but that the best was left.
Love with bright smiles and fond encircling arms
Banished from saddened hearts all dire alarms,
And from the ragged reb dispelled were sighs
As love and pride beamed forth from those sweet eyes,
That saw in him a hero true and grand
Who'd done great deeds for their dear native land.
—Joseph Tyrone Derry, formerly of the Oglethorpe Infantry[1]

The Angels Are in Sympathy with You

Shortly after the end of the war, Columbus resident Elizabeth Rutherford began reading *The Initials*, a novel about life in Napoleonic Bavaria written by Baroness Jemima von Tautphoeus of Great Britain. A passage in the book caught Rutherford's eye. The paragraphs described the care and decoration of heroes's graves on All Saints Day.

Miss Rutherford, known as "Lizzie," had been active in the Columbus Soldiers' Aid Society, which had been formed during the war to collect clothing and other supplies for Georgia troops in the field and to nurse convalescing soldiers in the local hospitals. After the conflict's end, the Society maintained Confederate graves in Linwood Cemetery.

During a conversation with other Columbus ladies, Lizzie mentioned what she had read in *The Initials*. Elizabeth's cousin, Mary Ann Williams, likely related her own poignant story during the discussion. Mrs. Williams's

---

[1] Joseph Tyrone Derry, *Story of the Confederate States: Or, History of the War for Southern Independence* (Richmond VA: B. F. Johnson Publishing Company, 1895) 148.

husband had been a colonel in the Confederate army. He had died of disease in January 1862 and was laid to rest in Linwood Cemetery. The widow and her four children visited the cemetery almost every day to lay flowers on the colonel's grave. One daughter would pull the weeds from nearby soldiers' burial sites, then cover them with flowers. Sadly, the little girl also died shortly thereafter. Her grieving mother continued to care for the graves, which her daughter had called "her soldiers."

The women excitedly called a meeting of the Soldier's Aid Society. Lizzie was unable to attend, so she entrusted Mrs. Williams to present to the group a plan for setting aside a certain day each year to clean and decorate the graves of Confederate soldiers. From this meeting, the Ladies Memorial Association was formed, and 26 April 1866, the anniversary of General Joseph E. Johnston's surrender, was selected to be the first Columbus "Remembrance Day." Colonel James N. Ramsey was approached to speak at the ceremony, and he accepted gladly.[2]

Federal occupation soldiers, alarmed at the prospect that such a gathering might lead to a disturbance, threatened to prevent the proceedings. Several ladies went to Ramsey, who assured them the ceremony would take place. "I will perform the duties assigned to me," he told the women, "and will assume all responsibility; and by the help of God and the presence of the women and children, I will tell the world of the heroic deeds and patriotic devotion of the fallen comrades."[3]

Despite the opposition of the federal authorities, the commemoration services went on as scheduled. Meeting first at St. Luke Methodist Church, the congregation moved to Linwood Cemetery. Dark clouds were building overhead as Colonel Ramsey began to speak. "Ladies and gentlemen," he began, "we meet to celebrate a sad anniversary. Heaven sympathizes with us, has draped the skies in mourning to suit the gloomy habits of our souls and bear a just remembrance to our fortunes. Amid the wreck of earthly hopes, the loss of liberty and the desolation of our homes, we are here to pay appropriate honor to the memory of our brave comrades who fell by the conqueror's sword."[4]

---

[2] Etta Blanchard Worsley, *Columbus on the Chattahoochee* (Columbus GA: Columbus Office Supply Company, 1951) 304–307.

[3] Anonymous, "Participant Tells Story of First Memorial Day," n.p, n.d., transcription contained in personal papers of Morgan Merrill, Cincinnati OH.

[4] See ibid.

Rain began to fall. Ramsey gazed skyward as the droplets coursed down. "Women of the South," he continued, "be encouraged, the angels are in sympathy with you, and are now mingling their tears with yours over the graves of our noble dead."[5]

Other Georgia towns followed the example of the Columbus Ladies Memorial Association and created their own remembrance societies and ceremonies. Across the former Confederacy, the custom of decorating and caring for veterans' graves spread (though many states chose different days for their observances). Picked up by officials in the Union Grand Army of the Republic, this commemoration has evolved through the years to become the national Memorial Day celebrated every May. Many Southern states celebrate Confederate Memorial Day, which falls on various dates in the different states. Georgia observes Confederate Memorial Day on 26 April, the anniversary of the original commemoration in Columbus.

Colonel James N. Ramsey, along with the other officers and men of the 1st Georgia Volunteer Infantry, have long ago passed from life's stage. Though the regiment's service was brief and did not have a major impact on the procession of the war, its members should be remembered for their suffering and for loyal belief in their homes, families, and way of life. Let us not forget them.

The Companies

Company A, "Newnan Guards"

The Newnan Guards, along with the Oglethorpe Infantry, Walker Light Infantry, and Washington Rifles, joined with the DeKalb Rifles of Stone Mountain to form the 12th Battalion Georgia Light Artillery, commanded by Major (later Lieutenant Colonel) Henry D. Capers. Now designated the Newnan Artillery, the company was the only one that received guns. A train wreck en route from Georgia to Jacksboro, Tennessee, resulted in the loss of several battalion horses. The Newnan Artillery was detached from the 12th and brigaded with General Henry Heth's division of General E. Kirby Smith's Army of East Tennessee. While under Heth's command, the company saw service during the invasion of Kentucky, from Lexington to

[5] Ibid.

the outskirts of Cincinnati. Afterwards, the Newnan Artillery was reunited with the 12th Battalion, which was sent to the coast of Georgia and South Carolina. In 1864 the battalion was sent to Virginia to be incorporated into General Clement Evan's Georgia Brigade. Acting once again as infantry, the Newnan Artillery (the company retained its designation) served with the rest of the battalion in the Army of Northern Virginia until its surrender at Appomattox Court House.[6]

The Newnan Guards were reconstituted as State Guards after the war. On 28 October 1891, an arsonist set several fires in Newnan. The goods from several stores were quickly removed and placed in the streets, and the company was called out to guard the merchandise.[7]

Company B, "Company D of the Southern Guard"

This company did not reorganize. Several members joined the 9th Georgia Artillery Battalion.

Company C, "Southern Rights Guard"

The Southern Rights Guard also elected to reorganize as artillery and joined the 14th Battalion Georgia Light Artillery, mustering in on 26 April 1862. Known as Company A, the Southern Rights Battery, they were commanded by Captain Joseph Palmer, late adjutant of the 1st Georgia. The 14th Battalion was assigned to General Braxton Bragg's Army of Tennessee, and participated in the battle of Perryville. Palmer's battery participated in General John Hunt Morgan's raid across northern Kentucky in December 1862. Commanded by Captain Minor W. Havis, the battery was assigned as part of the Army of Tennessee's artillery reserve and took part in all the campaigns of that command. The battery surrendered in North Carolina in late April 1865.[8]

---

[6] Clement A. Evans, ed., *Georgia*, vol. 6 of *Confederate Military History*, 12 vols. (Atlanta: Confederate Publishing Company, 1890) 23–24, 137–38, 144; Lillian Henderson, ed., *Roster of the Confederate Soldiers of Georgia, 1861–1865*, 6 vols. (Hapeville GA: Longing & Porter, Inc., 1959–1964) 1:252–53.

[7] Anonymous, "An Incendiary at Work," *New York Times*, 29 October 1891.

[8] Bobbe Hickson Nelson, *A Land So Dedicated: The History of Houston County, Georgia* (Perry GA: Southern Trellis, 1998) 112; Ruby C. Hodges, "First Georgia Infantry Regiment: southern Rights Guard, Later Southern Rights Battery," *United Daughters of the Confederacy Magazine* 50/2 (February 1987) 41–42; Terrelle M. Walker, comp., "Southern Rights Battery," http://www.thebriarpatch.com/wbts/havis/havis.html.

Company D, "Oglethorpe Infantry"

The Oglethorpe Infantry reenlisted at Camp Jackson (near Augusta) on 1 May 1862 as an artillery company and was attached to the 12th Battalion Georgia Light Artillery. Having received no guns, Captain J. V. H. Allen requested transfer to the 2nd South Carolina Artillery in Charleston. This request was granted, but the Oglethorpes were to be disappointed. The company left Jacksboro on 9 October 1862 for Augusta, where they remained until 9 December. Meanwhile, Colonel George A. Gordon, commander of the 13th Georgia Infantry Battalion in Savannah, was casting about for two more companies to upgrade his command's designation to a regiment. On 15 December 1862, the Oglethorpes were attached to Gordon's command, which became the 63rd Georgia Infantry Regiment. Designated Company A, the Augustans retained the name "Oglethorpe Light Artillery," as well as the red trim on their uniforms. For the next year and a half, the regiment served along the Georgia and South Carolina coast in the vicinity of Savannah. In early May 1864, the 63rd was ordered to Dalton, Georgia, where it became part of General W. H. T. Walker's brigade of General Joseph E. Johnston's Army of Tennessee. The company was involved in Johnston's (and later General John B. Hood's) Atlanta and Nashville campaigns. On 10 April 1865, the remnants of the 63rd were consolidated with the 57th Georgia Infantry and Colonel Charles H. Olmstead's 1st Georgia Regiment to form the 1st Georgia Volunteer Battalion. Olmstead surrendered in North Carolina with the remnants of the Army of Tennessee on 26 April 1865. Strangely enough, the Oglethorpes began and ended their Confederate service as members of the 1st Georgia.[9]

Several years after the end of the war, the unit was reconstituted as Companies A and B, Oglethorpe Infantry, State Guards. The company's original commanding officer, James O. Clarke, was elected captain of Company B. In June 1877, in recognition for his service, Company B was renamed the Clarke Light Infantry.[10]

---

[9] Walter A. Clark, *Under the Stars and Bars: Or Memories of Four Years Service with the Oglethorpes, of Augusta, Georgia* (Augusta GA: The Chronicle Printer, 1900) 79–80, 85, 97, 197; Henderson, *Roster of the Confederate Soldiers of Georgia*, 6:369; Evans, *Georgia*, 132.

[10] "Clarke's Light Infantry," *Augusta Chronicle and Sentinel*, 7 June 1877.

Company E, "Washington Rifles"

Thirty-three members of the Washington Rifles joined the 12th Battalion Georgia Light Artillery, forming the Washington Artillery, 3rd Company E, under Captain John Rudisill. While at Jacksboro, Tennessee (and acting as infantry), the battalion was ordered to Huntsville, Kentucky, where in conjunction with the 43rd Alabama it was successful in taking Union-held Fort Cliff. After returning to Jacksboro, the battalion was ordered to Savannah, where it was split into two companies due to its size. The Washington Artillery now became 3rd Company B. After a stint in Charleston, the company was reequipped as infantry and sent north to join the Army of Northern Virginia where it participated in the battles of Hanover Junction and Cold Harbor. Rudisill's company was attached to General Jubal Early's corps and forwarded to the Shenandoah Valley. Company B remained with Early through his 1864 Valley campaign and the siege of Petersburg. The unit surrendered with the Army of Northern Virginia at Appomattox Court House.[11]

Several other veterans of the Rifles also organized as an artillery unit, Martin's Battery, named in honor of Captain Robert Martin. The unit proceeded to Savannah, where they received two brass howitzers and four brass Napoleon guns. While there, Martin's Battery assisted in repulsing an attack on Fort McAllister on 1 February 1863. In early May 1863, the unit (now commanded by Captain Evan P. Howell) was ordered to Mississippi, where it was involved in the battle of Jackson on 14 May 1863. On 4 July the battery was enroute to Chattanooga when its train wrecked, killing eight men and all of the company's horses. Attached to General Braxton Bragg's Army of Tennessee, Howell's Battery was involved in the battle of Chickamauga. The battery remained with the Army of Tennessee through its subsequent campaigns. It surrendered in North Carolina on 26 April 1865.

Another group, including Captain S. A. H. Jones, Lt. Weaver Jones, and Sergeant P. R. Taliaferro, formed another company calling itself the Washington Rifles, which was designated Company E of the 32nd Georgia Infantry on 7 May 1862. The regiment served mostly in the Confederate Department of South Carolina, Georgia, and Florida, and was engaged at Fort Wagner, outside of Charleston, South Carolina. It participated in the

---

[11] Henderson, *Roster of the Confederate Soldiers of Georgia*, 1:252–53.

Battle of Olustee, Florida. The 32nd was attached to the Army of Tennessee when it surrendered on 26 April 1865.

The Washington Rifles reorganized as State Guards during the 1870s. The flag captured at Kalers Ford was returned by the federal government to Georgia in 1905 and is in the collection of the Georgia Capitol Museum in Atlanta.[12]

Company F, "Gate City Guards"

Several members joined the 9th Georgia Artillery Battalion and Cobb's Legion. The Guards reorganized in 1876 as a drill company and attended events across the United States and Europe. In 1879 the Gate City Guards toured several Northern cities in a goodwill gesture of peace and unity between the North and South. A new armory for the Guards was constructed in 1881, and in 1901 a monument to the unit was dedicated in Atlanta's Piedmont Park. The Gate City Guard still exists today; its membership comprises commissioned and warrant officers in the Georgia National Guard. The company's battleflag, lost during the retreat from Laurel Hill, is in the possession of the Atlanta History Center and is awaiting restoration.[13]

Company G, "Bainbridge Independents"

The company did not maintain its organization during the war. Several Bainbridge men went across the state line to join Florida units, such as the 8th Florida Infantry and the Milton Light Artillery. The Independents reorganized as state militia in July 1873, but they reportedly had difficulty getting weapons and other equipment from the state. The company received

---

[12] Isaac Hermann, *Memoirs of a Confederate Veteran 1861–1865* (Atlanta GA: Byrd Printing Company, 1911) 79, 81–84; Evans, *Georgia*, 146; US Government, National Park Service, "Civil War Soldiers and Sailors System," http://www.itd.nps.gov/cwss/; Thomas B. Irwin, comp., *Acts and Resolutions of the General Assembly of the State of Georgia, passed at the Regular Session of January, 1876* (Atlanta: H. G. Wright, Public Printer, 1876) 387.

[13] Wallace P. Reed, ed., *History of Atlanta, Georgia: With Illustrations and Biographical Sketches of Some of Its Prominent Men and Pioneers* (Syracuse NY: D. Mason & Company, Publishers, 1889) 481–82.

a new silk US flag on 11 November 1875. In January 1900, the Independents were designated Company I of the Georgia National Guard.[14]

Company H, "Dahlonega Volunteers"

On 25 March 1862, Captain Thomas Cabiness (a resident of Monroe County) came to Dahlonega, most likely in an attempt to reconstitute the Volunteers. Festivities including a parade, speeches, and a dinner were held in tribute to the company, during which several men signed enrollment papers. These men most likely ended up in Cobb's Legion, as the Volunteers never were reorganized. On 22 May 1862, Cabiness enlisted in the 11th Battalion Georgia Light Artillery.[15]

Company I, "Walker Light Infantry"

The Walker Light Infantry was the fourth company to join the 12th Georgia Artillery Battalion. This company remained with the battalion through to the surrender at Appomattox, alongside the Washington Artillery. It did not reorganize after the war.

Company K, "Quitman Guards"

On 6 May 1862, the Quitman Guards reenlisted as Company K of the 53rd Georgia Infantry Regiment, commanded by Colonel Leonard T. Doyal. The 53rd was assigned to General Paul J. Semmes's Brigade, McLaw's Division, of the Army of Northern Virginia. After the Peninsula Campaign, McLaw's Division became part of General James Longstreet's Corps, fighting at Antietam, Chancellorsville, and Gettysburg. When Longstreet's Corps was sent to reinforce General Braxton Bragg's Army of Tennessee, the 53rd found itself involved in the Battle of Chickamauga. After Longstreet's Corps returned to the Army of Northern Virginia, the regiment endured the battles of Spotsylvania Courthouse and Cold Harbor. Now part

---

[14] William Warren Rogers, *A Scalawag in Georgia, Richard Whitely and the Politics of Reconstruction* (Champaign: University of Illinois Press, 2007) 158; Jones, *History of Decatur County*, 323.

[15] Andrew W. Cain, *History of Lumpkin County, 1832–1932* (Atlanta GA: Stein Printing Company, 1932) 146; Henderson, *Roster of the Confederate Soldiers of Georgia*, 6:298.

of Brigadier General Goode Bryan's brigade, the 53rd was attached to General Jubal Early's Corps, and sent to the Shenandoah Valley, then later returned to Lee's army for the Petersburg siege. The Quitman Guards surrendered with General Lee at Appomattox Court House.[16]

The Quitman Guards were reconstituted as State Guards on 5 June 1872. In 1898, the Guards once more were part of a 1st Georgia Regiment, as they left for service in Cuba during the Spanish-American War. Under various designations, the Quitman Guards served in all subsequent American wars, and are now a unit of the Georgia National Guard.[17]

The Players

Colonel James Newton Ramsey

His health broken by the rigors of the Virginia campaigns,[18] Colonel Ramsey returned to his law practice in Columbus. Though several reports stated he was promoted to brigadier general, he never served in that capacity. In 1866, Ramsey was asked to speak at a service honoring Confederate dead held in Columbus's Linwood Cemetery.[19] During a sensational murder trial in 1868 that pitted twelve defendants against a United States military commission convened to prosecute the case, Ramsey was one of several defense attorneys on a team headed by former Confederate vice president Alexander Stephens. Among the counsels for the prosecution was former governor Joseph E. Brown. The defense was successful and the defendants were released.[20]

---

[16] Evans, *Georgia*, 125; Philip Katcher, *The Army of Robert E. Lee* (London: Arms and Armour Press, 1994) 220, 279–80, 285, 289, 295; Monroe County (GA) Historical Society, "History of Quitman Guards and Monroe Musketeers," http://www.thegagenweb.com/mchs/military-history.htm.

[17] See, e.g., Monroe County (GA) Historical Society, "History of Quitman Guards and Monroe Musketeers," http://www.thegagenweb.com/mchs/military-history.htm.

[18] James Madison Folsom, *Heroes and Martyrs of Georgia: Georgia's Record in the Revolution of 1861* (Macon GA: Burke, Boykin & Co., 1864; Baltimore MD: Butternut and Blue, 1995) 9.

[19] Nancy Telfair, *A History of Columbus, Georgia, 1828–1928* (Columbus GA: Historical Publishing Company, 1929) 152–53; Worsley, *Columbus on the Chattahoochee*, 310–13.

[20] Walter G. Cooper, *Official History of Fulton County* (Atlanta GA: W. W. Brown, 1934) 235–39.

Ramsey was unrepentant after the war. In 1868, speaking at the "Bush Arbor" Convention in Atlanta, which was called to protest the new Republican state government, Ramsey declared "that the true men of the South are ready to rally once more under the Rebel flag and try the issue of the cartridge box."[21] The *Atlanta Constitution* reported that Ramsey's speech resulted in a "wild, upheaving applause that shook the hall as he uttered thoughts that breathed and words that burned." James N. Ramsey died in Columbus on 10 November 1870 of "congestion," and was buried in Linwood Cemetery.[22]

Lieutenant Colonel James O. Clarke

Clarke returned to Augusta and raised a new infantry company, the Richmond County Guards, though he evidently did not retain command of this unit. He was commissioned second lieutenant on 29 July 1862 and served as drillmaster at Camp Randolph, outside of Calhoun, Georgia. Later he was transferred to Camp of Instruction Number 2, near Decatur. A post surgeon declared Clarke unfit for field service due to varicose veins. On 3 July 1863, Clarke wrote to Major Jonathon F. Andrews, his commanding officer, requesting he be appointed to captain, so as to outrank the other drillmasters. Instead, he received promotion to first lieutenant on 17 July.

After the war Clarke worked as a contractor in Augusta, and was named instructor of military tactics at the Academy of Richmond County. He was instrumental in reconstituting two companies of the Oglethorpe Infantry and was elected captain of Company B. He was later honored by having the company renamed the Clarke Light Infantry. Clarke died in his mid-sixties in Augusta on 6 December 1889, several weeks after suffering a stroke. Several military units, including his Clarke Light Infantry, escorted his hearse to Magnolia Cemetery. The funeral was said to have been "one of the most largely attended ever witnessed in Augusta."[23]

---

[21] *Speech of the Hon. Edwards Pierrepont in Favor of the Election of Gen. Grant* (New York: William C. Bryant & Co., Printers, 1868) 12.

[22] J. David Dameron, *General Henry Lewis Benning: "This was a man": A Biography of Georgia's Supreme Court Justice and Confederate General* (Bowie MD: Heritage Books, Inc., 2004) 254, 256. Ramsey lies in an unassuming grave covered with bricks, with just a simple stone reading "1st Ga. Regt."

[23] James O. Clarke and H. C. Foster service records, roll 143, Compiled Service Records of Confederate Soldiers Who Served in Organizations from the

Lieutenant Colonel George Harvey Thompson

Reports of Thompson's service after leaving the 1st are elusive although business records place him in Atlanta from March 1863 through May 1864. Thompson died on 18 December 1864. Articles about his father, Dr. Joseph Thompson of Atlanta, mention that George Harvey died while in Confederate service.[24]

Major James W. Anderson

The Newnan Guards, from which Anderson had been promoted, reenlisted as part of the 12th Georgia Battalion of Artillery. Anderson was elected first lieutenant of 2nd Company A of the 12th on 1 May 1862, and captain on 2 November. Anderson was wounded and taken prisoner on 29 September 1864 and sent to Point Lookout, Maryland. He was exchanged on 20 February 1865 and returned to his outfit just before Lee's surrender on 9 April. In the years following the end of the war he was active in reunions of 1st Georgia survivors. After serving for several years as sheriff of Coweta County, Anderson died of a stroke at age sixty-seven on 15 November 1902.[25]

Lieutenant William O. Fleming

State of Georgia, National Archives Microfilm Publication M266, Georgia Department of Archives and History, Morrow GA; Advertisements, *Augusta Chronicle and Sentinel*, 16 and 30 April 1862; Anonymous, "Clarke's Light Infantry," *Augusta Chronicle and Sentinel*, 7 June 1877; Anonymous, "Col. Jas. O. Clarke Dead," *Augusta Chronicle and Sentinel*, 7 December 1889; Anonymous, "Col. Jas. O. Clarke's Funeral," *Augusta Chronicle and Sentinel*, 10 December 1889; Bruce S. Allardice, *Confederate Colonels: A Biographical Register* (Columbia: University of Missouri Press, 2008) 101. The *Augusta Chronicle and Sentinel* stated that Clarke was sixty-five at the time of his death, while the monument on his gravesite says he was sixty-four.

[24]Confederate Papers Relating to Citizens or Business Firms, 1861–65, National Archives Microfilm Publication, Record Group 109. National Archives, Washington DC. M346, Document Number 12, George H. Thompson; Nellie Peters Black, *Richard Peters, His Ancestors and Descendents; 1810–1889* (Atlanta GA: Foote and Davies Company, 1904) 112; R. J. Massey, "Men Who Made Atlanta," *Atlanta Constitution*, 5 November 1905.

[25] Henderson, *Roster of the Confederate Soldiers of Georgia*, 1:212; Anonymous, "Captain J. W. Anderson Dies," *Atlanta Constitution*, 16 November 1902.

Fleming returned home to welcome his new daughter, Mary Caroline, born 4 January 1862. On 4 March he left his family once again as second lieutenant of the 50th Georgia Infantry, rising in rank to become lieutenant colonel of the regiment. As part of the Army of Northern Virginia, the 50th was involved in its battles from Second Manassas (Second Bull Run) to Gettysburg. Fleming resigned on 21 December 1863, after election to the Georgia legislature as a representative for Decatur County.

After his public service, Fleming returned to Bainbridge and raised a family that eventually included eleven children. When the Bainbridge Independents was reorganized in 1873, he was elected captain. In 1880, he was appointed judge of the Superior Court. William O. Fleming died on 4 May 1881 after contracting typhoid fever.[26]

Private Lavender R. Ray

Shortly after mustering out of the 1st Georgia, Ray enlisted in Company H of the 1st Georgia Cavalry and served under General Nathan B. Forrest. In a skirmish near Murfreesboro, Tennessee, in August 1862, Ray's horse was shot out from under him by an artillery shell, but he was unharmed. In July 1863, he was ordered to the Atlanta Arsenal and took charge of the facility's powder storehouse. Ray returned to the 1st Georgia Cavalry on 3 September 1864 as adjutant. One year later he was promoted to lieutenant and assigned as acting ordnance officer in General Alfred Iverson's brigade. On 18 January 1865, Ray was appointed acting ordnance officer for Iverson's Division in General Joseph Wheeler's cavalry corps.

Back in Coweta County at war's end, Ray studied law and became an attorney in 1866. He served as captain of the reconstituted Newnan Guards from 1876 to 1880. Ray was elected to the state legislature and served at various times in both houses.

In 1861, when Ray left the University of North Carolina at Chapel Hill to join the Newnan Guards, he had not completed his course of study. In recognition of his services during the war, the university bestowed upon him an honorary degree in 1911.

---

[26] Henderson, *Roster of the Confederate Soldiers of Georgia*, 1:272; William O. Fleming service record, roll 507, Confederate Soldiers from Georgia; Jones, *History of Decatur County*, 189, 323; Ancestry.com, genealogy entry for William O. Fleming, http://freepages.family.rootsweb.ancestry.com/~mkblewett/d0012/g0000071.html#I06047.

In 1916, after attending a Confederate veterans' reunion in Birmingham, Alabama, Ray became ill. He died in Atlanta on 27 May from complications of apoplexy.[27]

Ray's servant, Dick, stayed at his side throughout the war. Dick's expertise in cooking caused him to be in great demand after the conflict's end. "To know Dick was to be his friend," wrote Ray after Dick's death in 1906.[28]

Private Isaac Hermann

Once he recuperated from his illness, Hermann returned to Georgia, where he was invited to enlist with others from the Washington Rifles in an artillery company. Appointed bugler of Martin's (later Howell's) Battery, Hermann was frequently at odds with his commanding officers. With the battery, Hermann served at Fort McAllister on the Georgia coast and later was involved in the Battle of Jackson, Mississippi, where he was wounded in the arm and face. Returning to Georgia, he entered the Floyd House Hospital, where he was diagnosed with an "enlargement of the heart." Following his convalescence, Hermann remained at the hospital for several months and was appointed general ward master. Accused of being a deserter by Captain Evan P. Howell, Hermann returned to the army, but the post physician relieved him of duty due to poor health. Ordered to Atlanta, Hermann worked in the hospitals there. For the rest of the war, he performed various tasks for the army's medical staff.

Upon his return to Washington County, Hermann operated a small freight company for a short time and reopened his store in downtown Sandersville. During the years following, Hermann served as tax receiver and was on the Washington County Board of Education. In 1911 he published *Memoirs of a Veteran*, in which he related his wartime experiences. Hermann died in 1917.[29]

---

[27] Lucius Lamar Knight, *A Standard History of Georgia and Georgians*, 6 vols. (Chicago: The Lewis Publishing Company, 1917) 4:1960–61; Henderson, *Roster of the Confederate Soldiers of Georgia*, 1:221.

[28] Mary G. Jones and Lily Reynolds, eds., *Coweta County Chronicles for One Hundred Years* (Atlanta GA: The Stein Printing Company, 1928) 374.

[29] Hermann, *Memoirs of a Confederate Veteran*, 105, 142–53, 230–51; Henderson, *Roster of the Confederate Soldiers of Georgia*, 1:258; Ella Mitchell, *History of Washington County* (Atlanta GA: Byrd Press, 1924) 136.

Private James Stokes

At the time the regiment mustered out in Augusta, Stokes was still being held in a Staunton jail for the murder of Private Bernard Meyer. He was later transferred to a prison facility in Richmond, but he was released (without ever coming to trial) sometime near the end of May or beginning of June 1862. It was later asserted Stokes had been criminally insane when he shot Private Meyer and that he had displayed "evidences of it before and after that time." Stokes died in Monroe County, Georgia, in October of 1867.[30]

General Robert Seldon Garnett

With his death at Corricks Ford, Garnett became the first general officer killed on either side in the Civil War. Carried to the William Corrick house, his remains were placed in a coffin and preserved with salt, then escorted to Grafton, where family members retrieved the casket. Garnett lies next to his wife and child in Greenwood Cemetery, Brooklyn, New York.[31] His original monument bears no mention of his military service, but a veteran's stone placed later says "Brig Gen Robert S. Garnett CSA 1819 1861."

James "Tanner Jim" Parsons

Images of those traumatic days in July 1861 were burned into the memories of the Georgians. Parsons, their wilderness savior, was remembered fondly. "Parson proved himself to be a noble, patriotic host," recalled Isaac Hermann in his memoirs.[32] In a letter written shortly after the ordeal, Private James Kinmon wrote, "Though at first we suspected him of being a bribed spy for the enemy, we resolved to follow him even to the

---

[30] T. B. Cabiness to Lavender Ray, 13 June 1884, Hanvey Papers.

[31] W. Hunter Lesser, *Battle at Corricks Ford, Confederate Disaster and Loss of A Leader* (Parsons WV: McClain Printing Company, Inc., 1993) 19–21; W. Hunter Lesser, *Rebels at the Gate: Lee and McClellan on the Front Line of a Nation Divided* (Napierville IL: Sourcebooks, Inc., 2004) 302; Ezra J. Warner, *Generals in Gray* (Baton Rouge: Louisiana State University Press, 1959) 100.

[32] Hermann, *Memoirs of a Confederate Veteran*, 27.

enemy's camp. He proved to be the best friend we had."[33] Praised as a hero for guiding the Southern troops to safety, Parsons was afraid to return to his farm in Unionist West Virginia. Though it was reported that he had been killed by Northern sympathizers, Parsons made his way west to Iowa, where he was taken in by his brother, Robert Slack Parsons. Parsons did not come home to West Virginia until after war's end. He died in Tucker County on 25 August 1887.[34]

Colonel William Booth Taliaferro

Promoted to brigadier general on 4 March 1862, Taliaferro continued to battle with General Jackson, even though he was given a brigade in Jackson's Valley Army, which later became part of the Army of Northern Virginia. Taliaferro was wounded just before the Battle of Second Manassas, and after Fredericksburg was transferred to General P. G. T. Beauregard's command in Charleston. After the war he was both a judge and a member of the Virginia legislature, and he served on the boards of various colleges. Taliaferro died 17 February 1898 in Gloucester County, Virginia.[35]

General William Wing Loring

The charges preferred by General Thomas J. "Stonewall" Jackson were quietly dropped. Loring was given command of the Department of Southwestern Virginia, and later led divisions in the Army of Mississippi and the Army of Tennessee, earning the nickname "Old Blizzards" for his command "Give them blizzards, boys!" After the war, he traveled to Egypt, where he accepted a commission in the Khedive's army. Loring died in New

---

[33] "An Incomplete Letter from James Kinmon, July 1861," in Mills Lane, ed., *"Dear Mother: Don't grieve about me. If I get killed, I'll only be dead.," Letters from Georgia Soldiers in the Civil War* (Savannah GA: The Beehive Press, 1977) 24.

[34] Homer Floyd Fansler, *A History of Tucker County, West Virginia* (Parsons WV: McClain Printing Company, 1962) 165; J. W. Stokes, "The Retreat from Laurel Hill, West Virginia," *Southern Bivouac* 3/10 (October 1884): 66; Louise Frederick Hays, *History of Macon County* (Atlanta GA: Stein Printing Company, 1933) 334.

[35] Warner, *Generals in Gray*, 297–98.

York City on 30 December 1886 and was interred in St. Augustine, Florida.[36]

General Henry Rootes Jackson

Jackson returned to Georgia and accepted a commission as major general in the State Army. Reappointed brigadier general in the Confederate Army in 1863, Jackson served with the Army of Tennessee until his capture at Nashville. Following imprisonment at Fort Warren, Massachusetts, he returned to practice law in Georgia until 1885, when he was appointed minister to Mexico. Jackson died on 23 May 1898 in Savannah.[37]

The Places

Camp Oglethorpe

The camp continued in use for a short time as a staging area for new regiments. In May 1862, nine hundred Union prisoners from the Battle of Shiloh were forwarded to Macon, resulting in a new phase for the facility as a prisoner of war camp. Housing mostly commissioned officers, at one time Camp Oglethorpe contained over 2,300 detainees. By the latter half of 1864, with federal armies penetrating deep into Georgia, the camp was closed and the prisoners sent off to other locations. The location of Camp Oglethorpe was obliterated many years ago; the site is completely covered by a rail yard.[38]

Forts Pickens and Barrancas

Like many coastal fortifications, Fort Pickens remained a military post up until the 1940s. In 1886, the fort served as prison for the Apache leader Geronimo and several of his warriors. On 20 June 1899 a magazine exploded, destroying one of the fort's bastions. Several concrete gun batteries were added over the years between the Spanish American War and World War II.

---

[36] Ibid., 193–94; Sifakis, *Who Was Who in the Civil War*, 395.
[37] Warner, *Generals in Gray*, 149–50.
[38] Richard W. Iobst, *Civil War Macon: The History of a Confederate City* (Macon GA: Mercer University Press, 1999) 125–27, 129, 136, 142–43.

The site of two earlier British and Spanish forts, Fort Barrancas is located on the Pensacola Naval Air Station and is in an excellent state of preservation. The National Park Service administers the two forts as units of the Gulf Islands National Seashore.

Battlefield of Laurel Hill

The terrain around Camp Laurel Hill remains virtually unchanged, except for the installation of a water reservoir for the city of Belington. The Battle of Laurel Hill Association has placed interpretive markers in several locations around the site of the Confederate camp and sponsors an annual reenactment held on the third weekend of July.

Battlefield of Corricks Ford

The scene of the upper ford battle is now owned by Kingsford Corporation, which operates a charcoal plant on the site. The town of Parsons purchased the land at the lower, second crossing where General Garnett was killed. With the help of local preservation groups and the Corricks Ford Civil War Round Table, the town is creating a historic park to commemorate the battle.

Cheat Summit Fort

Federal forces abandoned the fort, also known as Fort Milroy, in April 1862. Logging and coal mining around the site destroyed much of the original outworks. The land surrounding the fortification was taken over by the US Forest Service in 1987, which has preserved the core earthworks. Cheat Summit Fort was listed in the National Register of Historic Places in 1990.[39]

Travelers Repose (Camp Bartow)

The original tavern house burned, and a new structure was built on the site in 1869. The house is now privately owned, but there is an interpretive marker in front. Remains of Confederate entrenchments still can be seen on

---

[39] US Government, National Forest Service, “Monongahela National Forest,” http://www.fs.fed.us/r9/mnf/rec/civilwar/cheatsummit.html.

the hills behind the house, and there is a Confederate cemetery close by. The nearby town of Bartow takes its name from the camp.

Bath, Hancock, Romney

The town of Bath is now known as Berkeley Springs, named for an old resort. Hancock and Romney still maintain their small-town character. A local group, the Bath-Romney Historical Preservation Association, was formed in recent years to commemorate the campaign and the soldiers who participated.

The Ordered Away

Written by Mrs. B. J. Jacobus of Macon, Georgia, to honor the Oglethorpe and Walker Light Infantries as they departed for Pensacola.

At the end of each street, a banner we meet,
The people all march in a mass,
But quickly aside, they step back with pride
To let the brave Companies pass.
The streets are dense filled, but the laughter is still'd,
The crowd is all going one way.
Their cheeks are blanched white, but they smile as they light
Lift their hats to the—Ordered away.
They smile while the dart deeply pierces their heart,
But each eye flashed back the war glance,
As they watch the brave file, march up with a smile,
'Neath their flag—with their muskets and lance.
The cannon's load roar, vibrates on our shore,
But the people are quiet today,
As startled they see, how fearless and free,
March the Companies—Ordered away.
Not a quiver or gleam of fear can be seen,
Tho' they go to meet death in disguise,
For the hot air is filled, with poison distilled,
'Neath the rays of fair Florida's skies.
Hark! the drum and the fife, awake to a new life,
The soldiers who—"can't get away,"
Who *wish* as they wave, their hats to the brave,
That *they*, were the—Ordered away.
As *our* parting grows near, let us quell back the tear,
Let our smiles shine as bright as of your,
Let us stand with the mass, salute as they pass,
And weep, when we see them no more.
Let no tear-drop or sigh, dim the light of our eye,
Or mourn from our lips—as they say,
While waving our hand, to our brave little band—

Good-bye—to the Ordered away.
Let them go, in God's name, in defence of their *fame*,
Brave death, at the cannon's wide mouth;
Let them honor and save, the land of the brave,
Plant freedom's bright flag in the *South*.
Let them go! While we weep and lone vigils keep,
We will bless them, and fervently pray,
To the God whom we trust, for our cause firm but just,
And our loved ones—the Ordered away.
When fierce battles storm, we will rise up each morn,
Teach our young some the saber to wield;
Should their brave fathers die, we will arm *them* to fly,
And fill up the gap in the field.
Then fathers and brothers, fond husbands and lovers,
March! march! Bravely on—*we* will stay,
Alone in our sorrow, to pray on each morrow,
For our loved ones—the Ordered away.[1]

[1] Mrs. B. J. Jacobus, "The Ordered Away," *Macon Daily Telegraph*, 8 April 1861.

Bibliography

Primary Sources

Blissit Family, 1861–1876. Papers. Accession 1977–0365M. Georgia Department of Archives and History, Morrow GA.

Collier, Joseph T. Personal Papers. Microfilm. Civil War Miscellany, drawer 283, roll 21. Georgia Department of Archives and History, Morrow GA.

Fleming, William Oliver. Letters. Southern Historical Collection, Manuscripts Department. Wilson Library, University of North Carolina, Chapel Hill NC. Quoted with permission of William Fleming.

Griffin, Len Mitchell. Papers. Civil War unit files, box 3, accession 3339–17. Georgia Department of Archives and History, Morrow GA.

Hanvey, George N. Papers. Manuscript Collection, Ms 494. Hargrett Rare Book and Manuscript Library, University of Georgia, Athens GA.

Johnson, William F. Personal Papers. Microfilm. Civil War Miscellany, drawer 283, roll 29. Georgia Department of Archives and History, Morrow GA.

Jones, S. B. Personal Papers. Microfilm. Civil War Miscellany, drawer 283, roll 30. Georgia Department of Archives and History, Morrow GA.

Lee, Robert Edward, 1861. Papers. Ms 494. Virginia Historical Society, Richmond VA.

Miller, A. J. Papers. Southern Historical Collection, Manuscripts Department. Wilson Library, University of North Carolina, Chapel Hill NC.

Norrell, James. Letters. Madeleine Anthony Collection, box 7, folder 10. Chestatee Regional Library System, Lumpkin County Library, Dahlonega GA.

Officers of the 1st Georgia Regiment to Governor Joseph E. Brown. Letter. Typewritten transcript. Private collection of Barry Colbaugh, Lula GA.

Ray, Lavender R., 1791–1954. Personal Papers. Box 2. Accession 1949 0012M. Georgia Department of Archives and History, Morrow GA.

Rice, Edmond Lee, editor. *Compiled Civil War Letters of James McDonald Campbell; of the 47th Alabama Infantry Regiment, with a brief sketch of his life*. Unpublished typescript. E495.5 47th.C3. Alabama Department of Archives and History, Montgomery AL.

Rodgers, Robert L. Personal Papers. Microfilm. Civil War Miscellany, drawer 283, roll 58. Georgia Department of Archives and History, Morrow GA.

Sneed, Archibald. Letter transcripts. Private collection of Cheryl Brundle, Macon GA.

Taliaferro, William Booth. Papers. Mss. 65 T15, box 3, folder 4. Special Collections Research Center, Earl Gregg Swem Library, College of William and Mary, Williamsburg VA.

Thomas, Ruby Felder Ray, compiler. *Letters and Diary of Lieut. Lavender R. Ray, 1861–1865, comp. and ed. by his daughter Ruby Felder Ray (Mrs. Eli. A. Thomas)*. Atlanta, 1949. Typewritten manuscript. E605.R263.A4. Georgia Department of Archives and History, Morrow GA.

Turner, Stephen. Personal Papers. Microfilm. Civil War Miscellany, drawer 283, roll 42. Georgia Department of Archives and History, Morrow GA.

Tyus, John L. Letter transcripts. Private collection of Lt. John Powell, USN.

Official Publications

Bohannon, Keith, et al. *Hallowed Banners; Historic Flags in the Georgia Capitol Collection*. Atlanta GA: Georgia Capitol Museum, Office of Secretary of State, 2005.

Campbell, W. J., State Printer. *Muster Roll of First Regiment Georgia Volunteers, 1861*. Atlanta GA: Constitution Publishing Company, 1890.

Candler, Allen D., compiler. *The Confederate Records of the State of Georgia*. 6 vols. Atlanta: Charles P. Byrd, State Printer, 1909–1910.

Compiled Service Records of Confederate General and Staff Officers and Non-Regimental Enlisted Men. National Archives Microfilm Publication, Record Group 109, M331, rolls 57 and 241. Georgia Department of Archives and History, Morrow GA.

Compiled Service Records of Confederate Soldiers Who Served in Organizations from the State of Georgia. 1st Georgia Infantry (Ramsey's). National Archives Microfilm Publication, Record Group 109, M266, rolls 143–145. Georgia Department of Archives and History, Morrow GA.

Confederate Papers Relating to Citizens or Business Firms, 1861–1865, National Archives Microfilm Publication, Record Group 109, M346, Document 12. National Archives, Washington DC.

Irwin, Thomas B., compiler. *Acts and Resolutions of the General Assembly of the State of Georgia, passed at the Regular Session of January, 1876.* Atlanta: H. G. Wright, Public Printer, 1876.

Letters received by the Confederate Adjutant and Inspector General 1861–1865. National Archives Microfilm Publication, Record Group 109, M474, roll 20. National Archives, Washington DC.

United States War Department, *Special Orders of the Adjutant and Inspector General's Office, Confederate States*. 5 vols. Washington: Government Printing Office, 1885–1887.

United States War Department, compiler. *The War of the Rebellion; a Compilation of the Official Records of the Union and Confederate Armies*. 128 vols. Washington: US Government Printing Office, 1880–1901.

Books

Allardice, Bruce S. *Confederate Colonels, A Biographical Register.* Columbia: University of Missouri Press, 2008.

Amann, William Frayne, ed. *Personnel of the Civil War*. Cranbury NJ: Thomas Yoseloff, Publisher, 1968.

Avery, Isaac W. *The History of the State of Georgia from 1850 to 1881.* New York: Brown & Derby, Publishers, 1881.

Black, Nellie Peters. *Richard Peters, His Ancestors and Descendants: 1810–1889*. Atlanta GA: Foote and Davies Company, 1904.

Boatner, Mark M. III. *The Civil War Dictionary*. New York: David McKay Company, Inc., 1959.

Bowers, John. *Stonewall Jackson: Portrait of a Soldier*. New York: William Morrow and Company, 1989.

Brinsfield, John Wesley, William C. Davis, Benedict Maryniak, and James I. Robertson, Jr., eds. *Faith in the Fight: Civil War Chaplains*. Mechanicsburg PA: Stackpole Books, 2003.

Bryan, Thomas Conn. *Confederate Georgia*. Athens GA: University of Georgia Press, 1953.

Cain, Andrew W. *History of Lumpkin County for the First Hundred Years, 1832–1932*. Atlanta GA: Stein Printing Company, 1932; Spartanburg SC: The Reprint Company, 1979.

Cantrell, Oscar A. *Sketches of the First Regiment Georgia Volunteers*. Atlanta: Intelligencer Steam Power Presses, 1864; facsimile copy, Georgia Department of Archives and History, Morrow GA.

Cashin, Edward J. *The Story of Augusta*. Augusta GA: Richmond County Board of Education, 1980.

Clark, Walter A. *Under the Stars and Bars: Or Memories of Four Years Service with the Oglethorpes, of Augusta, Georgia*. Augusta GA: The Chronicle Printer, 1900; Clearwater SC: Eastern Digital Press, 2001.

Clarke, Charles M. *The History of the Thirty-ninth Regiment Illinois Volunteer Veteran Infantry (Yates Phalanx) in the War of the Rebellion, 1861–1865*. Chicago: Veteran Association of the Regiment, 1889.

Clayton, Sarah "Sallie" Conley. *Requiem for a Lost City: A Memoir of Civil War Atlanta and the Old South*. Edited by Robert Scott Davis, Jr. Macon GA: Mercer University Press, 1999.

Coleman, James C., and Irene S. Coleman. *Guardians on the Gulf: Pensacola Fortifications, 1698–1980*. Pensacola FL: Pensacola Historical Society, 1982.

Cooper, Walter G. *Official History of Fulton County*. Atlanta: W. W. Brown, 1934; Spartanburg SC: The Reprint Company, 1978.

Corley, Florence Fleming. *Confederate City; Augusta, Georgia, 1860–1865*. Columbia: University of South Carolina Press, 1960.

Dabney, R. L. *Life and Campaigns of Lieut-Gen. Thomas J. Jackson (Stonewall Jackson)*. New York: Blelock and Co., 1866.

Dameron, J. David. *General Henry Lewis Benning: "This was a man": A Biography of Georgia's Supreme Court Justice and Confederate General*. Bowie MD: Heritage Books, Inc., 2004.

DeLeon, T. C. *Four Years in Rebel Capitals*. Mobile AL: The Gossip Printing Company, 1890; Alexandria VA: Time-Life Books, 1983.

Derry, Joseph T. *Story of the Confederate States: Or, History of the War for Southern Independence*. Richmond VA: B. F. Johnson Publishing Company, 1895; New York: Arno Press Inc., 1979.

———. *The Strife of Brothers, a Poem*. Atlanta: The Franklin Printing and Publishing Company, 1904.

Dewberry, Ray. *History of the 14th Georgia Infantry Regiment*. Westminster MD: Heritage Books, Inc., 2004.

Dowdey, Clifford, and Louis H. Manarin, eds. *The Wartime Papers of R. E. Lee*. Boston: Little Brown and Company, 1961.

Dyer, Thomas G. *Secret Yankees: The Union Circle in Confederate Atlanta.* Baltimore: The Johns Hopkins University Press, 1999.

Evans, Clement A., ed. *Virginia.* Vol. 3, *Confederate Military History.* Atlanta: Confederate Publishing Company, 1890.

———. *Georgia.* Vol. 6, *Confederate Military History.* Atlanta: Confederate Publishing Company, 1890.

Fairman, Henry Clay. *Chronicles of The Old Guard of the Gate City Guard, Atlanta, Georgia, 1858–1915.* Atlanta: Byrd Printing Company, 1915.

Fansler, Homer Floyd. *A History of Tucker County, West Virginia.* Parsons WV: McClain Printing Company, 1962.

Field, Ron. *The Confederate Army 1861–1865 (2): Florida, Alabama and Georgia, Men at Arms Series.* Oxford: Osprey Publishing, 2005.

Folsom, James Madison. *Heroes and Martyrs of Georgia: Georgia's Record in the Revolution of 1861.* Macon GA: Burke, Boykin & Co., 1864; Baltimore: Butternut and Blue, 1995.

Freeman, Douglas Southall. *Lee's Lieutenants: A Study in Command.* 3 vols. New York: Charles Scribner's Sons, 1942; 1970.

Garrett, Franklin M. *Atlanta and Environs: A Chronicle of Its People and Events.* 2 vols. Athens: University of Georgia Press, 1969.

Grice, Warren, ed. *A History of Houston County, Georgia.* Perry GA: n.p., 1934.

Hays, Louise Frederick. *History of Macon County.* Atlanta: Stein Printing Company, 1933.

Henderson, Lillian, editor. *Roster of the Confederate Soldiers of Georgia, 1861–1865.* 6 vols. Hapeville GA: Longing & Porter, Inc., 1959–1964.

Hermann, Isaac. *Memoirs of a Confederate Veteran 1861–1865.* Atlanta: Byrd Printing Company, 1911; Lakemont GA: CSA Press, 1975.

Hewitt, John H. *War: A poem, with copious notes, founded on the Revolution of 1861–62, (up to the Battles before Richmond, Inclusive).* Richmond VA: West and Johnson, 1862.

Holcomb, Brent H. Vol. 2, *Marriage and Death Notices from the "Southern Christian Advocate," 1861–1867.* Greenville SC: Southern Historical Press, 1980.

Iobst, Richard W. *Civil War Macon: The History of a Confederate City.* Macon GA: Mercer University Press, 1999.

Jones, Frank S. *History of Decatur County Georgia.* Spartanburg SC: The Reprint Company, 1980.

Jones, Mary G., and Lily Reynolds, eds. *Coweta County Chronicles for One Hundred Years*. Atlanta: The Stein Printing Company, 1928.

Jones, Terry L. *Lee's Tigers: The Louisiana Infantry in the Army of Northern Virginia*. Baton Rouge: Louisiana State University Press, 1987.

Katcher, Philip. *American Civil War Armies (5); Men at Arms Series*. Oxford: Osprey Publishing, 1989.

———. *Flags of the American Civil War (1); Confederate, Men at Arms Series*. Oxford: Osprey Publishing, 1992.

———. *The Army of Robert E. Lee*. London: Arms and Armour Press, 1994.

Knight, Lucius Lamar. *A Standard History of Georgia and Georgians*. 6 vols. Chicago: The Lewis Publishing Company, 1917.

Krick, Robert K. *Lee's Colonels: A Biographical Register of the Field Officers of the Army of Northern Virginia*. 2nd ed. Dayton OH: Press of Morningside Bookstore, 1984.

Lane, Mills, ed. *"Dear Mother: Don't grieve about me. If I get killed, I'll only be dead." Letters from Georgia Soldiers in the Civil War*. Savannah GA: The Beehive Press, 1977.

Lesser, W. Hunter. *Battle at Corricks Ford: Confederate Disaster and Loss of a Leader*. Parsons WV: McClain Printing Company, Inc., 1993.

———. *Rebels at the Gate: Lee and McClellan on the Front Line of a Nation Divided*. Napierville IL: Sourcebooks, Inc., 2004.

Livingston, Gary. *Cradled in Glory: Georgia Military Institute, 1851–1865*. Cooperstown NY: Caisson Press, 1997.

Lyle, Thomas E., Larry O. Blair, and Debra S. Lyle. *Organizational Summary of Military Organizations From Georgia in the Confederate States of America*. Louisville TN: Byrons Printing, 1999.

Martin, John H. *Columbus, Geo., From Its Selection as a "Trading Town" in 1827, to Its Partial Destruction by Wilson's Raid, in 1865*. Columbus GA: Thomas Gilbert, Book Printer and Binder, 1874.

McWhiney, Grady. *Braxton Bragg and Confederate Defeat*. 2 vols. Tuscaloosa: University of Alabama Press, 1969.

Merrill, Catharine. *The Soldier of Indiana in the War for the Union*. 2 vols. Indianapolis IN: Merrill and Company, 1866.

Mitchell, Ella. *History of Washington County*. Atlanta: n.p., 1924; Greenville SC: The Southern Historical Press, Inc., 2000.

Monroe County Historical Society. *Monroe County, Georgia: A History.* Forsyth GA: n.p., 1979.

Moore, Frank, ed. *The Rebellion Record: A Diary of American Events, with Documents, Narratives, Illustrative Incidents, Poetry, Etc.* New York: G. P. Putnam, 1861.

Nelson, Bobbe Hickson. *A Land So Dedicated: The History of Houston County, Georgia.* Perry GA: Southern Trellis, 1998.

Nevins, Allan. *Prologue to Civil War 1859–1861.* Vol. 2, *The Emergence of Lincoln.* New York: Charles Scribners Sons, 1947–1950.

Newell, Clayton R. *Lee vs. McClellan: The First Campaign.* Washington: Regnery Publishing, Inc., 1996.

Newnan-Coweta Historical Society. *History of Coweta County, Georgia.* Roswell GA: Wolfe Associates, 1988.

Parks, Joseph H. *Joseph E. Brown of Georgia.* Baton Rouge: Louisiana State University Press, 1977.

Pearce, George F. *Pensacola during the Civil War: A Thorn in the Side of the Confederacy.* Gainesville FL: University Press of Florida, 2000.

Phillips, Ulrich Bonnell. *The Life of Robert Toombs.* New York: The MacMillan Company, 1913.

Poland, Charles P., Jr. *The Glories of War: Small Battle and Early Heroes of 1861.* Bloomington IN: AuthorHouse, 2004.

Raab, James W. *W. W. Loring: Florida's Forgotten General.* Manhattan KS: Sunflower University Press, 1996.

Radical Rule: Military Outrage in Georgia. Louisville KY: John P. Morton and Company, 1868.

Rankin, Thomas M. *Stonewall Jackson's Romney Campaign; January 1–February 20, 1862.* Lynchburg VA: H. E. Howard, Inc., 1994.

Reed, Wallace P., ed. *History of Atlanta, Georgia: With Illustrations and Biographical Sketches of Some of its Prominent Men and Pioneers.* Syracuse NY: D. Mason & Company, Publishers, 1889.

Rigdon, John. *Historical Sketch and Roster of the Georgia 1st Infantry Regiment (Ramsey's).* Clearwater SC: Eastern Digital Resources, 2006.

Riley, Elihu S. *"Stonewall Jackson": A Thesaurus of Anecdotes of and Incidents in the Life of Lieut. General Thomas Jonathan Jackson, CSA.* Annapolis MD: s.n., 1920.

Robertson, James I. *Stonewall Jackson: The Man, the Soldier, the Legend.* New York: MacMillan Publishing USA, 1997.

Rodgers, Thomas G., and Richard M. Harrison. *Never Give up This Field: Georgia Troops in the Civil War*. Norcross GA: Wordsworth Group, 1989.

Rogers, William Warren. *A Scalawag in Georgia, Richard Whitely and the Politics of Reconstruction*. Champaign IL: University of Illinois Press, 2007.

Sarris, Jonathan Dean. *A Separate Civil War: Communities in Conflict in the Mountain South*. Charlottesville VA: University of Virginia Press, 2006.

Sauers, Richard A. *The Devastating Hand of War: Romney, West Virginia during the Civil War*. Glen Ferris WV: Gauley Mount Press, 2000.

Sifakis, Stewart. *Compendium of the Confederate Armies, South Carolina and Georgia*. New York: Facts On File, 1995.

———. *Who Was Who in the Civil War*. New York: Facts On File, 1988.

Smedlund, William S. *Camp Fires of Georgia's Troops, 1861–1865*. Marietta GA: Kennesaw Mountain Press, 1994.

Smith, Gordon Burns. *Counties and Commanders*. Pt. 1, Vol. 2, *History of the Georgia Militia, 1783–1861*. Milledgeville GA: Boyd Publishing, 2001.

———. *Counties and Commanders*. Pt. 2, Vol. 3, *History of the Georgia Militia, 1783–1861*. Milledgeville GA: Boyd Publishing, 2001.

———. *The Companies*. Vol. 4, *History of the Georgia Militia, 1783–1861*. Millegeville GA: Boyd Publishing, 2001.

Speech of the Hon. Edwards Pierrepont in Favor of the Election of Gen. Grant. New York: William C. Bryant & Co., Printers, 1868.

Stephens, Alexander Hamilton. *The Reviewers Reviewed: A Supplement to the "War Between the States," etc., With an Appendix in Review of "Reconstruction," So Called*. New York: D. Appleton and Company, 1872.

Stutler, Boyd B. *West Virginia in the Civil War*. Charleston WV: Education Foundation, Inc., 1966.

Tanner, Robert G. *Stonewall in the Valley; Thomas J. 'Stonewall' Jackson's Shenandoah Valley Campaign, Spring 1862*. Garden City NY: Doubleday and Company, 1976.

Telfair, Nancy. *A History of Columbus, Georgia, 1828–1928*. Columbus GA: Historical Publishing Company, 1929.

Warner, Ezra T. *Generals in Gray*. Baton Rouge: Louisiana State University Press, 1959.

Watkins, Sam. *1861 vs. 1882, "Co. Aytch": Maury Grays First Tennessee Regiment or A Sideshow of the Big Show*. Nashville: Cumberland Presbyterian Publishing House, 1882; Dayton OH: Press of Morningside Bookshop, 1992.

Wiggins, David N. Vol. 1, *Georgia's Confederate Sons*. Carrolton GA: University of West Georgia Press, 2007.

Worsley, Etta Blanchard. *Columbus on the Chattahoochee*. Columbus GA: Columbus Office Supply Company, 1951.

Zinn, Jack. *R. E. Lee's Cheat Mountain Campaign*. Parsons WV: McClain Printing Company, 1974.

Articles

Andrews, Garnett. "A Battle Planned But Not Fought." *Confederate Veteran Magazine* 5/11 (June 1897): 292–295.

Bruffey, E. C. "Lost Gate City Guard of Georgia Resembled Lost Battalion of A.E.F." *Atlanta Journal*, n.d. 1918.

Bloch, Anny. "Mercy on Rude Streams: Jewish Emigrants From Alsace-Lorraine to the Lower Mississippi Region and the Concept of Fidelity." *Southern Jewish History Journal* 2 (1999): 79–105.

Fleming, Martin K. "The Northwestern Virginia Campaign of 1861." *Blue & Gray Magazine* 10/6 (August 1993): 10–17, 48–54, 59–65.

Hagy, P. S. "The Cheat Mountain Campaign." *Confederate Veteran Magazine* 23 (March 1915): 122–123.

———. "The Laurel Hill Retreat in 1861." *Confederate Veteran Magazine* 24/4 (April 1916): 169–173.

Hodges, Ruby C. "First Georgia Infantry Regiment: Southern Rights Guard, Later Southern Rights Battery." *United Daughters of the Confederacy Magazine* 50/2 (February 1987): 41–42.

Howison, Robert R. "History of the War, Chapter V." *Southern Literary Messenger* 37/2 (February 1864): 68–78.

———. "History of the War, Chapter V." *Southern Literary Messenger* 37/3 (March 1864): 129–139.

Jones, A. C. "The Mountain Campaign Failure." *Confederate Veteran Magazine* 22/7 (July 1914): 305–306.

———. "The Mountain Campaign Failure." *Confederate Veteran Magazine* 22/8 (August 1914): 368.

Long, A. L. "Lee's West Virginia Campaign." In *Annals of the War*, edited by Alexander K. McClure. Edison NJ: Blue & Grey Press, 1996. 82–94.

"Participant Tells Story of First Memorial Day." Newspaper article, n.p., n.d. Personal papers of Morgan Merrill, Cincinnati OH.

Pillsbury, John B. "Garnett's Retreat After Rich Mountain." *Atlanta Journal*, 25 May 1901.

Stokes, J. W. "The Retreat from Laurel Hill,West Virginia." *Southern Bivouac* 3/10 (October 1884): 61–66.

Taliaferro, William B. "Annals of the War. Chapters of Unwritten History. Garnett in West Virginia." Typescript from the *Philadelphia Weekly Times*, 11 March 1882. Personal collection of W. Hunter Lesser.

Woods, John H., ed. "Soldier and Prisoner, Two Confederate Memoirs by Robert H. Little." Unpublished typescript. Chicago: University of Chicago, 2000.

Other Resources

Bohannon, Keith, comp. "1st Georgia (Ramsey's) Infantry Regiment Bibliography." Personal papers. Carrollton GA: n.p., 2007.

Hambrecht, F. Terry, comp. *Biographical Register of Physicians Who Served the Confederacy in a Medical Capacity*. Unpublished database. Rockville MD: n.p., 2008.

"Muster Roll of Co. K, 1st Regt. "Quitman Guards." Quitman Guards Collection. Monroe County Historical Society, Forsyth GA: n.p., n.d.

Persons, Henry R., Jr., comp. "First (Ramsey's) Regiment Georgia Volunteer Infantry." Bibliography, personal papers. Severn MD: n.p., 2006.

Sturkey, O. Lee, comp. "Gravesites of Georgia Civil War Soldiers." Personal research. McCormick SC: n.p., n.d.. Indexed cards now in the author's possession.

"Timeline of James Newton Ramsey." Personal papers of Loretta Andrews, Asheville NC: n.p., n.d.

Newspapers

Atlanta Constitution
Atlanta Daily Intelligencer
Atlanta Gate City Guardian
Atlanta Journal
Atlanta Southern Confederacy

Augusta Chronicle and Sentinel
Augusta Daily Constitutionalist
Columbus Daily Enquirer
Columbus Daily Sun
Columbus Daily Times
Columbus Weekly Times
Cumberland Evening Times
Forsyth Monroe Advertiser
Frank Leslie's Illustrated Newspaper (New York)
Griffin Middle Georgian
Macon Georgia Weekly Telegraph
Macon Daily Telegraph
New York Illustrated News
New York Times
Newnan Banner
Pensacola Tribune
Raleigh North Carolina Standard
Richmond Daily Dispatch
Richmond Examiner
Rome Weekly Courier
Sandersville Central Georgian
Savannah Republican
Staunton Spectator and Daily Advisor

Secondary Sources

Fielder, Herbert. *A Sketch of the Life and Times and Speeches of Joseph E. Brown*. Springfield MA: Press of Springfield Printing Company, 1883.

Johnson, Edward V., and Clarence C. Buel, eds. *Battles and Leaders of the Civil War*. 4 vols. New York: The Century Company, 1884–1887.

Miller, Francis Trevelyan, ed. *Armies and Leaders*. Vol. 10., *The Photographic History of the Civil War*. New York: The Review of Reviews Co., 1911.

National Cyclopaedia of American Biography Volume 5. New York: James T. White & Co., 1894.

Northen, William J., ed. *Men of Mark in Georgia*. 6 vols. Atlanta: A. B. Caldwell, Publisher, 1907–1912.

Roddy, Ray. *The Georgia Volunteer Infantry, 1861–1865*. Kearney NE: Morris Publishing, 1998.

Southern Historical Society Association. *Memoirs of Georgia*. 2 vols. Atlanta: The Southern Historical Press, 1895.

State of Georgia, Adjutant General, Military Record Book 1841–1862. Microfilm. Drawer 40, roll 17. Georgia Department of Archives and History, Morrow GA.

Washington County Historical Society. *Cotton to Kaolin; A History of Washington County, Georgia, 1784–1989*. Edited by Mary Alice Jordan. Roswell GA: W. H. Wolfe Associates, 1989.

Wiggins, David N. *Remembering Georgia's Confederates*. Mt. Pleasant SC: Arcadia Publishing, 2005.

Wiley, Bell I. *The Life of Johnny Reb; The Common Soldier of the Confederacy*. Baton Rouge: Louisiana State University Press, 1978.

Internet Research Web Sites

Ancestry.com: http://www.ancestry.com

Augusta Chronicle Online Archives: http://www.augustaarchives.com

"Find-a-Grave," Jim Tipton, editor: http://findagrave.com

Footnote: http://www.footnote.com

Heritage Quest Online: http://www.heritagequestonline.com

Internet Archives; American Libraries: http://www.archive.org/details/americana

Library of Congress, Civil War Maps: http://memory.loc.gov/ammem/collections/civil_war_maps

———. Prints and Photographs Online Catalog: http://www.loc.gov/rr/print/catalog.html

Making of America (MOA), University of Michigan: http://www.hti.umich.edu/m/moagrp

Manuscripts Department, Louis Round Wilson Library, University of North Carolina at Chapel Hill: http://www.lib.unc.edu/mss/shc/index.html

Monroe County Historical Society, Monroe County, Georgia: http://http://www.thegagenweb.com/mchs

National Archives and Records Administration: http://www.archives.gov

National Forest Service, Monongahela National Forest: http://www.fs.feditor.us/r9/mnf/rec/civilwar/cheatsummit.html

National Park Service, Civil War Soldiers and Sailors System: http://www.itd.nps.gov/cwss
———. Gulf Islands National Seashore: http://www.nps.gov/guis/planyourvisit/fort-barrancas.htm
NewspaperARCHIVE.Com: http://newspaperarchive.com
"Southern Rights Battery," Terrelle M. Walker, editor: http://www.thebriarpatch.com/wbts/havis/havis.html
University of North Carolina at Chapel Hill, Manuscripts Department, Wilson Library: http://www.lib.unc.edu/mss
University of Richmond: http://dlxs.richmond.edu/r/rdd/
Virginia Center for Digital History, The Valley of the Shadow: http://www.vcdh.virginia.edu/.

Appendix A

Organizations

Pensacola, mid-April–early June 1861
Troops in and near Pensacola, Brigadier General Braxton Bragg[1]
Second Brigade, Colonel Henry D. Clayton
First Georgia Infantry, Colonel James N. Ramsey

Laurel Hill Campaign, 24 June–20 July 1861
Army of the Northwest, Brigadier General Robert S. Garnett
First Georgia Infantry, Colonel James N. Ramsey

Cheat Mountain Campaign, 9–16 September 1861
Department of Western Virginia, General Robert E. Lee
Army of the Northwest, Brigadier General William W. Loring
Monterey Division, Brigadier General Henry R. Jackson
First Brigade, Brigadier General Henry R. Jackson
First Georgia Infantry, Colonel James N. Ramsey

Battle of Greenbrier River, 3 October 1861
Army of the Northwest, Monterey Division, Brigadier General Henry R. Jackson
Right Wing, Colonel Edward Johnson
First Georgia Infantry, Major George H. Thompson

Romney Campaign, 1 January–7 February 1862
Valley District, Major General Thomas J. Jackson
Army of the Northwest, Brigadier General William W. Loring
Fifth Brigade, Colonel William B. Taliaferro
First Georgia Infantry, Colonel James N. Ramsey

---

[1] General Braxton Bragg's command in and around Pensacola did not have a formal name until it was designated part of the Department of Alabama and West Florida on 29 October 1861, and officially named the Army of Pensacola on 22 December 1861. See William Frayne Amann, ed., *Personnel of the Civil War* (Cranbury NJ: Thomas Yoseloff, Publisher, 1968) 192.

Appendix B

Regimental Casualties

The statistics below come from a search of the *Compiled Service Records of Confederate Soldiers Who Served in Organizations From the State of Georgia*, held by the National Archives, compared with the rosters in Appendix C. Many of these records are woefully incomplete, with numerous files missing material. In a great number of cases the records contain no entries at all. Several 1st Georgia soldiers fall under two or more categories, but have been only placed under the first one listed in their record in order to avoid duplication. At least one soldier, Benjamin Russell of the Bainbridge Independents, was discharged but later reenlisted in the regiment. For the purposes of this chart, the regimental musicians have been included in their respective original companies.

Surprisingly, the 1st Georgia suffered very few casualties from battle. Combining killed in action with the two wounded categories, the regiment only had twelve combat losses. The larger share of those captured were lost during the retreat from Laurel Hill in July 1861.

The lion's share of those soldiers who left the ranks succumbed to disease. If it is assumed that most of the men who were discharged for unknown reasons left due to illness, and that those who died in service for unknown reasons did so because of disease, then sickness becomes the great ravager of the regiment. If these categories are combined with those soldiers who were known to be discharged for disability and those who died of disease, fully two-thirds of the regiment's losses can be attributed to illness.

Perhaps not unexpectedly, the two events that caused the most attrition from the ranks of the 1st Georgia were the retreat from Laurel Hill in July 1861, and Jackson's Romney Campaign over January and February 1862. Fifty-two men were discharged for various reasons during a two-month period following Garnett's and Ramsey's retreat, and thirty others died, for a total of eighty-two losses. For the period of two months from 1 January to 28 February 1862 covering Jackson's operations, fifty-nine soldiers were discharged and seventeen died. Taken together, these two operations accounted for almost half of the regiment's total losses.

APPENDIX C

1st Regiment Georgia Volunteer Infantry (Ramsey's) *Company Rosters*

The following roster of the 1,330 officers and men of the 1st Georgia Volunteer Infantry has been assembled from various sources, such as the *Compiled Service Records of Confederate Soldiers Who Served Organizations from the State of Georgia*, held by the National Archives; the *Roster of the Confederate Soldiers of Georgia, 1861–1865, Volume I*; *Muster Roll of First Regt. GA Volunteers, 1861*; the "Civil War Soldiers and Sailors System" website through the National Park Service, as well as several period newspaper accounts. The author is especially indebted to Mr. O. Lee Sturkey, who donated his extensive research on Georgia soldier burial sites. A full list of sources is included the end of this appendix.

Listings marked with (1) are for those soldiers who were original members of each company when the regiment was formed on 3 April 1861; the official date for their muster is 18 March 1861. Men who mustered out with the regiment on 10 March 1862 in Augusta are marked (2); the official date of the regiment's disbandment is recorded as 15 March. Other enlistment and departure dates are given where known. Commissioned and non-commissioned field, staff, and company officers are presented in order of rank. Privates are listed alphabetically. Military units are from Georgia unless otherwise specified. All burials are in the state of Georgia unless otherwise specified. Every effort has been made for accuracy, but in many cases contradictory information has been found. Where a dissimilarity of records is present, such as alternate spelling of names, it is posted in brackets [ ]. In the case of each soldier's date of birth, many records only state an age. In these cases, the year has been estimated. For example, a soldier who was twenty years of age at the time of enlistment will have a date of birth such as "B. about 1841."

Abbreviations

Adj.	Adjutant
ANV	Army of Northern Virginia
Appt.	Appointed
AQM	Assistant QM
Art.	Artillery
AWOL	Absent Without Leave
B.	Born
Bd.	Buried
Bn.	Battalion
Cap.	Captured
Cav.	Cavalry
Co.	Company
Cpl.	Corporal
Cty.	County
D.	Died
Dis.	Discharged
Elec.	Elected
Enl.	Enlisted
Ens.	Ensign
Exch.	Exchanged
Inf.	Infantry
KIA	Killed In Action
Lt.	Lieutenant
Par.	Paroled
Prom.	Promoted
Pvt.	Private
QM	Quartermaster
Reenl.	Reenlisted
Regt.	Regiment
Sgt.	Sgt.
Surr.	Surrendered
Tfd.	Transferred
WIA	Wounded In Action

Field Officers and Staff

Officers

Ramsey, James Newton (1, 2): 2nd Lt., Co. D of the Southern Guard. Elec. Col. 3 April 1861. [resigned 3 December 1861—See Appendix D] B. 21 June 1821. D. 10 November 1870. Bd. Linwood Cemetery, Columbus, Muscogee Cty.

Clarke, James O. (1): Capt., Oglethorpe Inf. Elec. Lt. Col. 3 April 1861; resigned November 1861. [promoted Col.—See Appendix D] Appt. 2nd Lt. and Drill Master, Camp of Instruction, Camp Randolph, Calhoun GA 29 July 1862. Tfd. to Camp of Instruction Number 2, Decatur GA. Prom. 1st Lt. and Drill Master 17 July 1863. B. 1825. D. 6 December, 1889. Bd. Magnolia Cemetery, Augusta, Richmond Cty.

Thompson, George Harvey (1, 2): Capt., GA State Army. Elec. Maj. 3 April 1861. Elec. Lt. Col. 11 December 1861. B. 16 January 1838. D. in service 18 December 1864, unit unknown.

Anderson, James W. (1, 2): 1st Lt., Newnan Guards. Appt. Adj. 3 April 1861. Elec. Maj. 11 December 1861. Elec. 1st Lt. of 2nd Co. A, 12th Bn. Light Art. 1 May 1862; Capt. 6 November 1862. WIA and captured Winchester VA 19 September 1864. Tfd. to Point Lookout MD for exchange 20 February 1865. B. 1835. D. 1903. Bd. Oak Hill Cemetery, Newnan, Coweta Cty.

Westmoreland, Willis Furman (1, 2): Appt. Surgeon, 3 April 1861. Resigned June 1861. Appt. Surgeon of the 10th Inf. Regt. 26 June 1861. Resigned 21 September 1861. Appt. Surgeon, CSA 26 September 1862; ordered to report to Surgeon Gen., having been assigned to duty in Atlanta. Ordered to Medical College Hospital Atlanta 31 December 1862. Served variously hospitals Milner, Barnesville and Albany. On duty November 1864 Columbus, MS hospital. Serving as Surgeon in charge of Medical College Hospital #2, Atlanta GA January 1865. B. 1 January 1828. D. 26 [27] June 1890.

Campbell, Dr. James McDonald: Appt. Chaplain 5 April 1861. Joined regiment Pensacola, FL. Elec. Capt., Co. E, 47th Regt. AL Inf. WIA Cedar Mountain VA 8 [9] August 1862. Prom. Maj. of Regt. B. 8 October 1830. KIA by a sharpshooter at Spotsylvania Courthouse, VA 10 [15] May 1864.

Staff

Thompson, Joseph Jr. (1, 2): Pvt., Gate City Guards. Appt. Regimental Sgt. Maj. 4 April 1861. Appt. Lt. September 1861. Dis. 5 November 1861. Elec. Lt. of Co. 2nd Regt. State Troops. Remained two months when he went to TX with Maj. Dunnwoody, Mining Bureau. On ordnance duty in TX as 1st Lt. under Gen. Hugher. Surr. Shreveport LA April 1865. B. about 1842.

Dunn, Andrew (1, 2): 2nd Cpl., Quitman Guards. Appt. Regimental QM Sgt. 16 August [September] 1861; Capt. QM Department 16 September 1861. B. 1835. D. 1878. Bd. Rest Haven Cemetery, Forsyth, Monroe Cty.

Collier, Joseph T. (1, 2): Pvt., Southern Rights Guard. Appt. Ordnance Sgt. Appt. 2nd Cpl. of Co. A, 19th Bn. Cav., 24 July 1862. Tfd. to Co. F, 10th Regt. Confederate Cav. January 1863. Par. Hillsboro NC 3 May 1865.

Crane, George W. (1, 2): 2nd Lt., Oglethorpe Inf. Appt. QM. Reenl., unit unknown. Appt. Maj. QM Department. B. about 1828.

Culler, Philip Benjamin Derrill Hart (1, 2): Pvt., Southern Rights Guard. Appt. Assistant Surgeon 5 April 1861; Surgeon June 1861. Enl. Co. D, 12th State Guards Cav. [Robinson]. B. 17 December 1815. D. 4 November 1876. Bd. Evergreen Cemetery, Perry, Houston Cty.

Cunningham, Hardy C. (1, 2): Pvt., Co. D of the Southern Guard. Appt. Regimental Commissary 5 May [April] 1861. Appt. Capt. and ACS and assigned to duty Macon GA 17 April 1862, where he was serving 15 March 1864.

Hines, David P. (1, 2): Pvt., Bainbridge Independents. Appt. Assistant Surgeon 5 April 1861. B. 1826. D. 1866. Bd. Oak City Cemetery, Bainbridge, Decatur Cty.

Hughs, Harry [Hughes] (1, 2): Pvt., Oglethorpe Inf. Appt. Regimental Hospital Sgt., Regimental QM. B. about 1836.

McKinley, Charles A. (1, 2): Pvt., Newnan Guards. Appt. Regimental Hospital Steward 1861. Enl. Co. A, 56th Inf. Regt. 25 April 1862. Tfd. to Academy Hospital 21 July 1862. Appt. Assistant Surgeon of the 12th Bn. Light Art., 1862; Assistant Surgeon, PACS, 4 December 1862. On duty Talladega AL 12 September 1864. B. 1839.

Connally, David Hudnall [Conley, Conally] (1): Pvt., Gate City Guards. Appt. Regimental Hospital Steward 16 April 1861. Detailed as Hospital Steward, Richmond VA, December 1861. On detached duty 11 March 1862. Enl. Cav., unit unknown. Confirmed Assistant Surgeon by CSA Senate 4 April 1863. B. 3 December 1837. D. 21 June 1912. Bd. Oakwood Cemetary, Tyler, Smith Cty., TX.

Musicians

Keller, Joseph Raburn [Rayburn Kellar] (1, 2): Pvt. Newnan Guards. Appt. Regimental Drum Maj. 1861. Enl. 2nd Co. A, 12th Bn. Light Art. 1 May 1862. Appt. Cpl. 1862. Tfd. to band. Appt. Drum Maj. Surr. Appomattox VA, 9 April 1865. B. about 1843.

Clue, Julius: Pvt., Southern Rights Guard. Appt. Regimental Bandsman.

Luckie, William H. (1, 2): Pvt., Newnan Guards. Tfd. to regimental band 1861. Enl. Co. E, 27th Bn. Inf. 2 May 1864. On sick furlough 31 December 1864.

Mitchell, John Wesley [Wesly J.] (1): Pvt., Newnan Guards. Appt. 4th Sgt. Appt. Regimental Musician 7 May 1861. Dis. Winchester VA 8 February 1862. Enl. 2nd Co. A, 12th Bn. Light Art. 1 May 1862. B. 12 March 1831. D. 10 December 1876. Bd. Oak Hill Cemetery, Newnan, Coweta Cty.

Rote, M. [Roate] (1, 2): Pvt., Gate City Guards. Tfd. to regimental band 1861. B. about 1833. [D. near Culpepper VA 1861.]

Thomson, J. F.: Regimental Bandsman.

Well, M. J.: Regimental Bandsman.

Co. A, "Newnan Guards," Coweta County

Officers

Hanvey, George McDuffie (1, 2): Capt. Elec. Capt. of 2nd Co. A, 12th Bn. Light Art. 1 May 1862; Maj. 6 November 1862. WIA and captured Monocacy, MD 9 July 1864. Released Johnson's Island OH 25 July 1865. B. 2 November 1824. D. 16 November 1900. Bd. Oakland Cemetery, Atlanta, Fulton Cty.

Swint, Thomas (1, 2): 2nd Lt. Elec. 1st Lt. 3 [6] April 1861. Elec. 1st Lt. Co. H, 7th State Guards, then 1st Lt. Co. E, Coweta Militia Bn. WIA Griswoldville. B. 1 August 1825. D. 23 April 1909. Bd. Oak Hill Cemetery, Newnan, Coweta Cty.

Brown, Andrew P. (1, 2): Jr. 2nd (or 3rd) Lt. Elec. 2nd Lt. 3 April 1861. Elec. 2nd Lt. of 2nd Co. A, 12th Bn. Light Art. 1 May 1862; 1st Lt. 6 November 1862. B. about 1843. KIA Fort Sumter SC 28 October 1863.

Palmer, Oscar [Palmas/Palmes] (1, 2): 1st Sgt. Reduced to private. Enl. 2nd Co. A, 12th Bn. Light Art. 1 May 1862. Tfd. to band. Surr. Appomattox VA 9 April 1865. B. about 1831. D. Savannah, 28 March 1887.

Dent, William B. W., Jr. (1, 2): 2nd Sgt. WIA Cheat Mountain, VA 12 September 1861. Enl. Co. C, 2nd State Guards Cav., 1 August 1863. Appt. Purchasing Agent, CSA B. 25 November 1837. D. 20 December 1907. Bd. Oak Hill Cemetery, Newnan, Coweta Cty.

Martin, Charles (1, 2): 3rd Sgt. Enl. Co. C, 16th Inf. Regt. 1862. Appt. Adj. B. about 1840. KIA Sharpsburg, MD 17 September 1862. [KIA at Front Royal VA 1861.]

Brown, Peter J. (1, 2): 1st Cpl. Appt. First Sgt. Enl. Co. K, Phillips' Legion of Cav., 10 May 1862. Tfd. to Co. K, 3 June 1862. WIA Funkstown MD 12 July 1863. D. Staunton, VA 1 August 1863.

Mitchell, William A. (1, 2): 2nd Cpl. Appt. 3rd Sgt. Enl. 2nd Co. A, 12th Bn. Light Art. 1 May 1862. Tfd. to battalion band. Surr. Appomattox VA 9 April 1865. B. 1 November 1839. D. 7 October 1898. Bd. Oak Hill Cemetery, Newnan, Coweta Cty.

Alexander, Thomas G. (1, 2): 3rd Cpl. Enl. 2nd Co. A, 12th Bn. Light Art. 1 May 1862. Appt. Comm. Sgt. 1862. Surr. Appomattox VA 9 April 1865. B. about 1837. Bd. Senoia Town Cemetery, Coweta Cty.

Calhoun, Abner Wellborn (1): 4th Cpl. Dis. Winchester, VA 31 December 1861. Enl. 2nd Co. A, 12th Bn. Light Art. 1 May 1862. Appt. Sgt. Maj. 2 June 1864. WIA Winchester VA 19 September 1864. WIA Hatcher's Run, VA 6 February 1865. Surr. Appomattox VA 9 April 1865. B. 16 April 1845. D. 21 August 1910. Bd. Oakland Cemetery, Atlanta, Fulton Cty.

Privates

Addy, Reuben, L. (1, 2): Enl. Co. G, 53rd Inf. Regt. 30 April 1862. Appt. 1st Sgt. 13 March 1863. WIA Baker's Creek MS 16 May 1863. WIA at the Wilderness VA 6 May 1864. Appt. Regimental Ens. 15 June 1864. Appt. Color Bearer. Cap., date and place not given. Released near Sandusky OH 18 June 1865.

Allen, George M. (1): B. about 1826. D. Monterey, VA 11 August 1861.

Arnold, John M. (2): Enl. 1 November 1861. Enl. Co. C, 6th Regt. LA Cav. Elec. 1st Lt.

Askew, William S.: Enl. 7 May 1861. Cap. 12 [13] July 1861, but escaped. Dis. for disability at Monterey VA 21 August 1861. Enl. Co. F, 16th Bn. Cav., 2 May 1862. Cap. Knoxville TN 4 December 1863. Sent to Camp Morton IN. Tfd. to Co. F, 13th Regt. Cav. 2 May 1864. Appt. 4th Cpl. Tfd. from Camp Morton IN to Fort Delaware DE, and paroled there February 1865. Received Boulware & Cox's Wharves James River VA for exchange, 10–12 March 1865. B. 1 January 1841. D. Newnan, GA April 1917. Bd. Oak Hill Cemetery, Newnan, Coweta Cty.

Barnes, Robert S. (2): Enl. 1 June 1861. Enl. 2nd Co. A, 12th Bn. Light Art. 1 May 1862. Dis. 1863. B. 7 May 1836. D. 1 August 1919. Bd. Sardis Baptist Cemetery, Palmetto, Campbell Cty (now Fulton).

Barnes, William E. (1, 2): Enl. 2nd Co. A, 12th Bn. Light Art. 1 May 1862. WIA Cold Harbor VA 2 June 1864. Surr. Tallahassee FL 10 May 1865. Par. Thomasville GA 16 May 1865. B. 7 October 1842. D. 22 March 1887. Bd. West End Cemetery, Quitman, Brooks Cty.

Bass, James N. (1, 2): Enl. Co. H, 56th Inf. Regt. 13 May 1862. Appt. Adj. 15 May 1862. Assigned as 1st Lt. and Acting Inspector Gen. of Cumming's Brigade, Stevenson's Division 4 November 1864. D. 22 September 1888.

Beadles, Joseph N. (2): Enl. 7 May 1861. Appt. Cpl. Enl. 2nd Co. A, 12th Bn. Light Art. 1 May 1862. Appt. Sgt. B. about 1842. KIA Monocacy MD 9 July 1864.

Beadles, William Sterling (2): Enl. 7 May 1861. Elec. Jr. 2nd (or 3rd) Lt. of 2nd Co. A, 12th Bn. Light Art. 1 May 1862; 2nd Lt. September 1863. WIA in leg and

Cap. Monocacy MD 9 July 1864. Leg amputated Frederick City MD 11 July 1864. Par. West's Buildings Hospital, Baltimore MD for exchange 21 September 1864. B. 24 November 1839. D. 9 October 1881. Bd. Fayetteville Town Cemetery, Fayette Cty.

Belisle, John H. (1, 2): Enl. 2nd Co. A, 12th Bn. Light Art. 1 May 1862. Tfd. to Co. H, 66th Inf. Regt. 15 September 1863. Appt. Sgt. Cap. near Atlanta GA 7 August 1864. Enl. Co. E, 5th Regt. US Volunteers Camp Chase OH 25 April 1865.

Belisle, Lorenzo D. (1, 2): Elec. Capt. of Co. H, 66th [64th] Inf. Regt. 9 August 1863. Listed as WIA and permanently disabled at Peachtree Creek GA 20 July 1864. On detail duty due to disability, Macon GA from 1864 to close of war. B. 4 January 1837. D. 26 September 1913. Bd. Memory Hill Cemetery, Milledgeville, Baldwin Cty.

Bevis, George H. (1, 2): Enl. 2nd Co. A, 12th Bn. Light Art. 1 May 1862. B. about 1842. KIA Kernstown VA 24 July 1864.

Bolton, Charles A. (2): Enl. 1 June 1861. Enl. Co. B, 1st Bn., State Guards Inf. [Co. B, Ordnance Bn. for defense of Columbus, GA,], 4 August 1863.

Brewster, Blake Dempsey (1, 2): Appt. 1st Cpl. of Co. A, 56th Inf. Regt. 25 April 1862; 4th Sgt. Cap. Vicksburg MS 4 July 1863, and paroled 8 July 1863. Cap. Nashville TN 16 December 1864. Released Camp Chase OH 12 June 1865. D. 17 January 1929.

Brewster, Daniel Ferguson (2): Enl. 1 June 1861. Enl. Co. A, 56th Inf. Regt. 25 April 1862. Appt. Sgt. Maj. Cap. Vicksburg MS 4 July 1863, and paroled 8 July 1863. Appt. Acting ADC 24 September 1864, and serving as such 20 November 1864. B. 17 December 1831. D. 4 April 1919. Bd. Brewster Family Cemetery, near Newnan, Coweta Cty.

Brewster, James J. Pendleton (2): Enl. 1 June 1861. Elec. Capt. of Co. A, 56th Inf. Regt. 25 April 1862. Elec. Maj. (to rank from 10 August 1862.), 20 August 1862. Cap. Vicksburg MS 4 July 1863, and paroled 8 July 1863. WIA in leg, necessitating amputation above knee, Kennesaw Mountain GA 27 June 1864. Report dated Atlanta GA 20 August 1864, shows him absent, wounded. B. 1834. D. 1917. Bd. Oak Hill Cemetery, Newnan, Coweta Cty.

Brewster, William: Enl. 1 July 1861. Dis. Unger's Store VA 12 January 1862. Enl. Co. A, 56th Inf. Regt. B. 23 September 1827. D. 17 March 1895. Bd. Brewster Family Cemetery, near Newnan, Coweta Cty.

Brooks, David H. (1, 2): Enl. 2nd Co. A, 12th Bn. Light Art. 1 May 1862. Elec. 2nd Lt. 27 May 1863. B. about 1843. KIA Monocacy MD 9 July 1864.

Brooks, John Newell (1): Tfd. to Co. A, 7th Inf. Regt. 7 June 1861. AWOL January to 28 February 1865. B. about 1846.

Brown, Thomas Y.: Enl. 1 June 1861. WIA Cheat Mountain VA 12 September 1861. D. Camp Bartow VA 25 September 1861.

Calhoun, Thomas J. (1): Tfd. to Co. B, 5th Inf. Regt. 4 January 1862. On detached duty Montgomery AL 12 February 1862 to 30 December 1864. Appt. QM for Wither's Brigade. B. 1841.

Cannon, George W. (1): Dis. Winchester VA 26 December 1861. Enl. Co. G, 53rd Inf. Regt. 30 April 1862. D. of smallpox Culpeper VA 18 November 1862.

Cantrell, Oscar A. (2): Enl. 1 June 1861. Elec. Jr. 2nd (or 3rd) Lt. of Co. A, 56th Inf. Regt. 25 April 1862; 1st Lt. Cap. Nashville TN 16 December 1864. Released Johnson's Island OH 16 June 1865. B. 1836.

Carmical, Robert Y. [Carmichael] (1): Dis. Winchester VA 2 February 1862. Appt. 4th Cpl. of Co. D, 53rd Inf. Regt. 6 May 1862. WIA Sharpsburg MD 17 September 1862. Absent, wounded, 31 October 1862. In hospital or light duty Lynchburg VA until D. 3 July 1863. B. about 1837. Bd. Confederate Cemetery, Lynchburg, Campbell Cty, VA.

Chapman, J. T. (1, 2): Enl. 2nd Co. A, 12th Bn. Light Art.

Clarke, Benjamin McPherson: Enl. 7 May 1861. Dis. Laurel Hill VA 6 July 1861. Enl. Co. F 2nd State Guards Cav., 3 August 1863. B. 19 February 1842. D. 16 June 1885. Bd. Oak Hill Cemetery, Newnan, Coweta Cty.

Clements, Thelbert M. (1): Dis. Winchester VA 8 February 1862. Enl. 2nd Co. A, 12th Bn. Light Art. 1 May 1862. Appt. 5th Sgt. 1862. WIA and disabled Cold Harbor VA 2 June 1864. Par. Albany GA 20 May 1865. B. about 1829.

Colquitt, George W. (1): WIA Corricks Ford VA. Tfd. to Co. G, 7th Inf. Regt. 4 August 1861. WIA Garnett's Farm VA 28 June 1862. WIA Gettysburg PA 2 July 1863. Retired 25 July 1864.

Conyers, John F. (2): Enl. 7 May 1861. Enl. 2nd Co. A, 12th Bn. Light Art. 1 May 1862. Appt. Adj. 41st Inf. Regt. 13 January 1864. B. about 1838. D. 1885.

Copeland, Jonathan C. "John" (1, 2): Appt. 1st Sgt. of Co. C, 56th Inf. Regt. 10 May 1862. Cap. Vicksburg MS 4 July 1863, and paroled 8 July 1863. B. 14 November 1836. D. 28 January 1922. Bd. Bowdon First Methodist Church Cemetery, Bowdon, Carroll Cty.

Culpepper, John L. (1): D. Winchester, VA 24 February 1862.

Davis, James J. (2): Enl. 1 June 1861. Dis. for disability at Winchester VA 18 January 1862. Enl. 2nd Co. A, 12th Bn. Light Art. 1 May 1862. Appt. Cpl. B. about 1832.

Davis, Jeptha Vining, Jr. (2): Enl. 7 May 1861. Appt. Cpl. of 2nd Co. A, 12th Bn. Light Art. 1 May 1862. WIA Monocacy MD 9 July 1864. On wounded furlough close of war. B. 24 October 1839. D. 18 July 1876. Bd. Davis Family Cemetery, near Newnan, Coweta Cty.

Davis, Jesse M. (1): B. about 1842. D. Staunton VA 4 October 1861.

Davis, Minor Maury Stevens (2): Enl. 7 May 1861. Enl. 2nd Co. A, 12th Bn. Light Art. 1 May 1862. Appt. Assistant Surgeon. Severely scalded in train collision Ringgold GA 6 July 1862. Dis. 6 February 1863. Rejoined 12th Bn. 5 May 1863. Detailed "to care for negroes" on James Island from September to December 1863. Cap. and paroled Athens GA 8 May 1865. B. 7 December 1837. D. 3 December 1892.

Dennis, Francis Marion "Caesar" (1 [16 April 1861], 2): Enl. 2nd Co. A, 12th Bn. Light Art. 1 May 1862. Prom. Lt. WIA Monocacy MD 9 July 1864; Smithville VA 29 August 1864. B. 13 February 1841. D. 13 April 1915. Bd. Dennis Family Cemetery, near Corinth, Coweta Cty.

Dent, John T.: Enl. 7 May 1861. Dis. 31 December 1861. Appt. QM Montgomery AL.

Dent, Joseph H. (2): Enl. 15 September 1861. Enl. 3rd Co. C, 12th Bn. Light Art. 1 May 1862. Appt. Cpl. WIA Fort Steadman VA. Cap., date and place not given. Par. Burkeville VA 17 April 1865. B. about 1845.

Duncan, Benjamin R. [also shown as Rush M. Duncan] (1): Cap. during retreat from Laurel Hill July 1861. Par. 24 July 1861 and sent home. D. August 1861.

Dyer, W. J. N. (1, 2).

Echols, William S. (1, 2): Enl. 2nd Co. A, 12th Bn. Light Art. 1 May 1862. WIA through thigh KY 28 August 1862. [WIA in TN]

Elmore, Jacob S. (1): Dis. Ungers Store, VA 12 January 1862. Appt. 1st Sgt. of Co. G, 53rd Inf. Regt. 30 April 1862. Elec. Jr. 2nd (or 3rd) Lt. 13 March 1863; 2nd Lt. 28 July 1863; 1st Lt. 25 November 1863. Cap. Sailor's Creek VA 6 April 1865. Released Johnson's Island OH 18 June 1865. D. 12 January 1911. Bd. Mt. Pilgrim Lutheran Church Cemetery, near Senoia, Coweta Cty.

Favor, John D. (2): Enl. 7 May 1861. Enl. 2nd Co. A, 12th Bn. Light Art. 1 May 1862. KIA Cold Harbor VA 2 June 1864.

Freeman, Alvan Dean [Alvin] (2): Enl. 7 May 1861. Appt. 2nd Sgt. Appt. 1st Sgt. of 2nd Co. A, 12th Bn. Light Art. 1 May 1862. Appt. Sgt. Maj. WIA and captured Monocacy MD 9 July 1864. Exch. Appt. Brevet Jr. 2nd (or 3rd) Lt. of 2nd Co. A, 12th Bn. Light Art. February 1865. Surr. Appomattox VA 9 April 1865. B. 15 March 1841. D. 11 October 1917. Bd. Oak Hill Cemetery, Newnan, Coweta Cty.

Garrison, James F. (1, 2): Enl. Forrest's Cav. Appt. Lt.

Goodwyn, John B. [Goodwin] (2): Enl. 7 May 1861. Appt. 1st Sgt. of 2nd Co. A, 12th Bn. Light Art. 1 May 1862. WIA collision Ringgold GA 6 July 1862; Cold Harbor VA 2 June 1864. WIA and captured Monocacy MD 9 July 1864.

Received Venus Point, Savannah River GA for Exch. 15 February 1865. Surr. Appomattox VA 9 April 1865. B. about 1839.

Goodwyn, Thomas D. [Goodwin] (2): Enl. Co. D, 53rd Inf. Regt. 6 May 1862. Appt. 4th Cpl. 1862. WIA in finger, necessitating amputation, Knoxville TN 29 November 1863. Tfd. to 2nd Co. A, 12th Bn. Light Art., Exch. for William Walden, 10 June 1864. Cap. Sailor's Creek VA 6 April 1865. Released Point Lookout MD 12 June 1865. B. about 1841.

Grace, William F. (1, 2): Enl. 2nd Co. A, 12th Bn. Light Art. 1 May 1862. Appt. Cpl. Surr. Greensboro NC 26 April 1865. D. 1885.

Griswold, Lyman (2): Enl. 1 July 1861.

Haas, Solomon (1, 2): Enl. 2nd Co. A, 12th Bn. Light Art. 1 May 1862. Appt. QM Sgt. Dis. after furnishing Patrick Dougherty as substitute, 19 November 1862. B. Germany about 1841. D. Los Angeles CA 21 November 1909. Bd. Hollywood, Los Angeles Cty., CA.

Hartsfield, Wiley F., Jr. (1, 2): Elec. 2nd Lt. of Co. H, 53rd Inf. Regt. 5 May 1862; Maj. 8 November 1863; Lt. Col. 3 December 1863. WIA The Wilderness VA 6 May 1864. Elec. Col. KIA Sailor's Creek VA 6 April 1865.

Hollis, James F. (1 [18 May]): Dis. Staunton VA 23 September 1861. Enl. 2nd Co. A, 12th Bn. Light Art. 1 May 1862. WIA Monocacy MD 9 July 1864. WIA Winchester VA 19 September 1864. Furloughed for 60 days due to wounds 5 April 1865.

Huckaby, George W. [Huckaba] (1): WIA Laurel Hill VA 8 [12] July 1861. D. Seneca [Staunton] VA 20 August 1861.

Jackson, James M. (1, 2): Appt. Sgt. of Co. H, 1st Regt. Cav. 19 April 1862. Elec. 2nd Lt. 5 August 1863. WIA 12 December 1863. Applied for extension of furlough due to fracture of left thigh 13 January 1865. D. 1885.

Johnson, Marcus S. (1): Dis. for disability at Richmond VA 31 July 1861. Appt. 3rd Sgt. of Co. K, 4th Regt. State Troops, 25 October 1861. [41st Inf. Regt.] Mustered out April 1862. Appt. 4th Sgt. of Co. C, 34th Inf. Regt. 13 May 1862. Elec. Jr. 2nd (or 3rd) Lt. 30 June 1862. Cap. Vicksburg MS 4 July 1863, and Par. there 8 July 1863. Elec. 2nd Lt. 25 November 1863; 1st Lt. 5 February 1864. WIA Kennesaw Mountain GA 27 June 1864. Elec. Capt. January 1865. Surr. Greensboro NC 26 April 1865. B. about 1833.

Jones, Harrison (1, 2): Enl. 2nd Co. A, 12th Bn. Light Art. 1 May 1862. WIA Cold Harbor VA 2 June 1864. On wounded furlough from hospital 1 November 1864. B. 22 April 1843. D. 2 March 1923. Bd. Hampton Town Cemetery, Henry Cty.

Jones, Thomas Franklin: Enl. 7 May 1861. Dis. for disability at Monterey VA 21 August 1861. Appt. 2nd Sgt. of Co. F, 16th Bn. Cav., 15 May 1862. Tfd. to

Co. F, 13th Regt. Cav. 21 May 1864. Severely wounded in arm Morristown TN 28 October 1864. B about 1839.

Keller, James Wood (1, 2): Appt. 4th Cpl. Enl. 2nd Co. A, 12th Bn. Light Art. 1 May 1862. B. about 1835. D. Knoxville TN 7 November 1862. Bd. Oak Hill Cemetery, Newnan, Coweta Cty.

Legg, David Crawford (1, 2): Enl. Co. A, 9th Bn. Light Art. 30 April 1862. Appt. Sgt. Cap. Cumberland Gap TN 20 September 1863. Released Camp Douglas IL 16 June 1865.

Leigh, Anselem B. [Anselm] (1, 2): Enl. 2nd Co. A, 12th Bn. Light Art. 1 May 1862. WIA Monocacy MD 9 July 1864. Cap. Fredericksburg VA 10 July 1864. Exch. Venus Point, Savannah River GA 15 November 1864. Furloughed for 60 days due to wounds 6 April 1865. B. 14 May 1824. D. 9 December 1905. Bd. Oak Hill Cemetery, Newnan, Coweta Cty.

Leigh, Benjamin Walter (1, 2): Appt. Cpl. Enl. 2nd Co. A, 12th Bn. Light Art. 1 May 1862. Appt. Cpl.; Sgt. Dis. due to tuberculosis Coosawhatchie SC 4 February 1864. B. 18 January 1843. D. of disease at home 5 May 1864. Bd. Leigh-Potts Family Cemetery, near Newnan, Coweta Cty.

Little, Robert Henry (1, 2): Enl. Co. I, 44th Regt. AL Inf., 24 April 1862. Prom. 2nd Sgt. June 1862. WIA Sharpsburg MD 17 September 1862. AWOL May 1863. Reduced to private 1 June 1863. Cap. Chattanooga 29 October 1863. Prisoner of War Camp Morton IN, until 4 March 1865. After parole forwarded to City Point VA for exchange. B. 10 December 1837. D. Houston TX 25 March 1926. Bd. Denman Cemetery, Sparta, Bell Cty., TX (remains relocated to Resthaven Cemetery, Belton TX).

Mann, Josiah L. (1, 2): Elec. Jr. 2nd (or 3rd) Lt. 3 April 1861. Elec. Jr. 2nd (or 3rd) Lt. of 2nd Co. A, 12th Bn. Light Art. 1 May 1862; 2nd Lt. March 1863; 1st Lt. KIA Winchester VA 19 September 1864.

Martin, William M. (1): Dis. for disability at Staunton, VA 11 October 1861. Enl. 2nd Co. A, 12th Bn. Light Art. 1 May 1862. WIA Monocacy MD 9 July 1864. Surr. Appomattox, VA 9 April 1865. B. 31 July 1835. Date inscribed on tombstone states D. 27 November 1864. Bd. Martin Family Cemetery, near Palmetto, Coweta Cty.

McIver, David S. (1, 2): Enl. 2nd Co. A, 12th Bn. Light Art. 1 May 1862. Appt. Assistant Surgeon. Surr. Appomattox VA 9 April 1865. B. 1838. D. 7 February, 1872 [1873]. Bd. Myrtle Hill Cemetery, Troup Cty.

Meyer, Bernard H.: Enl. 1 June 1861. Murdered in Shaw's Pass VA 16 June 1861. Bd. Newnan, Coweta Cty.

Mobley, Eleazer Eldridge (1, 2): Appt. Cpl. of 2nd Co. A, 12th Bn. Light Art. 1 May 1862. Cap. Fort Steadman VA 25 March 1865. Released Point Lookout MD 29 June 1865.

Moncrief, William J. (1): Dis. Staunton VA 23 September 1861. Enl. 2nd Co. A, 12th Bn. Light Art. 1 May 1862. Deserted Fisher's Hill VA 16 October 1864. Took oath of allegiance to US Government New Creek VA 24 October 1864. B. about 1842.

Moody, George J. (1, 2): B. about 1842.

Moody, James P. (1, 2): Enl. 2nd Co. A, 12th Bn. Light Art. 1 May 1862. Cap. James Island SC 16 July 1863. B. about 1846. D. Point Lookout MD 16 September 1864. Bd. Point Lookout Confederate Cemetery, Point Lookout, St. Mary's Cty., MD.

Moore, George W. (1): Tfd. to Co. F, Cobb's Legion Inf. and elected 1st Lt. 18 September 1861; Capt. 25 June 1862. Cap. Knoxville TN 29 November 1863. Tfd. from Camp Chase OH to Fort Delaware DE and released 30 May 1865. B. about 1839.

Neil, Michael J. (1, 2): Tfd. to regimental band December 1861. Appt. Sgt. of 2nd Co. A, 12th Bn. Light Art. 1 May 1862. Cap. Battery Wagner SC July 1863. Par. Montgomery AL 17 May 1865.

Newnan, John B. [Newman] (1, 2): Elec. Jr. 2nd (or 3rd) Lt. of Co. D, 53rd Inf. Regt. 6 May 1862; 2nd Lt. 27 October 1862; 1st Lt. 1863. B. 17 November 1820. KIA Knoxville TN 29 November 1863. Bd. Woodlawn Cemetery, Eastman, Dodge Cty.

Orr, Isaac Newton D. (2): Enl. 16 August 1861. Enl. Co. F, 16th Bn. Cav., 1 May 1862. Dis. August 1862. B. 12 November 1840. D. 4 July 1917. Bd. Oak Hill Cemetery, Newnan, Coweta Cty.

Orr, Nicholas T. (2): Enl. 7 May 1861. Enl. 2nd Co. A, 12th Bn. Light Art. 1 May 1862. B. about 1838. KIA Monocacy MD 9 July 1864.

Orr, William Benjamin (1, 2): Appt. 1st Sgt. of Co. F, 16th Bn. Cav. 14 May 1862. Cap. Blountville TN 22 September 1863. Tfd. to Co. F, 13th Regt. Cav. 21 May 1864. Exch. Fort Delaware DE 18 September 1864. Furloughed home. B. 14 October 1838. D. Newnan GA 5 October 1916. Bd. Oak Hill Cemetery, Newnan, Coweta Cty.

Perkins, William T. (1): B. about 1838. D. McDowell, VA 30 August 1861.

Persons, Henry Turner: Enl. 1 June 1861. Dis. Monterey VA 21 August 1861. Enl. Co. D, Phillips' Legion of Cav. Cap. Warrenton VA 24 May 1863. Par. Washington DC 10 June 1863. Received James River VA for exchange 12 June 1863. WIA Funkstown MD 10 July 1863. B. 22 April 1845.

Price, Joseph R. (1, 2): Cap. 13 July 1861. Par. 31 August 1861.

Price, Q. H. (1): D. McDowell, VA August 1861.

Ragan, William (1, 2).

Ragsdale, Charles David [David C.] (1, 2): Enl. Co. K, 1st Regt. Cav. 3 May 1862.

Ramey, George W.: Enl. 7 May 1861. Dis. for disability at Camp Bartow VA 19 November [31 October] 1861. Enl. State Troops. Appt. Lt. B. 1839. D. 1895. Bd. Oak Hill Cemetery, Newnan, Coweta Cty.

Ransom, Columbus F. (1, 2): Enl. 2nd Co. A,12th Bn. Light Art. 1 May 1862. WIA Monocacy MD 9 July 1864. Cap. Frederick City MD 10 July 1864. Received Savannah River GA for Exch. 15 November 1864.

Rawls, Thomas F. (2): Enl. 1 June 1861. Elec. 1st Lt. of Co. G, 53rd Inf. Regt. 30 April 1862. Furloughed for 60 days 5 February 1863. WIA Gettysburg PA 2 July 1863. D. from wounds Richmond VA 28 July 1863. Bd. Hollywood Cemetery, Richmond, Henrico Cty., VA.

Ray, John D. (2): Enl. 7 May 1861. Enl. Co. H, 1st Cav., Hill's Cav. Brigade. Appt. Capt. B. 17 March 1841. D. 4 October 1911. Bd. Oak hill Cemetary, Newnan, Coweta Cty.

Ray, Lavender Roy (2): Enl. 6 July 1861. Enl. Co. H, 1st Regt. Cav. 19 April 1862. Appt. Sgt. 1862 or 1863. Detailed for duty Ordnance Department and ordered to report to Maj. M. H. Wright in Atlanta GA 18 July 1863. Appt. Adj. of the 1st Regt. Cav. 3 September 1864. Assigned to duty as Lt. and Acting Ordnance Officer of Iverson's Brigade 16 October 1864; as Lt. and Ordnance Officer of Young's Cav. Division. Ordered to report to S. P. Kerr, Chief Ordnance Officer, Wheeler's Corps Cav., for duty as Acting Ordnance Officer, Iverson's Division 18 January 1865. Ordered to proceed to Athens GA to procure ordnance and ordnance stores, 9 April 1865. Par. Augusta GA 2 May 1865. B. Newnan GA 15 December 1842. D. Atlanta, GA 27 May 1916. Bd. Oak Hill Cemetery, Newnan, Coweta Cty.

Robinson, Christopher C. [Robison] (1, 2): Appt. 1st Sgt. of Co. C, 34th Inf. Regt. 13 May 1862. Dis. having been elected sheriff of Coweta Cty GA 3 April 1864. B. about 1832.

Sackett, Edward A. (1): Prom. to Cpl. WIA and captured 13 July 1861. Par. and sent home 24 July 1861.

Sims, Martin W. Thompson [Semmes/Simmes] (1): Dis. for disability at Monterey VA 30 [21] August, 1861. Enl. 2nd Co. A, 12th Bn. Light Art. 1 May 1862. WIA 1863. Sent to Charleston SC hospital 20 August 1863. Enl. Co. D, Phillips' Legion Cav., 27 February 1864. Surr. Greensboro NC 26 April 1865. B. 7 February 1835. D. 7 December 1899. Bd. Oak Hill Cemetery, Newnan, Coweta Cty.

Smith, Hugh W. (1, 2): Enl. 20th Inf. Regt. Appt. Sgt. KIA Louisa Court House VA.

Smith, Nathaniel T. (1, 2): Enl. 6th Inf. Regt. Appt. Sgt. KIA July 1863 Gettysburg PA.

Smith, William H. (1, 2): Enl. 6th Inf. Regt. Appt. Sgt. KIA near Richmond VA.

Speer, Simeon F. (1, 2): Appt. 5th Sgt. of Gibson's [Scogins's] Battery Griffin Light Art. 7 May 1862.

Stallings, Andrew J. (2): Enl. 1 June 1861. Elec. 1st Lt. of Co. F, 16th Bn. Cav., 14 May 1862. WIA Blountville TN 21 September 1863. Tfd. to Co. F, 13th Regt. Cav. 21 May 1864. B. 6 March 1832. D. 19 August 1869. Bd. Stallings Family Cemetery, near Dresden, Coweta Cty.

Stokes, Augustus W. (1, 2): Enl. Co. H, 56th Inf. Regt. 13 May 1862. Cap. Vicksburg MS 4 July 1863, and Par. 8 July 1863. B. about 1838.

Sumner, John C. [Summers] (2): Enl. 2 September 1861. Appt. 4th Sgt. of Co. D, 53rd [56th] Inf. Regt. 6 May 1862. Elec. 2nd Lt. 29 November 1864. Cap. Sailor's Creek VA 6 April 1865. Released Johnson's Island OH 20 June 1865. B. 30 September 1837. Bd. Senoia Town Cemetery, Coweta Cty.

Swint, Daniel [Swent] (1, 2): Appt. Sgt. Enl. 2nd Co. A, 12th Bn. Light Art. 1 May 1862 Appt. Sgt. WIA in arm, necessitating amputation, Cold Harbor VA 2 June 1864. B. 1844. D. 1890. Bd. Oak Hill Cemetery, Newnan, Coweta Cty.

Taylor, Robert P. (1, 2): Elec. Capt. of Co. G, 53rd Inf. Regt. 30 April 1862; Lt. Col. 14 October 1863. B. about 1837. KIA Knoxville TN 29 November 1863.

Tench, James A.: Enl. 1 June [7 May] 1861. B. 1 June 1842. D. Monterey VA 26 July 1861. Bd. Tench Family Cemetery, near Newnan, Coweta Cty.

Tench, John W. (2): Enl. 1 June 1861. Elec. Jr. 2nd (or 3rd) Lt. of Co. K, 1st Regt. Cav. 1 May 1862. Appt. Adj. WIA near Steubenville KY June 1863. Elec. Maj. December 1864. Judge Advocate of Martin's Division Cav. Par. Charlotte, NC 3 May 1865.

Tench, Reuben Monmorenci "Montie" [Rhubin/Robert]: Enl. 1 June 1861. Dis. Winchester VA 1 December 1861. Appt. 2nd Sgt. of Co. K, 1st Regt. Cav. 1 May 1862. WIA Murfreesboro TN 2 July 1862. B. 3 November 1844. D. 16 May 1910. Bd. Tench Family Cemetery, near Newnan, Coweta Cty.

Thomas, Montgomery L.: Enl. 7 May 1861. Dis. Staunton VA 25 August 1861. Enl. Co. I, 37th Inf. Regt. March 3, 1864. Appt. Acting Sgt.-Maj. WIA Franklin TN Elec. 1st Lt. Surr. Greensboro NC 26 April 1865. B. 13 June 1843. D. 10 June 1885. Bd. Oak Hill Cemetery, Newnan, Coweta Cty.

Thompson, James C. (2): Enl. 15 September 1861. Tfd. to regimental band 1861. Appt. Bugler of 2nd Co. A, 12th Bn. Light Art. 1 May 1862. Tfd. to band. Surr. Appomattox VA 9 April 1865. B. 15 January 1831. D. 20 June 1900. Bd. Oak Hill Cemetery, Newnan, Coweta Cty.

Thompson, Young H. J. (2): Enl. 15 September 1861. Tfd. to regimental band 1861. Appt. Regimental Bugler. Enl. 2nd Co. A, 12th Bn. Light Art. 1 May 1862. Appt. Cpl. Tfd. to battalion band. Surr. Appomattox VA 9 April 1865. B. about 1834. D. 28 June 1894. Bd. Oak Hill Cemetery, Newnan, Coweta Cty.

Thurmond, David H.: Enl. 7 May 1861. B. 18 April 1843. D. of disease McDowell VA 3 August 1861. Bd. Oak Hill Cemetery, Newnan, Coweta Cty.

Thurmond, Joel M.: Enl. 1 June 1861. B. 29 April 1839. D. of disease Staunton VA 6 December [August] 1861. Bd. Oak Hill Cemetery, Newnan, Coweta Cty.

Tomlin, Arken A. [Tamlin, Arcael/Arkin] (1, 2): Enl. Co. K, 1st Regt. Cav. 1 May 1862. Appt. 4th Sgt.

Turnipseed, Hiram W. [Harmon] (1, 2): Enl. Co. G [D], 53rd Inf. Regt. 30 April 1862. Appt. 4th Sgt. August 1863. Cap. Sailor's Creek VA 6 April 1865. Released Point Lookout MD 20 June 1865.

Welsh, Francis S. [Welch] (1, 2): Enl. 2nd Co. A, 12th Bn. Light Art. 1 May 1862. WIA and captured Monocacy MD 9 July 1864. Par. Point Lookout MD and Tfrd. to Aiken's Landing VA for exchange 15 March 1865. Received Boulware & Cox's Wharves, James River VA 18 March 1865.

Welsh, Joseph J [Welch] (1, 2): Appt. Regimental Sgt. Maj. September 1861. Appt. Sgt. of 2nd Co. A, 12th Bn. Light Art. 1 May 1862. WIA Monocacy MD 9 July 1864. On wounded furlough 31 August 1864. B. about 1842.

Whatley, William R. [Watley] (2): Enl. 7 May 1861. Enl. 2nd Co. A, 12th Bn. Light Art. 1 May 1862. WIA Cold Harbor VA 2 June 1864. B. about 1843. D. Richmond VA 9 July 1864.

Wilkinson, Henry Q. (1): Dis. Winchester VA 1 [16] February 1862. Enl. 2nd Co. A, 12th Bn. Light Art. 1 May 1862. Surr. Appomattox VA 9 April 1865.

Williams, Augustus R. (2): Enl. 7 May 1861. Enl. 2nd Co. A, 12th Bn. Light Art. 1 May 1862. Absent on furlough from hospital 31 August 1864. B. about 1836.

Williams, Madison F. (1, 2): Enl. 2nd Co. A, 12th Bn. Light Art. 1 May 1862. WIA, date and place not given. Cap. Farmville VA 6 April 1865. Released Newport News VA 25 June 1865. D. February 1887.

Wood, Rufus Peoples (2): Enl. 15 August 1861. Enl. 37th GA Militia (inactive). B. 10 June 1825. D. 28 February 1879. Bd. Wood Family Cemetery, near Texas, Heard Cty (GA).

Wood, Winston B. (1 [1 June]): Dis. for disability at Monterey VA 25 August 1861. Elec. 1st Lt. of 3rd Co. C, 12th Bn. Light Art. 1 May 1862. Resigned, disability, 20 October 1862. Enl. State Troops. Appt. Capt. B. 15 March 1835. D. 10 April 1873. [D. of wounds during war.] Bd. Oak Hill Cemetery, Newnan, Coweta Cty.

Wood, Wyatt H.: Enl. 15 August 1861. Dis. Unger's Store VA 12 January 1862. Enl. 3rd Co. C, 12th Bn. Light Art. 1 May 1862. Appt. Cpl.; Sgt.; 1st Sgt. Deserted 1 November 1864.

Word, Albert R. (2): Enl. 7 May 1861. Appt. Cpl. of 2nd Co. A, 12th Bn. Light Art. 1 May 1862. B. about 1844.

Wright, Moses H. [Mathew/Matthew] (1): B. about 1828. D. of disease at Jordan Springs VA 25 [26] January 1862.

Wright, William C. (1, 2): Enl. Co. K, 1st Regt. Cav. 1 May 1862. WIA Murfreesboro TN 13 July 1862. Par. Charlotte NC 3 May 1865. B. about 1835.

Co. B, "Co. D, Southern Guard," Muscogee County

Officers

Wilkins, Francis G. (1): Capt. Resigned due to ill health 6 March 1862. Appt. 1st Cpl. of Capt. F. S. Chapman's Co. GA Defenders, CSA, 15 August 1863. Appt. Col. State Troops. B. 1833. D. 1894. Bd. Linwood Cemetery, Columbus, Muscogee Cty.

Atkinson, George W. (1): 1st Lt. Cap. 13 July 1861. Exch. Beverly VA 16 July 1861. Resigned 2 September 1861. Elec. Capt. of Co. C, 9th Bn. Light Art. 1 April 1862. Resigned to join ranks as a private 20 June 1863. Enl. Co. E, 5th Regt. State Guards Inf. 1 August 1863. Assigned to QM's Department. B. about 1832.

Turman, William R. (1): 2nd Lt. Cap. 13 July 1861. Par. Beverly VA 16 July 1861. B. about 1832.

Wall, Lawrence W. (1, 2): Jr. 2nd (or 3rd) Lt. Cap. 13 July 1861. Par. Beverly VA 16 [20] July 1861. Prom. to 2nd Lt. Appt. 1st Sgt. of Co. A, 3rd Regt. Cav. 10 April 1862. Columbus GA hospital 31 December 1864. B. 1822. D. Jacksonville FL 22 May 1883. Bd. Linwood Cemetery, Columbus, Muscogee Cty.

Dennis, James W. (1, 2): 1st Sgt. Elec. 1st Lt. 3 [29] September 3. Appt. 1st Sgt. of Co. I, 3rd Regt. Cav. 16 May 1862. Tfd. to Co. K. Appt. 1st Lt. and Acting Adj. Par. Charlotte NC 26 April 1865. B. 1840. D. 1889. Bd. Linwood Cemetery, Columbus, Muscogee Cty.

Wiley, James M. (1): 2nd Sgt. Dis. 18 August 1861. Enl. Co. H, 11th Inf. Regt. 25 September 1861. WIA at The Wilderness VA 6 May 1864. On wounded furlough 31 August 1864.

Lovelace, James J. [Loveless] (1): 3rd Sgt. Dis. for disability 20 November 1861.

Althisar, Charles H. [Althiser/Althison] (1, 2): 4th Sgt. Enl. Co. B, Columbus Iron Works Bn.

Thompson, William H. (1, 2): 1st Cpl. Appt. 2nd Sgt.

Jones, Seaborn L. (1, 2): 2nd Cpl. Enl. Co. H, 54th Inf. Regt. 13 August 1863. B. 25 January 1826. D. 31 July 1909. Bd. Harmony Primitive Baptist Church, near Cataula, Harris Cty.

Taylor, George F. (1, 2): 3rd Cpl. Enl. Co. F, 12th Bn. Light Art. 26 November 1863. WIA Winchester VA 19 September 1864. Absent, wounded, 1 November 1864.

Wilson, Clayton (1, 2): 4th Cpl.

Privates

Allen, William F.: B. about 1842.

Arnold, Lovick P. [Lorick] (1, 2).

Atwood, James H. (1, 2): Listed as AWOL following retreat from Laurel Hill VA 30 July 1861.

Baker, Charles W. (1, 2).

Baker, William H.

Banks, Reason (1): Dis. for disability 29 August 1861. [D. 20 August 1861.]

Barker, John (1, 2).

Barrow, Charles (2): Enl. 18 December 1861. B. about 1823.

Benton, William.

Brooks, Wilkins (1, 2).

Bryant, William H. (1, 2): Bd. Pine Grove Cemetery, Eatonton, Putnam Cty.

Bussey, Jesse Frank (1, 2): Enl. Co. C, 9th Bn. Light Art. 1 April 1862. Appt. 5th Sgt. Bd. Cedar Hill Cemetery, Dawson, Terrell Cty.

Clegg, James (1, 2): B. about 1834.

Clegg, J. H. H. (1, 2).

Clinton, Robert H.: (1) Deserted 11 [15] June 1861.

Cohen, James (1, 2).

Cohen, Joseph.

Collier, Frank (1): Musician. Dis. for disability 21 August 1861.

Conley, Luke [Conley] (1, 2): Enl. Co. C, 9th Bn. Light Art. 1 April 1862. Took oath of allegiance to US Government Bermuda Hundred VA and furnished transportation to Rouse's Point VA 19 December 1864.

Cook, Seaborn (1): Cap. 13 July 1861. Par. Beverly VA 20 July 1861. Enl. Co. H, 3rd Bn. Inf. 19 February 1862. No record of transfer. Enl. Co. B, 15th Regt. Confederate Cav. 10 April 1864.

Cook, Solon.

Cook, Willis.

Cooper, George W. (1): D. of illness in Staunton VA hospital 1 August 1861.

Currence, Junius A. [Currance/Currants] (1): Deserted Staunton VA 13 [18] June 1861.

Denson, Burrell Mc. [Burwell] (1, 2): Enl. Co. H, 3rd Bn. Inf. 26 March 1862. Tfd. to Co. K, 37th Inf. Regt. 6 May 1863. Appt. 1st Cpl. 1 January 1864; Sgt. 1864. B. about 1839. KIA New Hope Church GA 28 May 1864.

Deshaser, Richard (1): Drummed out of camp for theft 22 July 1861, by vote of company.

Edwards, Charles (1, 2): Cap. 13 July 1861.

Edwards, Christopher (1, 2).

Etchison, Stephen [Atchison/Etchinson/Etehurn] (1): Cap. 13 July 1861. Par. Beverly VA 20 July 1861.

Ferguson, Nathaniel C. (1, 2): B. about 1829.

Fletcher, John (1): Dis. for disability 19 December 1861.

Flynn, John E. [Flinn] (1): Cap. 13 July 1861. Par. Beverly VA 20 July 1861. Enl. Co. H, 1st GA Local Defense Troops (Augusta). D. 25 July 1910. Bd. Clear Springs Baptist Church Cemetery, near Roswell, Milton Cty. (now Fulton Cty).

Foran, James (1): Dis. for disability 21 [26] August 1861. B. 1812. D. 16 March 1888. Bd. Linwood Cemetery, Columbus, Muscogee Cty.

Foran, John (2): Enl. 1 September 1861. B. 1838. D. 29 June 1905. Bd. Linwood Cemetery, Columbus, Muscogee Cty.

Foran, Patrick (1): Dis. for disability 21 August [5 September] 1861. B. about 1811.

Ford, Manley W. [Manly] (2): Enl. 1 June 1861.

Foster, Frank (1, 2).

Foyle, William L. (1, 2).

Frazier, Andrew L. [Frasier, H. L.] (1, 2).

Hagans, Joseph B. [Hagins] (1): Dis. for disability 18 June 1861. Enl. Co. H, 31st Inf. Regt. 27 November 1861. Cap. Sharpsburg MD 17 September 1862. Exch. 11 November 1862. D. November 1863.

Hall, Moses H. (1, 2): Cap. 13 July 1861. Par. Beverly VA 20 July 1861. Enl. Co. H, 3rd Bn. Inf. 21 March 1862. Tfd. to Co. K, 37th Inf. Regt. 6 May 1863. Cap. Calhoun GA 17 May 1864. Tfd. to Rock Island IL, where he took oath of allegiance to US Government and Enl. US Navy, 10 June 1864. B. about 1838.

Hall, William (1): Cap. 13 July 1861. Par. Beverly VA 20 July 1861.

Hammons, George [Hammond] (1, 2): B. about 1843.

Hellings, John P. (1, 2): Elec. 2nd Lt. 1862 [remained a private]. Enl. Co. C, 9th Bn. Light Art. 1 April 1862. Appt. Sgt. With Gen. Breckinridge's Division 29 February–31 August 1864.

Henderson, James (1): Dis. for disability 10 August 1861.

Henley, Frank (1, 2).

Hodgins, Americus V. (2): Enl. 1 October 1861.

Hodgins, Leonidas (1, 2).

Holmes, C. W.

Holmes, Joseph W.: B. about 1839.

Holstead, William H. (1, 2): Cap. 8 January 1862. Exch. 1862. Enl. Co. H, 3rd Bn. Inf. 24 March 1862. Tfd. to Co. K, 37th Inf. Regt. 20 July 1863. Surr. Greensboro NC 26 April 1865. B. about 1841.

Jones, J. G.

Kelley, William (1, 2).

Key, Peter (1): Cap. 13 July 1861. Par. Beverly West VA 20 July 1861. Absent, a paroled prisoner, 11 March 1862.

Key, Randolph [Kerr] (1, 2): Appt. 1st Sgt. 3 [30] September 1861.

Lawrence, Drewry L. (1, 2).

Lawrence, James P. (1, 2).

Lynah, James [Linah, Lynch] (1): Dis. for disability 21 July 1861.

Magnus, George [Magnes/Magney] (1): Cap. 13 July 1861. Par. Beverly VA 20 July 1861. Dis. 2 December 1861.

Malone, Milton (1, 2).

Massey, Richard (1, 2): Enl. Co. D, 1st Regular Inf. Cap. Jericho Ford VA 22 May 1864. Exch. Point Lookout MD 15 March 1865.

Mathews, Levi P. (1): Dis. for disability 1 August 1861.

McCurdy, John C. (1): Cap. 13 July 1861. Par. Beverly VA 20 July 1861. Dis. 14 July 1861 [1862]

McDaniel, Alexander (1, 2).

McElrath, James [McElreath] (1, 2): Appt. Cpl. of Co. C, 9th Bn. Light Art. 1 April 1862. Appt. Sgt. Received Washington DC, a Confederate deserter, where he took oath of allegiance to US Government and was furnished transportation to New Orleans LA 26 January 1865.

McKay, William A. (1, 2).

Morgan, Evan.

Morgan, Rans.

Morris, John (2): Enl. 1 June 1861. D. 9 May 1905. Bd. Mt. Pilgrim Baptist Church Cemetery, near Buena Vista (Fort Benning), Marion Cty.

Morrison, Alexander C. (1, 2): Enl. Co. C, 46th Inf. Regt. 10 May 1862. Dis. after furnishing substitute, 27 April 1863. B. about 1838.

Morrison, Jeptha H. (1, 2): Enl. Co. C, 46th Inf. Regt. 10 May 1862. Detailed QM Department Columbus GA June 1864. On detail Ordnance Department Columbus GA 26 April 1865. B. about 1843.

Murphy, Matthew W. (1, 2): Appt. 4th Sgt. of Co. C, 9th Bn. Light Art. 1 April 1862. Detailed Columbus GA Arsenal 24 March 1865. B. 22 August 1843. D. 27 December 1874. Bd. Linwood Cemetery, Columbus, Muscogee Cty.

Nix, James H. (1, 2): B. about 1843.

Ogletree, Vincent G. (1, 2): Enl. Co. E, 5th Regt. State Guards Inf. 4 August 1863. B. about 1833.

Phelps, Levi D. (1): B. about 1842. D. Winchester VA 8 February 1862.

Pursell, David P. [Purcell] (1): Dis. for disability 21 July 1861. Appt. 1st Sgt. of Co. F, 17th Inf. Regt. 14 August 1861. WIA Garnett's Farm VA 27 June 1862. Absent, detached Jackson Hospital, Richmond VA, due to disability 28 February 1865. B. about 1833.

Reagan, William R. [Ragan] (1, 2).

Reese, John Chappel (1): Appt. 5th Sgt. 30 September 1861. Dis. 16 January 1862. Enl. Co. I, Floyd's Legion State Guards Inf. Bd. Rose Hill Cemetery, Rockmart, Polk Cty.

Ridenhour, Augustus B. [Ridenhall/Rydenhour] (1): B. about 1839. D. Monterey, VA 21 August 1861.

Sanford, A. P. [Sandland] (1, 2).

Sauls, John B. (1, 2).

Seals, John W. [Seats] (1, 2).

Simmons, Lewis (1, 2).

Smith, Isaac.

Smith, James T. (1, 2): Appt. Cpl. Appt. 1st Sgt. of Co. G, 28th Bn., GA Siege Art. 14 September 1863.

Smith, Jason T. (1): D. 6 May 1861 Pensacola FL.

Smith, Shadrach (1, 2).

Smith, Thomas J. (1, 2): Enl. Co. C, 9th Bn. Light Art. 1 April 1862. Cap. Macon GA 20 April 1865. B. about 1842.

Sturdevant, Thomas [Sturtevant] (1): Dis. for disability 21 July 1861.

Sunderland, A. P.

Sweet, Thomas (1, 2): [2nd Cpl.] B. about 1839.

Tucker, John W. (1): D. in Staunton VA hospital 1 July 1861.

Watson, M. G. (1, 2): [3rd Cpl.]

Watts, J. R. [G. R.] (1, 2).

Webb, William J. (1): Cap. 13 July 1861. Par. Beverly VA 20 July 1861.

Welch, William (1): WIA in leg at Cheat Mountain, VA 12 September 1861. Dis. 16 January 1862. Enl. Co. F, 64th Inf. Regt. 11 April 1863. Richmond VA. Hospitalized 31 October 1864. B. about 1842.

West, Riley (2): Enl. 1 September 1861. B. about 1837.

White, Jacob P. (1, 2): Enl. Co. B, Columbus Naval Iron Works Bn. B. 1842. D. 1891. Bd. Laurel Grove Cemetery, Savannah, Chatham Cty.

Wiggins, Jeptha C. (1, 2): Enl. Co. H, 3rd Bn. Inf. 31 March 1862. Tfd. to Co. K, 37th Inf. Regt. 6 May 1863. Cap. Missionary Ridge TN 25 November 1863. Released Rock Island IL 18 May 1865.

Williams, Benjamin Henry (1, 2) [Dis. 14 July 1861 or 1862]: Cap. 13 July 1861. Par. Beverly VA 20 July 1861. Enl. Co. G, 9th Regt. GA Militia July 1864.

Williams, Benjamin Sherold (1, 2): Cap. 13 July 1861. Par. B. 2 June 1829. D. 9 September 1861. Bd. Linwood Cemetery, Columbus, Muscogee Cty.

Williamson, William S. (1, 2).

Wilson, Henry: Enl. 1 June 1861.

Wood, James [Woods] (1, 2): B. about 1835.

Wright, James A. (1, 2): Reported AWOL 30 July 1861.

Young, Leonard H. (1, 2).

Co. C, "Southern Rights Guard," Houston County

Officers

Houser, John Andrew (1, 2): Capt. B. 1 August 1827. D. 15 March 1910. Bd. Oaklawn Cemetery, Ft. Valley, Peach Cty.

Palmer, Joseph (1, 2): 1st Lt. Appt. Regimental Adj. 11 December 1861. Elec. Capt. of Co. A, 14th Bn. Light Art., Southern Rights Battery, 26 April 1862; Promoted Maj. 1863. Surr. Greensboro NC 26 April 1865. B. 10 July 1835, Pineville, Berkeley Cty., SC. D. 1 July 1898. Bd. Evergreen Cemetery, Perry, Houston Cty.

Gilbert, Julius Caesar (1): 2nd Lt. Resigned prior to 15 March 1862. Elec. 1st Lt. of Co. A, 8th Regt. State Guards Inf. 7 July 1863. Mustered out February 1864. Enl. Co. G, 8th Regt. Militia June 1864. Appt. Surgeon. Dis. May 1865. B. 4 January 1841. D. 17 March 1895. Bd. Evergreen Cemetery, Perry, Houston Cty.

Felder, John Richard (1): Jr. 2nd (or 3rd) Lt. B. about 1833. D. of disease McDowell VA 24 August 1861.

Killen, Samuel D. [James] (1): 1st Sgt. Cap. 13 July 1861. Par. Beverly Northwestern (now West) VA 20 July 1861. Reduced to private. Listed as a paroled prisoner, 11 March 1862. Elec. Capt. of Co. A, 8th Regt. State Guards Inf. 7 July 1863. Mustered out February 1864. Appt. Comm. Sgt. of the 64th Inf. Regt. 4 February 1864. Cap. Sailor's Creek VA 6 April 1865. Released

Newport News VA 14 June 1865. B. 16 February 1823. D. 5 April 1880. Bd. Evergreen Cemetery, Perry, Houston Cty.

Havis, Minor W. (1, 2): 2nd Sgt. Appt. 1st Sgt. 6 December 1861. Elec. Sr. 1st Lt. of Co. A, 14th Bn. Light Art., Southern Rights Battery, 26 April 1862. Elec. Capt. 12 October 1862. Surr. Greensboro NC 26 April 1865. B. 23 April 1829. D. 27 November 1889.

King, Sylvester Capers (1, 2): 3rd Sgt. Appt. 3rd Sgt. of Co. A, 14th Bn. Light Art., Southern Rights Battery, 26 April 1862. Tfd. to Co. G, 14 October 1862. Surr. Greensboro NC 26 April 1865. [Enl. Cav.]

King, Wesley F. (1, 2): 4th Sgt. Reenl., command not given. D. in service.

Duncan, James R., Jr. (1): 5th Sgt. Elec. Jr. 2nd (or 3rd) Lt. 18 October 1861. Resigned 10 November 1861. Elec. Jr. 1st Lt. of Co. A, 14th Bn. Light Art., Southern Rights Battery, 26 April 1862. Surr. Greensboro NC 26 April 1865. B. 23 October 1837. D. 17 July 1899. Bd. Evergreen Cemetery, Perry, Houston Cty.

King, Alfred A. (1, 2): 1st Cpl. Enl. Co. A, 14th Bn. Light Art., Southern Rights Battery, 26 April 1862. WIA, date and place not given. Surr. Greensboro NC 26 April 1865. B. about 1837. Bd. Evergreen Cemetery, Perry, Houston Cty.

King, Francis Marion (1, 2): 2nd Cpl. Enl. Co. B, 2nd Regt. SC, Art. 2 May 1862. WIA, date and place not given. Surr. Greensboro NC 26 April 1865. Bd. Evergreen Cemetery, Perry, Houston Cty.

Jordan, Stephen E. (1): 3rd Cpl. Dis. 11 January 1862. B. 1835. Bd. Evergreen Cemetery, Perry, Houston Cty.

Killen, Thomas M. (1, 2): 4th Cpl. Appt. 1st Sgt. of Co. A, 8th Regt. State Guards Inf. 7 July 1863. Mustered out February 1864. Appt. 1st Sgt. of Co. G, 8th Regt. GA, Militia June 1864. Surr. May 1865. B. 19 September 1837. D. 14 April 1902. Bd. Evergreen Cemetery, Perry, Houston Cty.

Davis, Henry B. (1): 5th Cpl. Dis. 24 [11] August 1861. B. about 1833.

Privates:

Alcott, David G. [Alcut/Albert] (1, 2).

Anderson, Reuel Wooten. [Rural/Ryel] (2): Enl. 20 [10] August 1861. Elec. 1st Lt. 11 December 1861. Elec. Sr. 1st Lt. of Co. A, 14th Bn. Light Art., Southern Rights Battery, 26 April 1862. Elec. Capt. Surr. Greensboro NC 26 April 1865. Bd. Orange Hill Cemetery, Hawkinsville, Pulaski Cty.

Barrett, J. Franklin A. (1, 2): Appt. Sgt. of Terrell's Battery Light Art. 11 March 1862. Surr. Greensboro NC 26 April 1865.

Barrett, James E. (2): Enl. 18 September 1861. Enl. Co. A, 14th Bn. Light Art., Southern Rights Battery, 26 April 1862. Appt. Guidon bearer. Surr. Greensboro NC 26 April 1865.

Barrineua, S.

Baskin, Alonzo P. [Baskins] (1, 2): Appt. 5th Sgt. 18 October 1861. Enl. Co. A, 14th Bn. Light Art., Southern Rights Battery, 26 April 1862. Appt. Cpl. Surr. Greensboro NC 26 April 1865. B. 20 January 1844.

Baskin, John O. [Baskins, James] (2): Enl. 18 September 1861. Enl. Co. F, 31st Inf. Regt. 5 May 1862. WIA Fredericksburg, VA 13 December 1862. Appt. 3rd Cpl. Cap. Gettysburg, PA 4 July 1863. Par. Fort Delaware, DE, February 1865. Received Boulware & Cox's Wharves, James River, VA 10–12 March 1865. B. 23 October 1843. D. 25 June 1905. Bd. Orange Hill Cemetery, Hawkinsville, Pulaski Cty.

Baskin, Joseph C. [Baskins] (2): Enl. 18 September 1861. Enl. Co. A, 8th Regt. State Guards Inf. 1 August 1863. Mustered out February 1864. Enl. Co. G, 8th Regt. GA, Militia June 1864. Surr. May 1865. B. 4 March 1837.

Bateman, Simon E. (1, 2): Enl. Co. A, 14th Bn. Light Art., Southern Rights Battery, 26 April 1862. Surr. Greensboro NC 26 April 1865. B. about 1843. Bd. Evergreen Cemetery, Perry, Houston Cty.

Bechtholdt, Lewis [Bechtold/Becholat, Louis] (1): Cap. 13 July 1861. Par. Beverly VA 20 July 1861. Dis. Richmond VA 3 August 1861. Enl. Co. A, 14th Bn. Light Art., Southern Rights Battery, 1 May 1864. Surr. Greensboro NC 26 April 1865.

Belvin, Thomas Sumter [Sumpter] (1): Tfd. to Co. C, 6th Inf. Regt. 14 February 1862. Dis. 5 September 1862. Enl. Co. K, 11th Inf. Regt. 7 October 1862. Appt. Sgt. Cap. The Wilderness VA 6 May 1864. B. 1 June 1842. D. of dropsy Fort Delaware, DE, 16 May 1864. Bd. Marshallville Methodist Church Cemetery, Marshallville, Macon Cty.

Bolton, Matthew Perryman (1, 2): Enl. Co. H, 45th Inf. Regt. March 1862. Appt. 5th Sgt. 1 January 1865. Elec. Lt. 1865. Cap. Hatcher's Run VA 25 March 1865. Released Johnson's Island OH 17 June 1865. [Enl. Cav.] B. about 1839.

Bolton, Thomas M.: Enl. 1 September 1861. Dis. 24 January 1862. B. about 1838.

Britt, Pinckney C. (1, 2): Enl. Co. A, 14th Bn. Light Art., Southern Rights Battery, 26 April 1862. Surr. Greensboro NC 26 April 1865.

Brown, D. Homer (1, 2): Enl. Terrell's [Anderson's] Battery Light Art. 18 May 1862. Tfd. to Co. A, 14th Bn. Light Art., Southern Rights Battery, 1 September 1862. Tfd. to Co. G, 1863. Surr. Greensboro NC 26 April 1865. Bd. Evergreen Cemetery, Perry, Houston Cty.

Butler, Joseph C. (1, 2): Enl. Co. K, 11th Inf. Regt. 11 March 1862. WIA at Cold Harbor VA 1 June 1864. [KIA.]

Choate, Charles T. [Choat] (1, 2): Enl. Co. A, 14th Bn. Light Art., Southern Rights Battery, 26 April 1862. Surr. Greensboro NC 26 April 1865.

Clark, James D. [Clarke]: Enl. 10 November 1861. Dis. 26 January 1862. Enl. Cav. B. about 1832.

Clark, John W. [Clarke] (1 [Dis. 28 January 1862], 2): Enl. Co. A, 14th Bn. Light Art., Southern Rights Battery, 26 April 1862. Appt. Cpl. Surr. Greensboro NC 26 April 1865. B. 5 May 1838. D. 19 April 1910. Bd. Evergreen Cemetery, Perry, Houston Cty.

Clark, William.

Cliett, Alcephron C. [Cliot, Alciphron] (1): AWOL as of 31 July 1861. Enl. GA State Troops. B. about 1842.

Collier, Edwin S. (1): Tfd. to Co. E, 24 June 1861. Deserted 3 October 1861. [Other reports show KIA.] Bd. Indian Springs Town Cemetery, Butts Cty.

Collier, Lawson F. (1, 2): Enl. Co. C, 19th Bn. Cav., 24 July 1862. Tfd. to Co. H, 10th Regt. Confederate Cav. January 1863. Elec. 2nd Lt. 9 November 1863. Par. Hillsboro NC, 3 May 1865.

Cooper, William D. H. (2): Enl. 20 August [1 September] 1861. Enl. Massenburg's Battery Light Art., [Jackson Art.], 17 May 1862. Appt. Cpl. On detached duty 1 May to 31 October 1864. [Enl. Cav.]

Cox, William R. (2): Enl. 1 September 1861. Enl. Co. A, 14th Bn. Light Art., Southern Rights Battery, 26 April 1862. Surr. Greensboro NC 26 April 1865. B. about 1844.

Cross, Hardy (2): Enl. 10 September 1861.

Culler, Derrill H. (1, 2): Enl. Co. D, 12th (Robinson's) Regt. State Guards, Cav. 4 August 1863. B. about 1839.

Davis, John Gamble (2): Enl. 10 [20] June 1861. Enl. Co. H, 45th Inf. Regt. 22 April 1862. Appt. Sgt. Maj. April 1862. On furlough 28 September 1862–3 January 1863. Bd. Evergreen Cemetery, Perry, Houston Cty.

Davis, William Richardson (1, 2): Enl. Co. B, 11th Bn. Light Art. 1 September 1862. Tfd. to Co. G, 8th Regt. Cav. 5 January 1865. [Appt. Sgt. Maj. Inf. Regt.] B. 31 August 1842. D. 26 December 1920. Bd. Evergreen Cemetery, Perry, Houston Cty.

Dennard, Charles W. [Denward] (1): B. 18 March 1838. D. Houston Cty. GA 24 August 1861. Bd. Evergreen Cemetery, Perry, Houston Cty.

Doolittle, George R. (1, 2): Enl. Co. A, 14th Bn. Light Art., Southern Rights Battery, 26 April 1862. Surr. Greensboro NC 26 April 1865. D. October 1885.

Drake, John S. [Duke] (1, 2): Enl. Co. G, 32nd Inf., 6 May 1861. Elec. Capt., command not given. B. 29 April 1841. D. 6 May 1816. Bd. Poplar Springs Methodist Church Cemetery, near Adrian, Johnson Cty.

Duncan, Clinton C. (1, 2): Appt. 2nd Sgt. 13 December 1861. Appt. 1st Sgt. of Co. A, 14th Bn. Light Art., Southern Rights Battery, 26 April 1862. Surr. Greensboro NC 26 April 1865. B. 5 December 1839. D. 8 May 1910. Bd. Evergreen Cemetery, Perry, Houston Cty.

Duncan, Edward E. (2): Enl. 14 [18] May 1861. Enl. Co. A, 14th Bn. Light Art., Southern Rights Battery, 26 April 1862. WIA and Cap. Perryville KY 8 October 1862. Exch. Surr. Greensboro, NC 26 April 1865. Bd. Evergreen Cemetery, Perry, Houston Cty.

English, Solomon: Enl. 20 August [30 September] 1861. Dis. 21 January 1862. Enl. Co. A, 3rd Regt. Cav. 16 April 1862. Admitted to 2nd Division, 20th Army Corps Hospital, 3 January 1865. Sent to Gen. Hospital 16 January 1865. Admitted to Gen. Field Hospital, 20th Army Corps, 19 January 1865. B. 1 April 1833. D. 15 July 1901. Bd. Sowhatchie Cemetery, near Cedar Springs, Early Cty.

Ezell, Ezekiel H. (1, 2): Appt. Maj. and QM CSA, from GA, to rank from 14 October 1862, and ordered to report to Gen. Leadbetter. Relieved from duty by Special Order dated 11 December 1862, and ordered to report to the Chief QM for duty. Appears on Return of Department of Trans-MS, for September 1864, which shows him Chief QM for Department Headquarters On duty Shreveport LA 13 February 1865, and Par. there 9 June 1865. B. 6 April 1834. D. 29 June 1900. Bd. Byron Town Cemetery, Peach Cty.

Feagin, Henry S. [Feagan] (1, 2): Appt. 6th Sgt. of Co. A, 14th Bn. Light Art., Southern Rights Battery, 26 April 1862. B. about 1841.

Felder, Hamblin Ragin (1, 2): Enl. Co. A, 14th Bn. Light Art., Southern Rights Battery, 26 April 1862. Elec. Jr. 2nd (or 3rd) Lt. Surr. Greensboro NC 26 April 1865. B. 1 March 1835. D. 14 March 1890. Bd. Evergreen Cemetery, Perry, Houston Cty.

Felder, Lawrence A. (1): B. about 1843. D. of disease Augusta Cty., VA 11 September 1861. Bd. Evergreen Cemetery, Perry, Houston Cty.

Felder, Rufus McPherson (1): B. about 1839. KIA Cheat Mountain VA 12 [13] September 1861. Bd. Evergreen Cemetery, Perry, Houston Cty.

Felder, William McDaniel [McDonald] (1, 2): Enl. GA State Troops. [Enl. Art.]

Fisher, Sam (1): Drummer. B. 1842. D. 10 October 1931.

Flanders, Theodore F. [Flanderow/Flanderon] (1): Cap. 13 July 1861. Par. Beverly VA 20 July 1861.

Frazier, H. S. (1, 2): Enl. Pvt. Battery, State Troops.

Fry, Albert H. (2): Enl. 18 September 1861. Enl. Co. A, 14th Bn. Light Art., Southern Rights Battery, 26 April 1862. Appt. 1st Cpl.; Sgt. WIA, date and place not given. Surr. Greensboro NC 26 April 1865. B. 27 January 1832.

Fullenwider, Sydney F. [Fulenwider] (2): Enl. 10 October [November] 1861. B. about 1838.

Giles, Samuel Andrew [Andrew Samuel] (2): Enl. 1 June 1861. Appt. 2nd Sgt. of Co. A, 14th Bn. Light Art., Southern Rights Battery, 26 April 1862. Appt. Sgt. Maj. Surr. Greensboro NC 26 April 1865. [Appt. Sgt. Maj. of Palmers Art. Bn.] B. 21 October 1841. D. 24 March 1897. Bd. Evergreen Cemetery, Perry, Houston Cty.

Giles, John Mason (1): Dis. 27 May [10 December] 1861. Appt. Ens. and Brevet 2nd Lt. of Co. A, 8th Regt. State Guards Inf. 7 July 1863. Mustered out February 1864. Enl. Co. G, 8th Regt. GA, Militia June 1864. Dis. May 1865. B. 21 February 1818. D. 25 May 1866. Bd. Evergreen Cemetery, Perry, Houston Cty.

Graves, John A (1): Cap. 13 July 1861. D. Beverly VA 26 July [3 August] 1861.

Gray, Simon (1): D. Monterey VA 26 July 1861. Bd. Gray-Varner Family Cemetery, near Centerville, Houston Cty.

Gunn, Daniel F. (2): Enl. 20 June 1861. Appt. Brigade Ordnance Sgt. Enl. Co. A, 8th Regt. State Guards Inf. 7 July 1863. Mustered out February 1864. Enl. Co. G, 8th Regt. GA, Militia June 1864. Dis. May 1865. B. 10 August 1833. D. 23 March 1896. Bd. New Park Cemetery, Fort Gaines, Clay Cty.

Haren, John C. [Haron, Horan, Haran, Heron] (1, 2): Enl. GA State Troops.

Hardy, Thomas Mc. [Thomas Mack] (1): Dis. 26 January 1862. Enl. Co. A, 14th Bn. Light Art., Southern Rights Battery, 26 April 1862. Appt. QM Sgt. Surr. Greensboro NC 26 April 1865. [Enl. Cav.] B. about 1836.

Hardy, William S. (1): Dis. 26 January 1862. Enl. Cav. B. about 1833.

Harvey, Henry H. (2): Enl. 10 September 1861. B. about 1839.

Henson, A. O.: Enl. SC Art.

Holmes, John B. (2): Enl. 20 October 1861. Enl. Co. A, 14th Bn. Light Art., Southern Rights Battery, 26 April 1862. Appt. Cpl. WIA and Cap. Perryville KY 8 October 1862. Exch. Surr. Greensboro NC 26 April 1865.

Holmes, Robert M. (2): Enl. 1 September 1861. Enl. Trans-Mississippi Army.

Houser, Andrew O. (1, 2): Enl. SC Art. B. about 1842.

Hudson, Matthew C. (2): Enl. 18 September 1861. Enl. Co. A, 14th Bn. Light Art., Southern Rights Battery, 26 April 1862. Surr. Greensboro NC 26 April 1865.

Jones, William C. (1, 2): B. about 1843.

Kendrick, Benjamin C. (1, 2): Appt. 7th Sgt. of Co. A, 14th Bn. Light Art., Southern Rights Battery, 26 April 1862. Surr. Greensboro NC 26 April 1865. B. 1838. D. 1921. Bd. Unadilla Town Cemetery, Dooly Cty.

Kendrick, James Dawson (1, 2): Appt. 4th Cpl. of Co. A, 14th Bn. Light Art., Southern Rights Battery, 26 April 1862. WIA, date and place not given. Surr. Greensboro NC 26 April 1865. B. 1843. D. 1 August 1876. Bd. Oak Lawn Cemetery, Fort Valley, Peach Cty.

Kendrick, John H. (1, 2): Enl. Co. A, 14th Bn. Light Art., Southern Rights Battery. Bd. Orange Hill Cemetery, Hawkinsville, Pulaski Cty.

Kendrick, Martin (1): B. 6 November 1822. D. 5 [6] August 1861 near Staunton VA. Bd. Henderson Town Cemetery, Houston Cty.

Killen, George W.: Enl. 11 April 1861. Cap. 13 July 1861. Par. Beverly VA 13 August 1861. Dis. 29 August 1861. Enl. Engineer Corps. B. about 1839.

Killen, John N.: Enl. 4 [1] June 1861. Cap. 13 July 1861. Par. Beverly, VA 24 July 1861. Enl. Cav. B. 1840. D. 1912. Bd. Evergreen Cemetery, Perry, Houston Cty.

Klewe, Julius [Klive/Clive] (1, 2): Tfd. to Regimental Band 1861.

Manning, Willoughby (1, 2): B. 28 September 1838. D. 9 November 1903. Bd. Westview Cemetery, Atlanta, Fulton Cty.

McDaniel, Henry T. [McDanils] (1): Cap. 13 July 1861. Par. Beverly VA 20 July 1861. Roll for 11 March 1862 shows him "Paroled, now in Georgia." Reenl., command not given. D. in service.

McDaniel, Thomas (1).

McPherson, Lewis W. (1): Dis. 21 January 1862.

Noel, William B.: Enl. 20 August 1861. Dis. 21 January 1862.

Norwood, Archibald S.: Enl. 1 September 1861. B. about 1845. D. of disease 16 December [16 October] 1861. Bd. Evergreen Cemetery, Perry, Houston Cty.

Norwood, Sylvester T.: Enl. 1 September 1861. B. 3 February 1945. D. 16 December 1861. Bd. Evergreen Cemetery, Perry, Houston Cty.

Norwood, William Henry (1, 2): Appt. 4th Sgt. of Co. A, 14th Bn. Light Art., Southern Rights Battery, 26 April 1862; 1st Sgt. WIA, date and place not given. Surr. Greensboro NC 26 April 1865. B. 22 August 1840. D. 31 December 1920. Bd. Evergreen Cemetery, Perry, Houston Cty.

Patten, William C. [Patton] (1, 2): Enl. 1 September 1861. Dis. 29 December 1861.

Paul, George (1): Dis. 28 December 1861. Enl. Co. A, 14th Bn. Light Art., Southern Rights Battery, 26 April 1862. Artificer for battery. Surr. Greensboro NC 26 April 1865. B. 22 October 1829. D. 9 February 1902. Bd. Evergreen Cemetery, Perry, Houston Cty.

Peddy, William B. [Piddy] (1, 2): Enl. Co. A, 14th Bn. Light Art., Southern Rights Battery, 26 April 1862. Surr. Greensboro, NC 26 April 1865.

Powers, John H. (1): Dis. 3 [10] August 1861. Elec. Capt. of Co. E. 7th Regt. State Troops, 16 November 1861. Mustered out May 1862. B. about 1821.

Pugh, Joseph S. (1): Dis. 30 October 1861.

Rainey, Watkins Leigh (1, 2): Enl. Co. A, 14th Bn. Light Art., Southern Rights Battery, 26 April 1862. WIA Seven Days Fight near Richmond VA June 1862. On detail duty in Columbus GA Arsenal, due to disability from wound, 30 June 1864, to close of war. B. about 1840.

Rainey, William H. [Rainy] (1, 2): Enl. Co. D, 10th GA Bn. B. 8 May 1839. KIA action near Atlanta, 16 August 1864. Bd. Evergreen Cemetery, Perry, Houston Cty.

Rice, James R. (1, 2): Appt. 5th Sgt. 13 December 1861. Appt. 5th Sgt. of Co. A, 14th Bn. Light Art., Southern Rights Battery, 26 April 1862. Elec. 2nd Lt. 30 June 1862. Surr. Greensboro NC 26 April 1865.

Riley, John H. (1, 2): Enl. SC Art. B. about 1841. Bd. Evergreen Cemetery, Perry, Houston Cty.

Rutherford, Eugenius H. (1, 2): Reenl., command not given. B. about 1841.

Shearin, Martin L. [Shearan/Shearen/Swearine] (1): Dis. 13 [15] December 1861.

Smith, Eason Jr. (1, 2): Enl. Co. A, 14th Bn. Light Art., Southern Rights Battery, 26 April 1862. Surr. Greensboro NC 26 April 1865. B. 25 December 1835. D. 11 June 1912. Bd. Snow Springs Baptist Church Cemetery, near Unadilla, Dooly Cty.

Smith, James N.: Enl. 1 September 1861. Dis. 29 [30] January 1862. Enl. Co. A, 14th Bn. Light Art., Southern Rights Battery, 26 April 1862. Surr. Greensboro NC 26 April 1865. B. about 1838.

Smith, John N.: Enl. Co. A, 14th Bn. Light Art., Southern Rights Battery. Later Enl. Co. E, 3rd Inf. Regt. B. 18 November 1818. D. 5 June 1895.

Spencer, John C. (1, 2): Enl. Cav.

Spier, John R. [Spear/Speir] (1 [D. September, 1861], 2): Bd. Evergreen Cemetery, Perry, Houston Cty.

Sturges, George W. [Sturees/Sturgess/Sturgis] (1): Dis. 12 [18] February 1862. Elec. Jr. 2nd (or 3rd) Lt. of Co. A, 8th Regt. State Guards Inf. 7 July 1863. Mustered out February 1864. Appt. Cpl. of Massenburg's Battery Light Art. (Jackson Art.), 11 February 1864. B. 7 April 1826. D. 29 June 1880. Bd. Oaklawn Cemetery, Fort Valley, Peach Cty.

Swift, Charles T. (1): Dis. 11 January 1862. Enl. Co. A, 14th Bn. Light Art., Southern Rights Battery, 26 April 1862. Appt. Capt. and Commissary

Subsistence 12 October 1862. Sent to Gen. Hospital 18 February 1864. B. about 1835.

Swift, William Tyre, Jr. (1): D. near Pensacola FL 29 May 1861. B. about 1839.

Taylor, Sidney Seals (1, 2): Enl. Co. G, 62nd Inf. Regt. 31 May 1862. Appt. 1st Cpl. Tfd. to Co. G, 8th Regt. Cav. 11 July 1864. Par. Raleigh NC 20 April 1865. B. about 1843. Bd. Filton Cemetery, Montezuma, Macon Cty.

Tharpe, Albert A. [Thorpe/or Tharp] (2): Enl. 1 September 1861. Appt. 3rd Cpl. of Co. A, 14th Bn. Light Art., Southern Rights Battery, 26 April 1862. WIA Missionary Ridge TN 25 November 1863. Appt. Sgt. Cap. Macon, GA 20–21 April 1865. Par. 1865. B. 28 March 1844. D. 3 July 1914. Bd. Evergreen Cemetery, Perry, Houston Cty.

Tharpe, James Davis [Thorpe/Tharp] (1, 2): Enl. 4 August 1863, Co. D, 12th State Guards Cav. (Robinson's). Mustered out 4 February 1864. B. 9 May 1829. D. 25 February 1908. Bd. Evergreen Cemetery, Perry, Houston Cty.

Thompson, Marshall H. (1, 2): Elec. Jr. 2nd (or 3rd) Lt. of Co. G, 62nd Inf. Regt. 31 May 1862. Tfd. to Co. G, 8th Regt. Cav. 11 July 1864. Elec. 1st Lt. Par. 20 April 1865.

Tull, Francis M. (1): Dis. 26 January 1862. Appt. 2nd Sgt. of Co. G, 62nd Inf. Regt. 31 May 1862. Tfd. to Co. G, 8th Regt. Cav. October 1864. Par. Headquarters 2nd Military District, Department of NC, Bunn's House, 20 April 1865.

Westbrook, Alatia C. (2): Enl. 20 August [September] 1861. Reenl., command not given.

Westcott, Albert (1, 2): B. about 1840.

Wimberly, Joseph W. (1, 2): B. about 1826. Bd. Henderson Town Cemetery, Houston Cty.

Co. D, "Oglethorpe Inf.," Richmond County

Officers

Adams, Horton B. (1, 2): Capt. Elec. 3 April 1861. Tendered resignation due to ill health 6 February 1862. Recalled resignation 26 February; left Augusta to rejoin company 28 February 1862. B. 27 October 1825. D. 20 July 1899. Bd. Magnolia Cemetery, Augusta, Richmond Cty.

Allen, Joseph V. H. (1, 2): 1st Lt. Elec. Capt. of 1st Co. A, 12th Bn. Light Art. 10 April 1862; Capt. of Co. A, 63rd Inf. Regt.; Maj. 6 July 1863. Furloughed for 30 days due to sickness 25 February 1864. B. 22 May 1830. D. 19 February 1883. Bd. Magnolia Cemetery, Augusta, Richmond Cty.

Crane, George W. (1): 2nd Lt. B. about 1828.

Analty, E. W. (1): 3rd Lt.

Simmons, Sterling B. (1, 2): 1st Sgt. Appt. Ens. 29 April 1861. Elec. Jr. 2nd (or 3rd) Lt. 23 September 1861. Enl. Brook's Art. Battery. B. 18 January 1832. D. 30 April 1867. Bd. Magnolia Cemetery, Augusta, Richmond Cty.

Setze, A. J.[Setz] (1, 2): 2nd Sgt. Appt. 1st Sgt. 1861. Elec. 2nd Lt. 19 December 1861. Enl. Cav., unit unknown. Appt. Lt.

Mustin, Milton. A. (1): 3rd Sgt. B. about 1835.

Holmes, William Samuel [Willis]. (1): 4th Sgt. Appt. 3rd Sgt. 1861. Appt. 1st Sgt. 24 September 1861. B. 24 November 1834. D. of disease Staunton VA 8 December 1861. Bd. Magnolia Cemetery, Augusta, Richmond Cty.

Foreman, Solomon. C. (1, 2): 1st Cpl. [4th Sgt.] Appt. 3rd Sgt. Appt. 2nd Sgt. 24 September 1861. Elec. Jr. 2nd (or 3rd) Lt. 19 December 1861; 2nd Lt. 1 February 1862. Appt. 4th Cpl. of 1st Co. A, 12th Bn. Light Art. 10 April 1862. Tfd. to Co. A, 63rd Inf. Regt. October 1862. Appt. 3rd Cpl. February 1863; 2nd Cpl. 1 February 1864; 3rd Sgt. 10 April 1865. Surr. Greensboro NC 26 April 1865. B. about 1831.

Picquet, Louis A. (1, 2): 2nd Cpl. Appt. 1st Cpl. 1861. Appt. 4th Sgt. 24 September 1861. Elec. Jr. 2nd (or 3rd) Lt. 1 February 1862. Elec. 2nd Lt. of 1st Co. A, 12th Bn. Light Art. 10 April 1862. Tfd. to Co. A, 63rd Inf. Regt. October 1862. Elec. 1st Lt. 3 April 1863; Capt. 6 July 1863. WIA in leg, necessitating amputation, New Hope Church GA 28 May 1864. Made application for artificial limb 19 September 1864. B. about 1836.

Sheppard, Samuel H. [Shepard] (1, 2): 3rd Cpl. Appt. 2nd Cpl. 1861. Enl. Co. A, 21st Bn. Cav., 20 September 1863. Tfd. to Co. A, 7th Regt. Cav. 13 February 1864: Appt. clerk in QM Department 1864. B. 8 March 1838. D. 2 March 1907. Bd. Magnolia Cemetery, Augusta, Richmond Cty.

Clarke, Horace A. [Clark] (1): 4th Cpl. Appt. 3rd Cpl. 1861. Elec. 2nd Lt. of Co. F, 1st Regt. Regulars, 15 October 1861; 1st Lt. 4 July 1863; Capt. August 1864. Cap. Macon GA 21 April 1865. B. about 1841.

Privates:

Adams, Dillard (1): B. about 1838. D. Laurel Hill VA 8 July 1861.

Andrews, Albert E. (1): Tfd. to Co. D, 3rd Inf. Regt. 30 June 1861. Dis. 26 December 1861. Appt. Cpl. Co. B, 9th State Guards. Appt. Capt. Co. C, 27th Inf. Bn. Appt. Surgeon and assigned to duty with Federal prisoners Madison GA May 1863. Appt. Capt. of 51st GA Bn. B. 4 July 1837. D. 15 September 1897. Bd. Madison Town Cemetery, Morgan Cty.

Averill, Alfred M. [Averall/Averil/Averett] (1): Dis. for disability Warrington FL 12 June 1861. Appt. 5th Sgt. of Co. I, Cobb's Legion of Cav., 27 February 1862. Dis. due to heart disease 15 September 1862.

Bailey, A. W. (2): Enl. 1 June 1861. Listed as "Commissioned MS" 15 March 1862.

Beall, Fontenoy Augustus [Bell] (2): Enl. 1 June 1861. Listed as "Commissioned MS" B. 22 March 1836. D. 8 January 1876. Bd. Magnolia Cemetery, Augusta, Richmond Cty.

Bignon, Armand F. (1, 2): Enl. Capt. Barnes' Co., 1st Regt. Local Troops Inf. (Augusta) 31 July 1863. B. 22 March 1833. D. 19 January 1884. Bd. Magnolia Cemetery, Augusta, Richmond Cty.

Blanchard, Adiel W. (1, 2): Enl. 1st Co. A, 12th Bn. Light Art. 10 April 1862. Tfd. to Co. A, 63rd Inf. Regt. 1 October 1862. Elec. Jr. 2nd (or 3rd) Lt. 3 April 1863; 2nd Lt. 6 July 1863; 1st Lt. 15 July 1863. WIA Kennesaw Mountain GA 27 June 1864. Elec. Capt. of Co. K, 1st Consolidated Inf. Regt. 10 April 1865. Surr. Greensboro NC 26 April 1865. B. about 1837. D. 25 February 1925. Bd. Magnolia Cemetery, Augusta, Richmond Cty.

Booker, R. M. (1): Dis. prior to 16 April 1861. Commissioned Regular Service, CSA.

Bradford, Charles A.: Enl. 1 June 1861. Dis. 13 November 1861.

Brown, Milton A. (1, 2): Enl. Co. E, Cobb's Legion Inf. B. 14 December 1841. D. 29 October 1912. Bd. Gough Town Cemetery, Burke Cty.

Brown, Samuel M. (1): Dis. April 1861. Appt. 4th Cpl. of Co. B, 1st Regt. 1st Brigade State Troops, 30 September 1861.

Bryson, William (1, 2): Enl. Co. I, Cobb's Legion Cav., 3 April 1862. Tfd. May 1862.to 9th Regt. Cav. WIA Hanover VA 27 May 1862. B. 1841. D. 4 December 1904.

Bunch, John M. (1, 2): Elec. 1st Lt. of Co. A, 21st Bn. Cav., 15 April 1862; Capt. Tfd. to Co. A, 7th Regt. Cav. 13 February 1864. Cap. Trevillian Station, VA 11 June 1864. Released Fort Delaware, DE, 17 June 1865.

Burgess, Thomas (2): Enl. 1 June 1861. Enl. Cobb's Legion.

Burroughs, A. J.: Enl. 12 August 1861. Dis. 30 January 1862.

Catlin, Charles W. (2): Enl. 30 April 1861.

Cherry, Henry A. (1, 2): Enl. 1st Co. A, 12th Bn. Light Art. 10 April 1862. Tfd. to Co. A, 63rd Inf. Regt. October 1862. Absent, sick, November–December 1863. AWOL 22 January 1864. B. 1841. D. 1881. Bd. Magnolia Cemetery, Augusta, Richmond Cty.

Clark, Frank W. [Clarke] (1): On detached duty Staunton VA hospital 31 December 1861–11 March 1862.

Clark, Walter Augustus [Clarke] (1, 2): Appt. 9th Cpl. of 1st Co. A, 12th Bn. Light Art. 10 April 1862. Tfd. to Co. A, 63rd Inf. Regt. October 1862. Appt. 8th Cpl. February 1863; Assistant Surgeon 1 March 1863; 2nd Sgt. 17 April 1863; 1st Sgt. 15 July 1863 Elec. 1st Lt. 10 April 1865. Surr. Greensboro NC 26

April 1865. B. March 1842 [1843]. D. 1914. Bd. Hepzibah Town Cemetery, Richmond Cty.

Clark, William Howard [Clarke, John W.] (2): Enl. 6 August 1861. Enl. Co. C, 57th Inf. Regt. 8 May 1862. D. Knoxville TN 10 November 1862.

Clayton, Edvardus F. (1, 2): Enl. 1st Co. A, (subsequently 2nd Co. D.) 12th Bn. Light Art. 10 April 1862. Tfd. to Co. A, 63rd Inf. Regt. 1862; to 2nd Co. B, 12th Bn. Light Art. September 1862. Appt. Sgt. Maj. November 1862; Adj. 19 July 1864. B. 31 July 1840. KIA Fort Steadman VA 25 March 1865. Bd. Magnolia Cemetery, Augusta, Richmond Cty.

Cloyd, T. S. (2): Enl. 1 June 1861.

Cloyd, W. I. (1, 2): [KIA July 1861.]

Coffin, John R. (1, 2): Enl. 1st Co. A, 12th Bn. Light Art. 10 April 1862. Tfd. to Co. A, 63rd Inf. Regt. October 1862. Appt. Regimental Musician 1862. Cap. Cartersville GA 24 July 1864. Forwarded to Provost Marshal Gen., Department of Cumberland 25 July 1864. B. about 1845.

Craig, Cicero S. [C. H. Crag/Craige] (1, 2): Appt. Sr. 2nd Lt. Co. I, 3rd NC Inf. [Enl. 63rd Inf. Regt.]

Craig, William (1, 2): Enl. 63rd Inf. Regt.

Crumpton, John B.: Enl. 16 April 1861. Dis., date not given. B. about 1840.

Daniel, Wilberforce [Daniels] (2): Enl. 16 April 1861. Appt. Sgt. 24 September 1861. Enl. 1st Co. A, 12th Bn. Light Art. 10 April 1862. Elec. Jr. 2nd (or 3rd) Lt. 1 May 1862. Tfd. to Co. A, 63rd Inf. Regt. as Jr. 2nd (or 3rd) Lt., 1 October 1862. Elec. 1st Lt. 3 April 1863; Capt. 10 April 1865. Surr. Greensboro NC 26 April 1865. B. about 1834.

Darby, Edward (1): Dis. 31 December 1861.

Derry, Joseph Tyrone (1, 2): Enl. 1st Co. A, 12th Bn. Light Art. 10 April 1862. Tfd. to Co. A, 63rd Inf. Regt. December 1862. Cap. Kennesaw Mountain GA 27 June 1864. Released Camp Douglas IL 16 June 1865. B. 12 December 1841. D. 16 February 1926. Bd. Riverside Cemetery, Macon, Bibb Cty.

Doughty, Charles W. (2): Enl. 1 June 1861. Tfd. to Co. I, 5 October 1861. Appt. QM of the 12th Bn. Light Art. 15 August 1862. Elec. 1st Lt. of 2nd Co. D, 12th Bn. Light Art. 19 January 1863. WIA and permanently disabled Cold Harbor VA 2 June 1864. Par. Augusta GA 19 May 1865. B. 21 July 1839. D. 14 February 1914. Bd. Magnolia Cemetery, Augusta, Richmond Cty.

Doughty, Joshua J. (2): Enl. 1 June 1861. Enl. Co. F, 12th Bn. Light Art. 1 May 1862. Elec. 2nd Lt.; 1st Lt. 14 January 1863. WIA and permanently disabled Monocacy MD 9 July 1864. Cap. near Washington DC 12 July 1864. Par. Fort Delaware DE, 28 September 1864. Received Varina VA 5 October 1864. Unable to return to service due to wounds. B. about 1842.

Doyle, B. B.: Enl. 1 [12] August 1861. On detached duty Staunton VA hospital 31 December 1861–15 March 1862.

Doyle, W. R. (2): Enl. 1 June 1861. Enl. Co. A, 63rd Inf. Regt.

Dunbar, Elmore A. (1, 2): Appt. 1st Cpl. of 1st Co. A, 12th Bn. Light Art. 10 April 1862. Tfd. to Co. A, 63rd Inf. Regt. November 1862. Appt. 3rd Sgt.; Ens., 63rd Inf. Regt. 2 August 1864, to rank from 29 July 1864.

Duncan, Jonathon P., Jr. (2): Enl. 23 April 1861. Reenl., command not known. KIA in VA.

Dye, Samuel Henry (1): Tfd. to Co. G, Cobb's Legion Inf. 9 June 1861. Appt. Comm. Sgt. Enl. 28th GA Militia, (Inactive). Appt. Capt., GA Militia 1864. Surr. Appomattox VA 9 April 1865. Bd. Old Madison Cemetery, Madison, Morgan Cty.

Evans, George W. (2): Enl. 7 July 1861. Enl. Co. C, 48th Inf. Regt. 20 March 1862. Appt. AQM 22 March 1862; Serving as Capt. and AQM of Sorrell's Brigade, Mahone's Division 5 March 1865. Surr. Appomattox VA 9 April 1865. B. 1844. D. 1886. Bd. Magnolia Cemetery, Augusta, Richmond Cty.

Eve, Robert Campbell (1): On detached duty Staunton VA hospital 15 March 1862. Enl. 1st Co. A, 12th Bn. Light Art. 10 April 1862. Tfd. to Co. A, 63rd Inf. Regt. October 1862. Appt. Assistant Surgeon 20 April 1863. On duty as Assistant Surgeon, CSA, Staunton VA September 1864. B. 15 May 1843. D. 31 January 1885. Bd. Magnolia Cemetery, Augusta, Richmond Cty.

Eve, Sterling Combs (1): Appt. Assistant Surgeon and ordered to report to Surgeon Gen. for assignment 21 September 1861. On duty 16 November 1862 Gen. Hospital #16, Richmond VA. On duty 1 January 1863 1st GA Hospital, Richmond. On duty 3 November 1863 Gen. Hospital, Wilmington NC. Ordered to report for duty Officer's Hospital Augusta 21 June 1864, and was serving as Assistant Surgeon charge of hospital 26 August 1864. Surr. in NC April 1865. B. 1840. D. 8 February 1884. Bd. Magnolia Cemetery, Augusta, Richmond Cty.

Fleming, L. F. (1, 2): Enl. 1st Co. A, 12th Bn. Light Art. 10 April 1862. Tfd. to Co. A, 63rd Inf. Regt. October 1862; to Co. E, 20th Bn. Cav., January 1864; to Co. C, 1864; to Co. E, 62nd Inf. Regt. 1864; to Co. E, 8th Regt. Cav. November 1864. Disabled railroad accident. Listed as absent to procure a remount 31 December 1864.

Foster, Henry Clay (2): Enl. 4 May 1861. Enl. 1st Co. A, 12th Bn. Light Art. 10 April 1862. Tfd. to Co. A, 63rd Inf. Regt. October 1862. WIA Atlanta GA 22 July 1864. B. 2 November 1843. D. 27 August 1890. Bd. Magnolia Cemetery, Augusta, Richmond Cty.

Foster, John Preston (2): Enl. Co. A, Hampton's Legion SC Cav. 6 [14] June 1861. Tfd. to Co. D, 1st Inf. Regt. (Ramsey's), 25 December 1861. B. 22 September 1837. D. 6 December 1878. Bd. Magnolia Cemetery, Augusta, Richmond Cty.

Foster, William Harrison (1, 2): Enl. 1st Co. A, 12th Bn. Light Art. 10 April 1862. Tfd. to Co. A, 63rd Inf. Regt. October 1862. Appt. 10th Cpl. August 1863; 9th Cpl. October 1863; 8th Cpl. February 1864. Surr. Greensboro NC 26 April 1865. B. March 3, 1841. D. 17 June 1903. Bd. Magnolia Cemetery, Augusta, Richmond Cty.

Gibbs, George G. [Gobbs]: Enl. 28 April 1861. B. about 1837.

Goodrich, Charles M. (1 [Enl. 1 June 1861]): D. Monterey, VA 13 August 1861.

Goodrich, J. P. (1, 2): Enl. 63rd Inf. Regt.

Goodrich, William (1, 2): Enl. 63rd Inf. Regt. B. about 1845. B. about 1839.

Goodwin, Charles Johnston: Enl. 27 May [26] 1861. Dis. 24 July 1861. Enl. Co. A, 34th GA. B. 15 September 1831. D. 17 October 1894. Bd. Marshallville Methodist Church Cemetery, Marshallville, Macon Cty.

Goodwin, Charles M.: Enl. 26 April 1861.

Griffin, William A. (1, 2): Appt. Cpl. 16 December 1861; 5th Sgt. 1 February 1862. Appt. 4th Sgt. of Co. N, 5th Inf. Regt. 15 May 1862. Tfd. to Co. C, 2nd Bn. Sharpshooters as 4th Sgt. 2 June 1862. Appt. 2nd Sgt. 25 January 1863; 1st Sgt. 1 March 1863. WIA right arm Atlanta GA 2 August 1864. Listed as sick, in hospital 31 August 1864. Dis.

Haigh, William [Haight] (1, 2): Appt. cpl. B. about 1822.

Hall, Albert G. (1, 2): Enl. Co. N, 5th Inf. Regt. 16 May 1862. Tfd. to Co. C, 2nd Bn. Sharpshooters May 1862. Dis. by furnishing John Sullivan as substitute, 14 January 1863. B. about 1838.

Hall, Edward H. (1, 2): Enl. 2nd Bn. Sharpshooters. B. about 1831.

Harrell, J. J. (2): Enl. 16 [19] August 1861.

Hight, Francis M.: Enl. 19 August 1861. Dis. 12 January 1862. Appt. 1st Sgt. of Co. C, 48th Inf. Regt. 28 February 1862. Elec. Jr. 2nd (or 3rd) Lt. 19 June 1862; 2nd Lt. 18 August 1862. Resigned, disability, 8 April 1863. B. about 1843.

Hill, John C. (1 [Enl. 1 June 1861], 2): Enl. 1st Co. A, 12th Bn. Light Art. 10 April 1862. Tfd. to Co. A, 63rd Inf. Regt. October 1862. Appt. Cpl.; 5th Sgt. August 1863; 4th Sgt. February 1864. B. 1839. D. 1908. Bd. Magnolia Cemetery, Augusta, Richmond Cty.

Hitt, Virginius Gadsden (1): On detached duty Staunton VA hospital 15 March 1862. Appt. 2nd Cpl. of 1st Co. A, 12th Bn. GA Light Art. 10 April 1862. Tfd. to Co. A, 63rd Inf. Regt. October 1862. Appt. Assistant Surgeon 21 April 1863. Assigned to duty as Assistant Surgeon of Capt. Douthat's Co., VA Light Art. 24 November 1863. Assigned to duty with 9th Bn. Light Art. 31 October

1864. Surr. Appomattox VA 9 April 1865. B. 14 June 1840. D. 17 January 1905. Bd. Magnolia Cemetery, Augusta, Richmond Cty.

Hull, Ellis Harrison (1): Dis. 1861. Enl. Co. K, 20th Inf. Regt. 8 August 1861. Elec. Jr. 2nd (or 3rd) Lt. of Co. A, 66th Inf. Regt. 1 August 1863; 2nd Lt. 1 November 1863.

Hungerford, John T. (1, 2): Enl. 1st Co. A, 12th Bn. Light Art. 10 April 1862. Tfd. to Co. A, 63rd Inf. Regt. October 1862. Sick garrison hospital 29 February 1864. B. about 1843.

Jackson, Andrew Muler [Andrew Miller] (1, 2): Enl. Co. C, 52nd Inf. Enl. Co. C, 11th State Guards Bn. B. about 1841. Bd. Salem Methodist Church Cemetery, near Dawsonville, Dawson Cty.

Jackson, H. B. (1, 2): Enl. 1st Co. A, 12th Bn. Light Art. 10 April 1862. Tfd. to Co. A, 63rd Inf. Regt. October 1862. WIA New Hope Church GA 27 May 1864. On detached duty with Co. F, 1st Regt. Troops and Defenses Macon GA AWOL 20 November 1864. B. about 1826.

Jackson, W. F. (1): Dis. Berryville, VA hospital.

Johnson, Whitson G. [Johnston/William] (1, 2): Appt. Cpl. 30 June 1861; Sgt. 19 December 1861; 1st Sgt. 1 February 1862. Elec. 1st Lt. Co. A, 12th GA Art. Bn. April, 1862. Co. connected to Co. A, 63rd Inf., October 1862. Resigned due to acute rheumatism 3 April 1863. B. 22 December 1835. D. 13 December 1893. Bd. Lexington Town Cemetery, Oglethorpe Cty.

Jones, George A. (2): Enl. 1 June 1861. B. about 1840.

Jones, William E. (2): Enl. 18 June 1861. B. about 1838.

Jones, William H. (1): Appt. Cpl. 16 December 1861. Appt. 4th Sgt. of Co. I, Cobb's Legion of Cav. 14 February 1862. Tfd. to 9th Regt. Cav. WIA Savannah GA 10 December 1864.

Kean, Matthew (1, 2): Enl. 63rd Inf. Regt.

Kennedy, W. H. [Kennady] (1, 2): Enl. 63rd Inf. Regt.

Lamar, James J. (1): B. about 1828. D. Monterey, VA 19 November 1861.

Lamar, William T. (2): Enl. 1 June 1861. Enl. 1st Co. A, 12th Bn. Light Art. 10 April 1862. Appt. 6th Cpl. of Co. A, 63rd Inf. Regt. October 1862. Elec. 2nd Lt. Surr. Greensboro NC 26 April 1865. B. 18 May 1844. D. 23 April 1910. Bd. West View Cemetery, Augusta, Richmond Cty.

Leonhardt, George G. (2): Enl. 7 August 1861. Appt. 3rd Cpl. of 1st Co. A, 12th Bn. Light Art. 10 April 1862. Tfd. to Co. A, 63rd Inf. Regt. October 1862. Appt. 2nd Cpl. 21 April 1863. WIA Atlanta GA 22 July 1864. Surr. Greensboro NC 26 April 1865. B. about 1839. D. 10 May 1875.

Little, Daniel W. (1, 2): Enl. 1st Co. A, 12th Bn. Light Art. 10 April 1862. Tfd. to Co. A, 63rd Inf. Regt. October 1862. B. about 1835.

Love, P. E. (2): Enl. 7 July 1861. Enl. Cav. D. 1885.

Marshall, Anthony D. (1, 2): Enl. 1st Co. A, 12th Bn. Light Art. 10 April 1862. Tfd. to Co. A, 63rd. Inf. Regt. October 1862. Cap. Kennesaw Mountain GA 27 June 1864. Tfd. from Camp Douglas IL to New Orleans, LA 4 May 1865, and Exch. there 23 May 1865.

Marshall, Charles D. (1): Dis. April 1861.

Marshall, C. O. (1): Dis. 4 December 1861.

McCarty, C. E. [McCarthy] (1, 2).

McGraw, James T. [McGran] (2): Enl. 1 June 1861. Enl. 1st Co. A, 12th Bn. Light Art. 10 April 1862. Tfd. to Co. A, 63rd Inf. Regt. October 1862. Appt. 5th Cpl. February 1863. On government detail duty Columbus GA 31 December 1864.

McLaughlin, George W. [Laughlin] (1, 2): Appt. 1st Sgt. of 1st Co. A, 12th Bn. Light Art. 10 April 1862. Tfd. to Co. A, 63rd Inf. Regt. October 1862. Appt. Acting Adj. April 1863. Elec. Jr. 2nd (or 3rd) Lt. 15 July 1863. Appt. Sgt. Maj. 1863; Assistant Adj. 8 November 1863. Elec. 1st Lt. of Co. A, 63rd Inf. Regt. 10 April 1865. B. about 1842.

Miller, E. O. [Burt] (1, 2): Appt. 4th Cpl. 24 September 1861. Appt. 10th Cpl. of 1st Co. A, 12th Bn. Light Art. 10 April 1862. Tfd. to Co. A, 63rd Inf. Regt. October 1862. Appt. 9th Cpl. February 1863; 2nd Cpl. August 1863; 1st Cpl. February 1864. B. 1841. D. 1914. Bd. Magnolia Cemetery, Augusta, Richmond Cty.

Miller, D. B.: Enl. 63rd Inf. Regt. Appt. Sgt.

Miller, Josiah (1, 2): Enl. Co. I, Cobb's Legion of Cav., 14 April 1862. Tfd. to 9th Regt. Cav. Cap. Brandy Station, VA 9 June 1863. Par. Old Capitol Prison, Washington DC 25 June 1863. WIA The Wilderness VA 6 May 1864. WIA Ream's Station VA 25 August 1864. Absent on horse detail 31 October 1864.

Miller, William J. (1): B. 7 March 1844. D. Augusta 22 August 1861. Bd. Magnolia Cemetery, Augusta, Richmond Cty.

Mongen, Daniel W. [Mongin/Mungen]: Enl. 6 August 1861. Dis. 19 December 1861.

Morris, Richard B. (1, 2): Appt. 1st Cpl. of 1st Co. A, 12th Bn. Light Art. 10 April 1862. Tfd. to Co. A, 63rd Inf. Regt. October 1862. Appt. 6th Sgt. August 1863; 5th Sgt. February 1864; 1st Sgt. 10 April 1865. Surr. Greensboro NC 26 April 1865. B. 28 September 1841. D. 7 August 1926. Bd. Magnolia Cemetery, Augusta, Richmond Cty.

Morris, William B. (1): Dis. for disability. Enl. 1st Co. A, 12th Bn. Light Art. 10 April 1862. Tfd. to Co. A, 63rd Inf. Regt. October 1862. WIA Kennesaw Mountain GA 27 June 1864. Surr. Greensboro NC 26 April 1865. B. 20

September 1843. D. 18 January 1923. Bd. Magnolia Cemetery, Augusta, Richmond Cty.

Morris, Zachariah B. (1, 2): Enl. Co. A, 21st Bn. Cav., 1 January 1864. Tfd. to Co. A, 7th Regt. Cav. 13 February 1864. [Enl. 63rd Inf. Regt.]

Mosher, George D. (1, 2): Enl. 1st Co. A, 12th Bn. Light Art. 10 April 1862. Tfd. to Co. A, 63rd Inf. Regt. October 1862. WIA Atlanta GA 18 July 1864. B. about 1842. D. Chatham Cty. 10 April 1916.

Murphy, Moses Collins [Murphey] (2): Enl. 1 June 1861. Enl. Cav. B. 29 July 1838. D. 7 December 1915. Bd. Magnolia Cemetery, Augusta, Richmond Cty.

Mustin, Milton A. (1): Appt. 3rd Sgt. B. about 1835.

Newberry, John T. (1): Cap. 13 July 1861. Par. Beverly VA 20 July 1861. Dis. 27 September 1861. B. about 1829.

Peay, William Edward [Prary] (1, 2): Enl. 1st Co. A, 12th Bn. Light Art. 1 January 1863. Dis. 10 October 1863. B. 3 September 1843. D. 22 October 1868. Bd. Magnolia Cemetery, Augusta, Richmond Cty.

Pierce, George Foster, Jr. [Pearce] (2): Enl. 16 April 1861. Enl. Co. G, Cobb's Legion Inf. 1862. Appt. Sgt. 1862. WIA Crampton's Pass MD 14 September 1862. Elec. 2nd Lt. 25 September 1862. WIA Chancellorsville VA 3 May 1863. Elec. 1st Lt. 8 January 1864. WIA The Wilderness VA 6 May 1864. Cap. Sailor's Creek VA 6 April 1865. Released Johnson's Island OH 19 June 1865. [Enl. 63rd Inf. Regt. and died during the war.]

Pitcher, Augustus M. [Pilcher] (1): Dis. 11 July 1861. Enl. 63rd Inf. Regt. KIA during the war.

Pope, F. M. [Papo] (1, 2).

Pournelle, George P. [Parnell/Pournell] (1, 2): Enl. 1st Co. A, 12th Bn. Light Art. 10 April 1862. Tfd. to Co. A, 63rd Inf. Regt. October 1862. KIA Kennesaw Mountain GA 27 June 1864.

Ramsey, William P. (1, 2): Enl. Co. B, 3rd Regt. Cav. 17 April 1862. B. 12 September 1829. D. 24 October 1922. Bd. Lawrence Family Cemetery, West Armuchee, Walker Cty.

Rankin, Jesse W. (1, 2): [4th Cpl.] Appt. 2nd Cpl. 16 April 1861. Appt. Acting Hospital Steward. B. 1839. D. 25 February 1892.

Ratcliff, James T. [Ratcriff/Radcliffe/Ratcliffe] (1, 2): Enl. 1st Co. A, 12th Bn. Light Art. 10 April 1862. Tfd. to Co. A, 63rd Inf. Regt. October 1862. B. about 1839. D. from disease Tuscumbia AL 5 November 1864.

Revell, J. H. [Revill] (2): Enl. 16 August 1861.

Rhodes, Andrew J. (2): Enl. 16 August 1861. Enl. Co. B, 57th Inf. Regt. 1862. Dislocated ankle 1862. On detail duty due to disability until the end of the war. B. about 1838.

Rhodes, John H. [Rhoden] (2): Enl. 16 August 1861. Enl. Co. F, 12th Bn. Light Art. 8 May 1862. Appt. 2nd Cpl. 1862; 5th Sgt. Enl. Co. B, 57th Inf. B. about 1841. KIA Winchester VA 19 September 1864. Bd. Magnolia Cemetery, Augusta, Richmond Cty.

Rigsby, John W.: Enl. 1 June 1861. Dis. 18 January 1862. Enl. Co. E, 63rd Inf. Regt. 22 January 1863. On furlough Marion Cty., March–April 1865. B. 15 October 1825. Bd. Union Baptist Church Cemetery, near Buena Vista, Marion Cty.

Roberts, Charles Pleasant (1, 2): Appt. 3rd Cpl. 24 September 1861. Enl. Co. N, 5th Inf. Regt. 15 May 1862. Tfd. to Co. C, 2nd Bn. Sharpshooters 1862. Appt. Acting Sgt. Maj. 1 October 1862; Adj. 4 February 1864. Surr. Greensboro NC 26 April 1865. B. about 1843.

Roberts, J. P. (1, 2).

Roberts, James M. (1): Tfd. to Capt. Blodgett's Co. of Art. 11 September [18 October] 1861. B. about 1835.

Roebuck, James Z. [Z. J/W. J./J.C.]: Enl. 1 June 1861. On detached duty Staunton VA hospital 15 March 1862. Enl. 63rd Inf. Regt.

Roll, R. F.: Enl. 19 August 1861. KIA in action, July 1861.

Roll, W. A. (1, 2): B. about 1838.

Shain, James T. (1, 2): Enl. Co. A, 5th Inf. Regt. 13 May 1864.

Shead, Loring W. [Shed] (1, 2): Appt. Cpl. Enl. 63rd Inf. Regt.

Shepard, Samuel H. (1, 2).

Smith, Alva D. [Alonzo] (2): Enl. 12 August 1861. B. 17 January 1835. D. 2 January 1891. Bd. Magnolia Cemetery, Augusta, Richmond Cty.

Stone, Osborn M. (1, 2): Appt. 1st Cpl. 24 September 1861; Sgt. 16 December 1861. Appt. Sgt. of 1st Co. A, 12th Bn. Light Art. 10 April 1862. Tfd. to Co. A, 63rd Inf. Regt. October 1862. Elec. 1st Lt. of Co. E, 66th Inf. Regt. 9 September 1863. Resigned 31 August 1864. B. about 1837. Bd. Magnolia Cemetery, Augusta, Richmond Cty.

Stoy, Frederick W. [Story] (1): Dis. 19 December 1861. Enl. 63rd Inf. Regt. B. 28 June 1838. D. 13 December 1909. Bd. Magnolia Cemetery, Augusta, Richmond Cty.

Stoy, John W. [Story] (1, 2): Appt. cpl. 17 October 1861; Sgt. 19 December 1861. Appt. 5th Sgt. of 1st Co. A, 12th Bn. Light Art. 10 April 1862. Tfd. to Co. A, 63rd Inf. Regt. October 1862. Appt. 4th Sgt. April 1863; 3rd Sgt. August 1863. Cap. Atlanta GA 23 July 1864. Received James River VA for exchange 10–12 March 1865. B. about 1841.

Stread, Loring W. [Stroud/Shead] (1, 2): Appt. Cpl. Enl. 63rd Inf. Regt.

Thomas, James E. (2): Enl. 1 June 1861. Enl. 1st Co. A, 12th Bn. Light Art. 10 April 1862. Tfd. to Co. A, 63rd Inf. Regt. October 1862. B. 4 June 1840. D. 3 February 1880. Bd. Summerville Cemetery, Augusta, Richmond Cty.

Turpin, Miles (1, 2): Enl. 1st Co. A, 12th Bn. Light Art. 10 April 1862. Tfd. to Co. A, 63rd Inf. Regt. October 1862. Par. Augusta GA 30 May 1865. B. about 1843.

Tutt, Thomas J. (1, 2): Enl. Co. F, 12th Bn. Light Art. 18 April 1862. Elec. Jr. 2nd (or 3rd) Lt. 19 January 1863. WIA Cedar Creek VA 19 October 1864. B. about 1838. D. from wounds October 31 [November 1], 1864.

Verdery, George Jackson [Verderey] (2): Enl. 1 June 1861. Enl. 1st Co. A, 12th Bn. Light Art. 10 April 1862. Tfd. to Co. A, 63rd Inf. Regt. October 1862; to Co. D, 2nd Regt. Engineer Troops, CSA, 20 September 1863.

Verdery, R. W. [Verderey] (2): Enl. 16 August 1861.

Watkins, Benjamin H. (1): Tfd. to Co. I, Cobb's Legion of Cav., and Appt. 1st Sgt. 14 February 1862. Tfd. to 9th Regt. Cav. Surr. Greensboro NC 26 April 1865. B. about 1840.

Watkins, Charles D. (1, 2): Appt. Cpl. 1 February 1862. Enl. Co. I, Cobb's Legion of Cav., 25 March 1862. Tfd. to 9th Regt. Cav. B. about 1842.

Watkins, J. S. (1).

Whiting, William M. (1): Dis. 13 February 1862.

Wiley, Walter A. (1, 2).

Williams, Francis M.: Enl. 1 June 1861.

Williams, William G. (1, 2): Enl. 63rd Inf. Regt.

Williams, William T. (2): Enl. 1 June 1861. Enl. 1st Co. A, 12th Bn. Light Art. 10 April 1862. Tfd. to Co. A, 63rd Inf. Regt. October 1862. Dis. Thunderbolt GA 1 March 1863.

Wilson, James D. (1, 2).

Wilson, James E. (1, 2): Enl. 63rd Inf. Regt. B. about 1836.

Wilson, Joseph S. (1, 2).

Wing, Benjamin F. (1): AWOL as of date of regiment's disbandment. Mustered out with regiment. B. 13 January 1845. D. 5 December 1870. Bd. Magnolia Cemetery, Augusta, Richmond Cty.

Wing, Dean.

Winn, W. T. (1, 2): Enl. 63rd Inf. Regt.

Co. E, "Washington Rifles," Washington County

Officers

Jones, Seaborn Augustus Harrison (1, 2): Capt. Elec. Capt. of Co. E, 32nd Inf. Regt. 7 May 1862. Resigned 11 July 1862. B. 1806. D. 17 November 1862. Bd. Old City Cemetery, Sandersville, Washington Cty.

Rudisill, John Wiery (1, 2): 1st Lt. Elec. Capt. of 3rd Co. B, 12th Bn. Light Art. 1 May 1862. Cap. Fisher's Hill VA 22 September 1864. Imprisoned Harper's Ferry VA and Fort Delaware DE, where he was released 10 June 1865. B. about 1823.

Evans, Beverly Daniel (1, 2): 2nd Lt. Elec. Col. 13th Regt. GA Militia 8 September 1862. Mustered out 1862. Elec. Capt. of Co. H, 2nd Regt. State Troops, 16 February 1863; Lt. Col. 20 February 1863; Brevet Col. September 1864. Mustered out May 1865. B. 6 February 1826. D. 21 March 1897. Bd. Old City Cemetery, Sandersville, Washington Cty.

Carter, William Wooten (1): Jr. 2nd (or 3rd) Lt. Resigned 3 June 1861. Elec. Capt. of Co. C, 49th Inf. Regt. 4 March 1862. Resigned, disability, 31 July 1862. Enl. 20th Regt. GA Militia. B. 28 April 1825. D. 22 June 1898. Bd. Forest Grove (Warthen Family) Cemetery, near Sandersville, Washington Cty.

Jones, Charles Mc. (1): Ens. Cap. 13 July 1861. Par. Beverly VA 16 July 1861. Elec. Capt. of Co. H, 49th Inf. Regt. 4 March 1862. B. 1839. KIA Gettysburg PA 3 July 1863. Bd. Old City Cemetery, Sandersville, Washington Cty.

Rudisill, Benjamin Franklin (1): Appt. Surgeon. Dis. 13 December 1861. Appt. Assistant Surgeon of 12th Bn. Light Art. 29 May 1862. Resigned 31 December 1864. B. 27 November 1834. D. 26 [28] June 1901. Bd. Westview Cemetery, Forsyth, Monroe Cty.

Youngblood, John Thomas (1, 2): Color Bearer and Co. QM. Appt. 5th Sgt. B. 22 May 1822. D. 18 January 1890. Bd. Old City Cemetery, Sandersville, Washington Cty.

Howell, Evan Park (1, 2): 1st Sgt. Elec. Jr. 2nd (or 3rd) Lt. 4 July 1861. Elec. Sr. 1st Lt. of Martin's Battery Light Art. 10 May 1862; Capt. of Howell's Battery Light Art. 7 September 1865. On detached duty 31 December 1864. Par. Macon GA May 1865. B. 1839. D. 6 August 1905. Bd. Westview Cemetery, Atlanta, Fulton Cty.

Warthen, George Washington (1): 2nd Sgt. B. 17 January 1835. D. of typhoid Staunton VA hospital 23 [26] September 1861. Bd. Old City Cemetery, Sandersville, Washington Cty.

Medlock, Joseph Miller Grieves (1): 3rd Sgt. Appt. Regimental Comm. Sgt. Dis. 11 September 1861. B. 30 October 1833. D. 21 September 1913. Bd. Sylvania, Screven Cty.

Jernigan, Augustus Daniel (1): 4th Sgt. Dis. 24 [25] May 1861. Elec. 1st Lt. of Co. H, 49th Inf. Regt. 4 March 1862; Capt. 1862. Resigned due to ill health 7 July 1862. B. about 1827.

Gray, William J. (1): 1st Cpl. Dis. 6 October 1861. Elec. 1st Lt. of Capt. Horatio N. Hollifield's Battery Light Art. State Troops, 22 February 1862. Mustered out

Savannah GA May 1862. Enl. Capt. C. W. Slaten's Co., Macon Light Art. 3 May 1862. AWOL 5 October 1864–28 February 1865. B. 10 December 1833. Bd. Old City Cemetery, Sandersville, Washington Cty.

Sessions, Andrew Thompson (1, 2): 2nd Cpl. Elec. Jr. 2nd (or 3rd) Lt. of 3rd Co. B, 12th Bn. Light Art. 1 May 1862. B. about 1837. KIA Cedar Creek VA 19 October 1864.

Renfroe, William Haynes (1, 2): 3rd Cpl. Appt. 1st Sgt. of Co. E, 32nd Inf. Regt. 7 May 1862. Elec. 2nd Lt. 2 April 1864; 1st Lt. Surr. Greensboro NC 26 April 1865. B. 17 November 1839. D. 13 January 1900. Bd. Old City Cemetery, Sandersville, Washington Cty.

Wicker, John Richard (1, 2): 4th Cpl. Appt. Cpl. of Co. B, 7th Bn., State Guards Cav. 4 August 1863. B. 4 September 1829. D. 29 November 1905. Bd. Old City Cemetery, Sandersville, Washington Cty.

Privates

Allen, George R. (1, 2): Appt. 1st Sgt. of Co. G, 57th Inf. Regt. 6 May 1862.

Arnan, Francis M. B. about 1831.

Arnan, James M. [Arnau/Arnaw] (1, 2): Enl. 3rd Co. B, 12th Bn. Light Art. 1 May 1862. Appt. Cpl.

Asimop, Jonathon L.

Bailey, James Wimberly (2): Enl. 30 June 1861. Enl. Co. H, 49th Inf. Regt. 14 May 1862. Appt. 1st Sgt. 1 August 1862. Elec. Jr. 2nd (or 3rd) Lt. 7 August 1863. On furlough of indulgence 28 February 1865. Cap. Macon GA 20 [21] April 1865. B. 16 December 1840. D. 18 August 1904. Bd. Oak Grove Cemetery, Americus, Sumter Cty.

Barnes, Alfred Suspense (1, 2): Enl. 3rd Co. B, 12th Bn. Light Art. 1 May 1862. Tfd. to Co. B, 28th Inf. Regt. 1862. WIA Petersburg VA 30 July 1864. Listed as home on furlough close of war. Bd. Wrightsboro Town Cemetery, Johnson Cty.

Barnes, Marcellus A. (1, 2): B. 1839. D. 1913. Bd. Memory Hill Cemetery, Milledgeville, Baldwin Cty.

Barwick, William B. (1, 2): Enl. 3rd Co. B, 12th Bn. Light Art. 1 May 1862. Appt. Cpl. Tfd. to Martin's (later Howell's) Battery Light Art., 13 February 1863. Enl. 1st Inf. Reserves. Par. 17 May 1865 Thomasville GA. B. 1835. D. 17 December 1902. Bd. Old City Cemetery, Sandersville, Washington Cty.

Boatwright, Benjamin Sessions [Boatright] (1, 2): Appt. 3rd Sgt. of 2nd Co. C, 12th Bn. Light Art. 1 May 1862. Tfd. to 3rd Co. E, 28 December 1862. Elec. Jr. 2nd (or 3rd) Lt.; 2nd Lt.; Lt. commanding 3rd Co. B, 1864. WIA November 1864. WIA Hatcher's Run VA 7 February 1865. Cap. Jackson Hospital

Richmond VA 3 April 1865, and escaped 25 April 1865. B. 26 July 1842. D. 20 December 1920. Bd. Zeta Cemetery, Tennille, Washington Cty.

Brantley, Joseph L. (1, 2): Enl. Co. D, 59th Inf. B. 29 August 1828. D. 1 January 1916. Bd. Mt. Gilead Primitive Baptist Church Cemetery, near Tennille, Washington Cty.

Brown, James M. [Joseph]: Enl. 10 June 1861. Dis. 8 February 1862. Appt. 4th Sgt. of Co. B, 7th Bn., State Guards Cav. 4 August 1863. [Enl. Co. K, 5th Reserves, appointed Lt.]. B. 13 September 1834. D. 14 August 1924. Bd. Zeta Cemetery, Tennille, Washington Cty.

Cason, George D. (2): Enl. 30 June 1861. Enl. 3rd Co. B, 12th Bn. Light Art. 1 May 1862. Cap. Winchester VA 19 September 1864. Took oath of allegiance to US Government Point Lookout MD and released upon joining US Army 17 October 1864. Bd. Section C-1, Louisville City Cemetery, Jefferson Cty., KY. B. about 1841.

Cason, William (1, 2): Enl. 3rd Co. B, 12th Bn. Light Art. 1 May 1862. WIA and Cap. Monocacy MD 10 July 1864. Sent to Fort McHenry MD 1864. Tfd. from West's Bldgs. Hospital Baltimore MD to Point Lookout MD 1864. Received Venus Point, Savannah River GA for Exch. 15 November 1864. Cap. near Petersburg VA 25 March 1865. Released Point Lookout MD 24 June 1865. B. about 1833.

Clay, William S. (1): D. by accidental discharge of weapon at Laurel Hill VA 7 July 1861.

Cook, Abram Thomas (2): Enl. 30 June 1861. Enl. Co. H, 49th Inf. Regt. 1 April 1862. WIA Frazier's Farm VA 30 June 1862. Listed as being home on sick furlough 28 February 1865. B. 21 August 1840. D. 2 December 1916. Bd. Rutherford Primitive Baptist Church Cemetery, near Oconee, Washington.

Cullen, English W. [Cullens] (1, 2).

Cullen, John E. [Cullens] (1, 2): Appt. 5th Cpl. of Martin's (later Howell's) Battery Light Art., 10 May 1862; 4th Cpl.

Cullen, Wilson A. [Cullum] (2): Enl. 10 June 1861. B. about 1835.

Cullum, S. E. [Cullen] (1, 2).

Cummings, Green E. [Cuming/Commings] Enl. 10 June 1861. D. of disease Beverly VA 20 [21] June 1861. B. about 1824.

Curry, David (2): Enl. 1 November 1861. Enl. Co. F, 48th Inf. Bd. Powell's Chapel Methodist Church Cemetery, near Kite, Johnson Cty.

Curry, John A. (1, 2): B. about 1823.

Curry, John H.: Enl. 18 September 1861. B. 5 April 1845. D. Strasburg VA 24 [26] December 1861. Bd. Riddleville Town Cemetery, Washington Cty.

Curry, Sylvanus K.: Enl. 18 September 1861. Dis. 13 December 1861. Enl. Co. H, 2nd Regt. State Troops, 16 February 1863. Appt. 4th Sgt. 28 February 1863. Dis. 28 April 1863. B. about 1825.

Darden, Marion [Durden] (1, 2): KIA Hatcher's Run VA.

Dudley, John E. Q. (2): Enl. 10 June 1861. Enl. Martin's (later Howell's) Battery Light Art., 10 May 1862. Appt. Sgt.

Dudley, William H. (2): Enl. 10 May 1861. Enl. Martin's (later Howell's) Battery Light Art., 10 May 1862. Appt. 7th Sgt.; 6th Sgt.; 5th Sgt. B. 2 July 1841. D. 18 May 1911. Bd. Zidon Baptist Church Cemetery, Sandy Cross, Franklin Cty.

Durden, Stephen M.: Enl. 30 June 1861.

Fluker, Milton B. [Flucker] (1, 2): Enl. 3rd Co. B, 12th Bn. Light Art. 1 May 1862. Appt. 1st Sgt./Orderly Sgt. WIA Kernstown VA 23 July 1864. B. about 1842. KIA Fort Steadman VA 25 March 1865.

Fulford, Samuel D. (2): Enl. 30 June 1861. Appt. 4th Sgt. of Martin's (later Howell's) Battery Light Art., 10 May 1862; 2nd Sgt. B. about 1842. D. in service.

Fulford, Thomas B.: Enl. 30 June 1861. Dis. 22 August 1861. Enl. Co. G, 57th Inf. Regt. 6 May 1862. B. 22 September 1837. D. 2 April 1902. Bd. New Bethel Baptist Church Cemetery, near Riddlesville, Washington Cty.

Fulghum, Joseph H. (2): Enl. 10 June 1861. Enl. 3rd Co. B, 12th Bn. Light Art. 1 May 1862. Appt. Assistant Ordnance Sgt. of the 12th Bn. GA Light Art. WIA Monocacy MD 9 July 1864. Surr. Appomattox VA 9 April 1865.

Gaskins, Jasper A. [Gasken] (2): Enl. 30 June 1861. Enl. Co. G, 57th Inf. Regt. 6 May 1862. B. about 1842. KIA while on picket duty Vicksburg MS 10 June 1863.

Gilmore, Ebenezer T. (1 [Enl. 20 August 1861], 2): Enl. Martin's Battery Light Art. (later Howell's Battery), 10 May 1862. B. 9 May 1842. D. 10 October 1922. Bd. Memory Hill Cemetery, Milledgeville, Baldwin.

Gilmore, John Newton (1, 2): Appt. 1st Sgt. 4 July 1861. B. 1836. D. 1898. Bd. Old City Cemetery, Sandersville, Washington Cty.

Gilmore, Stephen Mathis (2): Enl. 10 June 1861. Enl. Martin's (later Howell's) Battery Light Art., 10 May 1862. Appt. Cpl. B. 20 September 1839. D. 20 January 1904. Bd. Poplar Springs Christian Church Cemetery, near Deepstep, Washington Cty.

Gilmore, Thomas Jefferson (1, 2): Enl. Martin's (later Howell's) Battery Light Art. 10 May 1862. Elec. 2nd Lt. B. 15 May 1838. D. 6 October 1882. Bd. Old City Cemetery, Sandersville, Washington Cty.

Goodown, James A. [Godown/Goodowns] (2): Enl. 10 June 1861. Enl. Martin's (later Howell's) Battery Light Art. 10 May 1862.

Gray, W. B. (1): Dis. 6 October 1861.

Grimes, William A. (1, 2): Enl. Martin's (later Howell's) Battery Light Art. 1 June 1862. B. about 1844. Bd. Zebulon Methodist Church Cemetery, near Linton, Hancock Cty.

Haines, M. J.

Haynes, Charles E. [Haines] (1, 2): Appt. Lt. 13th Inf. Regt.

Haynes, Samuel S. [Haines] (1, 2): Enl. Co. G, 2nd Cav. B. 14 August 1841. D. 3 June 1912. Bd. Bronwood Town Cemetery, Terrell Cty.

Haynes, Thomas Harris [Hayes] (1): Dis. 3 September 1861. Enl. Co. C, 49th Inf. Regt. 4 March 1862. Tfd. to 3rd Co. B, 12th Bn. Light Art. 1 May 1862. Acting Sgt. Maj. 31 August 1864. Par. Augusta GA 19 May 1865. B. 17 December 1839. D. 14 August 1877. Bd. Old City Cemetery, Sandersville, Washington Cty.

Hermann, Isaac [Harman]: Enl. 30 June 1861. Dis. 24 [25] January 1862. Enl. Martin's (later Howell's) Battery Light Art. 10 May 1862. Appt. Musician. WIA Jackson MS 14 May 1863. Admitted to Macon GA hospital 17 December 1863. On detail duty 23 April 1864. B. 1838 Alsace-Lorraine, France. D. 1917. Bd. Old City Cemetery, Sandersville, Washington Cty.

Hicklin, A. F. (2): Enl. 10 June 1861. Enl. 3rd Co. B, 12th Bn. Light Art. 1 May 1862. hospital 19 September 1864. WIA Hatcher's Run VA 6 February 1865. Cap. Richmond VA hospital 3 April 1865.

Hicklin, William P. (1): Dis. 10 [12] August 1861. Appt. 1st Sgt. of Capt. Horatio N. Hollifield's Battery Light Art. 22 February 1862. Appt. Ordnance Sgt. Mustered out Savannah GA May 1862. Enl. Co. G, 6th Regt. State Guards Inf. 4 August 1863. Appt. Sgt. Maj. 19 September 1863.

Hines, Augustus C. (2): Enl. 30 June 1861. Enl. Martin's (later Howell's) Battery Light Art. 10 May 1862. Appt. Cpl. home on sick furlough from hospital 31 December 1864. Par. Augusta GA 21 May 1865.

Hines, Richard: Enl. 30 June 1861. D. of pneumonia Winchester VA 24 January 1862.

Hines, Samuel W. T.: Enl. 30 June 1861. D. of pneumonia Winchester VA 29 January 1862.

Hines, William H. (2): Enl. 30 June 1861. Appt. 6th Sgt. of Martin's (later Howell's) Battery Light Art. 10 May 1862; 3rd Sgt.; 1st Sgt.; Lt. WIA Jonesboro GA 31 August 1864. Bd. Davisboro Town Cemetery, Washington Cty.

Howard, Wesley C. [Honard/Westley] (2): Enl. 30 June 1861. Enl. Capt. Horatio N. Hollifield's Battery Light Art. 1862. Mustered out Savannah GA May 1862. Enl. Martin's (later Howell's) Battery Light Art. 10 May 1862. Appt. Cpl. D. of chronic diarrhea LaGrange GA hospital 10 June 1864. Bd. Stonewall Cemetery, LaGrange, Troup Cty.

Jones, Stephen Benjamin (1, 2): Elec. Capt. of Co. F, 62nd Inf. Regt. 1 July 1862. Tfd. to Co. F, 8th Regt. Cav. 1864. B. 14 September 1835. D. 10 May 1882. Bd. Old City Cemetery, Sandersville, Washington Cty.

Jones, Weaver Harrison. (1, 2): Elec. 4th Sgt. 11 February 1862. Elec. 2nd Lt. of Co. E, 32nd Inf. Regt. 7 May 1862; 1st Lt. 11 July 1862. Granted certificate of disability for leave of absence 10 December 1863. B. 1841. D. Charleston SC, 4 October 1864. Bd. Magnolia Cemetery, Charleston, Charleston Cty., SC.

Jordan, John T. (1): Dis. 20 July 1861. Elec. 2nd Lt. of Co. C, 49th Inf. Regt. 4 March 1862; 1st Lt. 24 July 1862; Capt. 31 July 1862; Lt. Col. 23 February 1864; Colonel 24 March 1864. WIA Petersburg VA 2 April 1865. B. 1840. Bd. Sparta Town Cemetery, Hancock Cty.

Jordan, William Jasper [Jourdan] (1, 2): Appt. 2nd Sgt. of Co. E, 32 Inf. Regt. 7 May 1862. Sick at Savannah GA hospital 31 August 1862. B. about 1835. Bd. Magnolia Cemetery, Charleston, Charleston Cty., SC.

Jordon, John J. [Jordan] (1, 2).

Kelly, George W. [Kelley] (1, 2): Appt. 5th Cpl. of 3rd Co. B, 12th Bn. Light Art. 1 May 1862, Surr. Appomattox VA 9 April 1865. B. 24 July 1836. D. 29 January 1887. Bd. Watkinsville Cemetery, Watkinsville, Oconee Cty.

Kieve, Adolph H. (Also known as Adolph H. Wessalowsky [Weslosky/Wessolowski/Wessolonsky]—Kieve enlisted with his uncles in the 32nd Inf. Regt. and assumed their name.) (2): Enl. 18 September 1861. Enl. Co. G, 32nd Inf. Regt. 7 May 1862. Tfd. to Co. E 1862. Tfd. to regimental band 1862. Sick in hospital Savannah GA August 1862. D. of yellow fever Mount Pleasant SC 1864.

King, James R. (1, 2): Enl. 3rd Co. B, 12th Bn. Light Art. 15 July 1863. WIA Cold Harbor VA 1 June 1864. KIA Cedar Creek VA 19 October 1864.

Kinman, James Kendrick [Kinmon] (2): Enl. 30 June 1861. Appt. 1st Sgt. of 3rd Co. B, 12th Bn. Light Art. 1 May 1862. Elec. 2nd Lt. Cap. Winchester VA 19 September 1864. Released Fort Delaware DE 17 June 1865. B. 31 July 1840. D. 21 June 1915. Bd. Bartow Town Cemetery, Jefferson Cty.

Kinman, W. H. (1, 2).

Kittrell, Gabriel [Kitrell/Kitterell] (1, 2): Enl. Martin's (later Howell's) Battery Light Art. 10 May 1862. Bd. Union Hill Baptist Church Cemetery, near Wrightsville, Johnson Cty.

Knight, Walker G. (1, 2): Appt. 2nd Sgt. of 3rd Co. B, 12th Bn. Light Art. 14 May 1862. Cap. Monocacy MD 10 July 1864. Received Venus Point, Savannah River GA for Exch. 15 November 1864. On detail duty as Provost Guard Augusta GA 1865. B. 8 December 1840. D. 29 November 1909. Bd. Bethlehem Baptist/Warthen Methodist Church, Warthen, Washington Cty.

Lamb, Isaac (1, 2): Appt. Lt., Co. C, 53rd Inf. Regt.

Lamb, J. M. (2): Enl. 10 June 1861.

Lannelle, Robert.

Lawson, William Hugh (2): Enl. 5 [7] May 1861. Appt. 1st Cpl. 1 November 1861. Enl. Co. C, 49th Inf. Regt. 5 May 1862. Appt. 2nd Sgt. 21 May 1862; Sgt. Maj. 1 July 1862. Resigned 1864. Appt. 3rd Lt./Adj. Co. B, 7th Regt. State Guards Cav. Bn. Appt. Capt. Co. K, 5th Regt. GA Reserves. B. 28 May 1841. D. 2 February 1893. Bd. Old City Cemetery, Sandersville, Washington Cty.

Layton, John Wesley [Laton] (1, 2): Enl. 3rd Co. B, 12th Bn. Light Art. 1 May 1862. B. 7 February 1842. D. 19 December 1902. Bd. Piney Mount Methodist Church Cemetery, near Tennille, Washington Cty.

Lewis, J. R. (2): Enl. 18 September 1861.

Lewis, William B. (2): Enl. 30 June 1861. D. of disease 9 March 1861 Washington Cty.

Lewis, William H. (1, 2): Enl. Co. B, 59th Inf. Regt. 10 June 1862. B. 18 August 1832. D. of erysipelas Gen. Hospital #14 Richmond VA 26 December 1862. Bd. Powell Family Cemetery, near Warthen, Washington Cty.

Mason, George L. (2): Enl. 12 August 1861. Enl. Co. B, 7th Regt. State Guards Cav. Bn. Enl. Co. F, 62nd Inf. Regt. 1 September 1863. Tfd. to Co. F, 8th Regt. Cav. 11 July 1864. WIA 1864. Absent, wounded 31 August 1864. B. 2 December 1845. D. 21 November 1885. Bd. Young Family Cemetery, near Tennille, Washington Cty.

Massey, Nathan S. [Samuel N.] (1, 2): Enl. 3rd Co. B, 12th Bn. Light Art. 1 May 1862. B. about 1839 KIA Monocacy MD 9 July 1864.

Matthews, William Collins [Mathews] (2): Enl. 1 [21] August 1861. Enl. Co. G, 38th Inf. Regt. 1 July 1862. Appt. Ordnance Sgt. 27 July 1862. Elec. 2nd Lt. 1 February 1863. WIA Gettysburg PA 3 July 1863. Cap. Smithsburg MD 4 July 1863. Elec. Capt. 12 May 1864. Par. Johnson's Island OH and forwarded to Point Lookout MD for Exch. 14 March 1865. B. 25 July 1839. D. 13 September 1894. Bd. Old City Cemetery, Sandersville, Washington Cty.

McCroan, Henry M. [McCroam] (2): Enl. 10 June 1861.

McCroan, John J. [McCroon/McCroam/McCrom/McCrown] (1): D. Stribling Springs VA 6 December 1861.

McDonald, Alexander A. (1, 2): Enl. 3rd Co. B, 12th Bn. Light Art. 1 May 1862. Cap. Monocacy MD 10 July 1864. Exch. Point Lookout MD 30 October 1864.

McDonald, J. J. (1, 2).

Medlock, Eugene: Enl. 20 June 1861. B. 29 January 1844. D. of pneumonia 25 February 1862. Bd. Stonewall Cemetery, Winchester, Frederick Cty., VA.

Morgan, John Hardy (2): Enl. 20 June 1861. Enl. Co. G, 57th Inf. Cap. Vicksburg MS; Par. Listed AWOL December 1863. Enl. Thiot's Co., 12th Regt. State Guards Cav. [Wright]. B. 1 July 1825. D. 2 October 1902. Bd. Riddleville Town Cemetery, Washington Cty.

Newsome, J. J. [Newson] (1, 2): Elec. Sr. 1st Lt. of 3rd Co. B, 12th Bn. Light Art. 1 May 1862; Capt. 17 May 1863.

Newsome, Joseph K. [Newson] (1, 2): Appt. 3rd Sgt. of Co. B, 7th Bn., State Guards Cav. 4 August 1863. Listed as absent, sick, 31 January 1864.

Orr, Thomas A. (1, 2): Enl. Co. B, 7th Bn., State Guards Cav. 4 August 1863. B. about 1820. KIA Honey Hill SC.

Pannell, Robert J. [Parnell/Pannall] (1, 2): D. 1884.

Parker, William H. (1, 2): Enl. Co. G, 6th Regt. State Guards Inf. 4 August 1863. Mustered out 1864. Enl. Co. H, 2nd Regt. GA State Line. B. 15 December 1819. D. 1 November 1883. Bd. Waller Family Cemetery, near Sandersville, Washington.

Parker, William J. (1, 2): Appt. Capt. Cobb's Legion. KIA in action in VA.

Peacock, George W. (1, 2): Appt. 3rd Sgt. 18 September 1861. Elec. Jr. 2nd (or 3rd) Lt. of 3rd Co. B, 12th Bn. Light Art. 1 May 1862; 2nd Lt.; 1st Lt. WIA 4 October 1864. Surr. Appomattox VA 9 April 1865. B. 12 September 1838. D. 13 August 1916. Bd. Zeta Cemetery, Tennille, Washington Cty.

Pittman, William H. [Pitman] (1, 2): Enl. 3rd Co. B, 12th Bn. Light Art. 1 May 1862. WIA Winchester VA 19 September 1864; foot amputated. B. 2 June 1835. D. of bronchitis, 1864 [1880]. Bd. Swint-Pittman Family Cemetery, near Sandersville, Washington Cty.

Rawlings, Charles [Rawlins] (1, 2): Enl. Co. E, 32nd Inf. Regt. 7 May 1862.

Rawlings, William H. [Rawlins] (1): Cap. 13 July 1861. Par. Beverly VA 20 July 1861. B. 22 January 1828. D. 1863. Bd. Old City Cemetery, Sandersville, Washington Cty.

Renfroe, Josiah C. (1, 2).

Riddle, Anderson M. (2): Enl. 10 June 1861. Appt. 2nd Cpl. of Co. E, 32nd Inf. Regt. 7 May 1862; 2nd Sgt. of Co. B, 7th Bn., State Guards Cav. 4 August 1863. AWOL 24–31 January 1864. B. 3 August 1843. D. 6 February 1919. Bd. Davisboro Town Cemetery, Washington Cty.

Ridden, Madison H.

Roberts, John Benjamin (1, 2): Appt. 1st Cpl. 6 October 1861. Tfd. to regimental band 6 October 1861. Enl. 3rd Co. B, 12th Bn. Light Art. 1 May 1862. Tfd. to Co. C, 49th Inf. Regt. 1 January 1863. Appt. Musician 1863; Sgt. Maj. 23 January 1863. WIA Chancellorsville VA 3 May 1863. WIA Gettysburg PA 3 July 1863. Elec. 2nd Lt. 7 August 1863; 2nd Lt. of Co. D, 49th Inf. Regt. 9 October 1863; Capt. of Co. G, for gallantry, by Secretary of War on recommendation of Commanding Gen. 12 November 1864. Surr. Appomattox VA 9 April 1865. D. Atlanta GA 30 August, 1917.

Robertson, Rufus A. [Robison/Roberson] (1, 2).

Robinson, William R. [Roberson/Robison] (1 [Enl. 18 September 1861], 2): Enl. Co. G, 57th Inf. Regt. 6 May 1862. Cap. Washington Cty., GA 23 November 1864. Released Point Lookout MD 17 June 1865.

Robson, Hans T. [Roberson] (1 [Enl. 20 [25] May 1861], 2): Elec. Jr. 1st Lt. of 3rd Co. B, 12th Bn. Light Art. 1 May 1862. Cap. Fisher's Hill VA 22 September 1864. Released Fort Delaware DE 17 June 1865.

Robson, Jesse A. [Roberson] (1, 2): Appt. 3rd Cpl. of 3rd Co. B, 12th Bn. Light Art. 1 May 1862. WIA in leg, resulting in amputation, Hatcher's Run VA 6 February 1865. Cap. Jackson Hospital Richmond VA 3 April 1865. Par. Albany GA 18 May 1865. B. 1843. D. 1913. Bd. Brownwood Cemetery, Sandersville, Washington Cty.

Robson, William Green (1, 2): Appt. Regimental Comm. Sgt. 1861. Elec. 1st Lt. of Martin's (later Howell's) Battery Light Art. 10 May 1862. Absent with leave 31 December 1864. Home on furlough close of war. [Enl. Wither's Art. Bn., appointed Lt.] B. 7 October 1831. D. 7 October 1895. Bd. Old City Cemetery, Sandersville, Washington Cty.

Rogers, Artemus L. [Rodgers] (1 [Enl. 18 September 1861], 2): Enl. Co. H, 28th Inf. Regt. 20 June 1862. Detailed with Co. G, 2nd Regt. Confederate Engineer Troops, CSA, 21 August 1864. Appt. Cpl. 1864. B. 23 November 1827. D. 8 October 1877. Bd. Jenkins-Johnson Family Cemetery, near Harrison, Washington Cty.

Rohean, William G.

Scarborough, Alfred Miles [Scarboro] (1): Dis. 3 [14] September 1861. Enl. Co. B, 7th Bn., State Guards Cav. 4 August 1863. Listed as absent, sick, 31 January 1864. B. about 1841. Bd. Old City Cemetery, Sandersville, Washington Cty.

Sheppard, Junius J. [Shepherd]: Enl. 30 June 1861. Cap. 15 [16, 20] November 1861. Imprisoned Camp Chase OH. Tfd. to Vicksburg MS for Exch. 25 August 1862. Exch. Aiken's Landing 10 November 1862.

Sillers, J. S.

Slade, Samuel L. [Slate] (2): Enl. May 10 [19], 1861. Enl. 3rd Co. B, 12th Bn. Light Art. 1 May 1862. Appt. 4th Sgt. WIA Monocacy MD 9 July 1864. B. about 1835. D. from wounds 10 July 1864.

Smith, James Howard [John] (1, 2 [dis. 25 September 1861]).

Smith, James Polk (1, 2): Enl. 3rd Co. B, 12th Bn. Light Art. 1 May 1862. Tfd. to Martin's (later Howell's) Battery Light Art. Exch. for Stephen F. Jordan, 1 June 1863. B. 25 December 1842. D. 6 November 1913. Bd. Sparta Town Cemetery, Hancock Cty.

Smith, John Henry [James]: Enl. June 10 [30], 1861. Cap. 13 July 1861. Par. Beverly VA 24 July 1861. Dis. 29 January 1862. [Mustered out with regiment.] Enl. 3rd Co. B, 12th Bn. Light Art. 1 May 1862. B. about 1835.

Smith, Joseph Crafton (1, 2): Enl. 3rd Co. B, 12th Bn. Light Art. 14 May 1862. Elec. 2nd Lt. WIA Monocacy MD 9 July 1864. Surr. Appomattox VA 9 April 1865. B. 25 November 1834. D. 26 November 1900. Bd. Smith-Lampp Family Cemetery, Mt. Olive Community, Johnson Cty.

Smith, Samuel Jordan: B. 9[10] July 1829. D. 25 May 1881. Bd. Old City Cemetery, Sandersville, Washington Cty.

Smith, William A. (1, 2): Enl. Martin's (later Howell's) Battery Light Art. 10 May 1862. Appt. Cpl.; Sgt. On detached duty with Capt. Howell 31 December 1864. B. 21 December 1842. D. 1 May 1896. Bd. Kitrell Family Cemetery, near Wrightsville, Johnson Cty.

Solomon, Henry A. [Solomons] (1): Tfd. to Co. B, 14th Inf. Regt. 19 July [16 August] 1861. Elec. 1st Lt./Capt. B. about 1835. KIA Chancellorsville VA 3 May 1863. Bd. Gordon City Cemetery, Gordon, Wilkinson Cty.

Spillers, John S. [Sillers] (1, 2).

Stanley, Joel C. (1, 2): Enl. 3rd Co. B, 12th Bn. Light Art. 14 May 1862. Cap. Petersburg VA 2 April 1865. Released Newport News VA 25 June 1865. B. 25 May 1845. D. 20 February 1899. Bd. Stanley Family Cemetery, near Chappell's Pond, Laurens Cty.

Stubbs, Gabriel. W: B. 25 January 1807. D. 15 November 1882. Bd. Old City Cemetery, Sandersville, Washington Cty.

Stubbs, Jasper Newton (2): Enl. 10 June 1861. Appt. 1st Cpl. of 3rd Co. B, 12th GA Light Art. 1 May 1862. Appt. Sgt. Surr. Appomattox VA 9 April 1865. B. 18 October 1837. D. 3 July 1905. Bd. Harrison Baptist Church Cemetery, Harrison, Washington Cty.

Taliaferro, Patrick Rose [Talliaferro] (1, 2): Elec. 5th Sgt. 28 August [1 September] 1861. Elec. 1st Lt. of Co. E, 32nd Inf. Regt. 7 May 1862. Capt. 11 July 1862. Par. Greensboro NC. B. 19 January 1837. D. 18 May 1919. Bd. Old City Cemetery, Sandersville, Washington Cty.

Tarbutton, G. Augustus (1, 2): Enl. Hilliard's AL Legion. Appt. Capt. B. 1808. D. 8 December 1878. Bd. Old City Cemetery, Sandersville, Washington Cty.

Tarver, F. R. (2): Enl. 10 June 1861.

Tarver, Bird G. B. about 1838.

Tilford, T. B. [Tulford] (1, 2).

Tison, Thomas J. [Tyson] (2): Enl. 7 [15] May 1861. Enl. 3rd Co. B, 12th Bn. Light Art. 1 May 1862. WIA Fisher's Hill VA 22 September 1864. Surr. Appomattox VA 9 April 1865. B. 1830. D. 1900. Bd. Zeta Cemetery, Tennille, Washington Cty.

Tooke, Charlton C. [Took]: Enl. 30 June 1861. D. McDowell, VA 11 [20] September 1861.

Trawick, A. J. [H. J.] (1): Dis. February 1862. Enl. 3rd Co. B, 12th Bn. Light Art. 1 May 1862. Tfd. to Bn. band. Surr. Appomattox VA 9 April 1865.

Trawick, Jesse T. (1): B. about 1835. D. Monterey, VA 25 August 1861.

Tulford, Sam.

Turner, Noah A: Enl. 30 June 1861. B. about 1843. D. Monterey VA September 29, 1861.

Veal, Reuben H. (1): Dis. 5 [15] August 1861. Enl. Co. H, 49th Inf. Regt. 4 March 1862. B. about 1843. D. of disease Richmond VA 1863.

Wagner, W. H. [Wagoner] (1, 2): Appt. 5th Sgt. of 3rd Co. B, 12th Bn. Light Art. 1 May 1862; 2nd Sgt. Tfd. to Bn. band 1 July 1863.

Waitzfelder, Elkan (1, 2): B. about 1834.

Wall, Charles A. (1, 2): Appt. 2nd Sgt. 26 [28] September 1861. B. about 1836. Bd. Old City Cemetery, Sandersville, Washington Cty.

Wall, William G. (1, 2): B. about 1838.

Warthen, Richard Lee: B. 26 June 1827. D. 22 April 1914. Bd. Worthen Cemetery, Worthen, Washington Cty.

Warthen, Thomas Jefferson, Jr. [Wharthen] (1): Dis. 8 February 1862. Enl. Co. C, 49th Inf. Regt. 4 March 1862. Tfd. to Co. B, 28th Inf. Regt. 1863. Appt. 3rd Sgt. 1863; 2nd Sgt. Surr. Greensboro NC 26 April 1865. B. 5 July 1837. D. 19 November 1910. Bd. Mineral Springs Baptist Church Cemetery, Hamburg Community, Washington Cty.

Watkins, William E. (1, 2): Appt. 4th Sgt. of 3rd Co. B, 12th Bn. Light Art. 1 May 1862. Cap. near Petersburg VA 25 March 1865. Released Point Lookout MD 21 June 1865. B. 21 March 1820. D. 10 June 1902. Bd. Watkins-Wiggins-Holt Family Cemetery, near Deepstep, Washington Cty.

West, S. H.: Enl. January, 1863 Co. H, 1st GA State Line. B. 17 April 1842. D. 18 April 1926. Bd. Ebenezer Baptist Church Cemetery, near Cartecay, Gilmer Cty.

Whiddon, Benjamin [Whiddom/Widdon] (1, 2): Enl. Co. K, 5th Reserves. Appt. Capt. B. about 1830.

Whiddon, Madison M. M. [Whiddom/Widdon] (1): B. about 1837. D. Monterey VA 12 August 1861.

Whitaker, George W. H. (1, 2): Enl. Co. C, 20th Cav. Bn. Co. converted 11 July 1864, to Co. E, 8th Cav. [Enl. Co. B, 12th Art. Bn., Appt. Capt.] B. 1840. D. 1890. Bd. Old City Cemetery, Sandersville, Washington Cty.

Wicker, Thomas Oscar (1, 2 [Dis. 8 February 1862]): Appt. 4th Sgt. 25 May 1861. Appt. Capt./Adj. 28th Inf. B. 19 August 1835. D. Sandersville, GA 1 October 1900. Bd. Old City Cemetery, Sandersville, Washington Cty.

Wright, W.

Youngblood, Joseph T.: B. 26 April 1833. D. 11 March 1896. Bd. Old City Cemetery, Sandersville, Washington Cty.

Co. F, "Gate City Guards," Fulton County

Officers

Ezzard, William Lane (1): Capt. Resigned 18 December 1861. B. 1835. D. 1903.

Wylie, H. M. [Wyley/Wiley] (1): 1st Lt. Appt. Adj. 42nd Inf. B. about 1835. KIA Franklin TN December 1864.

Stone, Chester Able (1 [Enl. 10 June 1861], 2): 2nd Lt. Elec. Capt. 18 December 1861. Appt. 2nd Lt. and Drill Master Camp of Instruction Number 2 Decatur GA 29 July 1862. B. VT about 1837. D. 1900.

Leyden, William Austin [Loyden] (1): Jr. 2nd (or 3rd) Lt. Appt. 2nd Lt. Resigned 5 November 1861. Elec. Maj. 9th Bn. Light Art., 1862. B. May 1826. Bd. Oakland Cemetery, Atlanta, Fulton Cty.

Jackson, Thomas C. (1, 2): 1st Sgt. Elec. 2nd Lt. 18 December 1861. B. about 1833.

Mims, William (1, 2): 2nd Sgt. Elec. Jr. 2nd (or 3rd) Lt. 18 December 1861. B. about 1838.

Chisholm, A. Gaines (1, 2): 3rd Sgt. B. about 1836.

Sitton, Phillip Marion (1, 2): 4th Sgt.: Appt. Ordinance Sgt. 43rd Inf. B. 9 June 1828. D. 31 October 1887. Bd. Mt. Hope Cemetery, Dahlonega, Lumpkin Cty.

Jones, Peter F. (1, 2): 5th Sgt. Appt. 1st Sgt. 18 December 1861. B. about 1836.

Orme, Aquilla J. "Quill" (1): 1st Cpl. Appt. 3rd Sgt. Dis. 31 December 1861. B. about 1839.

Love, James M. (1, 2): 2nd Cpl. Enl. Co. B, Cobb's Legion of Cav. B. about 1835. D. December 1881.

Howell, Albert, Sr. (1): 3rd Cpl. Dis. 5 November 1861. Elec. Capt. of Co. A, 1st Regt. State Troops, 1 November 1862; Lt. Col. 22 July 1864. Surr. Columbus GA 12 April 1865. B. about 1842.

Krouse, Harry (1, 2): 4th Cpl. Enl. Co. A, 9th Bn. Light Art. 7 May 1862. Tfd. to Co. E, 15 May 1862. Appt. QM Sgt. Surr. Appomattox VA 9 April 1865. B. about 1838.

Privates

Angier, Alton C.: Enl. 1 June 1861. Dis. 9 February 1862. B. about 1843.

Atkinson, Edward L. (1): Dis. 20 August 1861. B. about 1840. D. Shenandoah Valley VA 1861.

Badger, G. D. (1, 2): Cap. 13 July 1861. Par. Beverly VA 20 [24] July 1861. B. about 1844.

Badger, Robert (1): D. Shenandoah Valley VA 1861.

Bankston, John A. (1, 2): Elec. Jr. 2nd (or 3rd) Lt. of 2nd Co. C, 1st Confederate Regt Inf. 2 May 1862; 2nd Lt. 20 June 1863; 1st Lt. 17 September 1863. B. about 1839. KIA Atlanta GA 22 July 1864.

Barrett, J. C. (1, 2): B. about 1839.

Barrett, Robert (1, 2).

Bass, U. D. (1, 2): B. about 1841.

Blackwell, James Madison (1, 2): Enl. 16 April 1864 Co. G, Cobb's Legion Cav. Reported absent on furlough 28 September 1864. B. about 1829.

Brooks, A. E. (2): Enl. 7 September 1861. Reenl., unit unknown.

Brown, David W.: Enl. 1 June 1861. B. about 1838. KIA Greenbrier River VA 3 October 1861.

Brown, J. W. (2): Enl. 1 August 1861.

Burns, James T. [Burner/Burnes] (1, 2): Enl. Co. E, 9th Bn. Light Art.

Burner, William (1, 2).

Calhoun, Pink M. (2): Enl. 1 August 1861.

Casey, M. C. [Cassey] (1, 2): B. about 1834.

Center, Edward A. (1, 2): Enl. Co. E, 9th Bn. Light Art. B. about 1839.

Center, Nathaniel (2): Enl. 1 August 1861. Enl. 2nd Co. C, 1st Confederate Inf. Regt. 5 May 1862. Elec. Jr. 2nd (or 3rd) Lt. [Enl. 9th Bn. Light Art.]

Chapman, Joseph A. (2): Enl. 1 August 1861. Reenl., unit unknown. Appt. Sgt.

Clingham, R. T. [Clinghan/Clingan] (1, 2): Enl. Cav. Regt. B. about 1835. KIA in battle near Richmond VA.

Connally, David Wilson [Conally/Connalley] (1, 2): Enl. Co. E, 10th Regt. Inf. Enl. Co. F, 1st Cav. [Enl. 15 April 1862 Co. C, 1st Confederate Inf.] Cap. Nashville TN 16 December 1864. Released Camp Douglas IL 20 June 1865. B. 1838. D. 7 March 1910. Bd. Connally Family Cemetery, East Point, Fulton Cty.

Connally, James Cornelius [Conally/Connelly] (2): Enl. 1 August 1861. Appt. 2nd Sgt. of 2nd Co. C, 1st Confederate Inf. Regt. 3 May 1862. Elec. Jr. 2nd (or 3rd) Lt. 20 November 1863; 2nd Lt. Surr. Greensboro NC 26 April 1865. Bd. Oakland Confederate Cemetary, Atlanta, Fulton Cty.

Connally, William [Connelly] (2): Enl. 1 August 1861. Reenl., unit unknown. Appt. Sgt.

Corley, W. L. (2): Enl. 1 June 1861. B. about 1838.

Craven, R. W. (1, 2): Appt. 1st Sgt. of 2nd Co. C, 1st Confederate Inf. Regt. 15 April 1862. Elec. 1st Lt. of Co. A, 64th Inf. Regt. 16 February 1863. Listed as on furlough 31 August 1863. B. about 1835.

Craven, V. W. (2) Enl. 1 August 1861.

Crenshaw, James L. [Crinshaw] (1, 2): Enl. Co. E, 9th Bn. Light Art. B. 30 December 1837. D. 17 March 1910. Bd. Westview Cemetery, Atlanta, Fulton Cty.

Crockett, James M. (1, 2): Cap. 13 July 1861. Par. Beverly VA 24 July 1861. B. about 1842.

Darnall, Thomas M. [Darnold] (1, 2): B. about 1839.

Dodd, Phillip [Philamon] (1, 2): Reenl., unit unknown. Appt. Sgt. B. about 1829.

Donald, Thomas.

Dudley, Albert H. (1): B. about 1842. D. Harrisonburg VA 3 January 1862.

Eddleman, Joseph [Eddlman/Edleman, John] (1 [Enl. 1 August 1861], 2).

Elengun, R. T.

Farlow, Robert (2): Enl. 1 August 1861.

Farrar, Frank W. [Farris] (1): B. about 1844. D. McDowell, VA 20 August 1861.

Farris, Joseph: D. Shenandoah Valley VA 1861.

Farris, L. C. (2): Enl. 1 August 1861.

Farris, Robert (1, 2): D. during the war.

Ferguson, John [Furgerson] (1, 2): B. about 1838.

Ferguson, Stephen H. [Furgerson/Ferguison/Fergurson] (1, 2): Enl. Co. E, 9th Bn. Light Art.

Fife, Robert A. (1): Dis. 25 August 1861. Enl. Co. B, Cobb's Legion of Cav. 3 April 1862. Tfd. to Co. G. Appt. Cpl. 1 November 1863. Surr. Greensboro NC 26 April 1865. B. about 1842. D. 1885.

Fish, Vines (1, 2): Enl. Co. E, 9th Bn. Light Art. B. about 1820. D. 8 August 1885.

Fitch, F. S. [Filch] (2): Enl. 1 June 1861. B. about 1833.

Friedenthal, Morris (1, 2): Enl. Co. B, Cobb's Legion of Cav. 3 [30] April 1862. Tfd. to Co. G. Surr. Greensboro NC 26 April 1865. B. about 1843.

Furcrow, N.

Furcrum, Henry C. [Furcron] (1, 2): B. about 1834.

Furcrum, J. H. [Turcrum] (1, 2): Assigned as orderly to Gen. J. E. B. Stuart. KIA Yellow Tavern VA.

Gantt, Adolphus [Gant/Gannt] (1, 2): Enl. Co. B, Cobb's Legion of Cav. B. about 1841.

Gatewood, Zacheus Butler (1): B. 10 October 1842. D. of disease Staunton VA 18 September 1861. Bd. Oakland Cemetery, Atlanta, Fulton Cty.

Glasgow, (First name unknown) (1): Fifer

Guard, David Samuel (1, 2): Enl. Co. B, Cobb's Legion of Cav. 16 April 1862. Appt. Cpl. Tfd. to Co. G. B. about 1831.

Gullatt, Henry [Gullett] (1, 2): B. about 1836.

Hammond, Richard H. (1, 2): B. about 1843.

Haralson, C. A. (1, 2): B. about 1826.

Harris, Samuel Y. (2): Enl. 1 August 1861. Enl. Co. M, Phillip's Legion 28 April 1862. Appt. 4th Sgt./1st Lt. Prom. Capt. 1 February 1863. Admitted to 1st Division Hospital 6 April 1865 for gunshot wound.

Harrison, Joseph W. (1, 2): B. about 1837.

Harwell, Jesse Campbell [Hawell] (2): Enl. 1 August 1861. Enl. Co. A, 9th Bn. Light Art. 22 April 1862. Tfd. to Co. E, 15 May 1862. Surr. Appomattox VA 9 April 1865.

Haynes, Richard O. (1, 2): B. about 1828. D. 1888.

Henson, Fielding E. (1): Dis. 2 February 1862. Enl. Co. A, 9th Bn. Light Art. 27 February 1862. B. about 1842. D. 1890.

Hibler, Marshall A. C. [Hibbler] (1, 2): Reenl., unit unknown. B. about 1835.

Hill, Edward T. (1, 2): Enl. Co. E, 9th Bn. Light Art. 1 June 1862. Appt. Cpl. Cap. Richmond VA hospital 3 April 1865, and Par. 27 April 1865. Jackson Hospital Richmond VA 28 May 1865. B. about 1840.

Hill, D. E.

Hill, John A. (2): Enl. 1 June 1861. Reenl., unit unknown. B. about 1836.

Humphrey, G. W. [Humphries].

Jackson, Marion (1, 2): Reenl., unit unknown.

Jackson, W. R. (2): Enl. 1 August 1861. B. about 1837.

Johnson, James H. (1, 2): Elec. 5th Sgt. 1 September 1861. Enl. Co. B, Cobb's Legion of Cav. B. about 1838.

Johnson, William W. (1, 2): Enl. 2nd Cav. Bn. B. about 1838.

Joiner, William Henry (1): Dis. 1 November 1861. Enl. Co. A, 57th Inf. B. about 1841. D. 8 October 1864. Bd. Brinson Family Cemetery, near Canoochee, Emanuel Cty.

Jones, L. L. (1): Dis. 1 November 1861. B. about 1843.

Jones, T. J.

Jones, S. S.

Jourdan, Warren [Jordan] (1): [Appt. 2nd Cpl.] Dis. 5 November 1861. B. about 1839.

Key, W. R.: Enl. 1 August 1861. Dis. 25 September 1861. Enl. 9th Art. Bn. Enl. 11th Inf. Regt.

King, H. L.

King, John J. (1, 2): Enl. Co. E, 9th Bn. Light Art. B. about 1838. KIA Lynchburg VA.

Lambert, J.

Langston, Jeptha N. [Lankston] (1, 2): Enl. Co. B, Cobb's Legion of Cav. 28 April 1862. Tfd. to Co. G. B. 1837. D. 26 December 1913. Bd. Oakland Cemetery, Atlanta, Fulton Cty.

Latimer, Charles T. [Latimore] (2): Enl. 1 August 1861. Enl. Capt. Jackson's Co. Forrest's Escort TN Cav. 26 October 1863. Surr. Citronelle AL 4 May 1865. Par. Gainesville AL 9 May 1865. [Enl. Co. B, Cobb's Legion of Cav.]

Leatherwood, J. N.

Leatherwood, Wiley M. (2): Enl. 1 June 1861. Enl. Co. B, Cobb's Legion of Cav. 4 April 1862. Tfd. to Co. G.

Lofton, George Augustus: Enl. 1 August 1861. Dis. 1 November 1861. Enl. Co. A, 9th Art. Bn. Appt. Lt. B. 25 December 1838.

Loyd, James W., Jr. (1, 2).

Mangum, M. C. [N. C.] (2): Enl. 1 June 1861. B. about 1838.

Mangum, N. M. (1, 2): KIA during the war.

McClendon, John.

Mitchell, Henry A. (1, 2): Enl. Co. G, Cobb's Legion Cav. 5 April 1862. Surr. Greensboro NC 26 April 1865. B. about 1841.

Mitchell, R. J. (1): Tfd. 9 November 1861 to GA State Troops as 2nd Lt. B. about 1838.

Montgomery, Joseph (2): Enl. 1 August 1861. Enl. Co. G, Cobb's Legion of Cav.

Moon, Thomas (1, 2): Reenl., unit unknown.

Moore, J. Thomas (2): Enl. 1 August 1861.

Moore, Samuel T. (2): Enl. 1 August 1861.

Ozburn, Seaborn K. [Ozborn/Osborne/Ozbourn] (2): Enl. 1 August 1861. Enl. State Troops, unit unknown.

Ozburn, William H. [Ozborn/Osborne/Ozbourn] (1, 2): Enl. 14th Art. Bn. B. about 1842.

Peck, William F. (2—[Dis. 29 October 1861]): Enl. 1 August 1861. B. 1840. D. 1889 [1888]. Bd. Oakland Cemetery, Atlanta, Fulton Cty.

Pillsbury, John B. [Pillsberry/Pittsbury] (1, 2): Enl. Scogin's [Griffin] Art. Battery. [Enl. Gibson's Battery.] B. 1835. D. 1906. Bd. Oak Grove Cemetery, Americus, Sumter Cty.

Pitsburg, J. H.

Prince, David (1, 2): Reenl., unit unknown.

Rogers, James L. [Rodgers/Roggers] (1, 2): Reenl., unit unknown. B. about 1841.

Sanders, John L. [Saunders] (2): Enl. 1 August 1861. Enl. Co. A, 9th Bn. Light Art. 29 April 1862. Tfd. to Co. E, 15 May 1862. Par. Farmville VA April 1865.

Smith, U.

Smith, Zachariah H. (1, 2): Enl. Co. I, Cobb's Legion Inf. B. about 1835. Bd. Rock Mills Methodist Church Cemetery, near Jewell, Hancock Cty.

Stegall, Richard (2): Enl. 1 October 1861.

Stokes, James W. (1, 2): Enl. Co. B, Cobb's Legion of Cav. B. about 1843.

Strick, R. [Streck, G. A.]: Reenl., unit unknown. B. about 1835.

Suttles, Alf (1, 2): Reenl., unit unknown.

Tanner, Joseph Branch [Benjamin] (2): Enl. 1 August 1861. Enl. Co. E, 9th Bn. Light Art. B. 10 March 1842. D. Forest Park, 22 November 1911. Bd. Tanners Cemetery, Conley, Clayton Cty.

Tanner, William J. (2): Enl. 1 August 1861. Appt. Comm. Sgt. of 9th Bn. Light Art. B. 10 May 1836. D. 7 August 1916. Bd. Pleasant Grove Methodist Church Cemetery, near Union Crossroads, Harellson Cty.

Thornton, Jesse [Jim] (1, 2): Reenl., unit unknown. B. about 1834. D. at home during the war.

Thurman, David R. [Thurmon/Thurmond] (2): Enl. 1 August 1861. B. about 1839.

Tomlinson, W. A. (1, 2): Enl. Cav. Regt. B. about 1840.

Turner, James J. [Jonathon] (1, 2): Enl. Co. B, Cobb's Legion of Cav., 8 April 1862. Tfd. to Co. G. Cap. Sussex Court House VA 12 December 1864. B. about 1836. D. Point Lookout MD 20 January 1865.

Turner, Stephen (1, 2): Enl. Co. B, Cobb's Legion of Cav., 19 April 1862. Tfd. to Co. G. Absent on horse detail, 20 September 1864. B. about 1844.

Wallace, Charles (2): Enl. 1 May 1861. Elec. 1st Lt. of Co. D, 2nd Regt. Engineer Troops CSA Cap. and Par. Athens GA 8 May 1865. [Enl. Co. B, Cobb's Legion of Cav.] B. about 1843.

Warwick, John N. (1, 2): Reenl., unit unknown. B. about 1836.

White, H. S. (1, 2): Appt. 3rd Cpl. 11 November 1861. B. about 1839.

White, M. (1, 2): Enl. Cobb's Legion. KIA.

Wing, Hiram Clark (1, 2): B. about 1833. D. 18 September 1912. Bd. Oakland Cemetery, Atlanta, Fulton Cty.

Wing, M. S.

Wittgenstein, Louis M. [Witgenstein] (1): B. about 1843. D. Staunton VA 15 August 1861.
Wood, Jesse.
Woods, M. V. [Wood] (1, 2): Enl. Co. B, Cobb's Legion of Cav. B. about 1842.
Wylie, John H. [Wiley]: Enl. 1 August 1861. D. of pneumonia Stribling Springs VA 14 November, 1861.
Young, David (1, 2): B. about 1826.

Co. G, "Bainbridge Independents," Decatur County

Officers

Evans, John [Jonathon] W. (1, 2): Capt. Elec. Col. of the 64th Inf. Regt. 26 May 1863. B. about 1826. KIA at The Crater near Petersburg VA 30 July 1864.
Colbert, James Henry (1, 2): 1st Lt. Enl. Sims' Regt. State Troops. B. 1836. D. 1884. Bd. Oak City Cemetery, Bainbridge, Decatur Cty.
Griffin, Len M. [Levi] (1, 2): 2nd Lt. Enl. Co. G, 5th Regt. Cav. 23 February 1864. Cap. Bear Creek Station GA 16 November 1864. Released Point Lookout MD 27 June 1865. B. 12 October 1829. D. 7 August 1891. Bd. Oak City Cemetery, Bainbridge, Decatur Cty.
Fleming, William Oliver (1): Jr. 2nd (or 3rd) Lt. Resigned 2 January 1862. Elec. 1st Lt. of Co. F, 50th Inf. Regt. 4 March 1862; Capt. 8 October 1862; Maj. 30 July 1863; Lt. Col. 24 August 1863. Resigned 21 [22] December 1863. B. 2 April 1835. D. 4 May 1881. Bd. Oak City Cemetery, Bainbridge, Decatur Cty.
Granniss, Horace M. [Grannis] (1, 2): 1st Sgt. B. about 1840.
Belcher, Simeon Little (1, 2): 2nd Sgt. Enl. Co. K, 2nd Regt. Cav. 1 April 1862. Tfd. to 3rd Regt. Confederate Cav. 20 February 1863. Elec. 2nd Lt. 6th Regt. State Guards Inf. 4 August 1863. B. 10 October 1834. D. 18 December 1910. Bd. Oak City Cemetery, Bainbridge, Decatur Cty.
Neal, Thomas Jefferson (1, 2): 3rd Sgt. Appt. 3rd Sgt. of Co. K, 2nd Regt. Cav. 11 March 1862. B. about 1836.
Griffin, Thomas J. (1, 2): 4th Sgt. Enl. Co. K, 2nd Regt. Cav. March 1862. Elec. 2nd Lt. Commanding Co. December 1864. Par. Tallahassee FL 10 May 1865. B. about 1840. D. 1867.
Thompson, Thomas J. (1, 2): 5th Sgt. Appt. Ens. 11 [13] February 1862. Elec. Lt. "Palestine Rangers." B. about 1836.
Bates, Mortimer W. (1, 2): 1st Cpl. Enl. Capt. Dunham's Co., Milton Light Art. (FL) 6 May 1862. Elec. 2nd Lt. Par., Bainbridge GA 20 May 1865. B. 2 January 1840. D. 29 April 1904. Bd. Oak City Cemetery, Bainbridge, Decatur Cty.

Peabody, Edward R. (1, 2): 2nd Cpl. Appt. AQM, CSA, 19 June 1863. Assigned to duty with 64th Inf. Regt. as QM. Relieved by operation of Special Order 219, A. & IGO, 15 September 1864. Appt. Capt. & AQM, Forney's Brigade, Mahone's Division. Surr. Appomattox VA 9 April 1865. B. about 1835. D. 8 January 1892. Bd. Oak City Cemetery, Bainbridge, Decatur Cty.

Phillips, Joseph (1, 2): 3rd Cpl. Enl. Co. K, 2nd Regt. Cav. 1 April 1862. Surr. Tallahassee FL 10 May 1865. Par. Bainbridge GA 20 May 1865. B. about 1842.

Hunnewell, Theodore B. [Honeywell] (1, 2): 4th Cpl. Enl. Capt. Dunham's Co., Milton Light Art. (FL), 6 May 1862. Appt. Sgt. Par. Bainbridge GA 20 May 1865. B. 7 September 1841. D. 19 February 1877. Bd. Oak City Cemetery, Bainbridge, Decatur Cty.

Privates

Adams, Thomas Holmes (1): Cap. 13 July 1861. Par. Beverly VA 24 July 1861. Dis. 19 October 1861. Exch. December 1861 then Enl. Dunham's Artillery. Tfd. to Able's Artillery. Surrendered Greensboro NC May 1865. [Enl. 2nd Cav. Regt.] B. 19 December 1841.

Andrews, Frederick Wilson (2): Enl. 17 August 1861. Enl. Co. B, 8th Regt. FL Inf., 10 May 1862. WIA Gettysburg PA 3 July 1863. In Charlottesville and Richmond VA hospitals on account of wounds, July–August 1863. Surr. Appomattox VA 9 April 1865. B. 5 August 1836. D. 9 November 1873. Bd. Oak City Cemetery, Bainbridge, Decatur Cty.

Arline, Arthur R. D.: Enl. 1 September 1861. D. McDowell, VA 29 December 1861.

Arnett, Samuel W. (1, 2): Enl. Co. I, 31st Inf. Regt. 3 May 1862. Dis. 4 December 1862. Appt. 1st Cpl. of Co. G, 64th Inf. Regt. September 1863; Ordnance Sgt. WIA Crater, near Petersburg VA 30 July 1864. B. 14 February 1844. D. 11 October 1906. Bd. Cedar Hill Cemetery, Dawson, Terrell Cty.

Ashmore, Sanford [Ashemore] (1, 2): Enl. Co. E, 2nd Regt. FL Cav. 8 May 1862. Surr. Baldwin FL 17 May 1865. [Enl. Capt. Dunham's Co., Milton Light Art. (FL).] B. about 1839. D. 1872.

Barfield, Charles (1): B. about 1837. D. Monterey, VA hospital 12 August 1861.

Barrineau, Isaac S. [Barrimore/Bauneau] (1, 2): Appt. 3rd Sgt. of Co. B, 8th Regt. FL Inf. 10 May 1862; 1st Sgt. 17 September 1862. WIA 1863. In Quincy FL hospital wounded September 1863. B. about 1839. KIA Cold Harbor VA 3 June 1864.

Bates, Mark W. (1, 2): Enl. Capt. Dunham's Co., Milton Light Art. (FL), 6 May 1862. Appt. 5th Cpl. B. about 1842.

Beach, Charles L. (1, 2): Enl. Capt. Dunham's Co., Milton Light Art. (FL), 6 May 1862. Tfd. to Capt. Abell's Co. FL Light Art. 5 March 1863. Surr. Greensboro NC 26 April 1865. B. about 1840.

Beck, Patrick H. C.: Enl. 17 [20] May 1861. B. about 1839. D. Winchester, VA 21 December 1861.

Beck, William J. (2): Enl. 17 [20] May 1861. Reenl., unit unknown. B. about 1835.

Belcher, Daniel S. (1, 2): Enl. 1 August 1861. Enl. Co. K, 2nd Regt. Cav. 1 April 1862. WIA and D. Fort Donelson TN 10 March 1863.

Blount, Cornelius W. (2): Enl. 1 September 1861.

Bradford, Charles N. (1): Dis. 9 February 1862. Enl. Campbell's Independent Co. Siege Art. 21 March 1863. Appt. Cpl. 26 March 1863. Surr. Tallahassee FL 10 May 1865, and Par. there 18 May 1865. B. about 1836. D. 1868.

Bradwell, Alexander Moultrie (2): Enl. 17 August 1861. Enl. Co. B, 8th Regt. FL Inf. 10 May 1862. Cap. Gettysburg PA 3 July 1863. Released Fort Delaware DE 10 June 1865.

Bradwell, Thomas Marion (1, 2): Enl. Co. K, 2nd Regt. Cav. 5 May 1862. Surr. Tallahassee FL 10 May 1865. Par. Bainbridge GA 20 May 1865. B. 5 February 1835. D. 4 May 1920.

Brockett, Jesse L.: Enl. 17 August 1861. Dis. 9 February 1862. Appt. Sgt. of Co. B, 29th Bn. Cav. 25 July 1863. Par. Bainbridge GA 20 May 1865. B. 7 December 1840. D. 2 August 1908. Bd. Oak City Cemetery, Bainbridge, Decatur Cty.

Bruce, Donald (1, 2): Enl. Capt. Dunham's Co., Milton Light Art. (FL) 6 May 1862. Tfd. to Capt. Abell's Co. FL Light Art. 5 March 1863. Appt. 5th Cpl. 1864. Surr. Greensboro NC 26 April 1865. B. about 1839.

Buntyn, Franklin [Bunting/Buynton] (1, 2): Reenl., unit unknown. B. about 1838.

Butler, David K. (1, 2): Enl. Co. K, 2nd Regt. Cav. 26 April 1862. Cap. Millersburg TN 22 May 1863. Par. Fort McHenry MD 3 June 1863 and sent to Fortress Monroe VA. Received City Point VA for Exch. 5 June 1865. Appears also on roll of Co. C, 2nd Regt. Cav., but no record of transfer found. B. 7 November 1838. D. 18 April 1903. Bd. Camilla Town Cemetery, Mitchell Cty.

Byrd, James A. (1): Dis. Staunton VA hospital 2 [7] December 1861. Appt. Adj. of the 64th Inf. Regt. 19 June 1863. B. about 1823.

Chulian, M.: Bass Drummer.

Cloud, Green B. (1): B. about 1840. D. of measles Highland Cty. VA 19 July 1861. [D. Monterey VA August 1861.]

Cody, Albert (1, 2): Enl. Nelson's Independent Co. of Cav., 18 April 1862. Cap. Mechanicsburg MS 11 June 1863. B. about 1840. D. of smallpox Military Prison Alton IL 16 August 1863. Bd. Confederate Cemetery, Alton, Madison Cty., IL.

Cody, John G. (1, 2): Enl. Co. B, 29th Bn. Cav., 23 September 1863. Par. Bainbridge GA 20 May 1865. B. about 1829.

Colbert, Benjamin F. (1, 2): Enl. Capt. Dunham's Co., Milton Light Art. (FL) 6 May 1862. Appt. 4th Cpl. Surr. Bainbridge GA 10 May 1865. B. 5 September 1838. D. 11 July 1904. Bd. Oak City Cemetery, Bainbridge, Decatur Cty.

Cook, Ariel (2): Enl. 1 September 1861. Enl. Co. B, 8th Regt. FL Inf. 20 May 1862. Par. Bainbridge GA 20 May 1865. B. 22 December 1844. D. 27 April 1910. Bd. Attaplugus Town Cemetery, Decatur Cty.

Cox, Simon (2): Enl. 1 September 1861. Enl. Co. B, 8th Regt. FL Inf. 10 May 1862. Surr. Appomattox VA 9 April 1865.

Crawford, Richard H. W. (1, 2): Enl. Capt. Dunham's Co., Milton Light Art. (FL) 6 May 1862. Tfd. to Capt. Abell's Co. FL Light Art. 5 March 1863. Appt. 1st Cpl. 1864; Sgt. Surr. Greensboro NC 26 April 1865. B. 1837.

Creamer, William A. (1, 2): Enl. Co. K, 2nd Regt. Cav. 28 January 1863. Substitute for T. J. Williams. Cap. near Sugar Creek TN 9 October 1863. Par. Camp Morton IN and forwarded to Point Lookout MD for Exch. 19 February 1865. B. about 1820.

Crossly, John T. [Cropley/Croply/Crossby] (1): Left company in Atlanta GA on sick leave 2 June 1861. Never heard from again. B. about 1834.

Dickinson, William H. [Dickenson] (1, 2): Enl. Capt. Dunham's Co., Milton Light Art. (FL) 6 May 1862. Appt. Cpl. Par. Bainbridge GA 20 May 1865. B. 26 April 1839. D. 5 July 1899. Bd. Oak City Cemetery, Bainbridge, Decatur Cty.

Dowd, James [David] (1, 2): B. about 1837.

Evans, M. F.

Evans, Robert Fort (2): Enl. 13 [15] May 1861. B. about 1839.

Evans, Seth (1, 2): Enl. Capt. Dunham's Co., Milton Light Art. (FL), 6 May 1862. Par. Tallahassee FL 24 May 1865. B. about 1836.

Fox, George R. (1): Dis. 13 August 1861. B. about 1845. [D. Pensacola FL May 1861.]

Fulford, Francis M. (1): B. about 1840. D. Monterey VA hospital 13 August 1861.

Gaines, William A. (2): Enl. 17 August 1861. Enl. Co. K, 2nd Regt. Cav. 1 April 1862. Appt. Cpl. Cap. Murfreesboro TN 31 December 1862. Exch. Camp Douglas IL April 1864, and was on detached duty 15 January 1865 to close of war. Par. Bainbridge GA 20 May 1865. [Enl. Capt. Dunham's Co., Milton Light Art. (FL).] B. 14 December 1842. D. Bainbridge 7 January 1926. Bd. Oak City Cemetery, Bainbridge, Decatur Cty.

Gandy, Theodore (1, 2): Cap. 13 July 1861. Par. Beverly VA 24 July 1861. Enl. Campbell's Independent Co. Siege Art. 21 March 1863. Surr. Tallahassee FL 10 May 1865, and Par. 19 May 1865. B. about 1840.

Gassett, M. A. (1, 2): B. about 1832.

Gibson, James (1): B. about 1840. D. VA 27 January 1862. Bd. Stonewall Cemetery, Winchester, Frederick Cty., VA.

Gray, Thomas J. (2): Enl. 1 September 1861.

Griffin, George D. (2): Enl. 1 September 1861. Enl. Capt. Dunham's Co., Milton Light Art. (FL) 6 May 1862. WIA in arm, necessitating amputation at Natural Bridge, St. John's River FL 6 March 1865. On sick furlough 5 May 1865. Surr. Tallahassee FL 10 May 1865, and Par. 16 May 1865. B. May, 1842. D. Bainbridge. Bd. Griffin Family Cemetery, near Attapulgus, Decatur Cty.

Griffin, Isaac Mitchell (2): Enl. 1 September 1861. Enl. Capt. Dunham's Co., Milton Light Art. (FL) 6 May 1862. Surr. Tallahassee FL 10 May 1865, and Par. 18 May 1865. B. 18 September 1824. D. 9 October 1906. Bd. Griffin Cemetery, Decatur Cty.

Griffin, Jesse R. (2): Enl. 17 August [1 September] 1861. Enl. Co. B, 8th Regt. FL Inf. 10 May 1862. Appt. Musician. Tfd. to Co. F, and Appt. 1st Sgt. 1 January 1864. WIA 1864. Treated Gen. Hospital Howard's Grove, Richmond VA for contusion of right hip 10 May–3 June 1864. Surr. Appomattox VA 9 April 1865.

Hahn, Moritz (1, 2): Cap. 13 July 1861. Par. 20 July 1861 Beverly VA. Exch. 13 January 1862. Enl. Co. K, 2nd Regt. Cav. March 1862. B. 1812. D. 1873. Bd. Oak City Cemetery, Bainbridge, Decatur Cty.

Hambry, J.

Harper, Thomas W. (1, 2): Appt. 4th Cpl. of Co. B, 8th Regt. FL Inf. 10 May 1862. Cap. Gettysburg, PA 2 July 1863. B. about 1835. D. from erysipelas Fort Delaware, DE 1 November 1863. [D. in prison in 1861.] Bd. Salem National Cemetery, Salem Cty., NJ.

Harrell, Jacob, "Jake" (1, 2): Enl. Co. K, 2nd Regt. Cav. 12 April 1862. Elec. 2nd Lt. of Co. B, 29th Bn. Cav. 23 September 1863. Detailed with Co. D 27 July 1864. Surr. Tallahassee FL 10 May 1865, and Par. 17 May 1865. B. about 1845. Bd. Oak City Cemetery, Bainbridge, Decatur Cty.

Harrell, William Washington (1): Dis. Greenbrier River VA 12 November 1861. Enl. Co. F, 50th Inf. Regt. 4 March 1862. B. 17 October 1822. D. 13 January 1913. Bd. Oak City Cemetery, Bainbridge, Decatur Cty.

Harris, John R. (2): Enl. 31 May 1861. B. about 1839.

Hayes, John Randolph, Jr. [Hays] (2): Enl. 25 August 1861. Enl. Capt. Dunham's Co., Milton Light Art. (FL) 13 May 1862. Appt. Sgt. Maj. Par. Bainbridge GA 20 May 1865. D. FL 1881.

Henry, Peter (1, 2): B. about 1833. D. 1881.

Hines, George W. (2): Enl. 15 [26] May 1861. Enl. Capt. Dunham's Co. Milton Light Art. (FL) 6 May 1862. Elec. 2nd Lt. Par. Bainbridge GA 20 May 1865. B. 1841. D. 1872 [1870]. Bd. Oak City Cemetery, Bainbridge, Decatur Cty.

Holloway, John W. [Holaway] (1, 2): Enl. Co. K, 2nd Regt. Cav. 20 March 1862. Cap. near Atlanta GA 21 July 1864. Released Camp Chase OH 6 June 1865. B. about 1834.

Honely, James E. [Hunaly/Hunley]: (2) Enl. 1 September 1861.

Hughes, Charles W. (1, 2): Appt. Fifer. B. about 1837.

Hutchinson, Thomas J. [Hutchison] (1): Dis. Monterey VA 25 August 1861. Enl. Capt. Dunham's Co., Milton Light Art. (FL) 6 May 1862. Surr. Tallahassee FL 10 May 1865. Par. 20 May 1865. B. about 1843.

Ingram, William J. [Ingraham] (1, 2): Enl. Co. B, 8th Regt. FL Inf. 10 May 1862. [Enl. Co. B, 6th Regt. FL Inf. 10 May 1862.] [Enl. Co. B, 5th Bn. FL Cav. 21 February 1863. Par. Tallahassee FL 12 May 1865. B. about 1840. D. 14 December 1864.]

Jackson, Levi Oscar [Levy, Oscar Levi] (1, 2): Enl. Capt. Dunham's Co., Milton Light Art. (FL) 6 May 1862. Surr. Tallahassee FL 10 May 1865. Par. Bainbridge GA 20 May 1865. B. about 1842.

Jeter, Thomas J. [Jater] (1, 2): Enl. Capt. Dunham's Co., Milton Light Art. (FL) 6 May 1862. Retired 28 October 1864. Assigned to duty with Surgeon charge of hospital Lake City FL 23 November 1864. B. about 1839. Bd. Laurel Hill Cemetery, Thomasville, Thomas Cty.

Jones, Elias (1 [Enl. 1 September 1861], 2): Enl. Hood's 29th Cav. WIA FL.

Jones, Thomas W. (2): Enl. 1 September 1861. Enl. Co. A, 20th Bn. Cav. 16 May 1862. Tfd. to Co. F, Cobb's Legion of Cav. 31 July 1863. Surr. Tallahassee FL 10 May 1865. Par. Thomasville GA 21 May 1865. [D. Monterey, VA August 1861.]

Kent, William Randy (1): Dis. Staunton VA hospital 8 November 1861. Enl. Campbell's Independent Co., GA Siege Art. 21 March 1863. Par. Bainbridge GA 20 May 1865. B. about 1840.

King, John W. (2): Enl. 1 September 1861. Enl. Capt. Dunham's Co., Milton Light Art. (FL) 6 May 1862. Cap. Nashville TN 18 December 1864. Tfd. To Camp Chase OH 4 January 1865. Took oath of allegiance to US and released 20 April 1865.

King, Wesley (2): Enl. 1 September 1861. Enl. Capt. Dunham's Co., Milton Light Art. (FL) 6 May 1862. Surr. Tallahassee FL 10 May 1865.

Kirbo, Franklin [Kirby, Frankling]: Enl. 1 September 1861. Dis. 9 February 1862. Enl. Pegram's Bn. Art. D. VA.

Kirbo, Reuben [Kirby, Ruben]: Enl. 1 September 1861. Dis. 9 February 1862. Enl. Pegram's Bn. Art. D. 1869.

Kirkland, Guilford [Gilford] (1, 2): Enl. Capt. Dunham's Co., Milton Light Art. (FL) 6 May 1862.

Lewis, James M. (1, 2): Enl. Co. I, 31st Inf. Regt. 13 May 1862. Elec. 2nd Lt. 25 June 1862. WIA Spotsylvania VA 12 May 1864. Retired to Invalid Corps 27 February 1865. Par. Thomasville GA 18 May 1865. B. 1833. D. 1901. Bd. Oak City Cemetery, Bainbridge, Decatur Cty.

Lucas, William H. (1, 2): Enl. Capt. Brailsford's Co., 1st Bn. Cav. 19 May 1862. Tfd. to Co. H, 5th Regt. Cav. 20 January 1863. B. about 1834.

Lyon, John H. (1): Dis. Monterey VA hospital 5 September 1861. Reenl., unit unknown. B. about 1824. D. VA.

Mann, Israel (2): Enl. 1 September 1861.

Mann, Milton M.: Enl. 1 September 1861. Dis. 11 February 1862.

McDaniel, James M.: Enl. 1 September 1861. Dis. 11 February 1862.

McIntyre, Thomas B. (2): Enl. 17 [20] May 1861. B. about 1840.

McLauchlin, Duncan M. [McLaughlin/McLochland] (1, 2): Enl. Robertson Art. Bn. B. 1824. D. 1891. Bd. Oak City Cemetery, Bainbridge, Decatur Cty.

McLauchlin, James [McLaughlin/McLochland] (2): Enl. 1 September 1861. Enl. Co. B, 8th Regt. FL Inf. 10 May 1862. WIA Gettysburg, PA 3 July 1863. Cap. and sent to US Hospital Winchester VA 30 July 1863. B. 1838. D. from wounds 1 [3] August 1863. Bd. Oak City Cemetery, Bainbridge, Decatur Cty.

Mims, Dr. (1, 2).

Montgomery, Ed (1): B. about 1838.

Munnerlyn, Charles J., Sr. (1): Dis. 17 May 1861. Enl. Co. D, 5th Bn. FL Cav. 21 April 1864. Appt. Lt. Col. of Munnerlyn's Commissary Bn. [to rank from 23 December 1864] 1 March 1865. Surr. Tallahassee FL 18 May 1865. B. 27 November 1847. D. 27 November 1916. Bd. Oak City Cemetery, Bainbridge, Decatur Cty.

Paulett, Alonzo [Paulet/Paulettee] (1, 2): B. about 1835. D. 1866.

Paulett, Nathaniel M [Paulet, Nathaniel M.]: B. about 1837.

Paulett, Marcellus N. (1, 2): Enl. Capt. Dunham's Co., Milton Light Art. (FL) 16 May 1862. Dis. Camp Dunham FL 25 December 1862.

Perry, John O. (1): Dis. 11 January 1862. Enl. Capt. Dunham's Co., Milton Light Art. (FL) 16 May 1862. Tfd. to Capt. Abell's Co., FL Light Art. 5 March 1863. Appt. Sgt. Surr. Greensboro NC 26 April 1865. B. 3 April 1835. D. 9 January 1912. Bd. Newton Town Cemetery, Baker Cty.

Peters, Francis M. (1): Dis. Greenbrier River VA 6 October 1861. B. about 1841.

Reynolds, James J. (1): B. about 1840. D. Staunton VA 16 September 1861. Bd. Oak City Cemetery, Bainbridge, Decatur Cty.

Roan, Patrick (1, 2): B. about 1839.

Robison, John W. [Robinson]: Enl. Co. H, 49th Inf. Regt. D. 6 January 1894. Bd. Stanley Family Cemetery, near Nicklesville, Laurens Cty.

Robinson, John J. [Robison] (1, 2): Enl. Co. K, 2nd Regt. Cav. 28 April 1862. B. about 1840.

Robinson, William A. [Robison] (2): Enl. 17 May 1861. Enl. Co. C, 19th Bn. Cav., 1 August 1862. Appt. Cpl. Tfd. to Co. E, 1862. Tfd. to Co. K, 10th Regt. Confederate Cav. 30 December 1862. Appt. Sgt. Par. Bainbridge GA 20 May 1865. B. 1839. D. 1910. Bd. Corinth Freewill Baptist Church Cemetery, near Iron City, Seminole Cty.

Russell, Benjamin Edward (1): Kettle Drummer. Dis. 12 May 1861. Reenl. 1 September 1861. Appt. Musician of Co. B, 8th Regt. FL Inf. 10 May 1862. Elec. 2nd Lt. 27 November 1863. Cap. Sailor's Creek VA 6 April 1865. Released Johnson's Island OH 19 June 1865. B. 5 October 1845. D. 4 December 1909. Bd. Oak City Cemetery, Bainbridge, Decatur Cty.

Sapp, James J. (1, 2): Enl. Co. I, 31st Inf. Regt. Prom. to 2nd Lt. B. 15 October 1836. D. 1 May 1913. Bd. Bethany Methodist Church Cemetery, near Camilla, Mitchell Cty.

Sapp, Pendleton "Penn" (2): Enl. 22 October 1861. Enl. Co. K, 32nd Inf. Regt. 7 May 1861. D. of double pleuro-pneumonia Savannah hospital 4 April 1863. Bd. Pelham Town Cemetery, Mitchell Cty.

Saucer, John (1): B. about 1842.

Shaw, James K. (2): Enl. 1 September 1861. Enl. Co. D, 5th Bn. FL Cav. 10 September 1863. Par. Tallahassee FL 15 May 1865.

Shaw, Robert (1): Dis. Monterey, VA 25 August 1861. B. about 1815.

Sheulain, Moses [Shelein/Shulaine/Sheline/Shenlain, Moritz]: Appt. Drummer 12 May 1861. Enl. 11th FL Inf. Regt. B. about 1845. KIA Petersburg VA 1865.

Smart, Edward H. [Edmond] (1, 2): Enl. Capt. Dunham's Co., Milton Light Art. (FL) 6 May 1862. Surr. Quincy FL 11 May 1865. B. about 1841. Bd. Oak City Cemetery, Bainbridge, Decatur Cty.

Smith, Gaspero [Gospero/Goopero]: Enl. 1 September 1861. B. 29 November 1843. D. McDowell, VA 16 October 1861. Bd. Attaplugus Town Cemetery, Decatur Cty.

Snead, Garnett A. [Sneed/Garnet] (2): Enl. 17 [22] May 1861. B. about 1839.

Stegall, B. C.

Summers, William D. (1, 2): B. about 1833.

Swain, James T. (1): B. about 1841. D. Camp Allegheny, VA 26 November 1861.

Swain, Stephen W. (1, 2): Enl. Capt. Dunham's Co., Milton Light Art. (FL) 6 May 1862. B. about 1835. KIA by shell from Federal gunboat, St. John's Bluff FL 17 September 1862.

Taylor, Green B.: Enl. 1 September 1861. Dis. 9 February 1862. Enl. Co. B, 8th Regt. FL Inf. 10 May 1862. Cap. Gettysburg PA 3 July 1863. Released Fort Delaware DE 10 June 1865. B. about 1826.

Thomas, James B. (1, 2): Enl. 2nd Co. A, 12th Bn. Light Art. 1 May 1862. Surr. Appomattox VA 9 April 1865. B. about 1835.

Trulock, Gordon Byron [Truluck] (1): Dis. 9 February 1862. Enl. Co. F, 50th Inf. Regt. 4 March 1862. Dis. 17 February 1863. Enl. Co. F, 29th Bn. Cav. 7 November 1863. Par. Bainbridge GA 10 May 1865. B. 5 June 1837. D. 4 October 1919. Bd. Whigham Cemetery, Whigham, Grady Cty.

Tyson, Samuel L. [Tison] (1, 2): Enl. Co. B, 11th Bn. Light Art. 10 May 1862. Appt. Sgt. Roll for February 1865 reads, "Detached to go to GA, to procure a horse for himself since 9 February 1865." [Enl. Cutt's Art.] B. about 1840.

Waller, Robert A. (1, 2): Elec. Capt. of Co. B, 8th Regt. FL Inf. 10 May 1862. B. about 1837. KIA Sharpsburg MD 17 September 1862.

White, Ulysses D. [Ulishus] (1, 2): Enl. Capt. Dunham's Co., Milton Light Art. (FL) 6 May 1862. Surr. Bainbridge GA 10 May 1865. B. about 1841.

Williams, Martin W. (2): Enl. 15 [25, 26] May 1861. Enl. Co. K, 2nd Regt. Cav. 12 April 1862. B. about 1843. KIA Murfreesboro TN.

Wimberly, Christopher C. (1, 2): Enl. Co. K, 2nd Regt. Cav. [Enl. Capt. Dunham's Co., Milton Light Art. (FL).] B. about 1843. Bd. Oak City Cemetery, Bainbridge, Decatur Cty.

Woodward, Edward (2): Enl. 1 September 1861.

Wright, Bird B., Jr. (1, 2): Enl. Co. B, 8th Regt. FL Inf. 10 May 1862. WIA Sharpsburg MD 17 September 1862. B. about 1836. D. Shepherdstown VA 20 [25] September 1862.

Co. H, "Dahlonega Volunteers," Lumpkin County

Officers

Harris, Alfred (1): Capt. Resigned due to being overage 22 April [May] 1861. B. about 1803. Bd. Mount Hope Cemetery, Dahlonega, Lumpkin Cty.

Cabaniss, Thomas Banks [Cabiness] (1, 2): Pvt., Quitman Guards. Elec. Capt. of Co. H, Dahlonega Volunteers, 22 [27] April [May] 1861. Enl. Co. A, 11th Bn. Light Art. 23 May 1862. Appt. Sgt. Maj., Lt. Assigned to Doles' Brigade as Ordnance Officer 6 October 1862. Surr. Appomattox VA 9 April 1865. B. 31 August 1835. D. 14 August 1915. Bd. Rest Haven Cemetery, Forsyth, Monroe Cty.

Hardin, Jacob M. (1): 1st Lt. Enl. Co. D, 55th Inf. Regt. B. about 1811. Bd. Mount Hope Cemetery, Dahlonega, Lumpkin Cty.

Kelly, Samuel A. (1, 2): 2nd Lt.: Enl. Co. D, 55th Inf. Regt. B. about 1834. Bd. Mount Hope Cemetery, Dahlonega, Lumpkin Cty.

Gibson, Samuel H. (1, 2): Jr. 2nd (or 3rd) Lt. Appt. 2nd Lt. 15 November 1861. B. about 1841.

Sudduth, George A. (1, 2): 1st Sgt. Enl. Cobb's Legion. B. about 1837.

Quillian, James Raymond (1, 2): 2nd Sgt. Appt. 1st Sgt. Enl. Co. F, 52nd Inf. Regt. March 1862. Elec. Jr. 2nd (or 3rd) Lt. 17 February 1863. Appt. Comm. Sgt. 1863. Cap. Vicksburg MS 4 July 1863 and Par. 7 July 1863. Listed absent with leave 31 December 1863. B. 9 October 1844. D. 20 April 1923. Bd. Stapleton Baptist Church Cemetery, Stapleton, Jefferson Cty.

Lance, Christopher C. (1): 3rd Sgt. B. about 1840. D. of disease Winchester VA 9 February 1862. Bd. Mount Hope Cemetery, Dahlonega, Lumpkin Cty.

Hester, William H. H. (1, 2): 4th Sgt. Appt. 3rd Sgt. 9 February 1862. Enl. Co. C, 52nd Inf. Regt. 11 March 1862. Appt. Sgt. Absent, sick, 31 July 1863. Appt. Cpl. of Co. F, 3rd Regt. State Guards Cav. B. 24 September 1835. D. 9 November 1899. Bd. Madison Town Cemetery, Morgan Cty.

Gibson, Timothy H. (1): 1st Cpl. Dis. 1 December 1861. B. about 1813.

Worley, Columbus Warren (1, 2): 2nd Cpl. Appt. 1st Cpl. 9 February 1862. Enl. Co. D, 52nd Inf. Regt. 20 June 1862. Elec. Jr. 2nd (or 3rd) Lt. 17 December 1862. WIA Atlanta GA 22 July 1864. Elec. 1st Lt. 1864. Resigned 10 November 1864. B. 12 August 1840. D. 20 June 1913. Bd. Carrollton City Cemetery, Carrollton, Carroll Cty.

Fitts, Charles W. [W. E.] (1): 3rd Cpl. Cap. 13 July 1861. Forwarded to Grafton VA for Exch. 15 August 1861. Dis. about 29 August 1861. B. about 1841.

Awtry, Henry S. (1, 2): 4th Cpl.: Enl. Co. H, Cobb's Legion Inf. B. 11 April 1841. D. 27 June 1895. Bd. Powder Springs Baptist Church Cemetery, Powder Springs, Cobb Cty.

Privates

Allison, J. LaFayette (1, 2): Appt. 3rd Cpl. 29 August 1861. B. about 1843.

Arrendale, Thomas W. [Arendale/Avendale/Avondale] (2): Enl. 24 July 1861. B. about 1836.

Beck, David Lou Allen. (2): Enl. 24 July 1861. WIA left groin Greenbrier VA 3 October 1861. B. 27 August 1834. D. 3 April 1877. Bd. Gayton-Beck Cemetery, Lumpkin Cty.

Beck, John M. (2): Enl. 24 July 1861. Enl. Co. C, 52nd Inf. Regt. 15 April 1862. Cap. Vicksburg MS 4 July 1863, and Par. 6 July 1863. Exch. 8 October 1863.

Deserted 20 December 1863. Enl. Co. F, 11th Regt. Cav. B. 18 December 1835. D. 10 March 1919. Bd. Sweetwater Baptist Church Cemetery, near Amichola Falls, Dawson Cty.

Bell, Joseph H. (1, 2): B. 1843.

Bowen, John C. [Bowell] (1, 2): B. about 1837.

Brookshire, John C.: Enl. Co. C, 52nd Inf. Regt. D. at home November [December] 1863. Bd. Mount Hope Cemetery, Dahlonega, Lumpkin Cty.

Brown, Joseph Benjamin (2): Enl. 24 July 1861. Enl. Co. D, 62nd Inf. Regt. 11 May 1862. Appt. 1st Sgt. of Co. D, 1st Regt. State Troops, 24 January 1863. Dis. November 1863 [1 January 1864]. Enl. Co. E, 11th Regt. Cav. 4 May 1864. On sick furlough 30 March 1865 to close of war. B. February 1837. D. 21 December 1913. Bd. Old Bethlehem Baptist Church Cemetery, near Dahlonega, Lumpkin Cty.

Brown, William R. (1): Dis. at Laurel Hill VA 10 [24] June 1861. Enl. Co. I, 6th Regt. State Guards. B. 15 July 1821. D. 5 February 1875. Bd. Oaklawn Cemetery, Fort Valley, Peach Cty.

Bryson, James D. (1, 2): B. about 1843.

Burns, George Washington [Burnes] (2): Enl. 24 July 1861. Enl. Co. N, 38th Inf. Regt. 15 May 1862. Tfd. to Co. I, 1862. WIA Cold Harbor VA 27 June 1862. Cap. Mine Run VA 12 May 1864. Par. Point Lookout MD February 1865. Received Boulware & Cox's Wharves, James River VA for Exch. 12 March 1865. Home on furlough close of war. B. 10 August 1840. D. 19 February 1924. Bd. Mount Hope Cemetery, Dahlonega, Lumpkin Cty.

Burns, Robert C. [Burnes] (2): Enl. 24 July 1861. Enl. Co. G, Smith's Legion Cav., 1862. Co. converted to Co. G, 6th Regt. Cav. Appt. 3rd Sgt. of Co. D, 1st Regt. State Troops, 24 January 1863; 2nd Sgt. April 1864. Elec. Capt. March 1865. On detail duty close of war. B. 28 April 1836. D. 17 January 1921. Bd. Mount Hope Cemetery, Dahlonega, Lumpkin Cty.

Calhoun, Edward L. (1, 2): B. about 1837.

Campbell, Benjamin H. (1, 2): Appt. 4th Cpl. of Co. C, 52nd Inf. Regt. 11 March 1862. Cap. Vicksburg MS 4 July 1863, and Par. 7 July 1863. Exch. 8 October 1863. Appt. Regimental Ens. 28 October 1864 (to rank from 26 September). Par. Kingston GA 12 March 1865. B. 30 April 1840. D. 18 March 1914. Bd. Cleveland Town Cemetery, White Cty.

Carder, Abner [Carden/Cardin] (1, 2): Enl. Co. D, 1st Regt. State Troops 1 July 1863. B. about 1837.

Cardin, E. I. (1, 2).

Carroll, William A. (1, 2): Cap. 13 July 1861. Par. Beverly VA 24 July 1861. B. about 1838.

Carter, Alfred R. (2): Enl. 24 July 1861. Appt. 5th Sgt. of Co. C, 52nd Inf. Regt. 11 March 1862. D. in service.

Carter, Joshua E. (2): Enl. 24 July 1861. Enl. Co. C, 52nd Inf. Regt. 10 July 1862. D. 16 November 1862.

Cook, William H. (1, 2): Enl. Co. C, 52nd Inf. Regt. 15 April 1862. Cap. Vicksburg MS 4 July 1863 and Par. July 1863. Exch. 8 October 1863. Appt. 5th Sgt. November 1863. Cap. Nashville TN 16 December 1864. Released Camp Chase OH 12 June 1865. B. 1 November 1820. D. 20 June 1907. Bd. Timber Ridge Baptist Church, near Gillsville, Hall Cty.

Cousins, Jonathan F. [Cousine] (1): Dis. 1861, date unknown. Enl. Co. C, 6th Inf. Regt. 14 February 1862. Prom. 2nd Lt. 1864. Par. 1865. B. about 1843. Bd. Byron Town Cemetery, Peach Cty.

Crawford, Abel W. (1): Tfd. to Co. K, 7th Inf. Regt. 31 May 1861. Relieved from duty by Conscript Act 16 July 1862. B. about 1843.

Crenshaw, William C. (1, 2): B. about 1843.

Davis, Benjamin James [Jeff] (1, 2): Appt. 1st Cpl. 1 December 1861; 4th Sgt. 9 February 1862. Appt. 2nd Sgt. of Co. G, Cobb's Legion of Cav. 18 April 1862. WIA Ream's Station VA 25 August 1864. On wounded furlough September 1864–April 1865. B. 10 May 1830. D. 23 June 1898. Bd. White Methodist Church Cemetery, near Santee, White Cty.

Dockrey, James [Dickery] (2): Enl. 24 July 1861.

Douglas, William Jones [Douglass] (1, 2): Enl. Co. C, 8th Inf. Regt. B. 8 August 1841. D. 21 May 1903. Bd. Macedonia Baptist Church Cemetery, near Empire, Dodge Cty.

Elrod, James, Jr. (1, 2).

Elrod, James, Sr. (1, 2).

Elrod, Joseph M. [Ellrod] (1): Dis. 4 March 1862. Enl. Co. D, 52nd Inf. Regt. 4 March 1862. Prom. 4th Sgt. Prom. 3rd Sgt. Cap. Vicksburg MS 4 July 1863. Par. 6 July 1863. Dis. prior to 31 December 1864. B. 8 December 1844. D. 23 March 1910. Bd. Mount Vernon Baptist Church Cemetery, near Dawsonville, Dawson Cty.

Elrod, Josiah [Ellrod] (2): Enl. 24 July 1861.

Elrod, Levi Garfield [Ellrod] (2): Enl. 24 July 1861.

Fincher, John W. (1, 2): Appt. 1st Sgt., Co. I, 43rd Inf. Regt. B. 24 October 1819. D. 5 May 1892.

Fitts, W. E. (1, 2): Cap. 13 July 1861. Par.

Fitzgerald, George (1, 2): B. about 1844.

Gartrell, Henry C. (1, 2): Enl. Co. C, 52nd Inf. Regt. March 1862. Appt. Cpl. Cap. Baker's Creek MS 16 May 1863. Par. Fort Delaware DE 3 July 1863.

Received City Point VA for Exch. 6 July 1863. Dis. 13 February 1864. Enl. Co. E, 11th Regt. Cav. 4 May 1864. B. about 1842. [KIA at Vicksburg MS.]

Goswick, John W. [Gosswick] (2): Enl. 21 July 1861. Elec. Jr. 2nd (or 3rd) Lt. of Co. I, 38th Inf. Regt. 6 May 1862; 1st Lt. 2 September 1862. Cap. Fredericksburg VA 13 December 1862. Exch. Elec. Capt. 25 February 1864. WIA Spotsylvania VA 12 May 1864. WIA near Canton GA 19 September 1864 [KIA]. Listed as home on wounded furlough close of war.

Graham, James S. (1, 2).

Graham, Robert A. (2): Enl. 24 July 1861. Elec. 1st Lt. 23 September [13 October] 1861. Elec. Capt. of Co. D, 1st Regt. State Troops 24 January 1863. Resigned 18 January 1864.

Gregory, George W.: Enl. 24 July 1861. B. about 1837. D. Winchester, VA 23 January 1862. Bd. Antioch Baptist Church Cemetery, near Dahlonega, Lumpkin Cty.

Hardin, Richard T. (1, 2): B. 10 June 1841. D. 24 July 1911. Bd. Bethel Methodist Church, near Dawsonville, Dawson Cty.

Hays, Sampson: Enl. 24 July 1861. Dis. Monterey VA 10 September 1861. B. 1826. D. 1869. Bd. Mount Hope Cemetery, Dahlonega, Lumpkin Cty.

Hayes, Benjamin: Dis. 20 August 1861.

Hayes, J. (1, 2).

Henslee, Theodore B. [Hensley, B. T.] (2): Enl. 24 July 1861. Enl. Co. G, 52nd Inf. Regt. 10 May 1862. Cap. Vicksburg MS 4 July 1863, and Par. 6 July 1863. Delivered to Mobile AL 4 August 1863.

Henslee, Charles B. [Hensley] (2): Enl. 24 July 1861. Enl. Co. C, 52nd Inf. Regt. 10 May 1862. Cap. Vicksburg MS 4 July 1863 and Par. July 1863. Exch. 8 October 1863. Cap. Cassville GA 20 May 1864. Took oath of allegiance to US Government and Enl. US Navy Rock Island IL 10 June 1864.

Hoffman, Samuel (1): Dis. 10 June 1861. B. about 1824.

Huntsinger, Robert (1, 2): B. about 1840.

Hydon, Augustus M. [Hyden] [2—Dis. 17 February 1862]: Enl. 24 July 1861. B. 19 September 1839. D. 12 March 1905. Bd. Harmony Baptist Church, near Dawsonville, Dawson Cty.

Jay, Nathan H.: Enl. 24 July 1861. Dis. 17 February 1862. Enl. Co. E, 11th Inf. Regt. B. 29 January 1841. D. 1 April 1914. Bd. Hopewell Methodist Church Cemetery, Murrayville, Hall Cty.

Jay, Robert H. (2): Enl. 24 July 1861. Enl. Co. I, 38th Inf. Regt. 15 May 1862. Appt. 3rd Sgt. 25 September 1862. WIA and Cap. Gettysburg PA 4 July 1863. Par. DeCamp General Hospital, David's Island, New York Harbor, 24 August 1863. Exch. City Point VA 28 August 1863. Appt. 2nd Sgt. May 1864. WIA and permanently disabled Monocacy MD 9 July 1864. Listed as home on wounded furlough 31 August 1864, to close of war. B. about 1843.

Knight, Robert H. [Kelight] (1, 2): Appt. 2nd Sgt. of Co. K, 45th Inf. Regt. March 1862; 1st Sgt. 1863. WIA Fort Steadman VA 25 March 1865. Admitted to Jackson Hospital Richmond VA where left foot was amputated 27 March 1865; Cap. there 3 April 1865, and Par. 13 June 1865. B. about 1838.

Lester, John G. A. [Lister] (1, 2): B. about 1836.

Lilly, Charles A. (2): Enl. 24 July 1861. B. 1843. D. July 1909. Bd. Alta Vista Cemetery, Gainesville, Hall Cty.

Lowe, William Henry H. [Low]: Enl. 24 July 1861. B. 1840. D. Oakland, Morgan Cty., VA 6 January 1862. Bd. Oakland Methodist Cemetery, Oakland, Morgan Cty., WV.

Maddox, Andrew J. (1): Cap. 13 July 1861. Par. Beverly VA 13 August 1861. Dis. 29 August 1861. Enl. Scogin's [Griffin's] Art. Battery. Enl. Co. K, 6th Regt. State Troops. B. 8 March 1837. D. 16 July 1915. Bd. Maddox Cemetery, Orchard hill, Spalding Cty.

Marshall, Thomas H. (1, 2): Appt. 8th Cpl. of Co. A, 14th Bn. Light Art., Southern Rights Battery, 26 April 1862. Surr. Greensboro NC 26 April 1865. B. 25 March 1843. D. 8 October 1928. Bd. Felton Cemetery, Montezuma, Macon Cty.

Marshall, William Henry (1, 2): Enl. Cav. (probably Cobb's Legion). B. 10 November 1839. D. Stewartstown NH 23 August 1911. Bd. Colebrook Village Cemetery, Coos Cty., NH.

Martin, John M. (1 [Enl. 24 July 1861], 2): Enl. Co. I, 38th Inf. Regt. 15 May 1862. Cap. Spotsylvania VA 20 May 1864. Tfd. from Point Lookout MD to Elmira NY 6 July 1864. D. of chronic diarrhea Elmira NY 24 October 1864 [15 July 1864]. Bd. Woodlawn Cemetery, Elmira, Chemung NY.

Martin, Van Buren (2): Enl. 24 July 1861. Enl. Co. I, 38th Inf. Regt. 15 May 1862. WIA Malvern Hill VA 1 July 1862. Cap. and Par. Fredericksburg VA 13 December 1862. Appt. 3rd Sgt. August 1863. WIA, disabled, and Cap. at Spotsylvania VA 10 May 1864. Exch. 31 August 1864. Listed as home on wounded furlough from 1864, to close of war. B. 7 March 1841. D. 21 October 1874. Bd. Soules Chapel Methodist Church Cemetery, near Dahlonega, Lumpkin Cty.

Mathews, James R. [Matthews] (1, 2): Appt. 4th Sgt. of Co. K, 45th Inf. Regt. March 1862. WIA Frazier's Farm VA 30 June 1862 WIA Fort Steadman VA 25 March 1865. [Enl. Cav.] B. about 1838.

McGinnis, J. George (1, 2): B. about 1843.

Morrison, John A. (1, 2): B. 24 May 1838. D. 26 April 1912. Bd. Alta Vista Cemetery, Gainesville, Hall Cty.

Mullinix, Elijah V. [Mullinax] (1, 2): Appt. 1st Cpl. of Co. D, 1st Regt. State Troops, 24 January 1863. Pvt. 15 July 1863. Listed as deserter 31 May 1864. B. about 1841. Bd. Westview Cemetery, Atlanta, Fulton Cty.

Mullinix, George W. [Mullinax] (2): Enl. 24 July 1861. Appt. 5th Sgt. of Co. D, 1st Regt. State Troops, 24 January 1863. Elec. 2nd Lt. 30 January 1864. B. 1834.

Nicholson, Nasman [Naman] (1, 2): B. about 1835.

Norrell, James M. [Narvell/Norvell] (2): Enl. 24 July 1861. B. about 1824.

Odom, George M. [Odum] (2): Enl. 24 July 1861. Enl. Co. C, 52nd Inf. Regt. 15 July 1862. Cap. Vicksburg MS 4 July 1863. Par. 16 July 1863. Exch. 8 October 1863. Listed AWOL as of 8 October 1863.

Palmer, Andrew J. (2): Enl. 24 July 1861.

Palmer, Francis M. (1, 2): B. about 1842.

Palmer, William M. (1, 2 [Dis. 27 January 1862]): Enl. 12th Bn. Light Art. Tfd. to 63rd Inf. Regt. B. about 1839.

Payne, John W. (1): Dis. 11 [20] August 1861. B. about 1841. Bd. Mount Hope Cemetery, Dahlonega, Lumpkin Cty.

Powell, Joseph M. [James M.] (1, 2): Enl. Co. K, 45th Inf. Regt. March 1862. WIA Fredericksburg, VA 13 December 1862. B. about 1839. D. of variola General Hospital Howard's Grove, Richmond VA 6 February 1863.

Pressley, John M. (2): Enl. 24 July 1861.

Pressley, Wesley: Enl. 24 July 1861. D. Romney VA 31 January 1862.

Rider, James LaFayette (1, 2): Enl. Co. D, 52nd Inf. Regt. 11 March 1862. Appt. 2nd Cpl. October 1863. Dis. 13 February 1864. Enl. Co. E, 11th Regt. Cav. 4 May 1864. B. about 1838. KIA.

Riley, Albert O. (1, 2): B. about 1843.

Robinson, Adam D. [Roberson/Robertson] (2): Enl. 24 July 1861. Enl. Co. D, 55th Inf. Regt. 12 May 1862. Cap. Cumberland Gap TN 9 September 1863. D. of fever Camp Douglas IL 26 April 1865. Bd. Chicago City Cemetery, Cook Cty., IL.

Robinson, Edward D. [Roberson/Robertson] (1): Dis. 27 January 1862. Appt. 1st Cpl. of Co. D, 55th Inf. Regt. 12 May 1862. Cap. Cumberland Gap TN 9 September 1863. Released Camp Douglas IL 15 June 1865. B. 22 May 1837. D. 13 January 1905. Bd. Yellow Creek Baptist Church, near Murrayville, Hall Cty.

Rowe, James H. [Row]: Enl. 24 July 1861. D. Winchester VA January 1862.

Smith, Andrew J. (2): Enl. 24 July 1861. Reenl., unit unknown. B. 14 November 1825. D. 31 March 1884. Bd. Smith Family Cemetery, near Flowery Branch, Hall Cty.

Smith, Thomas J. (2): Enl. 24 July 1861. Reenl., unit unknown.

Spencer, John W. (1, 2): Appt. 3rd Cpl. Appt. 2nd Cpl. 9 February 1862. Reenl., unit unknown. B. about 1843.

Starcher, Joseph W. (1): B. about 1832. D. Staunton VA 1861. [absent sick in Staunton as of 14 February 1862.]

Truelove, Benjamin J. (1 [Enl. 24 July 1861], 2 [also shown admitted to Chimbarazo Hospital No. 2 Richmond VA 7 March 1862]): Reenl., unit unknown. B. about 1839.

Truelove, William R. [Willburn R.] (1): Admitted to Chimbarazo Hospital No. 2 Richmond VA 7 March 1862. Reenl., unit unknown.

Tyner, John F. [Tiner] (2): Enl. 24 July 1861. Appt. 3rd Sgt. of Co. C, 52nd Inf. Regt. 14 May 1862. Cap. Vicksburg MS 4 July 1863, and Par. 16 July 1863. Exch. 8 October 1863. WIA and disabled New Hope Church GA 25 May 1864. Bd. Shady Grove Baptist Church Cemetery, near Coal Mountain, Forsyth Cty.

Walden, John W. [Waldren] (1, 2): B. about 1840.

Williams, Andrew J. (1, 2): Enl. Co. C, 52nd Inf. Regt. 15 April 1862. Cap. Vicksburg MS 4 July 1863 and Par. 6 July 1863. Exch. 8 October 1863. Dis. Dalton GA March 1864. B. about 1841.

Wood, Oliver J. (1, 2): Reenl., unit unknown. B. about 1843.

Wooten, Francis Marion [Wootten] (1): Tfd. to Co. D, 52nd Inf. Regt. 14 February 1862. Cap. Nicholasville KY 18 October 1862. Sent to Vicksburg MS for Exch. December 1862 B. 25 April 1843. D. Vicksburg MS 4 December 1862. [D. 24 September 1922.]

Worley, Martin Van Buren (1): Dis. Monterey VA 11 [20] August 1861. Reenl., unit unknown. WIA 1863. B. 28 June 1835. D. 1 December 1911.

Co. I, "Walker Light Infantry," Richmond County

Officers

Crump, Samuel H. (1, 2): Capt. Elec. Capt. of 2nd Co. B, 12th Bn. Light Art. 1 May 1862, Maj. 27 January 1863. Tfd. to Staff of Brigadier Gen. W. H. T. Walker 3 May 1863. Appt. Capt. and Assistant Inspector General 20 September 1863. Surr. Appomattox VA 9 April 1865. B. 23 August 1827. D. 19 September 1883. Bd. Magnolia Cemetery, Augusta, Richmond Cty.

Wheeler, William H. (1): 1st Lt. B. 15 October 1834. D. of disease Augusta GA 26 [27] December 1861.

Russell, Whiteford D. (1, 2): 2nd Lt. Prom. to 1st Lt. Elec. Capt. of Co. A, 21st Bn. Cav. 8 May 1862. Elec. Maj.; Lt. Col. Tfd. to Co. A, 7th Regt. Cav. 13 February 1864. WIA Trevillian Station VA 11 June 1864. B. 13 June 1839. D. from wounds 14 June 1864. Bd. Magnolia Cemetery, Augusta, Richmond Cty.

Hood, George M. (1, 2): Jr. 2nd (or 3rd) Lt. Elec. Jr. 1st Lt. of 1st Co. E, 12th Bn. Light Art. 1 May 1862; Capt. of Co. F, 19 January 1863. Confined Blackie Hospital Augusta GA 9 September 1864–5 January 1865. Applied for reinstatement to CSA 5 January 1865. Endorsement dated 23 March 1865, stated that if "this officer returns to his command within 20 days investigation will be made. Referred to writer 29 March 1865." B. about 1841.

Taliaferro, Joseph N. (1, 2): 1st Sgt. Elec. 1st Lt. 1 February 1862. Elec. 1st Lt. of 2nd Co. D, 12th Bn. Light Art. 1 May 1862; Capt. 28 December 1862. WIA Cold Harbor VA 2 June 1864. WIA and Cap. Monocacy MD 10 July 1864. Exch. Par. Augusta GA 20 May 1865. B. about 1838.

Godwin, Joseph T. (1, 2): 2nd Sgt. [2nd Cpl., then later Appt. 2nd Sgt.] Appt. 1st Sgt., 1 February 1862. Enl. 7th Regt. Cav. B. about 1830.

Calhoun, Charles A. (1, 2): 3rd Sgt. [1st Cpl., then later appt. 3rd Sgt.] B. about 1834.

Donophan, H. T. [Doniphan] (1, 2): 4th Sgt. Reduced to 5th Sgt.

Hitt, William M. (1): 1st Cpl. Cap. during retreat from Laurel Hill VA 15 July 1861. Par. Beverly VA 24 July 1861. Dis. 19 November 1861. Appt. 4th Cpl. of Co. F, 12th Bn. Light Art. 26 January 1863. Sent to hospital 28 June 1864. Detailed by order of Medical Examining Board Augusta GA 1 August 1864. Par. Augusta GA 22 May 1865.

Pugh, Nathan S. (1, 2): 2nd Cpl. Appt. 4th Sgt.; 2nd Sgt. Enl. Co. I, Cobb's Legion of Cav. 10 April 1862. Elec. Jr. 2nd (or 3rd) Lt. 10 September 1862. KIA PA June 1863.

Howard, Samuel A. (1, 2): 3rd Cpl. Appt. 6th Cpl. of Co. F, 12th Bn. Light Art. 17 April 1862. WIA Monocacy MD 9 July 1864. Appt. 3rd Cpl. 1864. Listed as AWOL as of 13 October 1864. Roll made by members of company shows he "served through war."

Williams, George A. (1, 2): 4th Cpl. Enl. Co. I, Cobb's Legion of Cav. 11 March 1862. Elec. 2nd Lt. 8 August 1862. WIA The Wilderness VA 4 May 1864. WIA Columbia SC 9 April 1865. Surr. Greensboro NC 26 April 1865.

Privates

Adams, Lewis (1, 2).

Allen, George Washington: Enl. 3 June 1861. WIA Laurel Hill VA 8 July 1861. [Cap. and sent to Beverly VA hospital and from there to Camp Chase OH where he was Par. and sent home.] Appt. Sgt. of Co. A, 14th Regt. AL, Inf. 28 September 1862; Ens. and 1st Lt., PACS, 12 April 1864. WIA, left shoulder permanently disabled at Salem Church, VA 3 May 1863. Retired due to wounds 14 September 1864. Appears on a Medical Certificate for retiring Invalid Officers, dated Opelika AL 15 March 1865, which shows "That said officer is permanently disabled for field duty because of wound left shoulder. Has been Conscript service since retirement and it is recommended that he continue on same duty." D. Atlanta GA 1926.

Arnett, B. T. (2): Enl. 3 June 1861. Enl. Co. F, 12th Bn. Light Art. 21 April 1862.

Bacon, J. C.: Enl. 3 June 1861.

Barney, George F. (2): Enl. 1 June 1861. B. about 1837.

Batchelor, William [Bachelor] (2): Enl. 1 August 1861. B. about 1841.

Beier, John B. [Bier] (1): Dis. for disability 12 October 1861.

Blackburn, William (2): Enl. 1 [3] June 1861. Reenl., unit unknown. KIA.

Blalock, A. E.: Appt. 3rd Sgt.

Bottom, Jordan B. [Bolton] (1, 2): Appt. musician of 2nd Co. D, 12th Bn. Light Art. 17 April 1862. Tfd. to regimental band. Surr. Appomattox VA 9 April 1865. B. 1842. D. 22 October 1903. Bd. Magnolia Cemetery, Augusta, Richmond Cty.

Bowden, William [Bowdon] (1, 2): Enl. Co. D. 12th Bn. Light Art. 17 May 1862. Tfd. to Co. F. WIA Battery Wayne 26 July 1863. WIA Monocacy MD 9 July 1864. WIA and Cap. near Petersburg VA 25 March 1865. Released Point Lookout MD 24 June 1865.

Brady, James (1): Cap. during retreat from Laurel Hill VA 15 July 1861. Par. 24 July 1861. Dis. 11 [23] November 1861. Reenl., unit unknown. Cap. Fort Pulaski 11 April 1862. Exch. Aiken's Landing VA 5 August 1862. Enl. 2nd Co. D, 12th Bn. Light Art. 12 March 1863. WIA 29 September [October] 1863. Cap. Frederick City MD 9 July 1864. Released Elmira NY 15 May 1865. B. Ireland.

Broadhurst, Edward (2): Enl. 3 June 1861. B. about 1840.

Broome, Joseph J. [Broom] (1): Tfd. to Co. I, Cobb's Legion of Cav. 13 February 1862. Surr. Greensboro NC 26 April 1865. B. 1822. D. 1890. Bd. Magnolia Cemetery, Augusta, Richmond Cty.

Brooks, Joseph.

Brown, Milton: [2nd Sgt.]

Buford, John L.

Bugg, G. F.: Enl. 1 September 1861. D. Staunton VA 7 December 1861. [KIA on Allegheny Mountain 11 December 1861.]

Bugg, William (2): Enl. 1 August 1861.

Calhoun, Charles A. (1, 2): Appt. 3rd Sgt.

Carey, S. J.

Carter, John (2): Enl. 30 June 1861. B. 16 December 1848. D. 21 October 1869. Bd. Magnolia Cemetery, Augusta, Richmond Cty.

Clarkson, William O. (1, 2): Enl. Co. I, Cobb's Legion of Cav. 10 April 1862. WIA Trevillian Station VA 11 June 1864. Clarkson was reportedly "killed by Federals after the war."

Cook, R. P. (1): D. Staunton VA 5 September 1861.

Deas, Robert C. [Dias] (2): Enl. 1 August 1861. Enl. Co. C, 20th Regt. Cav. Bn. Enl. Co. E, 8th Regt. Cav. B. 23 February 1843. D. 4 November 1911. Bd. Riverside Cemetery, near Lumber City, Telfair Cty.

Dwyer, Richard T. (1): Cap. Beverly VA 13 July 1861. Dis. 1 October 1861. Enl. Capt. Barnes' Battery Light Art. [Augusta Art.], 1st Regt. Local Defense Troops 31 July 1863. B. about 1844.

Easterling, James T. (1): AWOL as of date of regiment's disbandment. Reenl., unit unknown. B. about 1822.

Ebecke, John A. [Ebeche/Ebike] (2): Enl. 1 June 1861.

Eblis, (First name unknown): Enl. 3 June 1861.

Ellis, J. (1, 2).

Frazier, Benjamin Franklin [Fraser/Frazer] (1): Dis. 7 [11] February 1862. Enl. Co. A, 21st Bn. Cav. 8 May 1862. Tfd. to Co. A, 7th Regt. Cav. 13 February 1864. B. about 1839.

Fridell, H. S.: Enl. 3 June 1861. Dis. for disability 17 August 1861. [Shown as AWOL as of date of regiment's disbandment.]

Gallaher, Michael [Gallagher] (1): Dis. 25 December 1861. Enl. Barnes' Battery Light Art., [Augusta Art.], 1st Regt. Local Defense Troops 30 July 1863. [Enl. 12th Bn. Light Art.] B. about 1825.

Garrahan, James [Garahan] (1, 2): Prom. 1st Cpl. 1 February 1862. Appt. 3rd Sgt. of Co. F, 12th Bn. Light Art. 19 April 1862. WIA Monocacy MD 9 July 1864; Cap. 10 July 1864. Tfd. from Fort McHenry MD to Point Lookout MD 1 January 1865. Par. Boulware & Cox's Wharves, James River VA 18 March 1865.

Gibson, J. A.: Appt. 4th Sgt. B. about 1825.

Gibson, Rev. Thomas Harris (2): Enl. 3 June 1861. Appt. Adj. of the 48th Inf. Regt. 23 April 1864. Elec. Capt. of Co. D, 9 July 1864. Surr. Appomattox VA 9 April 1865. B. 20 January 1833. D. December 1870. Bd. Old Gibson Family Cemetery, near Thomson, McDuffie Cty.

Goodwin, William D. (1): Dis. for disability 16 February 1862. Reenl., unit unknown. B. about 1833.

Hamill, Thomas [Hammill/Hemel/Hemmill] (1, 2): Appt. 1st Sgt./Orderly Sgt. of Co. F, 12th Bn. Light Art. 19 April 1862. WIA and captured Winchester VA 19 September 1864. Right leg was amputated below knee 20 September 1864. Tfd. from Fort McHenry MD to Point Lookout MD for Exch. 20 February 1865.

Harter, D. W. (1): Cap. 13 July 1861. Par. Beverly VA 24 July 1861. Reenl., unit unknown.

Hicks, E. J. (1, 2).

Hill, Drew Ferdinand (1, 2): Appt. Cpl. 1 February 1862. Reenl., unit unknown. B. about 1842.

Hill, Henry (1): Drummer. D. 1864.

Hill, L. W. (2): Enl. 1 [3] June 1861. Enl. 12th Bn. Light Art. KIA Monocacy MD.

Hills, John.

Hitt, Daniel Webster (1): Dis. for disability 7 September [1 October] 1861. Enl. Co. A, 9th Regt. State Troops 1 November 1861. Dis. 1862. Enl. Co. A, 21st Bn. Cav. 1 April 1863. Tfd. to Co. A, 7th Regt. Cav. 13 February 1864. Listed as being at Augusta GA returning from recruiting service, close of war. [Enl. Cobb's Legion Cav.] B. 1843. D. 22 February 1921. Bd. Old City Cemetery, Sandersville, Washington Cty.

Hitt, Robert G. (2): Enl. 1 [3] July 1861. Enl. Co. F, 12th Bn. Light Art. 1 May 1862. WIA Cold Harbor VA 2 June 1864. Appt. Adj. 1865. Surr. Appomattox VA 9 April 1865. B. 1844. D. 1912. Bd. Magnolia Cemetery, Augusta, Richmond Cty.

Hoops, John [Hooper] (2): Enl. 1 June 1861. Enl. Co. A, 21st Bn. Cav., 8 May 1862. Tfd. to Co. A, 7th Regt. Cav. 13 February 1864. Sick at Augusta GA hospital 30 September 1864.

Jacobs, John J. [Jacob] (1, 2): Enl. Co. I, Cobb's Legion of Cav. 31 March 1862. WIA 1863. Surr. Greensboro NC 26 April 1865. B. about 1840. Bd. Magnolia Cemetery, Augusta, Richmond Cty.

Keefe, Owen.

Killingsworth, W. T.: B. 24 September 1824. D. 16 December 1885. Bd. Wilkinson-Lamar Family Cemetery, Augusta, Richmond Cty.

King, Emanuel Isaiah [Emanuel J.] (2): Enl. 1 August 1861. Enl. Co. F, 12th Bn. Light Art. 1 May 1862. WIA Cold Harbor VA 1 June 1864. Surr. Appomattox VA 9 April 1865. B. 14 June 1841. D. 21 April 1912. Bd. Marks Baptist Church Cemetery, Richmond Cty.

King, James (1, 2): Reenl., unit unknown. [KIA].

King, John W.: Enl. 1 August 1861. Enl. Co. F, 12th Bn. Light Art. 1 May 1862. KIA while carrying colors Monocacy MD 9 July 1864.

Lard, Benjamin F. (2): Enl. 1 [3] June 1861. Report shows KIA during the war.

Larus, Thomas P. [Larns]: Enl. Co. G, 3rd Bn. Inf. 14 April 1862. Appt. 1st Sgt. 8 January 1863. Tfd. to Co. A, 4th Bn., GA Sharpshooters 20 May 1863. Cap. Hoover's Gap TN 24 June 1863. Sent from Camp Chase OH to Fort Delaware DE 4 July 1863 and Par. 30 July 1863. Call for October 1864, last on file, shows him present. Record shows KIA.

Liverman, William N. (1, 2): Enl. Co. I, Cobb's Legion of Cav. 11 March 1862. B. about 1843. Unofficial records show he was killed while on scout duty SC 9 April 1865.

Martin, John M. (2): Enl. June 1 [3], 1861. Enl. 12th Bn. Light Art.

McCullis, Caleb [McCallis] (1, 2): Reenl., unit unknown.

McGraw, J. P. [McGrath]: Enl. June 1 [3], 1861. AWOL as of date of regiment's disbandment.

McMahan, R. D. [McMahon] (1, 2): Reenl., unit unknown.

Miller, J.

Milton, Thomas J. (1, 2): Enl. 12th Inf. Regt.

Morris, Thomas Washington (2): Enl. 1 August 1861.

Mosley, James R. [Mosely] (1): Absent sick as of date of regiment's disbandment. Enl. SC Regular Art.

Murphey, Thomas J. [Murphy] (1): Appt. 4th Sgt. of Co. I, Cobb's Legion of Cav. 13 February 1862. On horse detail September 19–31 October 1864.

Muse, E. N. (1): Dis. for disability 15 September 1861. Enl. VA Regt. B. about 1843.

Nehr, Emanuel A. (1, 2): Appt. 4th Cpl. 1 February 1862. Appt. 1st Sgt. of 2nd Co. B, (subsequently 2nd Co. D), 12th Bn. Light Art. 19 April 1862. Elec. 2nd Lt. 19 January 1863. WIA Monocacy MD 9 July 1864; WIA Winchester VA 19 September 1864, and sent to hospital. D. in service.

Nichols, John W., Sr. (1, 2): Appt. 1st Cpl. of Co. I, Cobb's Legion of Cav. 26 March 1862. Dis. 23 August 1862. B. 8 September 1836. D. 10 August 1905. Bd. Magnolia Cemetery, Augusta, Richmond Cty.

Nimmo, St. John (2): Enl. 1 [3] June 1861. Enl. 12th Bn. Light Art. Appt. Lt.

Oglesby, G. T.

O'Keefe, Owen O. (1): Dis. Appt. 4th Cpl. of Co. I, Cobb's Legion of Cav. 19 March 1862. WIA Sharpsburg MD 17 September 1862. Cap. Falmouth VA 31 March 1864. Par. Fort Delaware DE February 1865. Received Boulware & Cox's Wharves, James River VA for Exch. 10–12 March 1865.

O'Neil, Joshua [O'Neal/O'Neill] (1, 2).

Peck, Leroy Mortimer (1, 2): Appt. 2nd Cpl. Appt. 4th Sgt. 1 February 1862. Enl. Co. I, Cobb's Legion of Cav. 27 March 1862. Surr. Greensboro NC 26 April

1865. B. 23 February 1835. D. 12 March 1904. Bd. Laurel Grove Cemetery, Savannah, Chatham Cty.

Peck, S. M.

Perrin, T. S.

Philpot, John (2): Enl. 1 August 1861. B. about 1843.

Poole, William P. S. [Pool]: 1 [3] June 1861. WIA and Cap. Laurel Hill VA 12 July 1861. Forwarded to Grafton VA 15 August 1861. Dis. 29 August 1861. Reenl., unit unknown. B. 6 July 1840. D. 10 November 1899. Bd. Ways Baptist Church Cemetery, Stellaville, Jefferson Cty.

Price, J. A.

Prouty, William H. [Proutley] (1 [Enl. 1 August 1861], 2): WIA Laurel Hill 12 July 1861. Enl. 1st Co. A, 12th Bn. Light Art. 10 April 1862. Tfd. to Co. A, 63rd Inf. Regt. October 1862. Detailed QM Dept. as carpenter. Detailed to government works Thomasville GA 13 June 1863. Par. Greensboro NC 1 May 1865.

Quinn, James (2): Enl. 1 August 1861. Reenl., unit unknown.

Ramsey, Joseph Wood [Ramsay] (1, 2): Appt. 1st Sgt. of 2nd Co. D, 12th Bn. Light Art. 19 April 1862. WIA Cold Harbor VA 2 June 1864. Cap. near Petersburg VA 25 March 1865. Released Point Lookout MD 15 May 1865. B. 30 April 1842. D. 2 January 1898. Bd. Magnolia Cemetery, Augusta, Richmond Cty.

Reeves, Henry (1, 2): Enl. 12th Bn. Light Art.

Rogers, Henry C. [Rodgers] (1, 2): Appt. Sgt. 12th Bn. Light Art.

Savage, Daniel (1): Dis. 22 July 1861. Reenl., unit unknown. B. about 1839.

Schaefer, Paul.

Singer, Theodore H.: Enl. 3 June 1861. B. about 1844. Record shows KIA.

Small, William. B. about 1840.

Smith, Andrew J. (1, 2): Enl. VA Regt. D. 10 January 1895. [KIA.] Bd. Magnolia Cemetery, Augusta, Richmond Cty.

Smith, Hugh Sterling (1, 2): Served as Acting Drillmaster of the 48th Inf. Regt. March–10 May 1862, and was recommended for permanent appointment to this position. No record found of such appointment. [Enl. Co. B, 24th Bn. VA Partisan Rangers, Scott's Partisan Rangers]. WIA and disabled Sharpsburg MD 17 September 1862. Ran blockade from Mobile on *St. Neptune*. KIA, date/location unknown.

Steiner, Frank H. (1): Appt. Sgt. 1861. Dis. 22 July 1861. B. 20 March 1842. D. 22 June 1878. Bd. Magnolia Cemetery, Augusta, Richmond Cty.

Swank, L. (1): AWOL as of date of regiment's disbandment.

Tanner, George C. [Turner] (1, 2): Appt. Musician of Co. I, Cobb's Legion of Cav. 1 April 1862. Cap. Gettysburg PA 5 July 1863. [Cap. at Hunterstown PA June

1863.] Par. at Fort McHenry MD 10 July 1861 and Tfd. to Fort Delaware DE. WIA The Wilderness VA 5 May 1864. On detached duty 31 October 1864. B. about 1845. D. 6 April 1824. Bd. Confederate Cemetery, Marietta, Cobb Cty.

Walker, Paul V. B. (2): Enl. 1 August 1861. Enl. 2nd Co. D, 12th Bn. Light Art. 30 April 1863. Severely wounded Monocacy MD 9 July 1864. WIA Fisher's Hill VA 22 September 1864 and sent to hospital. Listed as home on wounded furlough close of war. B. about 1838.

Ward, W. H. (2): Enl. 3 June 1861.

Weigel, George P. [Weigh/Weigle] (1, 2): Enl. Co. A, 21st Bn. Cav. 19 September 1863. Tfd. to Co. A, 7th Regt. Cav. 13 February 1864. Cap. Trevillian Station VA 11 June 1864. Released Elmira, NY 21 June 1865. [Enl. Augusta Battery.] B. 20 February 1842. D. 20 November 1907. Bd. Magnolia Cemetery, Augusta, Richmond Cty.

Weigel, John M. (2): Enl. 1 August 1861. Enl. Co. A, 12th Bn., GA Art. 13 July 1862. Converted to Co. A, 13th Bn. GA Art. October 1862. Co. converted to Co. A, 63rd Inf. Regt. December 1863. Appt. 11th Cpl. July [August] 1863. WIA Kennesaw Mountain GA 27 June 1864. [Enl. Augusta Battery.] B. 1841. D. from wounds 13 July 1864. Bd. Magnolia Cemetery, Augusta, Richmond Cty.

Weigel, John M. Sr., (2): Enl. 1 August 1861. Enl. Co. A, 12th Bn., GA Art. 13 July 1862. Co. converted to Co. A, 63rd Inf. Regt. December 1863. WIA Kennesaw Mountain GA 27 June 1864. B. 29 May 1811. D. from wounds 11 July 1864. Bd. Magnolia Cemetery, Augusta, Richmond Cty.

White, Daniel: [Appt. 3rd Cpl.] B. about 1840.

Williams, Henry M. (1, 2): Enl. Co. I, Cobb's Legion of Cav. 14 April 1862. WIA 1863. WIA Columbia SC 9 April 1865.

Wing, Benjamin F. B. about 1845.

Co. K, "Quitman Guards," Monroe County

Officers

Pinckard, James S. (1, 2): Capt. Elec. 1st Lt. of Co. D, 8th Regt. State Guards 4 August 1863; Maj. 21 September 1863. B. 23 March 1810. D. 27 [29] July 1879. Bd. Rest Haven Cemetery, Forsyth, Monroe Cty.

Stephens, John Turner (1, 2): 1st Lt. Enl. Co. C, 8th Regt. State Troops. Prom. Capt., Maj. B. 24 December 1827. D. 20 October 1867. Bd. Rest Haven Cemetery, Forsyth, Monroe Cty.

Banks, Joseph Ralph (1): 2nd Lt. Enl. State Troops 1864. Elec. Lt., Capt. B. 19 March 1823. D. 3 July 1910. Bd. Rest Haven Cemetery, Forsyth, Monroe Cty.

Cabaniss, George A. (1, 2): Jr. 2nd (or 3rd) Lt. Prom. 2nd Lt. 1862. B. about 1833.

Ponder, James M. (1): 1st Sgt. Elec. 2nd [3rd] Lt. 10 October 1861. Resigned 10 [20] January 1862. Elec. Capt. of Co. K, 53rd Inf. Regt. 6 May 1862. Appt. AQM 9 July 1863; Brigade AQM October 1864. Appears on list of QMs & Commissaries, ANV dated 5 March 1865.

Sneed, Archibald Henderson [Snead] (1): 2nd Sgt. Tfd. to Savannah GA hospital as Chief Steward 21 January 1862. [Dis. 1 June 1861.] Appt. Hospital Steward 13 February 1862. B. 11 October 1829. D. 17 March 1889 [1884]. Bd. Rest Haven Cemetery, Forsyth, Monroe Cty.

Ensign, Nathan Raleigh (1, 2): 3rd Sgt. Enl. Cutts Bn. Art. B. 27 March 1832. D. Simsbury, CT 27 October 1889.

Smith, Francis M. (1, 2): 4th Sgt. B. about 1831.

Dumas, William Jefferson (1, 2): 5th Sgt. Appt. 1st Sgt. 10 October 1861. Elec. 2nd Lt. 20 January 1862. Elec. 1st Lt. of Co. K, 53rd Inf. Regt. 6 May 1862; Capt. 9 July 1863. Cap. Knoxville TN 29 November 1863. Released Fort Delaware DE 12 June 1865. B. January 1838. D. Monroe Cty. 21 July 1908. Bd. Rest Haven Cemetery, Forsyth, Monroe Cty.

Collier, Lewis G. (1): 1st Cpl. Sick hospital Warrington FL 30 May 1861. Returned to home 3 June 1861. B. about 1837. D. 6 January 1862. [D. July 1861]

Christian, J. R.: 2nd Cpl.

Tyus, John Lewis [Tynes] (1): 3rd Cpl. B. 30 December 1826. D. of disease Monroe Cty. 29 [30] July 1861. Bd. Rocky Creek Baptist Church Cemetery, near Forsyth, Monroe Cty.

Leary, Jefferson M. (1, 2): 4th Cpl. Appt. 1st Cpl. 6 January 1862 [Appt. 5th Sgt. 10 October 1861]. B. about 1837.

Privates

Alexander, Willis R. (1, 2): Enl. Co. A, 14th Inf. Regt. B. about 1835. KIA Fredericksburg VA.

Anthony, James S. (1, 2): Enl. Co. K, 53rd Inf. Regt. 6 May 1862. WIA Sharpsburg MD. WIA Gettysburg PA 2 July 1863 and Cap. 5 July 1863. Appt. 4th Cpl. October 1863; 3rd Cpl. August 1864. Par. Point Lookout MD 18 February 1865. Exch. James River VA 20–21 February 1865. B. 1832. D. 5 February 1878. Bd. Butler Methodist Church Cemetery, Butler, Taylor Cty.

Banks, Thomas J. (2): Enl. 2 August 1861. Enl. Co. D, 8th Regt. State Guards. B. about 1845.

Barron, Jonathan W. H. (1, 2): B. about 1838.

Bean, John A. (2): Enl. 2 August 1861. Enl. Co. K, 53rd Inf. Regt. 6 May 1862. Cap. Tazewell TN 31 January 1864. Tfd. from Rock Island IL to James River VA and Exch. 23 March 1865. B. about 1845. D. 1875.

Bean, Edward W.: D. April 1906. Bd. Magnolia Cemetery, Augusta, Richmond Cty.

Bird, Elijah S. (1, 2): B. about 1829.

Blissett, Elijah W. [Blissitt/Elisha] (1, 2): B. about 1831. D. during the war.

Brantley, Mark (1): B. about 1823. D. by accident while on train from Pensacola FL 3 June 1861.

Brown, Benjamin S. [R. S.] (1, 2): B. about 1839.

Cabaniss, Joseph W. [Cabiness] (2): Enl. 18 June 1861. Enl. Co. B, 45th Inf. Regt. 17 May 1862. WIA and Cap. Fort Gregg VA 2 April 1865. Released Elmira NY 7 July 1865.

Callaway, John E. [Calloway/Calaway] (1, 2 [expelled by vote of company 12 February 1861 and reported AWOL]): Enl. Co. D, 31st Inf. Regt. 14 May 1862. Tfd. to regimental band 1 June 1863. On duty with ambulance corps close of war. B. November 1835.

Chambliss, William L. (2): Enl. 4 June 1861. Enl. Co. A, 32nd Inf. Regt. 5 May 1862. Surr. Greensboro NC 26 April 1865. B. 1840. D. 28 May 1911. Bd. Juliette Methodist Church Cemetery, Forsyth, Monroe Cty.

Chambliss, Zachariah H. (1, 2): Appt. 1st Sgt. 20 January 1862. Elec. Jr. 2nd (or 3rd) Lt. of Co. K, 53rd Inf. Regt. 6 May 1862; 1st Lt. 9 July 1863. B. about 1836. KIA at The Wilderness, VA 6 May 1864.

Christian, E. Ralph [Chresham] (1, 2): Appt. 2nd Cpl. 16 [31] August 1861. B. about 1837.

Clements, John T. (2): Enl. 18 June 1861. Enl. Co. E, Third Bn. Volunteer Inf., unit unknown. B. about 1841. KIA at Chickamauga 1863. Bd. Confederate Cemetery, Forsyth, Monroe Cty.

Cleveland, Milton W. [Cleaveland] (1): Elec. 1st Lt. of Co. B, 45th Inf. Regt. 28 February 1862. B. 2 September 1836. KIA Glendale VA 30 June 1862. Bd. Cleveland-Scott Family Cemetery, near Forsyth, Monroe Cty.

Clowers, John F. [Clower] (2): Enl. 18 June 1861. Enl. Co. D, 8th Regt. State Guards. B. 3 August 1843. D. 10 March 1916. Bd. Westview Cemetery, Atlanta, Fulton Cty.

Coggins, Thomas.

Colbert, James P. [Calpert, Cobbert]: Enl. 2 August 1861. B. about 1839. D. Romney VA 28 [29] January 1862.

Cook, David M. W. (1, 2): B. about 1830.

Davidson, William T. (1, 2): B. about 18 35. [D. Pensacola FL July 1861].

Davis, Thomas W.: Enl. 2 August 1861. D. Winchester, VA 18 [12] February 1862.

Dillon, Henry (1, 2): Enl. 3rd Regt. Cav. B. about 1843. KIA during Seven Days Battles near Richmond VA.

Douglas, Samuel S. [Douglass] (1, 2): B. about 1822.

Dumas, Henry Turner (1, 2): Appt. 3rd Cpl. 13 February 1862. Enl. Co. K, 53rd Inf. Regt. 6 May 1862. B. about 1840.

Edge, Joseph G. (1, 2): Enl. Co. A, Cutts Bn. Art. B. about 1839.

English, Jason F. M. (2): Enl. 18 June 1861. Enl. Co. A, 57th Inf. Regt. Appt. 2nd Lt.

Evans, Edward F. (1): Left at Warrington FL hospital 30 May 1861. Dis. from hospital by order of Medical Director 27 June 1861. Reported AWOL from 21 November 1861 until date of regiment's disbandment. [Mustered out with regiment.] Enl. Co. B, 45th Inf. Regt. March 1862. Never mustered in. Enl. 32nd Inf. Regt. B. 1836. D. Charlotte NC August [September] 1863.

Fambro, James F. [Fambrough] (1, 2): Enl. Co. E, 2nd Regt. Cav. 2 April 1862. Appt. Capt. 8 July 1863. B. 23 October 1842. D. 17 March 1864. Bd. Greenwood Cemetery, near Forsyth, Monroe Cty.

Flewellen, James M. [Flewellin/Fluewallen] (1, 2): Enl. Co. K, 53rd Inf. Regt. 6 May 1862. WIA and Cap. Farmville [High Bridge] VA 6 April 1865. Released Newport News VA 26 June 1865. B. about 1836.

Ford, James W. (1): Appt. 3rd Cpl. 30 July [31 August] 1861. Dis. 14 February 1862. B. 1838. Bd. Rest Haven Cemetery, Forsyth, Monroe Cty.

Gaines, William Thomas: Enl. 4 June 1861. Dis. 16 February 1862. B. 1827. D. 1862.

Gates, Seth W.: Enl. 18 June 1861. D. Stribling Springs VA 9 August 1861.

Gibson, Daniel Newton (2): Enl. 18 June 1861. Enl. Co. D, 8th Regt. State Guards. B. about 1820. Bd. Rest Haven Cemetery, Forsyth, Monroe Cty.

Goggins, Thomas F. [Goggans] (2): Enl. 2 August 1861. Enl. Co. K, 53rd Inf. Regt. 6 May 1862. WIA Chancellorsville VA 3 May 1863. Cap. Cold Harbor VA 1 June 1864. Released Elmira NY 21 June 1865. B. about 1839.

Goings, Thomas J. [Gorings]: Enl. 4 June 1861. Dis. 13 September 1861. Enl. Co. K, 53rd Inf. Regt. 6 May 1862. WIA Gettysburg PA 2 July 1863. Surr. Appomattox VA 9 April 1865. B. about 1835.

Granberry, Thomas J. [Grandbury] (2): Enl. 18 June 1861. Enl. 54th Inf. Regt. Appt. Sgt. B. 14 April 1832. D. 6 June 1890. Bd. Glaze Family Cemetery, near Midland, Harris Cty.

Grant, John S. (1, 2).

Ham, Thomas Clinton (2): Enl. 18 June 1861. Enl. Co. H, 32nd Inf. Regt. 6 May 1862. Enl. Massenburg's Art. Battery [Jackson's Art.]. [Enl. Co. D, 31st Inf. Regt.] WIA, left leg permanently disabled Ocean Pond FL 20 February 1864. Never returned to company. B. 25 September 1825. D. 16 August 1898. Bd. Providence Congregational Methodist Church Cemetery, Jackson, Monroe Cty.

Harman, Archibald F. (1, 2): Reenl., unit unknown. KIA Gettysburg, 1863. B. about 1844.

Haynes, William A. (1): B. about 1839. D. Warrington FL hospital 29 June 1861.

Head, James Joshua [Joshua James] (1, 2): Appt. 2nd Sgt. of Gibson's Battery Light Art. 7 May 1862. Elec. Jr. 2nd (or 3rd) Lt. 7 October 1863. B. about 1839.

Hill, Benjamin Handy (1, 2): Enl. Co. K, 53rd Inf. Regt. 6 May 1862. B. about 1840. KIA Fort Sanders, Knoxville TN 29 November 1863. Bd. Joseph W. Hill Family Cemetery, Rocky Mount, Monroe Cty.

Hogan, Ridgeway W. (1, 2): Appt. Regimental QM Sgt. 16 September 1861. Enl. Co. K, 53rd Inf. Regt. 6 May 1862. Appt. Capt. and AQM CSA 4 June 1862. Relieved from duty with 53rd Inf. Regt. 17 June 1863, and assigned to duty Atlanta GA to aid collecting tax-in-kind. Serving as Post QM Atlanta GA 17 December 1863. Tax-in-kind service Griffin GA 24 July 1864. B. about 1837. D. 1881.

Huguley, Thomas J. [Huguly/Hughey/Hughley]: Enl. 18 June 1861. Tfd. to Co. E, 3rd Bn. Inf. 5 March 1862. Appears without remark on roll of Co. B, 45th Inf. Regt. dated 11 March 1862. Dis. after furnishing substitute 1 April 1863. B. 1842. D. 1881.

Ivey, James R. (1, 2): B. about 1832.

Ivey, William T. (1, 2): Appt. 4th Sgt. of Co. K, 53rd Inf. Regt. 6 May 1862. WIA Deep Bottom VA 20 July 1864. Listed absent sick 28 February 1865. B. about 1841. D. 1868.

James, Rufus J. (2): Enl. 18 June 1861. Enl. Co. I, 61st Inf. Regt. Appt. Lt. B. about 1842.

Johnson, William F.: Enl. 2 August 1861. D. Monterey VA 10 September 1861.

Joiner, Simon Joseph [Joyner] (1, 2 [AWOL since 21 November 1861]): Enl. Co. K, 53rd Inf. Regt. 6 May 1862. Dis. due to heart disease 24 December 1862. B. 1 May 1831. D. 11 January 1910. Bd. Jackson Town Cemetery, Butts Cty.

Jones, Jesse (2): Enl. 4 June 1861. B. about 1831.

Land, James N. (1, 2): B. about 1843.

Lane, Absalom [Lance] (1, 2): Enl. Co. K, 53rd Inf. Regt. 6 May 1862. B. about 1840. KIA Chancellorsville VA 3 May 1863.

Lane, Cullen (1, 2): Enl. Co. K, 53rd Inf. Regt. B. about 1845.

Lane, Matthew M. (1, 2): Enl. Co. K, 53rd Inf. Regt. 6 May 1862. B. about 1842.

Leary, Thomas W. (1, 2): Appt. Cpl., 3rd Sgt. of Co. K, 53rd Inf. Regt. 6 May 1862. Cap. High Bridge [Farmville] VA 6 April 1865. Released Newport News VA 26 June 1865. B. about 1835.

Levy, Mendel [Mendell] (2): Enl. 2 August 1861. Enl. Co. G, 59th Inf. Regt. 6 May 1862. Listed as on sick furlough from February 1865 to close of war. B. 1834.

Livingston, John W. (2): Enl. 4 June 1861. Enl. Co. D, 31st Inf. Regt. 26 April 1862. Appt. 4th Cpl. May 1862. Absent wounded, 5 November 1864.

Livingston, Thomas W. (1 [Enl. 4 June 1861], 2): B. about 1839.

Martin, James A. (1, 2): Appt. 1st Sgt. of Co. K, 53rd Inf. Regt. 6 May 1862. On detached duty on Macon & Western Railroad 28 February 1865. B. about 1837. D. Murdered in SC 1868.

McAfee, Jonathan A. [McAffee] (1, 2): Enl. Co. K, 53rd Inf. Regt. 6 May 1862. Listed AWOL Chambersburg PA 30 June 1863. B. 12 April 1841. D. 8 April 1928 [1882]. Bd. Culloden Town Cemetery, Monroe Cty.

McCommon, William J.: Enl. Co. A, 14th Inf. Regt. Bd. McCommon Family Cemetery, near Forsyth, Monroe Cty.

McCowen, Benjamin Butler (1, 2): Elec. 2nd Lt. of Co. K, 53rd Inf. Regt. 6 May 1862. B. about 1835. KIA Gettysburg PA 2 July 1863. Bd. McCowen Family Cemetery, near Forsyth, Monroe Cty.

McCowen, Thomas Grant (2): Enl. 10 [18] June 1861. Appt. 2nd Cpl. of Co. K, 53rd Inf. Regt. 6 May 1862. WIA Fredericksburg VA. WIA and disabled Knoxville TN 29 November 1863. Detailed Enrolling Officer August 1864. On detached duty 28 February 1865. B. 7 June 1842. D. 29 July 1895. Bd. Culloden Town Cemetery, Monroe Cty.

McGinty, Augustine C. (2): Enl. 18 June 1861. Enl. Co. B, 45th Inf. Regt. March 1862. KIA Richmond VA 1 June 1862. [KIA at Frazier's Farm VA 30 June 1862.]

McGough, Christopher Columbus (2): Enl. 18 June 1861. Elec. Jr. 2nd (or 3rd) Lt. of Co. B, 45th Inf. Regt. 25 September 1862; 2nd Lt. 2 January 1863. KIA Gettysburg PA 2 July 1863.

McMullan, John S.: Enl. Co. D, 32nd Inf. Regt. Enl. Co. A, 6th Inf. Regt.

McRae, A. T. (1): Dis. 1 January 1862 [December 1861]. B. about 1840.

Middlebrooks, Iverson A. (2): Enl. Co. H, 32nd Inf. Regt. 6 May 1862. Appt. 5th Sgt. 19 November 1864. Surr. Greensboro NC 26 April 1865. B. 16 February 1844. D. 10 October 1914. Bd. Greenwood Cemetery, Barnesville, Lamar Cty.

Milner, William J. [Millner] (1, 2): B. about 1842.

Morrison, Levi Willis [Morison] (1): Dis. 2 November 1861. Enl. State Troops. B. 17 November 1830. D. 24 August 1901. Bd. Morrison Family Cemetery, near Forsyth, Monroe Cty.

Nobles, Durant T. (2): Enl. 2 August 1861. Enl. Co. B, 45th Inf. Regt. 3 May 1862. Furloughed for 30 days on 11 February 1865. B. about 1839.

Pennington, James A. [Penington] (1, 2): Enl. Co. D, 45th Inf. Regt. 13 April 1862. Dis. 1862. B. about 1834. D. 1868.

Phillips, James R. D. (1, 2): Enl. Co. K, 53rd Inf. Regt. 6 May 1862. Unofficial records show he was Dis. after furnishing a substitute 1863. B. about 1838.

Phillips, William H. D. (1 [Enl. 18 June 1861], 2): Enl. Co. K, 53rd Inf. Regt.

Polhill, Frederick Taylor (1): Appt. Ens. Elec. 1st Lt. of Co. D, 45th Inf. Regt. 4 March 1862. Resigned 12 July 1862. Enl. Co. D, 8th Regt. State Guards 4 August 1863. Surr. by Maj. Gen. Sam Jones 10 May 1865. Par. Albany GA 23 May 1865. B. 20 August 1830. D. 1 November 1886. Bd. Rest Haven Cemetery, Forsyth, Monroe Cty.

Ponder, Daniel J. (2): Enl. 2 August 1861. Appt. 3rd Cpl. of Co. K, 53rd Inf. Regt. 6 May 1862; 1st Cpl. October 1863; 5th Sgt. August 1864. Listed absent, sick, 28 February 1865. B. 14 January 1843. D. of disease at home 6 May 1865. Bd. Ponder Family Cemetery, near Forsyth, Monroe Cty.

Ponder, Oliver H. P. (1, 2 [left sick at home 4 June 1861 and never rejoined company]): B. about 1822. D. 1862.

Potts, Moses A. (1, 2): Enl. Co. K, 53rd Inf. Regt. 6 May 1862. WIA Chancellorsville VA 3 May 1863. AWOL 1 June 1864. Deserted January 1865 at Coosawhatchie SC. B. about 1836.

Potts, Samuel W.: Enl. 18 June 1861. Dis. for disability 4 September 1861.

Reese, Joseph B. (1): Dis. 12 [14] February 1862. Enl. Co. F, 44th Inf. Regt. Appt. Capt. B. about 1838.

Rosenberger, Gustav [Rozenberger/Rosenburg] (1, 2): B. 1840.

Salby, Sam.

Sawley, Ariostus: Enl. 2 August 1861. D. on road between Monterey and Staunton VA 16 September 1861.

Saxon, John F. [Saxton] (1, 2): Enl. Co. K, 53rd Inf. Regt. 6 May 1862. WIA Malvern Hill VA. B. about 1837. D. Winder Hospital Richmond, VA 2 December 1862. Bd. Hollywood Cemetery, Richmond, Henrico Cty., VA.

Sharp, Cyrus H. (1, 2): Enl. Co. A, Cutts Bn. Art. WIA at Lost Mountain MD resulting in loss of leg. B. 11 June 1837. D. 2 March 1909. Bd. Forsyth City Cemetery, Forsyth, Monroe Cty.

Senter, Charles Wesley [Center/Seuter] (2): Enl. 4 June 1861. Enl. Co. A, 14th Inf. Regt. March 1862. Appt. 2nd Cpl. 3 July 1863. Surr. Appomattox VA 9 April 1865.

Senter, John Robert [Center, James] (1): Tfd. to Co. D, 45th Inf. Regt. 14 February [4 March] 1862. WIA Cedar Run VA 9 August 1862 [Chancellorsville VA.]. Admitted to Gen. Hospital Charlottesville VA 11 August 1862. D. from wounds 24 August 1862.

Sheram, Edward M. [Sherm/Sherum/Shuram/Shurrum/Sherrum] (2): Enl. 2 August 1861. Elec. Jr. 2nd (or 3rd) Lt. of Co. D, 45th Inf. Regt. 4 March 1862; 2nd Lt.

23 January 1865. Cap. Fort Steadman VA 25 March 1865. Released Johnson's Island OH 17 June 1865.

Sheram, George Washington [Shuram/Shurrum/Sherrum] (2): Enl. 18 June 1861. Enl. Co. K, 53rd Inf. Regt. 6 May 1862. WIA Malvern Hill VA 1 July 1862. WIA Chancellorsville VA 3 May 1863. Appt. 4th Cpl. 1863; 3rd Cpl. October 1863; 2nd Cpl. August 1864. AWOL 28 February 1865. Listed as home on sick furlough April 1865. B. 11 October 1839. D. Confederate Soldiers' Home Atlanta 2 October 1936. Bd. Greenwood Cemetery, Barnesville, Lamar Cty.

Sheram, John W. [Shuram/Shurrum/Sherrum] (1, 2): Appt. 1st Cpl. 20 January 1862. Appt. 1st Cpl. of Co. K, 53rd Inf. Regt. 6 May 1862. B. about 1838. KIA Malvern Hill VA 1 July 1862.

Simmons, James M. [Simons] (1, 2): Appt. 4th Cpl. of Co. K, 53rd Inf. Regt. 6 May 1862; 2nd Cpl. October 1863; 1st Cpl. August 1864. Arrested 28 February 1865. B. 1844. D. 1910. Bd. Black Springs Baptist Church Cemetery, Black Springs Community, Baldwin Cty.

Simmons, James W. [Simons] (1, 2): Appt. 5th Sgt. of Co. K, 53rd Inf. Regt. 6 May 1862. WIA Chancellorsville VA 3 May 1863. Tfd. to Co. B, 45th Inf. Regt. 11 April 1864. Furloughed for 60 days due to typhoid fever 28 March 1865. B. about 1839. D. 1870.

Simmons, Robert [Simons] (1, 2): Appt. 1st Cpl. 10 October 1861. Prom. 2nd Sgt. 20 January 1862. Appt. 2nd Sgt. of Co. K, 53rd Inf. Regt. 6 May 1862. B. about 1839. D. of smallpox Fredericksburg VA 8 January 1863 [December 1862].

Smith, Eugene P. (1): Dis. 16 February 1862. B. about 1839.

Smith, John H. (1, 2): Enl. Co. K, 53rd Inf. Regt. 6 May 1862. Appt. 2nd Sgt. 8 January 1863; 1st Sgt. November 1863. WIA and disabled at The Wilderness VA 6 May 1864. Tfd. to QM's Department. Listed AWOL 28 February 1865. B. about 1836.

Smith, Joseph M. (2): Enl. 18 June 1861. Enl. Co. K, 53rd Inf. Regt. 6 May 1862. WIA Knoxville TN 29 November 1863. Surr. Appomattox VA 9 April 1865.

Smith, Walker P. (2): Enl. 4 June 1861. Enl. Co. B, 1st Regt. Sharpshooter Bn. WIA New Hope Church August 1864, resulting loss of leg. B. 16 March 1843. D. 9 May 1907. Bd. Juliette Family Cemetery, Juliette, Monroe Cty.

Smith, William E.: Enl. 18 June 1861. Dis. 2 [23] August 1862.

Stanford, Jabez D. (1, 2): Enl. 3rd Regt. Cav. Bd. Rest Haven Cemetery, Forsyth, Monroe Cty.

Stephens, John W. (1 [Enl. 18 June 1861], 2): Enl. Co. K, 53rd Inf. Regt. 6 May 1862. Appt. QM Sgt. January 1864. Surr. Greensboro NC 26 April 1865. B. about 1840.

Stokes, James J. (1): Staunton VA jail as of 15 March 1862, charged with murder. Later removed to jail Richmond VA. Never came to trial, released about the time of Battle of Seven Pines VA. B. about 1843. D. October 1867 Monroe Co. [D. 1866.]

Sutton, Stephen M., Jr. (1 [Enl. 18 June 1861], 2): Enl. Co. D, 31st Inf. Regt. 26 April 1862. Appt. 3rd Cpl. 13 May 1862. B. about 1844. KIA The Wilderness VA 6 May 1864.

Swan, Thomas M. [Swann]: Enl. 2 August 1861. Dis. 16 February 1862. B. about 1823. D. 1870.

Tate, James G. (2): Enl. 18 June 1861. Enl. Co. K, 53rd Inf. Regt. 6 May 1862. WIA Sharpsburg MD 17 September 1862. B. about 1841. D. from wounds 28 September 1862.

Tate, William J. (2): Enl. 2 August 1861. Enl. Co. H, 32nd Inf. Regt. 6 May 1862. Appt. 2nd Cpl. 16 September 1864. Surr. Greensboro NC 26 April 1865. B. 19 September 1835.

Toney, Charles P. (1, 2): Enl. Co. B, 45th Inf. Regt. 17 May 1862. WIA Fredericksburg VA 13 December 1862. Elec. 2nd Lt. 2 January 1863; 1st Lt. 10 March 1864. On furlough of indulgence 6–28 February 1865. B. about 1840.

Toney, W. Henry [Neary] (2): Enl. 2 August 1861. Enl. Co. H, 32nd Inf. Regt. KIA Ocean Pond FL.

Turner, Asbury A. (1, 2): Appt. 4th Cpl. 31 August 1861 [6 January 1862]. Enl. Co. A, Cutts Bn. Art. B. about 1838.

Ward, Tandy F. [Kancey]: Enl. 2 August 1861. Tfd. to Co. D, 45th Inf. Regt. 4 March 1862. Cap., date and place not stated. Released Point Lookout MD 21 June 1865. B. about 1839.

Weathersby, George F. (1): Dis. Warrington FL hospital 27 June 1861. Enl. Co. A, 32nd Inf. Regt. B. about 1840.

Wheeler, Enoch "Ed" Hansen (2): Enl. 15 [18] June 1861. Enl. Co. K, 53rd Inf. Regt. 6 May 1862. Tfd. 15 November 1862 to Confederate States Shoe Depot, Richmond VA as shoemaker. Assigned 18 June 1863 to Second (Waller's) VA Inf. Bn., Richmond Local Defense Force. [Listed missing in action after battle of Gettysburg PA.] Second Bn. consolidated 2 September 1864 under Second (Scrugg's) VA Inf., Local Defense Force. Deserted at Fort Harrison VA about 16 October 1864. Imprisoned Fort Monroe VA. B. 3 May 1843. D. 18 April 1923. Bd. Ozark Cemetery, Houston, TX Cty., MS.

Wilder, J. D.: B. 1844. D. 28 March 1868. Bd. Wilder Family Cemetery, near Cairo, Grady Cty.

Williams, Francis M. (1): B. about 1833. D. Mt. Jackson VA 26 February 1862.

Wilson, Christopher Columbus [Willson] (1, 2): B. about 1831.

Wilson, Robert K.: Enl. 4 June 1861. Dis. 16 February 1862. Enl. Maxwell's Art. Appt. QM. WIA Savannah GA. B. about 1835.

Woodall, Thomas: Enl. 4 June 1861. B. about 1844. D. Monterey VA 13 September 1861.

Wooten, Floyd G. [Wooton] (1): AWOL from 21 November 1861 to 12 February 1862 at which time expelled by vote of company. [Tfd. to Co. D, 45th Inf. Regt. 4 March 1862.] Cap. Fort Steadman VA 25 March 1865. Released Point Lookout MD 22 June 1865. B. 1836. D. 9 April 1900. Bd. Old Salem Methodist Church Cemetery, near Bollingbroke, Monroe Cty.

Wynne, Napoleon B., Jr. [Wynn] (1, 2): [Wyne/Wynn]: Enl. 8th Inf. Regt. B. 20 February 1839. D. 13 March 1905. Bd. Rest Haven Cemetery, Forsyth, Monroe Cty.

Wynne, Napoleon B., Sr. [Wynn]. B. about 1839.

Young, David Pierce (1, 2): Cap. during retreat from Laurel Hill VA 13 July 1861. Par. Beverly VA 20 July 1861. B. 22 December 1822. D. 18 December 1909. Bd. Thomson Methodist Church Cemetery, Thomson, McDuffie Cty.

Young, M. N.: Cap. during retreat from Laurel Hill VA 13 July 1861.

Company Affiliation Unknown

The following names are filed in the National Archive's Compiled Service Records as members of Ramsey's First Georgia, but do not include company designations. All of these records show the soldiers receiving an enlistment bounty of fifty dollars.

The CSR's for the first group each contain a sheet titled "Receipt Roll for Bounty for re-enlisting for two years from the expiration of the present term of service." These soldiers were most likely part of the First Georgia, at least while it was in Winchester, VA, and are included in the total given at the beginning of this Appendix. Records marked (1) have the statement "Brief shows paid February 18, 1862," while those marked (2) have "Roll dated Winchester February 18, 1862."

Adam, B. H. (1)
Black, George W. (1)
Brown, John (2)
Clarke, Benjamin C. (1)
Clarke, Owen (1)
Green, Brownlee (1)
Gresham, James B. (1)
Hanvey, Grice C. (1)

Headley, Seth H. (1)
Heard, Stephen (1)
Henslevy, Basin T. (2)
Jacobs, William (2)
James, Silas (2)
Jones, C. A. (2)
Smith, Adam A. (1)

The men of the second group, though also recorded as being part of the First Georgia, are all shown as having been enlisted by "Maj J W Anderson" on 11, 12 or 13 March 1862, which is after the regiment mustered out of service. Their records are titled "Receipt Roll for re-enlistment for two years or the war," and each has the entry "Brief shows Paid March 12, 1862." As their service in the First Georgia cannot be confirmed by other sources, they are not included in the Appendix total, but are listed here in hopes that their true service may someday be verified. The date shown by each name is that of their enlistment.

Benton, H. S.: 12 March
Blackburn, John: 13 March
Blackson, G. W.: 12 March
Bowen, William A.: 11 March
Bowery, S.: 12 March
Brewster, W. J.: 12 March
Browning, John: 12 March
Brownlow, A. B.: 12 March
Calhoun, H. J.: 11 March
Cavern, John: 12 March
Chambless, B.: 12 March
Chandler, S. S.: 11 March
Chiltoney, R. R.: 11 March
Clayton, P. A.: 11 March
Clinch, T. C.: 11 March
Clinton, Alex: 12 March
Clower, Jesse: 11 March
Cook, S. A.: 12 March
Davidson, T.: 11 March
Davis, C.: 11 March
Dillard, Willis: 12 March
Dillon, Andrew: 13 March
Doles, Franklin: 12 March
Douglass, Stephen: 11 March
Doyall, P. A.: 11 March
Dozier, J. W.: 11 March
Dudley, John H.: 12 March
Duncan, Henry: 11 March
Ennis, Dudley A.: 12 March

Evereen, E. E.: 11 March
George, John: 12 March
Goode, E. A.: 11 March
Green, D.: 12 March
Greer, William: 12 March
Gregory, Benjamin: 11 March
Hammond, William: 11 March
Hance, E.: 12 March
Hanson, E. H.: 12 March
Heiskell, C. P.: 12 March
Hidle, Henvck: 11 March
Hooper, William: 11 March
Howard, H. C.: 13 March
Hull, John H.: 11 March
Hunter, V.: 12 March
Keith, Hal: 13 March
King, Thomas: 11 March
Lane, Noah: 12 March
Lane, Stephen: 12 March
Lane, William C.: 12 March
Mangum, John: 12 March
Martineau, J. A.: 11 March
McFall, David: 12 March
Pough, P.: 12 March
Ralls, J. R.: 12 March
Reese, Simon: 11 March
Respass, William O.: 11 March
Ripley, George: 11 March
Scott, Henry: 12 March
Spicer, John: 12 March
Summer, H.: 11 March
Thomas, E. E.: 11 March
Thurmond, Phillipson: 12 March
Vaughn, W. G.: 12 March.
Wadley, Washington: 11 March
Walker, J. W.: 12 March
Ward, Duncan: 12 March
Warren, W.: 12 March
Watson, B. B.: 11 March

West, S. C.: 12 March
White, Wade: 11 March
Whitehead, Amos: 12 March
Williams, W. G.: 11 March
Willis, Thomas: 13 March
Wooten, F. G.: 12 March
Wooten, P. C.: 12 March
Wright, John W.: 11 March

Sources

(Full titles of books listed in Bibliography)

"A Day in Camp." *Sandersville Central Georgian*, 10 April 1861, p. 2.

"A Great Company." *Atlanta Constitution*, 18 January 1889, p. 5.

Campbell, W. J. *Muster Roll of First Regiment Georgia Volunteers, 1861.* State Printer.

Clark, Walter A. *Under the Stars and Bars; or Memories of Four Years Service with the Oglethorpes, of Augusta, Georgia.* Augusta GA: The Chronicle Printer, 1900.

Compiled Service Records of Confederate General and Staff Officers and Non-Regimental Enlisted Men. Georgia Department of Archives and History, Morrow GA. National Archives Microfilm Publication, Record Group 109. M331, rolls 57 and 241. 1961.

Compiled Service Records of Confederate Soldiers Who Served in Organizations from the State of Georgia. First Georgia Infantry. Georgia Department of Archives and History, Morrow GA. National Archives Microfilm Publication, Record Group 109. M266, rolls 143–145. 1959.

"Corrected List of Washington Rifles." *Sandersonville Central Georgian*, 1 April 1861, p. 2.

"Departure of the Military." *Augusta Daily Constitutionalist*, 31 March 1861, p. 3.

"Early History of Quitman Guards." *Forsyth* (GA) *Monroe Advertiser*, 14 May 1909, p. 1.

Garrett, Franklin M. *Atlanta and Environs: A Chronicle of Its People and Events.* 2 Vols. Athens: University of Georgia Press, 1969. 1:517.

"Gate City Guards." *Atlanta Daily Intelligencer*, 1 April 1861, p. 2.

Hambrecht, F. Terry. *Biographical Register of Physicians Who Served the Confederacy in a Medical Capacity.* Unpublished database, Rockville MO: n.p., 2008.

Henderson, Lillian, ed. *Roster of the Confederate Soldiers of Georgia, 1861–1865.* 6 vols. Hapeville GA: Longing & Porter, Inc., 1959–1964. 1:212–306.

Hermann, Isaac. *Memoirs of a Confederate Veteran 1861–1865.* Atlanta: Byrd Printing Co., 1911. 276–78.

Jones, Frank S. *History of Decatur County Georgia.* Spartanburg SC: The Reprint Company, Publishers, 1980. 368–70.

"Letter from Capt. Wilkins." *Columbus* (GA) *Daily Sun*, 6 August 1861, p. 2.

"List of the Officers and Members of Co. D, Southern Guard." *Columbus Daily Enquirer*, 1 April 1861, p. 3.

"List of the Officers and Privates of the Gate-City Guards." *Atlanta Southern Confederacy*, 1 April 1861, p. 5.

Martin, John H. *Columbus, Geo., From Its Selection as a "Trading Town" 1827, to its Partial Destruction by Wilson's Raid, 1865.* Columbus GA: Thomas Gilbert, Book Printer and Binder, 1874. 128–29.

Monroe County Historical Society. *Monroe County, Georgia: A History.* Forsyth GA: n.p. 1970. 528–64.

———. *Muster Roll of Co. K, 1st Regt. "Quitman Guards."* Monroe County Historical Society, Quitman Guards Collection. Forsyth GA: n.p., n.d.

National Park Service. "Civil War Soldiers and Sailors System," http://www.itd.nps.gov/cwss (accessed July 2007).

Nelson, Bobbe Hickson. *A Land So Dedicated; the History of Houston County, Georgia.* Perry GA: Southern Trellis, 1998. 303–305.

Newnan-Coweta Historical Society. *History of Coweta County, Georgia.* Newnan-Coweta Historical Society. Roswell GA: Wolfe Associates, 1988.

"Newnan Guards List of Members who Left for Pensacola–1861." Handwritten paper signed by Lavender R. Ray, 8 December 1891. George M. Hanvey Papers. Hargrett Rare Book and Manuscript Library. Ms. 494. Manuscript collection, University of Georgia, Athens GA.

Ray, Lavender R. "Newnan Guards List of Members who left for Pensacola—1861," 8 December 1891. Hanvey Papers. Photocopy.

Rigdon, John. *Historical Sketch and Roster Of The Georgia 1st Infantry Regiment (Ramsey's).* Clearwater SC: Eastern Digital Resources, 2006. 38–221.

Sturkey, O. Lee, compiler. Card Catalog, "Gravesites of Georgia Civil War Soldiers." Personal research on indexed cards. In the author's possession.

Tipton, Jim. "Find-a-Grave." http:www.findagrave.com/cgi-bin/fg.cgi (accessed 5–11 July 2010).

Johnson, William F. *Personal Papers.* Morrow GA. Georgia Department of Archives and History. Civil War Miscellany, Drawer 283, roll 29. Microfilm.

APPENDIX D

When Did Colonel Ramsey Leave The Regiment?

There is much conflicting information as to when Colonel Ramsey and Lieutenant Colonel Clarke actually departed from the 1st Georgia Regiment. Some records state that Ramsey resigned in December 1861, with Clarke becoming colonel, while others indicate Ramsey stayed with the 1st until it mustered out in March of 1862.

Information which supports Ramsey's early departure includes a muster role compiled in 1887 for a reunion of the 1st, and is found in the collection of the Georgia Department of Archives and History which states that Ramsey resigned 3 December 1861. Bruce Allardice, in his monumental work *Confederate Colonels, a Biographical Register,* asserts that Ramsey resigned on that date, but remained with the army. Other sources, such as Robert K. Krick's *Lee's Colonels* and *Compendium of the Confederate Armies, South Carolina and Georgia* by Stewart Sifakis, show that Ramsey resigned and Clarke became Colonel of the 1st. In Clarke's Compiled Service Record (CSR), there is a letter written 3 July 1862, in which he says "I was Lt. Col. of the 1st Regt Georgia Vols which was disbanded at the expiration of its term of service...," which implies he was still with the regiment when it mustered out. In *Confederate Colonels*, Mr. Allardice says that "Clarke's service record is hard to reconcile. It appears he was under arrest in Nov. 1861 and submitted his resignation shortly thereafter, but while the resignation paperwork was being processed, Colonel Ramsey resigned and Clarke received a postdated commission as colonel. He never led the regiment at that rank." A roll of the regiment's officers in an 1885 Atlanta *Constitution* article lists "Lieutenant colonel—J. O. Clark, of Augusta, who was afterwards colonel."[2]

On 28 November 1861, Colonel Taliaferro reported that Clarke had been placed under arrest and had submitted his resignation, after which an election was held to fill the post. The above mentioned 1887 muster role lists Lt. Col. Clarke as

[2] Bruce S. Allardice, *Confederate Colonels, A Biographical Register* (Columbia MO: University of Missouri Press, 2008) 101, 316, quoted with permission; Robert K. Krick, *Lee's Colonels: A Biographical Register of the Field Officers of the Army of Northern Virginia*, 2nd ed. (Dayton OH: Press of Morningside Bookstore, 1984) 30, 81, 288, 346; Stewart Sifakis, *Compendium of the Confederate Armies, South Carolina and Georgia* (New York: Facts on File, 1995) 178; Confederate General and Staff Officers, roll 57, James O. Clarke service record; Anonymous, "Scarred Veterans of the First and Forty-Second Georgia," *Atlanta Constitution*, 23 July 1885, p. 7.

having resigned in November 1861. Clarke's CSR never lists him as colonel, and there are no entries in his CSR regarding the 1st after late November 1861. In a letter dated 21 March 1863, Clarke recommended former Oglethorpe Infantry private Henry C. Foster for a commission. Clarke signed the letter as "Late Lieut Col, 1st Regt Ga Vols." In another letter written 3 July 1863, requesting promotion to Captain, Clarke says "I was Lt Col of the 1st Regt Georgia Vols." Surely Clarke would have referred to himself as colonel if that rank had been accorded him.[3]

In *Roster of the Confederate Soldiers of Georgia, 1861–1865,* edited by Lillian Henderson, the entry for Ramsey is as follows: "Ramsey, James N.—2nd Lieutenant, Company B, March 18, 1861. Elected Colonel April 3, 1861. Mustered out at Augusta, Georgia March 18, 1862. (Other records show he resigned December 3, 1861.)" Other evidence that Ramsey remained with the 1st includes his CSR from the National Archives, which shows pay vouchers signed by him as Colonel of the 1st as late as 15 March 1862. Colonel Taliaferro himself records Ramsey's presence on 16 December, when in a letter to Lieutenant Colonel J. T. L. Preston he writes "I have now to state that Col Ramsay has returned . . ."[4]

Ramsey, for at least a week or two in late December, was in command of Taliaferro's Fifth Brigade. Correspondent "Nestor" of the Atlanta *Southern Confederacy* reported to his newspaper on 17 December: "Our brigade commanded now by Col. Ramsey of the First Georgia, is encamped two miles northwest from Winchester, on the road leading to Romney." Writing to his mother on Christmas Day, 1861, Private Lavender Ray reported, "Our brigade is now commanded by Col Ramsey." A letter dated 3 January 1862, in the Atlanta *Daily Intelligencer* states, "The First Georgia Regiment is now near Winchester, Virginia. Col. Ramsey, who commanded it, is now commanding the Brigade, formerly commanded by Gen. Jackson. Lieutenant-Colonel Clark has resigned, and our young and gallant friend, Major Thompson...has been promoted to that office...." And on 31 December

---

[3] US War Department, *The War of the Rebellion, a Compilation of the Official Records of the Union and Confederate Armies, 1880–1901*, 70 vols. (Washington DC: Government Printing Office, 1880–1901) vol. 51, pt. 2, pp. 395; First Georgia Survivors Association Pamphlet, Joseph T. Collier Papers, Civil War Miscellany, Personal Papers, drawer 283, reel 21, Georgia Department of Archives and History, Morrow GA; Confederate Soldiers from Georgia, roll 143, James O. Clarke service record and H. C. Foster service record; Confederate General and Staff Officers, roll 57, James O. Clarke service record.

[4] Henderson, *Roster of the Confederate Soldiers of Georgia*, 225; Confederate Soldiers from Georgia, roll 145, James N. Ramsey service record; William B. Taliaferro to Lt. Col. J. T. L. Preston, 16 December 1861, Confederate General and Staff Officers, Roll 241, William B. Taliaferro service record.

1861, Colonel Ramsey signed discharge papers for Private James T. Dent as "Col Cmdg 5th Brigade."[5]

Colonel Taliaferro was away only a short time, returning to the army by the start of General Thomas J. Jackson's Romney Campaign. The exposures of that campaign apparently led to another of Ramsey's frequent illnesses, resulting in his being confined to a sickbed in Richmond toward the latter part of January 1862. Sometime near the end of January or in early February, he was visited by Captain Francis G. Wilkins, who was enroute home to Georgia on leave. Wilkins reported that Ramsey was "prostrated by sickness." On 19 February 1862, the Confederate Adjutant and Inspector General's Office issued orders for Ramsey to rejoin his regiment. Colonel Ramsey himself does not mention resigning in his own account of the 1st Georgia's activities, which was included in James Folsom's *Heroes and Martyrs of Georgia: Georgia's Record in the Revolution of 1861*, published in 1864, but he does refer to Clarke's resignation.[6]

The weight of evidence seems to establish that Lieutenant Colonel Clarke submitted his resignation in late November 1861, leaving the regiment, and that Colonel Ramsey retained command of the 1st Georgia until the regiment mustered out on 10 March 1862. When Brigadier General Henry R. Jackson resigned on 2 December 1861, Colonel William B. Taliaferro was given command of the brigade. Taliaferro had requested leave and was most likely home on or shortly after 17 December, probably not returning to his command until the end of the month. As senior colonel, Ramsey would have assumed command of the brigade. Ramsey's absences from his regiment due to brigade command, along with his frequent illnesses, may have led to the appearance by some that the colonel had departed the army.[7]

---

[5] "Nestor," letter to the editor, *Southern Confederacy*, 29 December 1861; Lavender Ray to his mother, 25 December 1861, in Thomas, *Letters and Diary of Lieut. Lavender R. Ray*, 45; Untitled article, *Atlanta Daily Intelligencer*, 3 January 1862; Confederate Soldiers from Georgia, roll 143, James T. Dent service record.

[6] "Return of Capt. Wilkins," *Columbus Daily Sun,* 7 February 1862, p. 3; U.S. War Department, *Special Orders of the Adjutant and Inspector General's Office, Confederate States,* 2:207-209; Folsom, *Heroes and Martyrs of Georgia*, 6-10.

[7] William Booth Taliaferro to his wife, 27 November and 6 December 1861, Taliaferro Papers.

"Appendixes"

INDEX

Index

Index